Blood Matters

Blood Matters

Studies in European Literature
and Thought, 1400-1700

Edited by
Bonnie Lander Johnson
and
Eleanor Decamp

PENN

UNIVERSITY OF PENNSYLVANIA PRESS

PHILADELPHIA

Copyright © 2018 University of Pennsylvania Press

All rights reserved. Except for brief quotations used for purposes of review or scholarly citation, none of this book may be reproduced in any form by any means without written permission from the publisher.

Published by
University of Pennsylvania Press
Philadelphia, Pennsylvania 19104-4112
www.upenn.edu/pennpress

Printed in the United States of America on acid-free paper
10 9 8 7 6 5 4 3 2 1

Library of Congress Cataloging-in-Publication Data

Names: Lander Johnson, Bonnie, editor. | Decamp, Eleanor, editor.
Title: Blood matters: studies in European literature and thought, 1400–1700 / edited by Bonnie Lander Johnson and Eleanor Decamp.
Description: 1st edition. | Philadelphia: University of Pennsylvania Press, [2018] | Includes bibliographical references and index.
Identifiers: LCCN 2017049245 | ISBN 9780812250213 (hardcover: alk. paper)
Subjects: LCSH: Blood in literature. | Literature, Medieval—History and criticism. | European literature—Early modern, 1500-1700—History and criticism. | Blood—Symbolic aspects—History. | Blood—Religious aspects—History. | Blood—Social aspects—History.
Classification: LCC PN682.B56 B58 2018 | DDC 809/.933561—dc23
LC record available at https://lccn.loc.gov/2017049245

Dedicated to Laurie Maguire

Contents

Introduction 1
    Bonnie Lander Johnson and Eleanor Decamp

I. CIRCULATION

Chapter 1. Was the Heart "Dethroned"?: Harvey's Discoveries and the Politics of Blood, Heart, and Circulation 15
    Margaret Healy

Chapter 2. "The Lake of my Heart": Blood, Containment, and the Boundaries of the Person in the Writing of Dante and Catherine of Siena 31
    Heather Webb

Chapter 3. Sorting Pistol's Blood: Social Class and the Circulation of Character in Shakespeare's *2 Henry IV* and *Henry V* 43
    Katharine A. Craik

II. WOUNDS

Chapter 4. Mantled in Blood: Shakespeare's Bloodstains and Early Modern Textile Culture 61
    Hester Lees-Jeffries

Chapter 5. Rethinking Nosebleeds: Gendering Spontaneous
        Bleedings in Medieval and Early Modern Medicine   79
Gabriella Zuccolin and Helen King

Chapter 6. Screaming Bleeding Trees: Textual Wounding
        and the Epic Tradition   92
Joe Moshenska

III. CORRUPTION

Chapter 7. Corruption, Generation, and the Problem of
        Menstrua in Early Modern Alchemy   111
Tara Nummedal

Chapter 8. Bloody Students: Youth, Corruption, and Discipline
        in the Medieval Classroom   123
Ben Parsons

Chapter 9. Blood, Milk, Poison: *Romeo and Juliet*'s Tragedy
        of "Green" Desire and Corrupted Blood   134
Bonnie Lander Johnson

IV. PROOF

Chapter 10. "In Every Wound There is a Bloody Tongue":
        Cruentation in Early Modern Literature
        and Psychology   151
Lesel Dawson

Chapter 11. "In such abundance . . . that it fill a Bason":
        Early Modern Bleeding Bowls   167
Eleanor Decamp

Chapter 12. *Macbeth* and the Croxton *Play of the Sacrament*:
        Blood and Belief in Early English Stagecraft   183
Elisabeth Dutton

Chapter 13. Simular Proof, Tragicomic Turns,
   and *Cymbeline*'s Bloody Cloth   198
 Patricia Parker

V. SIGNS AND SUBSTANCE

Chapter 14. Blood of the Grape   211
 Frances E. Dolan

Chapter 15. Blood on the Butcher's Knife: Images of Pig Slaughter
   in Late Medieval Illustrated Calendars   224
 Dolly Jørgensen

Chapter 16. Queer Blood   238
 Helen Barr

Notes   249

Bibliography   309

List of Contributors   339

Index   343

Acknowledgments   353

Introduction

BONNIE LANDER JOHNSON AND ELEANOR DECAMP

This book emerges from a concern, shared by a number of medieval and early modern scholars across the world, that "blood" was and is a word whose copious signifying capacities remain desperately underexamined. Frequently conjured on stage and in the printed word as both literal substance and figurative description, "blood" rarely appears to be drawn from a single, shared historical interpretation. What exactly did our medieval and early modern predecessors define as the red stuff that runs in human veins? And just how vast was blood's potential application in figurative descriptions of the human condition?

Medical and social historians of the medieval and early modern periods are increasingly locating blood as a rich and complex area of inquiry; recent individual works, each devoted to one of blood's many functions, have focused on the role blood played in Galenic thought,[1] in the intersection between familial networks, gender, childcare, and reproduction,[2] and in women's health in both early modern England[3] and France.[4] Hannah R. Johnson and Jean E. Feerick have examined blood and race in medieval blood libels[5] and early modern colonialism;[6] Louise Noble and Richard Sugg have unearthed early modern literature's interest in blood as a medicinal substance;[7] and Bettina Bildhauer's interest in medieval German approaches to blood is wide-ranging.[8] All of these studies draw on work by Caroline Walker Bynum and Gail Kern Paster—and this collection is no less indebted. Bynum's *Wonderful Blood* (2007) has ensured that for medievalists blood is now a crucial consideration when thinking about literary and cultural constructions of gender, race, holiness, devotion, and the body. And Gail Kern Paster's *The Body Embarrassed* (1993) guaranteed that a generation of early modern scholars are attuned to the historical reality of the humoral body.[9]

It should come as no surprise that blood is emerging as a central concern for scholars working in the medieval and early modern periods; it was in these centuries that blood underwent some of its most significant and lasting conceptual transformations. Definitions of blood in Western European medical writing ca. 1400–1700 were slippery and changeable: blood was at once the red fluid in human veins, a humor, a fluid governing crucial Galenic models of bodily change such as plethora and purging, a waste product, a cause of corruption, a source of life, a medical cure, a fluid appearing under the guise of all other bodily fluids, and (after William Harvey's discovery of its circulation) blood caused the seventeenth century's greatest medical controversy. However, the period's many figurative uses of "blood" are even more difficult to pin down: the term appeared in almost every sphere of life and thought and ran through discourses as significant as divine right theory, doctrinal and liturgical controversy, political reform, and family and institutional organization. Any attempt to trace blood's "lexical unwieldiness"[10] in the literature, drama, and visual arts of the period must therefore grapple with a highly overdetermined sign.

However, recent scholarship on blood in the medieval and early modern periods is not in full conversation. The works mentioned here are separated by both period and discipline. *Blood Matters* is designed to recognize blood as a distinct category of inquiry and to draw together those scholars developing an expertise in the area who might otherwise not be in dialogue. The nature of blood, as a substance and an idea, requires interdisciplinarity; blood touches and is codified by every area of human experience. But it also demands an interperiod approach, especially where the years 1400–1700 are concerned. These centuries proved crucially transformative for those discursive sites in which blood played a key role: Eucharistic controversy, anatomical cultures, Counter-Reformation piety, the emergence of nation-states and colonialism, and the rise of primogeniture.

Charting the full range of blood's meanings in the history of European thought will be an ongoing project, requiring the expertise of scholars from a variety of disciplines and periods. This book is offered as the first wide-ranging, interdisciplinary study of blood in Western Europe ca. 1400–1700, bringing together historians, literary scholars, and drama specialists. In this volume theatrical practice and medical practice are found to converge in their approach to the regulation of blood as a source of identity and truth; medieval civic life intersects with seventeenth-century science and philosophy; the categories of class, race, gender, and sexuality find in the language of blood as many mechanisms for differentiation as for homogeneity; and fields as disparate as pedagogical theory, alchemical cultures, phlebotomy, wet-nursing, and wine production emerge as historically and intellectually analogous. The breadth of study here is not to demonstrate that blood has a bewildering omnipresence, which defies semantics, logic, and categorization, but to explore how it enables medieval and early modern thinking (and our own) to confront the contradictions and failures of scientific, artistic, and social constructs. And so through our bold intellectualization of blood matters we gain a tool for discourse itself.

Blood Matters takes seriously its interdisciplinary and interperiod agenda. The book seeks in blood's various qualities and behaviors those unifying ideas from which are emerging methodological approaches capable of bridging disciplinary and period divides. Blood is therefore not just the object of our inquiry: its conceptual and semiotic patterns shape individual chapters' analytical approach but also provide the terms through which separate disciplines can converse. Each of the book's five sections (Circulation, Wounds, Corruption, Proof, Signs and Substance) brings together work from at least two distinct specialisms and historical periods.

Circulation

Blood Matters takes as its starting point William Harvey (1578–1657), whose discovery of the circulation of the blood has been seen as marking the beginnings of modern science—not so much through the physiological reality he revealed but rather through the controversial nature of his inquiry, which rejected the early modern medical community's intellectual tradition of philosophical disputation in favor of empirical observation and experimentation. In her chapter on Harvey, Margaret Healy questions the recent critical attempt to read Harvey's discovery as a radical "dethroning" of the heart (and the centralized political authority represented by the heart) in favor of the more dispersed and circulating blood. Arguing that Harvey's anatomical observations were *not* an expression of commonwealth politics, Healy reveals instead how the language Harvey used to articulate his discovery drew upon a much longer tradition in which circulation and rotation have been used to describe a range of human states and experiences. Like Heather Webb, whose chapter analyses the figurative language of circulation in the writing of Dante and Catherine of Siena, Healy demonstrates how powerful—and how pliable—circulation was, and is, as a metaphor for the organization of human society, the distribution of its goods, and the regulation of its moral health.

By bringing these chapters together with Katharine Craik's study of class, blood-typing, and the circulation of personhood on the Shakespearean stage, *Blood Matters* interpolates Webb's medieval Italian account of charity's demands on the individual-in-community with the now long-standing New Historicist interest in the rise of the individual and, in so doing, pushes early modern criticism's concern with historical personhood into important areas of inquiry that it has for too long neglected. New Historicist descriptions of the emerging modern, Protestant individual have for some decades looked to early modern Galenic and medical lexicons to account for the increased isolation and containment of the self within the body. But recent work by Paster, Lesel Dawson, Nancy Selleck, and Richard Sugg has instead explored early modern descriptions of the body as intersubjective or "interpersonal," as open to and embedded within the physiological operations of other bodies.[11] While broadening the terms in which early modern identity is understood, these new accounts nonetheless remain bound by those physiological interpretations of the self so central to early modern scholarship's interest in embodiment.

More recently still, there has been an increased desire to reassess the scholarly assumption that Cartesian duality was accepted absolutely by early moderns, and to include in our accounts of physiological experience a proper historical sense of the soul as conditioned by, and in relationship with, the body. To this end, Webb's analysis of the medieval individual compelled by the demands of virtue to circulate both physiologically and spiritually within the community of the church offers a theologically inflected description of selfhood much needed in early modern discussions. The neglect of this virtue-based interpretation by early modern scholars cannot be sufficiently accounted for by pointing to the Protestant Reformation's isolation of the self from ecclesial intervention in the spiritual and moral affairs of individual Christians; charity and community remained central imperatives regardless of confessional allegiance.

What is perhaps most striking about the group of chapters on circulation is their shared view of blood as a substance whose figurative possibilities—and not just in the English language—are caught up in those social conflicts that emerge when theories or discourses of movement collide with discourses of authority. In Shakespeare and Dante, as much as in writing from the theological, political, and scientific fields, blood's circularity underpins descriptions of society as collective against opposing images of authority as fixed, centralized, or rigid. But as Katharine Craik's analysis of *Henry V* demonstrates, blood's circularity was also deployed as a way of protecting authority: the shared blood of noblemen was a more limited domain of circulation into which common blood was not usually admitted.

Blood's long history in figurative descriptions of human relationships and community organization stems in part from the equally long-standing role it played in the construction and depiction of personal identity. What the chapters in this section suggest is that in the late medieval and early modern periods, new negotiations between collective and individual identities were emerging through revolutions in scientific, doctrinal, and political thought. Blood offered a vital conceptual terrain through which to pose questions about the self as separate from and embedded within the blood that circulated in collective bodies, from the body of Christ, and the body politic, to the social bodies that underpinned economic negotiation and the world of the professional theater itself.

Wounds

Blood's role in the conception—and reconception—of individual and collective identity also emerges in the late medieval and early modern interest in wounds. As the chapters in this second section reveal, wounds were often interpreted as sites of rupture; not only material, biological rupture but also ontological: wounds were capable of determining where one form of selfhood ends and another begins. Beyond the distinction made by the chapters on circulation—that blood could both reveal and occlude where one person's identity starts and another person's ends—the chapters on wounds suggest that the eruption of blood from the body could initiate the emergence of new states of being altogether. This is evident both within the individual bleeding body (for Helen King and Gabriella Zuccolin, the bleeding wound forces the reconception of a body's gender, as much then as now) and in the conception of bleeding bodies more generally (for Hester Lees-Jeffries, the wound, depicted onstage through bloody clothing, can pose the question of where the self ends and the world begins). And, as Joe Moshenska argues in his study of the bleeding tree *topos*, the wound could even problematize the distinction between sentient beings, objects, and textual events.

The sight of blood emerging from a wound was, and will always be, arresting. Wounds register the vulnerability of the human body, reminding us how easily the skin, which ought properly to contain our blood, can be ruptured. A wound is evidence of how suddenly the vitality of a life can be drained away, as though all the complex particularities of personhood, one's experiences and thoughts, one's tastes, sentiments, and relationship to the world, were merely water on whose rapid course "I" fades quickly to nothingness. It is perhaps not surprising then that wounding emerged as an event that provided opportunities for poets and playwrights, as much as for physicians and theorists, to explore drastic moments of differentiation—between life and death, human and animal, man and woman, sensate being and insensate object, person and world. This may be as true for our own society as it was for any other, but, as this volume argues, the medieval and early modern period saw a rapid increase in the anxious questioning of those systems of thought—doctrinal, medical, moral, philosophical—that underpinned conceptions of the human person and its relationship to the world and to God. And it is for this period in particular that an image as condensed and startling as a wound could become the site of such questioning: the period's literature and drama abounds with that flowering of sophistication and playfulness capable of concentrating unwieldy conceptual challenges into the ornate rendering of a Classical *topos* or the fold and cut of a doublet.

Corruption

Despite the many different traditions in medieval and early modern medical theory and practice, one element of blood's behavior remained a consistent point of interest and concern: its capacity to be corrupted. The corruptibility of blood was both a material and moral truth and was crucially linked to its perceived role in the generation and development of life. As the chapters in this section all make clear, blood's role in sex and reproduction ensured that it was routinely described as a force capable of both generation and corruption because blood, like human sexuality, was built from the moral opposition fundamental to original sin. Where the blood of Christ was uniquely pure and redemptive, human blood was at once a source of purification and a substance forever tainted. Just as the remission of sin was the ultimate goal of all Christian endeavor, so the cleansing of blood's inherent corruption was the implicit goal of most of the period's numerous medical regimens.

As Tara Nummedal's work on alchemical bloods demonstrates, the duplicity of blood as both the source of life and the cause of corruption was concentrated most in medieval and early modern perceptions of menstrual blood. Despite the menstruating body's function as an exemplary model for nature's expulsive and self-regulating power (as King and Zuccolin also suggest), menstrual blood itself carried the period's anxieties about women's moral duplicity and biological weakness. Menstrual blood was understood to be the matter out of which new life was formed in the womb: this fact, together with the crucial role menses played in cleansing purgation, underpinned the view of menstrual blood as good, wholesome, vital, and perhaps, if not pure, then purifying. But menstrual blood and menstruating women were also thought to be corrupting: they could bring madness, disease, and death to those who touched or looked upon them. Nummedal's work highlights how much blood's important role in alchemy stemmed from its dual function as generative and corrupting, but also how alchemical bloods were used to express the period's uncertainties about sexuality, and female sexuality in particular.

Blood's dual function as generative and corruptible, especially in the realm of sexuality and reproduction, was a particular concern for medieval and early modern writers when they turned to the problems of adolescence. Ben Parsons's work on medieval pedagogy reveals that from at least the thirteenth century adolescence was "often seen as an anatomical and medical problem as much as a disciplinary one, a point at which the body is temporarily corrupted, and corrupts mind and morals in turn." Medieval and early modern thinking about moral and physiological corruption perceived blood as crucially linked to the appetites—for food, as much as for sex, objects, and social positioning—and the purity of blood during the formative stages of infancy, childhood, and youth was thought to shape the relative health of one's appetites into adolescence and adulthood. As Parsons's work illustrates, the corrupted appetites of the medieval adolescent were both cause and effect of their corrupted and too-prevalent blood—a view clearly still in circulation by the time Shakespeare was working. Bonnie Lander Johnson explores these concerns as they emerge in Shakespeare's *Romeo and Juliet*, arguing that the relative physiological and emotional success of children's passage through the stages of nourishment—blood, milk, food—had crucial implications for their later development and health.

Medieval and early modern writing on blood as a substance governing sexual and reproductive health is heavily influenced by the period's anxieties about women's bodies and the special monopoly women had over the production of life. This writing suggests how concerned the period's medical, pedagogical, and scientific writers were over the fact that human life was formed by women's blood. Menstrual blood was thought to be the raw materials for infant bodies and their first food; breast milk (blood under a different guise) nourished children until weaning, and the entire process was overseen primarily by mothers, midwives, and wet nurses. By the time children reached the schoolroom and the interventions of those pedagogues described in Parsons's chapter, their blood and appetites were already formed. While the wild behavior of youth had a clear physiological cause, it was also necessarily rooted in an understanding of humanity as fallen. On its own, the fallen state was attributable to a woman and her appetites, but, as the chapters in this section reveal, a person's ability to be redeemed of original sin—whether in marriage, the schoolroom or the alchemist's laboratory—was also greatly influenced by the relative corruption or purity of the women who formed their blood in the womb and at the breast.

Proof

Throughout the medieval and early modern period, blood's close association with human identity underpinned its function as a form of evidentiary proof. Blood was perceived as not just essential to, but also the essence of, the person in whose veins it ran. Blood was, as Lesel Dawson puts it, thought to "encode a subject's experiences and embody some quintessence of the self." This belief can be traced in part to blood's role as a carrier of *spiritus* and soul, but also to the fact that blood is normally hidden within the body. Blood is the secret, internal self. And it is the truth of this hidden self that is necessarily glimpsed when blood is shed. As Elisabeth Dutton observes, "blood cannot, in the ordinary run of things, be found outside the body; once it is outside the body, it demands attention and explanation." In the same way, when evidence was required to prove an uncertainty (whether in the legitimate context of judicial inquiry or the revenger's desire for truth about the beloved) blood was usually demanded as proof.

This book's focus on blood's role in the search for evidentiary proof expands upon a growing critical interest in the history of judicial reasoning, from the "rise of Protestant legalism" to changes in the judicial and moral status of evidentiary proof more generally.[12] The medieval and early modern period's trust in blood's ability to speak the truth is nowhere more evident than in its use of cruentation to prove guilt in murder trials. *Cruentation* was the term given to the instantaneous and fresh bleeding from the corpse of a murder victim when it was brought into the presence of its assailant. Such blood was interpreted as testimony to the murderer's guilt. Fundamentally, the phenomenon was understood as providential, as a truth revealed in blood by God. But, as Lesel Dawson argues, this explanation also underpinned more local assumptions about the nature of the fleshly body and the bonds by which bodies—living and dead—were connected to each other, materially and morally.

It might seem surprising that the same cultures that thought blood constituted a person's secret being also routinely drew blood for health purposes. More surprising still, the blood drawn in phlebotomy was perceived as waste matter, a "noisome" and unwanted presence in the streets of London. But, as Eleanor Decamp's chapter suggests, anxieties surrounding the opposing definitions of blood as both essential selfhood and waste can be detected in early modern London's efforts to regulate all areas of phlebotomy. If a person's blood was perceived as capable of carrying their essential selfhood, the "truth" of their being, but was also, once spent and absorbed into the general waste of a community's shed blood, considered merely an anonymous source of pollution, then the fleeting moment in which blood appears at the surface of the skin emerges as especially meaningful. Developing further the view of bloody rupture as ontologically significant (as advanced in this book's section on wounds), the four chapters on proof demonstrate how much blood's role in the assertion and loss of personal identity was bound up with its capacity for complex and unstable patterns of signification.

Blood's status as evidentiary proof is familiar to contemporary societies, even if the truths it can prove to us are quite different from those in the medieval and early modern period. The chapters by Dawson and Decamp illustrate how pervasive and deeply felt was the period's investment in blood's capacity to prove the truth (of criminal behavior, of a phlebotomist's trustworthiness and training). Then, as now, we need to know that we have recourse to substances and techniques through which we can access absolute truths. The urgency of this need was a familiar subject on the stage. As the chapters by Elisabeth Dutton and Patricia Parker demonstrate, both the medieval and early modern theaters used blood to interrogate the human need to know the truth—of one's faith, one's safety from sin, and (most famously on the Shakespearean stage) of a spouse's fidelity.

Dutton's and Parker's chapters on blood's complex status as proof on the stage foreground the theatrical quality of evidentiary proof more generally, while the chapters by Decamp and Dawson illustrate how "staged" the human requirement for truth can be even in the realms of professional practice and legal justice. The theatrical nature with which early modern medical men promoted their expertise is already well recognized, but Decamp's chapter highlights how far barbers' and surgeons' self-promotion extended: to the dressing of their shop windows, their use of instruments, and their treatment of the waste blood drawn from their clients. When phlebotomy practices emerged on the stage, they both replicated the medical "performances" apparent on the streets of London and recodified them within a new moral and semiotic terrain in which they came to articulate the widespread anxiety about the competence of those who let blood.

In a similar way, when acts of cruentation appeared on the stage, they became occasions for elaborating the remorse felt by murderers. The early modern criminal justice system was required to stage publicly the guilt of perpetrators, and the theater's adoption of these scenes navigates their role in the desires of audience members (at the theater and in the courtroom). Spectators not only wanted to see crime policed but to be part of the moral cleansing for which contrition is designed. In this way the stage gave playgoers what they needed—a chance to believe that guilt can be proved beyond doubt and that the recognition of such truth enables universal cleansing. But, as Parker's work on bloody cloths makes clear, the theater also denied this same desire by suggesting that blood, as a sign, could ultimately only stand for itself and not for certain proof of anything at all.

Signs and Substance

One of Christendom's central doctrines, the doctrine of Real Presence, has throughout the last two thousand years come under constant attack. But in the centuries with which this book is concerned, this doctrine met with the most radical dissent. By questioning Christ's Real Presence in the Eucharist, reformers initiated what we might call a culture of doubt, in which the relationship between signs and substances more generally came under scrutiny. The chapters in this final section all treat depictions of blood that exploit the period's sophisticated approach to the relationship between substance and sign. In doing so, they draw on a rich and varied scholarly tradition. But each chapter pushes into new territory: the role of blood in medieval butchery and its depiction in popular calendars, nationalist arguments over the production and consumption of wine, and the queering of England's most famous saint, Thomas Becket.

In the chapters by Frances Dolan and Dolly Jørgensen, blood crosses the sacred and secular boundaries, embedding sacred signification in earthly and profane objects and at the same time exposing such miraculous sign-making as fraudulent. Helen Barr's work on *The Canterbury Interlude* instead presents us with a definition of blood that resists substantiation altogether. *The Canterbury Interlude*, a fifteenth-century response to Chaucer's *Canterbury Tales*, "conflates the sacrificial, healing, and sacred blood of a saint with the polluted and contaminated blood of a figure associated with murder, swindling and sexual deviance."

This commixture of unlikely bloods raises profound questions about the ontology of sacred blood and the figures with which it was most associated. Barr argues that in the short time afforded by the pilgrimage, the Pardoner's blood produces a dizzying array of significations. But as he journeys home from Canterbury, the Pardoner wears his bloody head wound hidden beneath bandages. Where the miraculous blood from Becket's wound was copious and an arresting material reality, the Pardoner's blood remains unseen, defying categorization as substance. It is a "queer blood that refuses identification and legibility." So severed from material blood, the Pardoner's blood reaches a point of ceaseless self-referentiality.

In semiotic narratives of the history of language, the sixteenth and seventeenth centuries usually emerge as a moment when "the link that joins each object to its own appearance, each creature to its own body, each word to its own signified is radically called into question."[13] But while Protestantism's separation of sign from substance constitutes a major turning point in the history of sign-making, so too did Thomas Aquinas's earlier justifications of transubstantiation. The theologies of substance and accident developed by Aquinas and his successors explain a unique phenomenon, the Real Presence. But these descriptions of the extraordinary rely on and are coterminous with an emerging medieval understanding of the "ordinary" relationship between substance and sign as itself far from straightforward. What Giorgio Agamben has said of the Baroque period also applies to the centuries preceding it: "each thing is true only to the extent to which it signifies another." This "mortification" of the proper relationship between sign and thing is "a token of redemption that will be rescued on the Last Day, but whose cipher is already implicit in the act of creation.... God appears thus as the first and supreme emblematist, an 'arguto favellatore' (subtle, witty fabulist)."[14]

Blood is central to the semiotic project. Its presence in the Word and in wine (both the consecrated and, as Dolan suggests, the everyday) determines its role in the unique and divine events through which absolute links between substance and sign were made possible. The Reformation's radical distinction between flesh and bread, blood and wine, and the culture of doubt that ensued, confirmed blood's place in a conceptual paradigm in which transubstantiation is both possible and impossible. In this paradigm, the divine possibility of total congruence between sign and signified is always shadowed by the profane, or heretical, specter of their ultimate separation, just as the impossibility of any such unity between substance and sign is haunted by the truth it denies. Helen Barr's work confirms that literature well before the Baroque period knew and reveled in the fragility of its status as sign-system. The Pardoner's bleeding wound was, as much as Shakespeare's bloody cloths, circulating in a text that refused it any moment of substantiation, propelling it instead into ever more significations, each referring one to the next.

This uncertainty of language is also blood's uncertainty. In each of the categories explored in this book, blood both does and does not do what is asked of it. While blood's circulation enables us to construct ideas about the organization of communities and the movement of their resources, it also denies this collective impulse by instead closing off the circulation of relationship and wealth to those whose racial, class, or familial blood sets them apart. In its appearance at sites of wounding blood is a sign of life, confirming vitality and existence, but it is also a sign of that life's rapid fading. Similarly, the very (female) blood that gives life to infants is also the source of the world's corruption. And the blood we demand as evidence of an absolute truth can ultimately prove only how tenuous blood is as a sign: it cannot be trusted, and yet we cannot help but put our trust in it since there is little else in the natural world that can so signify the essential self or codify materially the experience of being.

Helen Barr's description of blood as a sign without substance might in fact speak to our own time as well as to the Renaissance. As much as contemporary biomedical discourses seek to isolate blood as anatomical matter disconnected from its role in the description of personal and social identity, we remain unable to locate definitively the material substance we call blood. Modern medicine may scrutinize, name, divide, replicate, and make useful blood's various components, but these processes and insights (limited to the professional few) and medicine's heightened comprehension of blood's homeostatic role in our health do little to help us unearth blood's meaning and humanity's relationship(s) to the red stuff. The growing scholarship on blood suggests that in fact "blood" works as hard at the metaphorical level as it does as pumped matter. It is, perhaps, blood's extraordinary figurative capacity that means it comes closest to being understood at those historical moments in which it undergoes the greatest redefinition.

PART I

Circulation

Chapter 1

Was the Heart "Dethroned"?

Harvey's Discoveries and the Politics of Blood, Heart, and Circulation

MARGARET HEALY

> Most Serene King!
> The animal's heart is the basis of life, its chief member, the sun of its microcosm; on the heart all its activity depends.... Equally is the king the basis of his kingdoms, the sun of his microcosm, the heart of the state; from him all power arises and all grace stems.

In 1641, William Harvey, famous anatomist and royal physician, was commanded by King Charles I to investigate the "marvel" of a particularly strange body—that belonging to a "lively" young nobleman of about 18 years.[1] As a child, Hugh Montgomery suffered a "great mishap from an unexpected fall, causing a fracture in the ribs on his left side"; he subsequently developed an abscess, which had left a permanent "very wide cavity" in his chest (250). It was reported that his lungs could be seen and touched through this hole. Fired by his prodigious scientific curiosity, Harvey was immediately on the case: he arranged a meeting and at his request the young man removed the metal plate covering the old wound. Harvey recorded that he was "astounded at the extraordinariness of the thing and [he] . . . scrutinised everything again and again" (250). It was clear to him that the visible part was not, in fact, the lungs but the beating heart itself: its pulsation and rhythmical movements corresponded exactly with the young man's pulse. Excited by his discovery, Harvey immediately conveyed the young nobleman "to his most serene Majesty" so that he "might see the heart moving to and fro and its ventricles pulsating, and touch it with his hand" (251). The king's fingers were duly inserted into the cavity to touch the beating heart and amazingly the young man did not flinch; ergo, the heart, "that most supreme member, is itself insensitive" (249)—it was simply muscle. For Harvey this was his most "wonderful experiment" (249)—a unique opportunity—for "so it came about that his serene Highness agreed with me that the heart is without any sense of feeling" (251); it also confirmed the anatomist's thesis (with the king as chief witness) that the key movement of the organ occurred in systole when the heart thrust its refreshed sanguine contents into the arterial system to invigorate the entire body. The centuries-old notion of the kingly feeling heart—seat of the sensitive soul and all the weighty symbolic baggage attached to that—had been dealt a fatal blow, ironically by the touch of that other king, Charles I, who was, of course, soon to experience his own demise. Succinctly capturing the emotional and intellectual significance accorded to the heart at this time, the king confided in Montgomery, "Sir, I wish I could perceive the thoughts of some of my nobilities' hearts as I have seen your heart."[2]

As Harvey's fulsome eulogy to Charles I prefacing his 1628 treatise on the circulation of the blood reveals, he was acutely aware of the potential political ramifications of his anatomical demonstrations (see epigraph). The human body and society, the microcosm and macrocosm, were perceived as intimately related in this period—man was the model of all things. *De Motu Cordis*'s Dedication explains: "almost all our concepts of humanity are modelled on our knowledge of man himself, and several of our concepts of royalty on our knowledge of the heart" (3). Aristotle had insisted on the primacy of the heart in the body—it was the noblest of organs and the foundation of life—and, for a self-proclaimed Aristotelian like Harvey ("in chief of all the Ancients, I follow Aristotle," *De generatione,* 20), challenging that wisdom was akin to rocking the king's throne. However, by dramatically invoking Harvey as "Disturber of the quiet of physicians! O seditious citizen of the physical commonwealth!, who first of all durst oppose an opinion confirmed for so many centuries by the consent of all," the translator of the 1653 English edition of *De Motu* confirmed that this anatomist's findings had, indeed, proved disturbing, shaking many centuries of tradition about monarchical government as well as the heart.[3]

This chapter investigates Harvey's "discoveries," assessing the political implications of his momentous revelations about the circulation of the blood.[4] In the process it challenges the notion, first advanced by Christopher Hill, that in 1649, emboldened by the execution of the king, Harvey performed a "somersault" and "dethroned" the heart, abolishing "the hierarchy of heart, liver and brain within the body", reascribing primacy of position and power to "democratic" blood, which—in his late writings—is one with the soul and circulates to nourish and invigorate all parts of the body.[5] Hill suggests that this has "republican" implications: "Harvey spoke no longer of 'the sovereignty of the heart' but of 'the prerogative and antiquity of the blood'."[6] This perceived volte-face has been described by John Rogers as Harvey's "acrobatic theoretical reversal."[7] Furthermore, Rogers argues that there was a thoroughgoing "conceptual alliance" between science and politics in the revolutionary years centered in "the dangerously antiauthoritarian logic of the Vitalist Moment." In his view, Harvey's "vitalist turn" in 1649 meant that blood was now—for the first time—"empowered by a vitalist infusion of spirit and energy" while the heart was "demoted unequivocally from its former status as privileged member."[8] For Rogers, this amounts to "a radical recharting of bodily order" in which "the blood has clearly usurped the heart as the center of the bodily polis and as the distributor of bodily nourishment."[9]

On the basis of a detailed examination of Harvey's writings and an analysis of the use of his ideas by three political theorists in the mid-seventeenth century, this chapter argues that there is insufficient evidence to support a theoretical "somersault" in Harvey's late writings and, furthermore, that it is difficult to decipher any sustained "ontological connection" between politics and science in the revolutionary years.[10] That said, however, a complex interplay of scientific with political and economic ideas is discernible. As this chapter will seek to illuminate, Harvey's pronouncements about the circulation of the blood appear to have captivated the minds of his contemporaries for a variety of reasons that came together in the mid-century years. But how far did ideology help to fashion Harvey's anatomical hypotheses, and how influential were his ideas in shaping the political utopias and dystopias propounded by such diverse thinkers as James Harrington, Gerrard Winstanley, and Thomas Hobbes? Finally, if not a "conceptual alliance," what can be conjectured about the nature of the relation between models of the physical body and the body politic in these turbulent years?

Harvey studied anatomy at Padua, following in the illustrious footsteps of Andreas Vesalius, author of *De Humani Corporis Fabrica* (1543), and his successor Realdo Colombo, whose *De Re Anatomica* (1559) had demonstrated that blood moved from the right to the left side of the heart by means of a transit across the lungs—a crucial insight that was later developed by Harvey.[11] Although Harvey formally announced his discovery of the circulation of the blood in 1628 when he published his *Exercitatio Anatomica de Motu Cordis et Sanguinis in Animalibus* (*The Movement of the Heart and Blood in Animals: An Anatomical Essay*), he had been investigating the cardiovascular system for many years prior to this. In 1615, he had been appointed Lumleian lecturer on anatomy and surgery by the London College of Physicians, and his lecture notes for his 1616 anatomy course provide valuable information about the formation of his ideas. It seems that by 1616 Harvey had both verified Colombo's thesis on the pulmonary transit of the blood (and had thus rejected the Galenic notion of an interventricular septum) and established that the heart's muscular contraction in systole powerfully ejected the blood outward (as opposed to sucking it in during diastole as was traditionally thought).[12] The lecture notes also repeatedly make the point that "spirit and blood is one thing"; "spirit, like flame, is no wise separated from" blood; and even declare that "the soul is in the blood. Innate heat is the author of life and where it most abounds there it exists principally and primarily."[13] Spirit here denotes both heat and motive power and is one with the blood and soul. Furthermore, by 1616, his investigations into fetal development as observed within chicken eggs—a major preoccupation throughout his life—had led him to conclude that blood was in being (and was, therefore, the prime life-giving particle) prior to the heart, liver, and brain: "Nor is the heart the chief part by virtue of its origin, for I think that the ventricles ... are made from the drop of blood which is found in the egg and the heart is fashioned along with the remaining parts, as sprouts come forth in an ear of corn" (251). These key observations challenged both Aristotelian and Galenic orthodoxy, rocking the boat of traditional medicine, so it is not surprising—especially given Harvey's respected status as a high-ranking member of the College of Physicians and his stated desire "to keep Galen's medicine in good order"—that they had to wait many years before publication in 1628.[14]

But what were the traditional beliefs about the heart and blood? First, Galen maintained that veins and arteries played completely different roles in the body and his teachings conveyed no idea of circulation. Instead, venous blood, made in and attracted from the liver, supplied nourishment to all parts of the body, while the arteries carried "vital, life-giving blood" from the heart to the rest of the body by a "pulsative power of the arteries."[15] There was no pulmonary circulation (through the lungs); rather, a small amount of nutritious blood diffused from the right to left ventricle of the heart via invisible pores in the interventricular septum. Galen viewed the left ventricle of the heart as the site where air was refined and warmed, and Aristotelian wisdom had made much of the heart as the first part to be created—essential to growth and life and the home of the sensitive soul.

In fact Harvey's *De Motu Cordis* appears to strive extremely hard not to destabilize any philosophical or political boat. Harvey is profusely deferential toward the ancient authorities, especially Aristotle, making careful compromises where dangerous controversy is sensed, obfuscating where necessary, and ultimately utilizing his discovery of the circulation of the blood to boost princely authority. Early in his treatise, for example, he tackles the troublesome observation—confirmed by the authority of "autopsia"—that blood is the primogenital particle: "If . . . you look at the structural development in the chicken's egg, the first thing to be seen . . . is merely a vesicle or auricle or throbbing drop of blood; it is only afterwards, with growth, that the heart becomes apparent" (28–29). He repeats several times that life begins with that "throbbing point" or "drop of blood" and declares, "if anyone wished to look more deeply into the matter, he will not style the heart the 'first to live' and 'last to die.' Instead he will say that the auricles . . . are alive before the heart proper, and die after it" (27). The auricles are, of course, made from that throbbing drop of blood; the implication, then, is that blood (rather than the heart) receives life first and is last to die. His 1651 treatise *De Generatione Animalium* renders explicit the consistency of his thinking on this matter: "Life . . . exists in the blood . . . it is most plain that the blood is the genital particle, the fountain of life, the first to live and the last to die, the chief habitation of the soul, in which (as its fountain-head) heat first and chiefly abounds and flourishes. . . . As I pointed out some time ago in my book on the movement of the blood" (243–44). It seems that in Harvey's mind there was no contradiction between his thesis as propounded in 1628 ("as I pointed out some time ago") and his position in 1651.

However, *De Motu Cordis* does carry out some interesting linguistic maneuvers in order, it would seem, to make compromises with Aristotle, mollify his critics, and boost princely authority. Halfway through the treatise, the heart morphs into "the starting point of life" by virtue of it being the organ that moves the blood throughout the circulatory system: "This organ deserves to be styled the starting point of life and the sun of our microcosm. . . . For it is by the heart's vigorous beat that the blood is moved, perfected, activated" (46). However, as the treatise progresses, Harvey raises the important but potentially troubling question, "Why is [blood] . . . there before all the rest? How does it come to possess all the vital and higher principles, and to be eager to move and be driven hither and thither, the object for which the heart appears to have been made?" (74). Then, having raised this significant conundrum, he simply declines to provide an answer, excusing himself on the grounds that this would take "a full-sized book" (75). Indeed, by the end of *De Motu Cordis*, echoing the treatise's dedication, the heart has been restored to its kingly status, thereby underpinning the other king's supreme authority: "Just as the king has the first and highest authority in the state, so the heart governs the whole body. It is, one might say, the source and root from which in the animal all power derives, and on which all power depends" (84).

In Harvey's construction, the heart-monarch's "kingship" is completely justified: the heart's continuous delivery of "spiritous," "vital" nourishment keeps the body healthy and alive. However, it is crucial that prior to this the treatise has detailed the pulmonary circulation and the role of the lungs in perfecting the blood, and clearly this is of immense importance to Harvey's ideas about how the blood is "framed," which has to do with "warmth, spirit [and] finish" (31). He declares: "the greatest cause of indecision and error in this matter seems to me to have a single one, namely the close connection of the heart and the lungs" (31). Hailing "immortal Galen" as "that most ingenious and learned authority" in the same chapter, he has nevertheless contradicted him in proposing the deep significance of the pulmonary "circulation" to the "finishing" of the blood (32)—in Galen's view that was the seminal function of the left ventricle.

Further, Harvey clearly states in *De Motu Cordis* that the "heart's one role is the transmission of the blood and its propulsion, by means of the arteries, to the extremities" (31); later, he reiterates, "I am obliged to conclude that in animals the blood is driven round a circuit with an unceasing, circular sort of movement, that this is an activity or function of the heart which it carries out by virtue of its pulsation, and that . . . constitutes the sole reason for the heart's pulsatile movement" (68). If the heart's "one" and "sole" function is distribution, Harvey is indirectly refuting the Aristotelian position that the heart also heats the blood, adds spirit, and finishes it. Through the course of the treatise the circulatory system of heart, lungs, blood, and vessels—but crucially not the heart alone—emerges as preeminent in terms of human life:

Harvey affirms in the conclusion of *De Motu Cordis* that "the lungs and the heart contain the storehouse, source and treasury of the blood, and the laboratory in which it is brought to perfection" (86). As Harvey foregrounds in a letter written in the 1650s, a key opponent, the French anatomist Jean Riolan, "exert[ed] himself to the utmost to deny a passage of blood through the lungs to the left ventricle of the heart."[16] It seems that acknowledging the crucial (but theoretically heterodox) role of the lungs and pulmonary circulation in the process of replenishing the blood was a major obstacle to the acceptance of Harvey's findings.

To return now to the "dethronement" thesis initially advanced by Hill who based Harvey's remarkable "somersault" on his second letter to Riolan (1649),[17] which was published in 1653 as *Two Anatomical Exercitations*. This crucial passage warrants close scrutiny:

> I will say and propound it without demonstration . . . that the heart, as it is the beginning of all things in the body, the spring, fountain, and first causer of life, is to be taken, as being joynd, together with the veins, and all the arteries, and the blood which is contain'd in them. Like as the brain, (together with all its sensible nervs, organs, and spinal marrow) is the adequate organ of the sense. . . . But if you understand by this word heart, the body of the heart, with the ventricles and ears, I do not think it to be the framer [fabricator] of the blood, and that it has not force, vertue, motion, or heat, as the gift of the heart; . . . I think the first cause of distention is innate heat in the blood it self . . . and . . . is the last thing that is extinct in the creature.[18]

As we have seen, Harvey's 1628 treatise had said very much the same thing only with not quite so much forthrightness; this certainly does not constitute "dethronement" of the heart.[19] That which Harvey is articulating here is more complex and sophisticated than the traditional hierarchy of organs: he is foregrounding the existence of anatomical and physiological "systems," and the circulatory system is prime among these as "the spring, fountain, and first causer of life": "These parts can in no way get warm again except through the circulation. . . . warming and spirituous blood flowing in from the arteries revives the parts, rewarms them, and restores their movement and sensation. . . . And, indeed, that is the chief use and object of the circulation, and for its sake the blood goes round on its continuous course and perpetual inflow and moves in a circle; namely, so that all parts, depending on it, may be kept by their prime heat in life . . . they are sustained and actuated by the inflow of warmth and the spirits of life."[20]

His major disagreement with Aristotle is, as he makes clear, that he does not think "the *heart* to be the effecter of all things" (*Anatomical Exercitations*, 78). It does not "frame," that is, make the blood or the "Spirit," or heat it: taken alone it does not "perfect" the blood. As he articulated in his earlier *De Motu Cordis*, the lungs and pulmonary circulation are essential to that process, but animal bodies are "nourished, preserved and perfected" (84) by the heart through its sole activity—"pulsatile movement" (68). As the 1628 tract several times reiterates, the "sole reason" for the heart's movement is the forward propulsion of spirit-imbued blood (31, 68).

As Hill suggests, with greater freedom of the printing presses from 1649, and in the absence of a monarchical "heart" (Charles was executed that year), Harvey probably felt more at liberty to present his thesis on the circulation of the blood with greater clarity from that point.[21] We should consider, too, that the authority of the king's touch itself had verified a few years prior to this that the heart was an unfeeling muscle—hardly the seat, then, of the sensitive soul and the passions as Aristotle believed. Harvey is willing overtly to disagree with the authority of Aristotle in his mid-century writings and this might constitute a minor kind of dethronement—but of the master philosopher, not monarchism. However, even in *De Generatione Animalium* (1651), we can observe his drive to make careful compromises with Aristotle in order to avoid offending his disciples: "If we admit the punctum saliens, together with the blood and veins, as one and the same instrument, visible in the first dawning of the foetus, to stand for the heart . . . it is plain that the heart understood in this manner is truly, as Aristotle said, the principal and primary part of the body of an animal, yet its first and chief part is blood" (163).

There is certainly no indication that from 1649 Harvey was using his anatomical observations deliberately to undermine authority and underpin republicanism; on the contrary, he takes inordinate care to speak "with the kind permission of our learned men and a reverence for antiquity."[22] There is considerable evidence to suggest that Harvey was anxious in the earlier part of the century to minimize the depressing effects on his physician's practice, income, and professional standing of his heterodox views. John Aubrey's *Brief Lives* confirms, for example, that Harvey's practice declined after publication of *De Motu Cordis* and that "he was thought to be mad."[23] His friend G. Ent, who published a tract in support of circulation in 1641, *Apologia pro Circulatione*

Sanguinis, reports a telling remark of Harvey's: "You are not ignorant, how great troubles my lucubrations, formerly published, have raised."[24] It seems to have taken twenty to thirty years for his discoveries to be (partially) accepted and for his reputation to be restored; it is not surprising in this context that Harvey attempted to minimize the negative effects of his discoveries in 1628 through careful linguistic maneuvers and compromises with ancient authority.

The rhetorical shift in Harvey's post-1649 printed works from obfuscation toward greater perspicuity and forthrightness does not constitute the thoroughgoing "rejection" of Aristotle and the "theoretical reversal" argued by Hill and Rogers.[25] Furthermore, throughout Harvey's career there is no change in what he perceives to be the blood's constitution—it does contain spirits in the 1616 and 1628 formulations and this is many times reiterated. Rogers has forcefully asserted, however, that Harveian blood underwent an "extraordinary" "vitalist turn" in 1649, now no longer merely "fluid" circulated by the heart it is rather "empowered by a vitalist infusion of spirit and energy."[26] In fact there was nothing revolutionary anyway about the notion of "self moving, spiritualized blood:"[27] it corresponds to the Aristotelian notion of entelechy and, as Harvey's *Anatomical Exercitations* clarifies, vital spirit was a traditional formulation agreed upon by all in the School of Physicians.[28] In Sir Thomas Elyot's popular Galenic medical text, *The Castle of Helth* (1534), for example, "spirit" is the "substance . . . stirring the powers of the body, to perform their operations" and "Vitall spirit" "proceedeth from the heart, and by the arteries or pulses is sent into the whole body."[29] In Harvey, as in Elyot and his ancient authorities, spirits are "every thing which enforces in a mans body, whatsoever hath the power or force of action in living bodies" (*Anatomical Exercitations*, 44). Where Harvey differs from his predecessors is in his insistence that blood and spirits and the soul are one thing and, as we have already seen, he was firmly of this belief when he penned his lecture notes in 1616: "spirit, like flame, is no wise separated from" blood; "the soul is in the blood. Innate heat is the author of life and where it most abounds there it exists principally and primarily."[30] In Harvey, soul acts through the medium of spirit, but spirit cannot be separated from blood—"as light is to the candle so is the spirit to the blood" (1616); "the blood and the Spirit signifie the same thing, though divers in essence, as good Wine and its Spirit [bouquet]" (1653).[31] He is constant on this crucial matter, then, from his first writings to his last.

The notion of vitalism contained in Harvey's writings, therefore, is consistent through time, and this contradicts the notion that it emerged in spectacular form in the revolutionary years, with "monistic vitalism"—self-moving matter infused with spirit—"tying" together a chain of politically diverse figures from Harvey to Harrington, Winstanley, Hobbes, and Cavendish.[32] In fact in his *Anatomical Exercitations* Harvey expends a great deal of ink examining the diverse and nuanced range of mid-century notions of the relations between spirit and matter. There are incorporeal and corporeal spirits, and some corporeal spirits are even believed to be of an "aerial consistence" (46). Harvey is sceptical of all but his own position—that spirit and matter are inseparable and are blood—but, in a manner similar to that of Thomas Hobbes in *Leviathan*, he reserves his deepest scorn for those who believe in "incorporeal spirits" of an "aethereal and celestial nature" that are imagined by "ignorant common people" to enter the body as an "influx" and are the "instrument of Nature" or "bonds of the Soul" (43, 48–49); *Leviathan* linked such ideas about incorporeal spirits with dangerous radicalism—"the rage of the multitude"—and it is likely that Harvey shared this conservative perspective.[33] In her introduction to *De Generatione Animalium*, which Harvey completed in the troubled climate of 1648, Gweneth Whitteridge states, "That Harvey's sympathies were wholeheartedly with the King is clear enough from the many courteously formal yet affectionate references which he makes to him in this book."[34] Harvey's "sympathies" were not those of a revolutionary: when he was making his will in the early 1650s he remarked to Sir Charles Scarburgh that he had intended to endow a professorship of experimental philosophy at Cambridge and a laboratory and herb garden, but if he did that "I should do nothing other than make Anabaptists, Fanatics and all manner of thieves and parricides my heirs."[35]

That said, it is strangely true that certain aspects of Harvey's anatomical discoveries proved deeply attractive to some political writers of a republican and radical bent, such as Harrington and Winstanley. However, Harrington's conception of an active spirit universe would have been anathema to monarchists like Harvey and Hobbes. Harrington's fragmentary treatise, *The Mechanics of Nature* (1660), outlines his "scheme of Nature" in which "SHE is a spirit," the "spirit of God" and "Soul of the World," and he proceeds to describe "innumerable ministerial Spirits"—good and evil ones—"aethereal Particles," but "perfectly mechanical," unlocked and set loose by an alchemical process of fermentation.[36] His emphasis is on a network of invisible spirits linking the entire cosmos, producing unity and cooperation. Harrington's philosophy of incorporeal spirits, then, is the one that Harvey held up for most ridicule a few years earlier.

If the link with Harvey was not a shared new conception of spirit-matter relations—"vitalist science" contributing to a "Vitalist moment" in the turbulent middle years of the seventeenth century—as described in Roger's *Matter of Revolution*, what was it? First, it seems that monarchists did not own the heart. In his most famous treatise of republicanism, *Oceana* (1656), Harrington significantly acknowledges "famous Harvey" and his "circulation of the blood" in *The Preliminaries* (9), and proceeds simply to replace Harvey's monarchical heart with the organ of representative government, parliament, foregrounding "perpetual circulation" as the mechanism that ensures the fair distribution of "life blood:"[37] "So the parliament is the heart which, consisting of two ventricles, the one greater and replenished with a grosser store, the other less and full of a purer, sucketh in and gusheth forth the life blood of Oceana by a perpetual circulation" (174). In Harrington's utopian commonwealth the center of the organizational structure is the agrarian constitution and the ballot, which mysteriously ensure rotation, perpetual motion, and immortality: "For neither by reason nor by her experience is it impossible that a commonwealth should be immortal, seeing the people, being the materials, never dies, and the form, which is motion, must without opposition be endless" (97). In *Oceana* six wise men are elected as senators of the people in order that "the wisdom of the few may be the light of mankind" (24), but their rotation is crucial; "perpetual circulation" in this utopia (as in Harvey's bodies) ensures health for, Harrington asserts, "if it be not in rotation both as to persons and things, it will be very sick" (123).

The heart was, in fact, a very flexible political metaphor, and the notion of circulation, resonant with ideas of rotation, distribution, and sharing, had broad appeal too. But circles and circular motion had important meanings for philosophers well before Harvey's anatomical demonstrations. From as far back as ancient Egyptian times, circles had connotations of divinity and immortality; this tenacious idea was later incorporated into Hermeticism and Platonism and elaborated by Marsilio Ficino for Renaissance humanism.[38] However, as the OED attests, the emergence of both "circulation" and "rotation" in the English vocabulary had a different but related source: the scientific wing of Hermeticism—early chemistry or alchemy. Thus "circulacioun" first appears in late medieval writings as "the operation" of changing the "body" (by heating or cooling) from one "element" into another; it also designated the "still" or vessel of distillation (OED 3). In 1605 Thomas Tymme's *Pract. Chymicall & Hermeticall Physicke* elaborated: "Circulation is to rectifie any thing to a higher perfection" through distillation (cited in OED 3), and in the same text he employed the term to signify "A rotation about an axis . . . orbital revolution": "The perpetuall circulation by which heaven is married to the earth" (cited in OED 1b). Thus by the time Harvey was conducting his anatomical experiments, rotation and circulation were well established as interchangeable terms for the chemical process of distillation and purification, which had been linked through correspondence to the revolution of the heavens. As the famous alchemist George Ripley had expressed it in 1471, "Things being in earth, without any doubt Be ingendered of rotacione of the heavens aboute" (*Compend of Alchemy*, cited in OED 2a). Of course advances in astronomy—notably those contained in Nicolaus Copernicus's *On the Revolutions of the Celestial Spheres* (1543)—had also served to focus attention on the rotation of the earth in relation to the sun; thus rotation was a highly topical issue in "new philosophy" by the turn of the seventeenth century.[39] I suggest that these prior connotations of circulation and rotation might help us better to understand Harvey's circle-preoccupied hypothesizing about the blood's movement.

In fact, carefully considered, blood does not trace a circle round the body, yet clearly Harvey was motivated to describe a circular movement—his writings suggest he was mesmerized by the idea of circularity and this likely preceded his anatomical theorizing: "in animals the blood is driven round a circuit with an unceasing, circular . . . movement" (*De Motu Cordis*, 68); "the blood . . . moves in a circle."[40] Indeed, this illuminating passage confirms that both heavenly correspondences and chemical processes were operative in Harvey's mind when he was theorizing about the blood's movement:

> We have as much right to call this movement of the blood circular as Aristotle had to say that the air and rain emulate the circular movement of the heavenly bodies. The moist earth, he wrote, is warmed by the sun and gives off vapours which condense as they are carried up aloft and in their condensed form fall again as rain and re-moisten the earth, so producing successions of fresh life from it. In similar fashion the circular movement of the sun . . . give rise to storms and atmospheric phenomena.
>
>   It may very well happen thus in the body with the movement of the blood. All parts may be nourished, warmed and activated by the hotter, perfect, vaporous, spirituous and . . . nutritious blood. On the other hand in parts the blood may be cooled, coagulated, and be figuratively worn out. From such parts it returns to its starting point, namely the heart, as if to its source or to the centre of the body's economy, to be restored to its fiery heat, . . . it is re-liquified

and becomes impregnated with spirits . . . From the heart it is redistributed. (*De Motu Cordis*, 46)

Harvey is clearly imagining the bodily microcosm as a type of "circulation" vessel or "still" and linking this with Aristotle's reflections about the circular motions of the planets constituting perfect motion. Interestingly, Harvey's medical colleague, the Hermetic philosopher Robert Fludd, wrote a tract called *Utriusque cosmi* in the 1620s about the micro- and macrocosm in which "divine circles and circular processes abound"; significantly, he was one of the earliest supporters of Harvey's theories.[41] In Harvey's later work *De Generatione Animalium*, he directly compared the nourishing circulation of the blood to the activities of the heavenly orbs: "truly no otherwise than the superior luminaries, the Sun and moon, give life to this inferior world by their continuous circular motions" (382).

In the seventeenth century the circle's symbolic currency was undoubtedly given a substantial additional boost by Harvey's circle-preoccupied writings.[42] Consider, for example, this passage from *De Generatione Animalium*:

> And whether we say that the soul is in the egg or whether we say not so, yet from this circuit it clearly appears that there is some principle at the beginning of this revolution from the hen to the egg and from the egg back again to the hen, which imparts an eternity to them. According to Aristotle it is that very thing which bears an analogy to the element of the stars. . . . For just as the mind or spirit which perpetually moves this vast world and unendingly drives around the same sun . . . so likewise in the race of chickens the *vis enthea*, or divine principle . . . now putting on the form of a hen, now that of an egg, yet this same virtue endures throughout all ages. (150)

It is not difficult to see how Harvey's circular reflections might have influenced Harrington's utopian commonwealth: Oceana is rendered healthy and "immortal" by rotation and perpetual motion (97). Indeed, it is appealing to conjecture that the form and organization of Harrington's ideal commonwealth was not a little inspired by Harvey's musings on chickens, eggs, and, of course, circles. Indeed, the 1653 English translation of *De Generatione Animalium* is prefaced by a poem, "To the Incomparable Dr Harvey," which demonstrates a contemporary fascination with circular movement associated with discovery, "motion," and liberty:

The Crimson Blood, was but a crimson Lake.
Which first from Thee did Tyde and Motion gaine,
And Veins became its Channel, not its Chaine.
With Drake and Candish hence thy Bays is curld,
Fam'd Circulator of the Lesser World.[43]

While mesmeric circles are not so obvious in the political writings of Winstanley, the closely associated notions of distribution, sharing, and nourishment are clearly visible, and if Harrington's republicanism was prepared to countenance an alternative ruling heart—parliament—the communist vision of this Leveller could not support one. His writings seek to abolish such "kingly bondage"—"that man's reign in the heart."[44] "That man" it seems is the "bewitching fancy" of believing in a "chair of government" other than oneself (349). However, Winstanley asserts that spirit "rises up in the heart" of each individual as "the light in man, the reasonable power" (375), presumably to overturn the usurper. The earth features prominently as a kind of surrogate heart in Winstanley's writings—the "common treasury"—whose nourishment must be distributed for survival: "For take away the free use of these and the body languishes, the spirit is brought into bondage and at length departs, and ceaseth his motional action in the body" (295).

Hobbes's preoccupation with distribution was of a rather different nature; where Winstanley saw a treasury of earth, he envisaged one of money as "the fruits of the earth" which must be distributed like blood. *Leviathan* declares: "The artificiall Man maintains his resemblance with the Naturall; whose veins receiving the Bloud from the severall Parts of the body, carry it to the Heart; where being made Vitall, the Heart by the arteries sends it out again, to enliven, and enable for motion all the Members of the same" (175).

The heart is "the Soveraigne Power" and Disease—"Pleurisie"—arises when the heart is denied money "for the necessary uses of the Commonwealth" (228). With the "publique Treasure" obstructed by "the tenacity of the people" the fleshy parts become congealed, the veins obstructed with stagnant blood, and the "heart" is forced to act violently: "to force a passage for the Bloud; and before it can do that, contenteth it selfe with the small refreshments of such things as coole for a time, till . . . it break at last the contumacy of the parts obstructed, and dissipateth the venome into sweate; or . . . the Patient dyeth" (229). So the "Soveraign" heart labors on behalf of neglectful people and without his "strong endeavour" circulation would cease and the body would perish. What this constitutes, of course, is an extraordinarily graphic justification for the "heart"/"Soveraign" being unstintingly supplied with money—compelling justification, that is, for taxation.

Hobbes's graphic evocation of the circulation of money certainly captured the late seventeenth-century imagination. The free circulation of money and trade rapidly became synonymous with the nation's health and wealth for commentators on both sides of the political divide, and by the 1730s Daniel Defoe was one tradesman among many associating the circulation of both with rich employment opportunities: "the prodigious numbers of People, which are by this means employ'd, more than otherwise would be, are the consequences of that circulation."[45] Meanwhile, Harrington's emphasis on the necessity of rotation to maintaining a healthy body politic (an idea that had, of course, originally taken root in classical Greece and Rome) had breathed new life into an ancient idea that was to prove highly tenacious: for example, in the American Revolution the founders of the republic urged in a public letter that "a rotation of power, a rotation of office . . . are the best and most effectual means to preserve the liberties of the people."[46] Rotation was now synonymous with freedom from tyranny—liberty—and it was soon to become a founding principle of the American Constitution.

* * *

To conclude, this investigation has found no evidence of a theoretical "somersault" in Harvey's writings or of a sustained "conceptual alliance" between politics and science in the turbulent mid-seventeenth-century years.[47] Further, while Harvey was innovative in his anatomical thinking, he appears to have been consistently conservative in his political allegiances. Any bid to yoke together such a diverse range of thinkers as Harvey, Harrington, Winstanley, and Hobbes under the nineteenth-century label "vitalism" serves to iron out significant seventeenth-century distinctions that are essential to a complex and nuanced understanding of the intersection of scientific and political thought in the revolutionary era. No one scientific theory drove the English revolution. However, as this chapter has demonstrated, in the search for a new sociopolitical model that would end strife and promote harmony, the richly symbolic heart, blood, and its distribution provided a particularly compelling toolbox of analogies through which to imagine and describe change; they became prime targets for appropriation by writers of various ideological persuasions who used them selectively and opportunistically—there were no "ontological connections" between particular anatomical and political models. Harvey's discoveries had chimed with influential ideas about circles and rotation already extant in early chemistry and astronomy—the "new philosophy"—and this chapter has uncovered a flexible imaginative interplay of early science with emergent ideas in politics and economics. Today, the linked notions of circulation and rotation still resonate powerfully with beliefs about distribution, fairness, social, political, and economic health, and liberty—an enduring legacy, but should it be attributed to Harvey?

Chapter 2

"The Lake of my Heart"

Blood, Containment, and the Boundaries of the Person in the Writing of Dante and Catherine of Siena

HEATHER WEBB

In Dante Alighieri's late medieval Italy, there was, of course, no concept that blood might circulate within the human body. Blood was continually being made from food consumed through the mouth, continually refined, and continually used. In its most rarefied forms, it was understood to form the spirits that coursed through the human body and effected perception and sensation.[1] In dynamic motion at the outlets of the body, the spirits came forth in voice and in breath and in the visual rays of the eyes; they entered into the body through the eyes, mouth, and senses. And it is here, in the bustle of motion from interior to exterior and back, that we do find some notion of circulation *avant la lettre*. But it is a circulation that must exceed the limits of an individual human body. This chapter will examine some medieval Italian visions of the flow of blood from the heart, both within the body and out into the world (and back), as an articulation of the porous boundaries of the human person, as constitutive of the human person.

In the first canto of Dante's *Inferno*, we find Dante alone in a dark wood, with "terror . . . in the lake of my heart."[2] The first thirty lines of the poem describe a very specific physical state that is also a spiritual state. The indicator of this particular condition is the heart, as well as its inhabiting spirits, subtle creatures formed of the most refined blood and inhaled air. Fear has caused all spirit and heat to withdraw from its usual traffic within the body and gather in the heart; such cessation of the heart's outward propulsions has deprived Dante of the ability to move through his world and to be aware of his surroundings. It is, in fact, the same state of immobilized, petrified terror he describes in his earlier poem, one of the so-called *rime petrose*, or stony poems, "Così nel mio parlar voglio esser aspro": "And the blood, that is dispersed through the veins / fleeing runs toward / the heart, that calls it; and so I become white."[3] Here in the first canto of the *Inferno*, the body is, in fact, described as *lasso*, or weary. It is bereft of strength, turned inward upon itself.

The story of the *Comedy* is the story of awakening from this condition. Dante begins by recognizing that he has somehow stumbled into the wrong place, "found myself now searching / through a dark wood, the right way blurred and lost."[4] Such an act of recognition signals that the heart is once again sending forth an adequate supply of blood and spirit to the brain, that, in fact, things are slowly beginning to move again within the body. There are two levels of output from the heart: the first is a flow of spirit, heat, and blood within the body; the second is an overflow of spirit that extends beyond the borders of the body, enabling perception and interaction with the external world. In the condition from which Dante awakens at the beginning of the *Inferno*, both of these processes have been compromised.[5]

The physical and spiritual health of a human person was understood, I will argue, to depend upon a delicate balance between the containment and dispersion of blood and blood-based spirit. As we have seen from the opening of the *Inferno*, excessive containment of blood and spirit within the heart is figured as a kind of petrification. The body's physiospiritual lassitude means not only that the body is not fully functional, but also that the person in question is unable to make and maintain relations with neighbors. Dante is, in fact, dangerously isolated and alone in that first canto of the *Inferno*. And, alone, he is powerless against the beasts that assail him, figurations of sin and signs of the deadly consequences of such isolation for his soul. Dante emerges from this solitude through a cry for help, a cry that can only take place physically by means of the movement of spirit out from the heart and into the surrounding world, where, it seems, Virgil had long been waiting.[6]

The *Inferno* goes on to tell the tale of an exploration of the horrors of self-enclosure, from the narcissism of the lustful to the traitors encased in ice and cannibalizing one another. Dante emerges from this to the realm of

"The Lake of my Heart" 33

Purgatorio, in which penitents must, first and foremost, reorient themselves within a communal body. This process is introduced and dramatized when Dante inquires after the identity of penitents he meets. Two penitents I will mention here respond by inscribing their personhood within the new confines of the broader communities of the saved as they describe their loss of individual physical containment through their spilled blood. Jacopo del Cassero responds to Dante's query about his identity and his promise to act on behalf of the pentient souls as follows:

> You need not swear to that.
> Granted your will is not cut short by "can't,"
> each of us trusts that you will bring some good.
> May I (who'll only speak till others do)
> entreat you, if you've seen those lands that lie
> between Romagna and the realm of Charles,
> that you, in all your kindness, pray for me
> in Fano—so entreaties offered there
> may give me strength to cleanse my grievous sins.
> I was from Fano. But the hollow wounds
> from which the blood by which I lived ran down,
> were dealt me by the Antenorians.
> I thought my safety was, with them, assured.
> . . .
> Towards the marsh I ran, where—brackish reeds
> entwining me—I fell, watching as, in this mire,
> a lake spread outwards, forming from my veins.
> (*Purgatorio*, V.64–84)[7]

Having lost his self-containment as his body is breached and his blood, which he describes as the seat of his selfhood, "the blood by which I lived," runs forth, he turns in his discourse toward the promise of a new, communal seat of selfhood. The otherwise horrifying scene of the dying man who must watch the lake of the heart referenced in *Inferno* I empty itself upon the earth, or in other words, who must bear witness to his own dispossession, is anticipatorily redeemed by the framing statement in which Jacopo places his faith in Dante's goodwill. In a spiritual correlative of the experience of watching that which he understood to be his singular personhood spilled onto the earth, he now locates his salvation not within the confines of his own individual (aerial) body, but within the collective space of Dante's goodwill and the prayers of those left behind in Fano. The myth of self-reliance is exposed as the marsh plants claim Jacopo's body and empty him beyond himself into the hands of others.

Bonconte da Montefeltro tells a similar tale of a death that tears him from autonomous existence and plunges him into a community of mutual reliance. He identifies himself in the following terms:

> I am—once Montefeltran—now Buonconte.
> Giovanna does not pray for me. None cares.
> And so, among all these, I walk, brow lowered.
>   (*Purgatorio*, V.88–90)[8]

When asked why his body was never found after the battle of Campaldino, he explains:

> "Ah!" he replied. "A stream—the Archiano—runs
> across the lower Casentino hills,
> born above Hermitage-in-Apennine.
> I'd got to where this river's title fails,
> fleeing on foot, and wounded in my throat,
> a line of blood behind me on the plain.
> And now I lost my sight. And all my words
> ended in uttering Maria's name.
> I fell—my flesh alone remaining there."
>   (*Purgatorio*, V.94–102)[9]

The torrent Archiano loses its name as it empties itself into the river Arno. In the same way, Buonconte loses all that is his father's, associated here with place and name, as blood runs from his throat and sight and speech fail him. If Dante elsewhere defines the state of being human with the word "fante" (*Purgatorio*, XXV.61) to designate a speaking subject, here it is clear that at death, Buonconte ceases to be human as before, renounces his Montefeltran rooting, but as his earthly body tumbles away from his soul, he empties all of what will endure into the pronunciation of a single word, a single name. As he speaks the name, Maria, he throws himself into the community of the faithful and takes on a new identity. Paradoxically, he can no longer speak, is no longer subject, but begins his new existence in Mary's name.

Against the visions of inflicted abjection in *Inferno*, in which sinners' bodies are robbed of their self-possession as punishment for excessive policing of boundaries in life, the penitent in *Purgatorio* are shown to derive their salvation precisely from their recognition, like Dante's in *Inferno* I, that a self-sufficient personhood is a myth. It is the loss of blood that figures the abandonment of that myth.

Catherine of Siena (1347–1380) describes a similar notion of the porous boundary of personhood as always necessarily imbricated in community; she does so by rendering Saint Paul's images of the body of the church bloody. In one of her letters, Catherine describes proper relations between Christ and his church as follows:

> In the middle of the vineyard [of the soul] He [Christ] placed the vessel of his heart, full of blood, to water the plants with it, so that they don't dry out. . . . What is [the vineyard] watered with? Not with water but with precious blood spilled with much fire of love. That blood is located in the vessel of the heart, as it is said.[10]

Christ's heart overflows, spilling into the fertile earth of the individual human soul.[11] While biblical accounts of the wounding of Christ do not indicate that the lance reached Christ's heart or that the heart was in fact wounded, it had become commonplace by this time for religious thinkers to assume that Christ's heart was wounded on the cross. Saint Bernard of Clairvaux was one of the first to make it clear that the lance wounding Christ's side touched his heart, and Saint Bonaventure speaks of living within the heart of Christ, envisioning the wound as an entryway.[12]

The heart and the blood that it contains and spills, here and in other letters, becomes a means of understanding and teaching the ethics of spiritual and political community. Catherine's vineyard houses a heart that overflows into multiple levels of meaning. First, the example shows that each individual soul must take its nourishment from Christ, making his heart and his blood its own source of life. Second, Christ's full heart is located at the center of the body of the church, compelling each Christian to join under the care of the leadership of the church or be severed from that life-giving body.

When Catherine locates the heart in the middle of the garden, her letter is organized to conform to the standard pattern for discussing the heart's properties; the entries in both Vincent of Beauvais's and Thomas of Cantimpré's encyclopedias begin by mentioning and interpreting the heart's central position within the body as a prelude to further conclusions about its primacy as an organ.[13] Christ's bleeding heart in the middle of the vineyard of the soul has the same function as the heart was understood to have within the intact human body; it is the only source that produces, contains, and gives forth life-giving blood. As in Albert the Great's *De Animalibus*, Dominican sources that would have formed Catherine's immediate cultural milieu repeated Aristotle's correlation between physical centrality and the center of power.[14]

"Blood is located in the heart," Catherine insists, referencing unidentified sources: "as it is said." Along with the centrality of the heart, the issue of the location of blood was a topic of debate between the proponents of Aristotelian and Galenic teachings on bodily function. Both Vincent and Thomas cite Aristotle and Avicenna's commentaries on Aristotle on this issue, arguing against the Galenic assertion that the liver also produced and held (nutritive) blood.[15] This idea that the "seat of the soul" was the only source of the substance essential for life opened the way to more unified modes of thinking about body and spirit. Christ's heart is designated as the sole source of nutrients for the vineyard, just as the human heart, in the Aristotelian vision, was said to be the unique source of blood for the body. As through the sacrament of the Eucharist, Christ's blood offers eternal life to the soul; the heart's blood offers life to the body. Like Christ, the heart is the principle or source of all power in the body. In short, the medieval recyclings of Aristotelian centralized physiology, employed to counter Galenic divisions of power between the heart and the liver (and also the brain), in this context take on new importance: the body reflects Christian teachings. Just as there is only one central source of life in the body, there is only one way to salvation and only one Christ. This structure of the Christian community recalls Paul: "We, though many, are one body in Christ, and individually members one of another" (Romans 12.5); but Catherine has departed significantly from Paul here. Christ is not the head of the human in Catherine's letters; he is the overflowing heart of the human soul and of the human body. He is the heart of the church. Not father, not husband, not master, Catherine's Christ is cast as a maternal source of blood and nourishment.[16]

Such a centralized theological structure found its reflection in an idealized central administrative body for the church. Papal politics of the time fell far short of the ideal, however. In a letter to the Count of Fondi, Catherine expresses her dismay over the count's reception of the cardinals who refused to accept Urban VI's election. In the face of this conflict of curial authorities, Catherine describes what she sees as a "natural" structure for the church: "We have said that we are vineyards, and how the vineyard is ornamented, and how God wishes it to be worked. Now where have we been placed? In the vineyard of the holy Church. There He has placed the worker, that is Christ-on-earth, who distributes the blood to us."[17] Catherine has indicated clearly who this "worker" is, as this is precisely the motivation for her letter: it is Urban VI.[18] The pope, as she saw it, was designated by providence; only he had the authority to distribute the blood from Christ's heart.

The personal vineyard is a microcosm of the whole: each individual plot is placed within the larger vineyard of the church. Christ's heart stands at the center of each plot, but also, paradoxically, at the center of the larger body of the church. Each individual plot is unified with the whole by means of the source or heart that is simultaneously at the center of the microcosm and the macrocosm. In this way, each Christian has an individual relationship with Christ and a communal relationship with Christ. The latter is administrated by the pope and the ministers of the church, principally through the sacraments and particularly through the community of blood.

Urban VI is, then, designated by God to work the garden and administer the distribution of life-giving blood. Catherine calls upon the Count of Fondi to recognize this function and, in so doing, save both himself and the church. In the production and distribution of blood, the functions of Christ and the functions of the pope together correspond, respectively, to the functions of the heart. As Catherine unfolds her vision, it becomes clear that each Christian must understand himself or herself as dependent on his or her status as a member of a universal body. Since the blood flowing from the heart was thought to be the source of heat, motion, and sensation within the body, any member of the body that became disconnected from the powers flowing from the heart would lose the capacity for movement, become insensate, and finally die. Vincent of Beauvais cites the physician al-Razi on this point: "The heart was made by God to be the fount and origin of natural heat and the heat proceeds from the heart to the entire body by the arteries, heating every member, and if any of the arteries leading to a member are cut, they will congeal and the movement and sensation beyond that point will harden and the member will be rendered dead."[19] An individual's power to move and to feel is a divine gift in this analysis, a gift that depends on the connection of the parts to their point of origin.

Catherine makes use of this unifying principle to try to convince one of the priors of Florence, Niccolò Soderini, to accept an offer of peace from the pope: "We putrid members . . . can clearly see that we cannot do without him [the pope]. . . . He who scorns this sweet Vicar scorns the blood. . . . How can you say that if you offend the body, you do not offend the blood that is in the body? Don't you know that it [the body] has within it the blood of Christ?"[20] Those who do not embrace the pope are rejecting Christ himself. In their scorn, they become like rotting limbs, having willfully disconnected themselves from the life-giving, animating blood that flows from the heart. By seeking to remove themselves from the body of the state, the rebels against Urban VI scorn the blood of salvation that flows from Christ himself. As in Dante's purgatorial tales of hubristic individuals who learn at the last moment to enter into the body of Christ and to take on that communal body as their own, Catherine argues that there is no individual access to Christ unless the individual is part of the greater community and is open to those who administer to the common needs of that community.

Another of Catherine's letters, addressed to her confessor, Raymond of Capua, reveals in dramatic terms the extreme permeability of persons that Catherine envisions through Christ's blood, and indeed, through the blood of an executed young man. The young man, referred to in the letter only as "the person you know about," was identified by one of Catherine's biographers as Niccolò di Toldo, a Perugian nobleman sentenced to death for supposedly creating discord in the city of Siena.[21] Niccolò was thought to be an agent of Perugia's vicar general and to be working to keep Siena from joining the league of republics against the papacy.[22]

Catherine begins by recounting her offer of spiritual comfort to the prisoner prior to his execution. The prisoner responds eagerly to her, which Catherine explains as the result of a divine "trick":

> But the immeasurable and fiery love of God fooled him, creating in him such affection and love in the desire for God that he could not endure without Him, saying, "Stay with me, and do not abandon me. And thus I will only fare well, and I will die content." And he laid his head upon my breast. I felt then a rush of pleasure [un giubilo] and the odour of his blood; and it was not without the odour of my own, which I wish to spill out for our sweet spouse Jesus.[23]

Niccolò is filled with such desire for God that he cannot be apart from *him*, saying to *Catherine*: "Stay with me." By citing the young man's words to her immediately after the male pronoun, Catherine asserts that, for Niccolò, she is Christ.[24] The divine trick allows her to take Christ's place in the condemned man's affections and desires. In this privileged moment of intimate contact, with Niccolò's head upon her chest, Catherine smells his blood mixed with the odor of her own.

This inhalation is the first in a series of perceptual encounters along the way to the young man's death and salvation. In its entirety, the letter depicts Catherine's sensory experience of the execution as parallel to Christ's reception of the soul upon Niccolò's death. The dramatized analogy, establishing Catherine's status as an earthly agent of Christ, can only be appreciated in light of the heart's role as container for the blood-based spirits in respiration and sensory perception. Thomas of Cantimpré states that "the heart is the origin of life, as Aristotle says, and the origin of every movement and every sensation is in the heart. . . . And breath occurs through the lungs by means of the origin that is in the heart, as inhaled air first goes to the interior of the heart."[25] In Thomas's account, the heart is the primary recipient of unmediated, inhaled air. Perceptual matter rushes into the heart along with the air; in the words of William of Auvergne, "The senses are like gates into the body through which ingressions and egressions . . . are made."[26] In moments of particular sensorial intensity, the gates were opened and the heart was flooded with spirits. In the embrace between Catherine and Niccolò, breath and spirits circulate between the two bodies, commingling the odor of two bloods.[27]

As Niccolò meets his death by decapitation, "his mouth said only 'Jesus' and 'Catherine.' And, as he spoke, I received his head in my hands, fixing my eye on the divine goodness and saying, 'I do!'"[28] In Catherine's rushed narration, Niccolò's naming of his desires, Jesus and Catherine, merges them into one entity in the moment he is decapitated by the executioner's blade and his head falls into Catherine's hands. This climactic moment is figured as the marriage of Niccolò to Catherine-as-Christ and to Christ himself. Looking up into the sky, Catherine witnesses the following:

> And then I saw God-and-Man, just as brightly as the sun, and He was open [at the side] and received the [man's] blood. . . . After He had received his blood and his desire, He received his soul, which He put into the open cask of His side. . . . With what sweetness and love He awaited this soul departed from its body! The eye of mercy was turned toward his soul as it entered into His side, bathed in his own blood which gained its merit in the blood of the Son of God! . . . As soon as he became concealed, my soul rested in

peace and quiet, in such an odour of blood that I could not bear to remove the blood that had come onto me, from Him/him.[29]

Niccolò's death and salvation have infused his blood into Christ's. The two bloods are made one within Christ's heart (Catherine refers to his heart as "the open cask of his side") such that the substance pouring forth onto Catherine's waiting body and into her receptive soul is the product of that union. She is covered, both inwardly and outwardly, soul and garments, with this blood; she states that she could not bear to remove the blood on her and that her soul rested in the odor of blood. As she physically receives Niccolò's head, her soul breathes in his blood in simultaneity with Christ's gathering in of that blood and the soul into his wounded, open heart. Just as the odor of Catherine's blood mixed with Niccolò's during their embrace, Christ's heart effects a unification of his blood with the prisoner's blood. In two stages, as Catherine breathes in Niccolò's blood and is subsequently drenched in his blood, her physical interactions with the repentant soul mirror Christ's reception of the soul and blood into the "open cask" of his heart. In these moments of particular proximity to death and to the possibility of salvation, blood, spirit, breath, and air circulate between three bodies. Catherine's receptive body is an intermediary between the two violently opened bodies of the criminal and his redeemer. Her heart is as open as Christ's but remains within the range of heightened natural function. Christ's wound is the ideal of availability and openness to penitent souls; Catherine as his agent on earth can practice openness to the penitent through the portals of her senses.

Catherine's letters were frequently intended for a male audience.[30] Nonetheless, she fashions herself as an example, focusing on the projective powers of her own heart to inspire a pope in need of guidance, to embolden her confessor, and to influence any man with the desire to fight for the church. By emphasizing her heart as the hottest (and thus most "masculine") part of her female body, Catherine writes about passing on her strength and giving new life to the church with her blood. In one of Catherine's letters to Pope Urban VI, written a few days before she died, she tells the following story, beginning with a declaration to God:

> "O eternal God, receive the sacrifice of my life into the mystical body of the holy church. I do not have anything to give except that which you have given to me. Take out my heart, then, and press it on the face of this spouse." And so eternal God, turning the eye

of his mercifulness, took out my heart and pressed it in the holy church. And he took it to himself with such force that, if he hadn't immediately (not wishing that the vessel of my body be broken) encircled it with his strength, my life would have been lost.[31]

This is one of the rare letters in which Catherine shares a personal experience of an encounter with the divine presence (another is the letter that describes Niccolò di Toldo's execution). Most of Catherine's writings offer spiritual advice to others or describe the general principles of universal salvation. We might, therefore, have reason to suspect that this turn toward the personal has a specific exhortative purpose. This letter was written during the Great Schism, as Catherine's health was failing. She needed to inspire the pope to act with strength for the good of the united church and hoped to do so by describing her own sacrifice.[32]

Catherine concludes the letter with a summary that reveals her purposes in sharing her vision with the pope: "Thanks be to the highest eternal God, who has placed us on the battlefield, like knights, to fight for his spouse."[33] Catherine claims that she and the pope have both been chosen by God—"he has placed us" to fight on God's behalf—encouraging the pope by suggesting that the two of them share an active role in saving the passive church, described as a bride. Catherine leads the fight, exhorting the pope to follow her in the rescue of their suffering bride. In another letter to Urban VI, she describes the church's condition as follows: "The sweet spouse that is his and yours, that for so long has been all pale . . . because of those who fed and feed at her breast, that for their defects have made her pale and infirm, having sucked the blood from her with their own self-love."[34] The church is depicted as pale from the loss of blood, the victim of corrupt priests who have sucked her dry of life and spirit while nursing at her breast. The church suffers from a lack of vigor and from internal cold. Catherine's heart, squeezed by God's hand onto the face of the church, could infuse that pallid creature with hot, life-giving blood. The powers required to aid the church, heat and vitality, were virtues traditionally associated with the male. Here Catherine is depicting herself as a valiant savior, the bold groom that she wishes the pope could be, fearless in aiding a defenseless church.

In other letters, Catherine refers to Christ as the "true sower," pouring blood from his heart onto the garden of the soul. The creative force within the universe is reflected in the creative force within the body, the heart. In her gift to the church, Catherine emulates Christ's attributes.[35] Just as Christ's blood brings new life to the soul, seeding the garden, Catherine's blood, also issuing directly from the heart, offers new life to a wasting institution.

Both Dante's and Catherine's texts are situated beyond the space of the everyday: they tell of the moment of death, of mystical encounter, of the transition from this life to the world beyond. But the articulations of personhood that are delineated in these boundary-places reflect back upon the lived worlds of these two late medieval thinkers. The human person, as these texts would suggest, is joined by blood into the relational congress of community and into the body of the church, literally and figuratively, physically and spiritually.

Chapter 3

Sorting Pistol's Blood

Social Class and the Circulation of Character in Shakespeare's *2 Henry IV* and *Henry V*

KATHARINE A. CRAIK

> There are severall degrees in bloud.

So Francis Markham wrote in his handbook for noblemen, *The Booke of Honour*, published in 1625.[1] Markham regarded the blood of early modern aristocrats and sovereigns as different from that which ran in the veins of plebeians, a reliable marker of how to tell (and keep) different sorts of people apart. The blood Markham has in mind is surely the literal stuff of family, where an unbroken bloodline secures an intimate sense of belonging or entitlement. But blood also has a rich metaphorical significance in the literature of the period, especially when it was used to deliberate the ways identity could be conferred—or contested—by social degree. This chapter considers how blood functioned as a class-marker in the Renaissance, exploring how it reveals the emotional landscapes and habits of thought of men and women in various social positions. If blood-degree secured the separation of one "severall" sort of person from another on a sliding scale of social placement, differentiating one person's worth from another's, it also functioned as a form of sympathetic identification for those whose blood approximated one another's. In William Shakespeare's *2 Henry IV* and *Henry V*, in particular, blood sheds light on what people share in common, or imagine themselves to share in common, when class hierarchies start to erode—especially under the painful pressures of war. In these plays, blood reveals the difficulties involved in determining not only where one social class starts and another ends, but also in determining where one person's identity starts and another person's ends. For as we will see, blood-degree seldom functions as a bounded terminus, but emerges instead as something sympathetically sorted or shared between people and groups who might normally appear separate. In this way, the bonds forged by blood allow us to trace the emergence of a new and unfamiliar version of dramatic personhood capable of circulating freely outside the fixed hierarchies of social class.

Recent scholarship has considered blood as a complex signifier of Renaissance identity whose changing shades, textures, and temperatures reveal the shifting characteristics of gender, personality, and nationality. Gail Kern Paster has used blood to explore early modern emotional topography, for example, focusing on "the reciprocal absorption of body by landscape and landscape by body" in the works of Shakespeare, Edmund Spenser, and their contemporaries. Here a series of complex analogies between blood, streams, and fountains demonstrate the proximity of animate and inanimate worlds which, in turn, have a profound effect on people's behavior, characters, and appetites.[2] Mary Floyd-Wilson has similarly explored how temperaments—including sanguine ones—were fashioned by locale, arguing that humoral identity is inseparable in the period from ethnographical identity.[3] More recently, Sara Read has considered how blood and blood loss shaped early modern women's social status by confirming the onset of puberty, sexual maturity, or menopause.[4] Meanwhile historians such as Patricia Crawford have explored how illegitimacy was understood to tarnish the nobility of elite families, and how hierarchical systems of blood-bonding enabled noblemen to detach themselves, financially and emotionally, from their baser-blooded offspring.[5] Despite this recent interest in how blood, blood flow, and bloodlines contributed to the formation and reformation of early modern subjectivities, few scholars have so far considered how blood worked in literature and drama as a place to negotiate social class.[6]

Early modern physicians, moral philosophers, and writers on conduct, including Markham, recognised the blood of the nobility as physically different from that of commoners. In accordance with the humoral model, the achievement of well-being involved maintaining the body's delicate equilibrium—and the blood of the laboring classes was considered thinner and less refined than that of their noble counterparts partly because they were thought to expend more sweat and tears. The humoral system of temperament is closely related to ideas about social class, for the thinner blood of commoners was thought to account for their relative coarseness of feeling, poverty of manners, and spiritual simplicity.[7] But blood does not function in any straightforward way, in Shakespeare's works, as a means of policing the boundaries between rich and poor. Part of the work of this chapter is indeed to consider how Shakespeare's exploration of blood-degree questions the humoral model with its tendency to categorize people into "types" and, in so doing, to fix their social worth. As we will see, the complex sympathies and antipathies Shakespeare sketches through bloodlines have interesting implications for our understanding of dramatic character in the early modern playhouse. For while social allegiances between some of Shakespeare's characters in *Henry IV* and *Henry V* are forged through bloodlines and blood bonds, others circulate freely between or even outside these categories, allowing us to conceptualize Shakespearean character beyond the value-laden vocabulary of humoral typology.

Blood is a vivid presence on stage in many interpretations of *Henry V*, and Henry's own cold-bloodedness is frequently remarked. But blood carries a more nuanced set of meanings in Shakespeare's theater, which respond in interesting ways to the cultural assumptions lying behind the separation of blood into "degrees"—especially the idea that high-class blood was more valuable than low-class blood. To many people, aristocratic blood must have looked precious and authentic while plebeian blood appeared composite and expendable. But the differences between "aristocratic" and "plebeian" blood were not always clear, and the flourishing of the latter seemed dependent on its separation from the former. As Mary Ellen Lamb has argued, indeed, plebeian identity was in various ways at this time being "invented or produced by elite and middling sorts as a means of coming to their own self-definition."[8] Part of this invention, I argue, involved sketching elaborate new versions of plebeian personhood hinging on blood-based systems of degree. As we will see, Shakespeare's Henry is deeply invested in just such an elaborate imaginative enterprise on the eve of Agincourt.

Within this scheme, however, the social class of one character remains startlingly indeterminable: Pistol, the ensign of the company, whose credentials as captain are repeatedly called into question and who sometimes resembles a counterfeit playing only "under the form of a soldier."[9] Taking Pistol's choleric nature as a starting point, together with his disputed status as ensign of the company, I argue that social hierarchies are disturbed rather than confirmed in the history plays through the rich blood-based vocabulary of social degree. Part of the way Shakespeare achieves this is by sketching, through Pistol, a new and untried version of dramatic personhood capable of circulating freely outside familiar class-based social strata. Pushing against the hierarchy of blood that Markham and others insisted upon and drawing on theories of rank and fellowship from contemporary military theory, Shakespeare used Pistol to put pressure on the faultlines between individuated "figure" and socially recognizable "type." Pistol's part is a notoriously difficult one in performance, partly because he looks both uncompromisingly singular and aggressive (like a gunman) and unnervingly shapeless ("like quicksilver").[10] Despite this, he need not remain the "obsolete and extinct creature" which Edward Dutton Cook called him in 1883.[11] Instead the classless Pistol can be seen to emerge as a dramatic rendering of those aspects of early modern selfhood that cannot be contained by cultural formulas, humoral theory, or rhetorical schemes. Pistol's extraordinary *figura* tests conventional, class-based ways of performing the human and humoral ways of describing character, as Shakespeare makes theatrical capital (to borrow the words of contemporary military strategist Francois de La Noue) out of "the astonishment that the pistol bringeth at the cracke."[12]

* * *

Pistol rivalled Falstaff in popularity in the early lives of both plays partly because his character was unique and irreplaceable, but also because he conformed to certain recognizable cultural and dramatic types. Readers of the history plays have suggested that Shakespeare may have known John Florio's 1611 description of the *pistólfo* as "a rouging beggar, a cantler, an upright man that liveth by cosenage."[13] Pistol indeed looks schematic, if not calculatedly unoriginal: he is a version of the *miles gloriosus*, or braggart soldier, and many of his lines (in mock epic, Senecan bombast, Latin, or garbled Italian) are snatched from other people, or from books and plays. Although Pistol's name looks singular and determined, it nevertheless works to fix his personality into a recognizable choleric type. As the king remarks in *Henry V*, "It sorts well with your fierceness" (4.1.63). Pistol's reckless energy, impetuosity, and quick temper make him—on the surface at least—a clear example of choleric personhood. For the choleric man, as the physician Nicolas Coeffeteau reminds us, is always "boyling, [and] full of bitterness," since choleric humours "doth inflame the whole blood, and all the spirits which flowe about the heart."[14]

Mistress Quickly indeed notes Pistol's "very bitter words" in *2 Henry IV* and begs him (in a typical malapropism) not to alleviate but rather to "aggravate your choler" (2.4.169, 60).

Choler was associated with drunkenness, rashness, and vengefulness, and persuaded men—often mistakenly—that they had been wronged, for it

> incites vs to a feeling of a contempt and sensible iniury, which we beleeue hath been vniustly done . . . this antipathy supplies the place of an iniury, and works the same effect that the imagination did to haue receiued some wrong.[15]

The conviction in one's imagination that one has been wronged works as powerfully as being wronged in fact—for both stir up equally powerful feelings of outrage. Even before Doll Tearsheet has unleashed her memorable string of insults against him ("Away, you cutpurse rascal, you filthy bung, away!"), Pistol has already threatened Mistress Quickly, using his typical blend of menace and sleazy humor, as he promises to "discharge upon her . . . with two bullets" (*2 Henry IV*, 2.4.112 and 124). Later he threatens Doll, Falstaff, and Bardolph:

> What, shall we have incision? Shall we imbrue? . . .
> Why then, let grievous, ghastly, gaping wounds
> Untwine the Sisters Three.
> (2.4.193–96)

Pistol's alliterative outpouring taps into the bombastic rhetoric of contemporary melodrama. If choler and the imagination work similar effects in the minds of men, Pistol seems inflamed by both bitter blood and his immersion in literature and stage plays. His choler allows him to appear colorfully out of the ordinary—but also obliges him to risk disappearing altogether by virtue of his unexceptionality. Falstaff indeed compares Pistol to a set of insignificant playthings (a "quoit," a "shove-groat shilling"): "Nay, an a do nothing but speak nothing, a shall be nothing here" (2.4.189–91). For Falstaff, at least, Pistol's "helter-skelter" of words does not make him a memorable, singular individual but instead cancels him out altogether (5.3.93).[16] Pistol's habit of turning himself into a drama serves finally to mark him out as the onstage "nothing" that he must remain, materializing only in the audience's imagination.

Perhaps finding oneself subject to "gross passion," as Pistol does, means falling among the innumerable coarser sort.[17] As the king will later make clear, nobility and gentleness involve "not swerving with the blood." The flexibility of the early modern humoral system did nevertheless allow for a kind of noble anger, since those who "haue much blood and spirits, and which abound in heate, are most commonly hardy and valiant."[18] Flashes of fire, or choleric outbursts, could therefore be either the reprehensible signs of a personality trait shared among the numberless masses, or might confirm that one's blood-degree was of the highest order. Linking the right sort of choler with venerable bloodlines, Exeter accordingly reminds Henry that

> Your brother kings and monarchs of the earth
> Do all expect that you should rouse yourself
> As did the former lions of your blood.
> (*Henry V*, 1.2.122–24)

For kings and monarchs, the rousing of the blood in righteous anger is a duty and a responsibility to the glorious dead. The French constable later marvels at the English soldiers' ability to "Decoct their cold blood to such valiant heat" and urges the French to find a way of stirring up their own "quick blood" (3.5.20–21). Strikingly, though, the vengeful English noblemen do not revert as a group to a choleric type based on a shared set of characteristics. Instead spectacular and charismatic aristocratic individuals emerge—such as the Duke of York, whose heroic (and markedly bloody) death is recounted by Exeter. "[A]ll blood he was" when Henry saw him,

> *Exeter*. In which array, brave soldier, doth he lie,
>   Larding the plain. And by his bloody side,
>   Yokefellow to his honour-owing wounds,
>   The noble Earl of Suffolk also lies.
>   Suffolk first died, and York, all haggled over,
>   Comes to him, where in gore he lay insteeped,
>   And takes him by the beard, kisses the gashes
>   That bloodily did yawn upon his face.
>   (*Henry V*, 4.6.7–14)

Exeter describes Suffolk and York as "yokefellows" in blood. But their togetherness does not signify their depletion or diminishment. Instead their copiously bleeding gashes serve as authentic markers of their shared nobility and honor, vividly realized here in a dramatic tableau.

Interestingly, Pistol uses the same word as Exeter when he addresses Nim and Bardolph as his "Yokefellows in arms" (2.3.48). Unlike York and Suffolk, however, Pistol's comrades are yoked together not by their heroic exemplarity but rather by their unexceptionality. They are going to France not in expectation of military glory but "like horseleeches, my boys, / To suck, to suck, the very blood to suck!" (2.3.49–50). Compound and creaturely, Pistol's comrades call to mind the rabble army in *1 Henry IV* whose soldiers Falstaff describes as "good enough to toss; food for powder, food for powder" (4.2.61–3) or the troops in *Troilus and Cressida* whom Pandarus calls "chaff and bran, chaff and bran! porridge after meat!" (1.2.222). Critics have often remarked upon the "callous impersonality" of the conscription scene in *2 Henry IV* in which the miserable Mouldy, Wart, Bullcalf, Feeble, and Shadow are appraised for their suitability for service.[19] Elizabethan captains continued to receive pay for a full company even when its numbers were depleted, and they were notoriously willing to pocket "dead pay."[20] Falstaff has already summoned an army of figments ("a number of shadows to fill up the muster-book"), and his main criteria for recruitment is still expendability: "O, give me the spare men, and spare me the great ones" (3.2.133, 259).

More chilling than this, however, is the eager declaration by Feeble, the woman's tailor, of his willingness to fight:

> By my troth, I care not. A man can die but once. We owe God a death. I'll ne'er bear a base mind. And't be my destiny, so; and 't be not, so. No man's too good to serv's prince. And let it go which way it will, he that dies this year is quit for the next. (*2 Henry IV*, 3.2.225–29)

Unlike the other recruits who are ready to bribe Bardolph to secure their release, Feeble accepts his place among a self-sacrificing community of soldiers eager to relinquish their lives like debts that must be paid.[21] When Falstaff gives the command to "Prick him" in the muster book, Feeble is momentarily marked out as singular—but only insofar as his blood is marked out for shedding: "it is time you were spent" (3.2.108, 115). For these "warriors for the working day" (4.3.110), being yoked together in arms does not lead to a spectacular and exemplary array of blood. Common soldiers' personhoods are instead yoked together in ways that make them appear plural, composite—and vulnerable. Blood-based ideas of social degree thus begin to shed light on a version of personhood that must be shared and circulated, rather than remaining singular or bounded. These soldiers risk bleeding into one another, their identities valuable only insofar as they are adjuncts. The story revealed by blood-degree is therefore not only the familiar one of friction between classes, but also the less familiar story of individuals with similar class origins striving to remain separate from one another.

Pistol's character is as forceful as Feeble's is feeble. But we have seen how his identity, too, seems shared and sorted thanks to its affinity to a humoral type—even as he strives to remain singular. To his companions in the Boar's Head, Pistol is a "rascally scald beggarly lousy pragging knave" and "a gull, a fool, a rogue" (*Henry V*, 5.1.5, 3.6.70). Doll describes him as the commoners' "scurvy companion," a "poor, base, rascally, cheating, lack-linen mate." She reacts with outrage to the suggestion that Pistol might be singled out as a captain, thus allowing him to jump up the ranks:

> An captains were of my mind, they would truncheon you out, for taking their names upon you before you have earned them. You a captain? You slave! For what? For tearing a poor whore's ruff in a bawdy-house? He a captain? Hang him, rogue, he lives upon mouldy stewed prunes and dried cakes. A captain? God's light, these villains will make the word as odious as the word "occupy," which was an excellent good word before it was ill sorted; therefore captains had need look to't. (*2 Henry IV*, 2.4.120, 136–46)

In Doll's conservative view of the social matrix, where a rank-bestowing name guarantees social uprightness, words (like people) become "ill-sorted" if they keep the wrong company. The very word "captain"—and hence the reputation of all captains—becomes odious merely by association. Doll tasks her superiors with remedying this ill-sortedness, but it is she herself who determines to "look to't" that differing types and titles are kept properly apart. In Doll's estimation, Pistol does not deserve the name of captain, which would allow him to stand apart from the scurvy company. Not quite his own man, Pistol must remain among his own typical and typically unexceptional sort.

But Pistol is not so readily put in his place. In a play crucially concerned with staking claims to titles, not least the title of the French throne, even his own name seems ill-sorted.[22] Pistol is a pizzle, as Mistress Quickly is quick to remind him, prone to discharge more than one kind of "flashing fire" when his "cock is up" (2.1.49–50). Most debate about Pistol's name has centered, however, around his title as "ancient Pistol" or (in its "modernized" form) "ensign Pistol."[23] The two words sounded similar in Elizabeth pronunciation, and Shakespeare elsewhere used them interchangeably.[24] Pistol holds the military rank of ensign, the soldier who bore the company's "colors" on a lance or pole so that the troops could locate their own commanders as well as those of the enemy.[25] The role was a highly regarded one, calling for considerable courage and integrity. As the military strategist and writer Thomas Digges wrote in 1590, "in assaulting a breach, the Ensign should endeavor himself to be the first and foremost."[26] The "colors" comprised heraldic or regimental insignia, but the term also referred to the "bloody flag," or *oriflamme*, a red banner of two or three points, which warned the enemy that no prisoners would be taken.[27] These are the colors Canterbury has in mind when he urges Henry to take decisive action against France, invoking the blood of the "valiant dead":

> Stand for your own; unwind your bloody flag;
> Look back into your mighty ancestors.
> *(Henry V*, 1.2.100–102)

Since the ensign was expected to take the place of the captain or lieutenant if they fell, he was always a man of noble birth.[28] But Pistol's rashness and equivocal title hardly qualify him to act as a guarantor of the king's flag of war. It is tempting, then, to conclude with Paul Jorgensen that Pistol simply bears an "outrageously reversed relationship to his office" and that Shakespeare was making comical capital out of the assumption (held dear by Doll) that high rank correlated with virtue and competence.[29]

Much of the humor of Pistol's scenes does indeed pivot on the incongruity between his supposed high rank on the one hand and his bombastic ferocity on the other. But Pistol's social class remains impossible to determine. Bemused in *2 Henry IV* by Pistol's blustering, Shallow can only conclude "I know not your breeding" (5.3.106). And in *Henry V*, when Pistol and the king meet on the eve of Agincourt, the king turns Pistol's question back upon him: "art thou officer, / Or art thou base, common, and popular?" Pistol's reply is typically riddling and equivocal: "As good a gentleman as the Emperor" (4.1.38–9 and 43). Pistol's subsequent exchange with the French soldier, just before the declaration of defeat, focuses again on quality and degree:

> *French Soldier.* Je pense que vous êtes le gentilhomme de bon qualité.
> *Pistol.* Qualité? "Calin o custure me!"
> *(Henry V*, 4.4.3–4)

Pistol's riposte is an Elizabethan corruption of a familiar Irish refrain (*cailin og a' stor*, "maiden, my treasure") which serves simply to deflect the French soldier's question. So when Fluellen describes Pistol as "a man of no estimation in the world" (3.6.14), he suggests not only that Pistol lacks firm social standing, but also, and more interestingly, that his social degree is impossible for others to guess. In some ways, Pistol looks as insignificant and as vulnerable to diminishment as the poor creatures pricked out as battle fodder. But his much-discussed name and indeterminable worth resist any such ready sorting, and the quality of his blood remains inestimable. The fact that Pistol is the ensign of the company entrusted with carrying (or perhaps even embodying) the king's colors suggests that there is much at stake behind these interrogations of his social status.[30] Pistol presents a new and unfamiliar version of dramatic character formed in important ways by blood while remaining capable of circulating beyond and outside the systems of class allegiance that blood-based identity normally implied. Pistol's social slipperiness suggests not only his brash assertiveness but also, as we have seen, his sheer invisibility—and makes him a remarkably risky choice as the man to "stand for" the king's own colors. The unbounded, unsortable, and defiantly unclassifiable Pistol indeed issues a more general challenge: how can we understand personhood in Shakespeare's theater in terms other than those arising from humoralism and the social typologies it implies?

* * *

As Markham reminds us, blood-degree is fixed and irremovable: "there are severall degrees in bloud." His blunt assertion about blood-based social hierarchy perhaps reflects the contemporary increase in the practice of exogamy, or marrying outside one's own class, for as Markham goes on to explain,

> as men liue and are borne here into the world, there is a great difference both in their Bloods and Beings: for the Legitimate is much better borne then the Bastard . . . the Nobleman, then the Plebeian.[31]

The better blood Markham imagines is partly figurative, for the noble way of "being" he imagines has as much to do with manners, morals, and values as it does with physiology. Insofar as blood forms part of noble hard-wiring, however, it allows Markham to assert that better birth offers a guarantee of a superior kind of life. We have seen that Shakespeare's Pistol offers an extraordinary riposte to this sketch of a blood-based social hierarchy and to the consensual and hierarchically ordered society it imagines. Pistol's name, language, and reputation all render him unclassifiably singular and colorfully present, affording him a social circularity inaccessible to the incontrovertibly better-born who must live their lives in their place. At the same time, however, Pistol's choleric personality and his habit of borrowing others' words and gestures risk shearing him altogether of originality.

One might expect the play's elite characters to have a stronger stake than Pistol in the blood-based hierarchy Markham describes. It is striking, then, that when Henry exhorts the English noblemen "into the breach," his instruction pivots on collapsing blood-degree so that base-born soldiers become indistinguishable from noblemen:

> On, on you noblest English,
> Whose blood is fet from fathers of war-proof . . .
> Dishonour not your mothers; now attest
> That those whom you called fathers did beget you.
> Be copy now to men of grosser blood,
> And teach them how to war.
> 					(*Henry V*, 3.1.17–25)

"Fet from fathers of war-proof," the blood of the English aristocracy is guaranteed to be legitimate and authentic. Such "gentlemen of blood and quality" should provide a copy, or an example, to "men of grosser blood." So far, so classifiable. But Henry also exhorts his men to

> Stiffen the sinews, conjure up the blood,
> Disguise fair nature with hard-favoured rage
> 					(3.1.7–8)

reminding them that the savage blood conjured by war creates not a blush appropriate to "fair nature" but rather a flush of rage. The idea of "conjuring" suggests the miraculous recovery of the blood of lost forefathers. But the phrase "conjure up the blood" does not appear in the folio playtext of *Henry V* and is only the generally accepted amendment for the phrase that actually appears: "commune up the blood." If this is a compositorial misreading of the minims in the middle of the word, probably copied from Shakespeare's foul papers, the slip is a happy one. For although "commune" may mean "fortify" or "make strong," from the Latin *communion*, it could also of course carry the sense of "bring together."³² We remember Exeter's description of York and Suffolk in Act 4 Scene 6 as noble "yokefellows"—and a similar sense of blood-bonding animates Henry's rhetoric here.

On the eve of Agincourt Henry again makes powerful rhetorical capital out of blood conjuring, or communing. He imagines mingling his own blood with that of his foot soldiers:

> For he today that sheds his blood with me
> Shall be my brother; be he ne'er so vile,
> This day shall gentle his condition.
> (4.3.60–63)

To belong to the king's military fraternity offers "vile" men the opportunity not only to save their souls, but also to "gentle" their conditions—and the two transformations seem similar in Henry's mind as he offers the common soldiers the alluring prospect of glorious immortality shared among a self-sacrificing community.³³ The more radical idea is that shedding one's blood alongside that of one's social superiors involves a magical transmigration of class, allowing "vile" types to ascend toward heroic individuality. This is a ruthlessly efficient form of conjuring, for Henry's purposes, in the theater of war. In this moment at least, grosser blood need not be diminished by being shared, but may instead borrow the extraordinary exemplarity of the finer sort. The alluring new identity Henry sketches for his foot soldiers recalls in interesting ways Pistol's strange indeterminacy. Henry imagines breaking the allegiances formed by blood, as Pistol does, in order to allow circulation between social "types" usually regarded as securely separate. Again, though, blood-bonding between classes involves the risk of exposure to fragility and diminishment as much as the prospect of heroic exemplarity. And in each case, the promise of a jubilantly classless identity involves the imminent threat of bloodshed.

Henry has in fact already tested this version of classless blood brother-hoods. Two scenes earlier he had walked, disguised, among the troops and had spoken with the foot soldier John Bates:

> *King Henry.* By my troth, I will speak my conscience of the King: I
>   think he would not wish himself any where but where he is.

Bates. Then I would he were here alone. So should he be sure to be
ransomed, and a many poor men's lives saved.
King Henry. I dare say you love him not so ill to wish him here
alone, howsoever you speak this to feel other men's minds.
Methinks I could not die anywhere so contented as in
the King's company, his cause being just and his quarrel
honourable.

(4.1.112–21)

The disguised king here claims his own aristocratic singularity and self-sufficiency: "I could not die anywhere so contented as in the King's company." At the same time, though, he is claiming he would willingly die only if he were a soldier "in the King's company," serving as one man among many. In a reversal of the blood brotherhood sketched in Act 3 Scene 1, where noble blood provides a copy to grosser, the king's contented death seems dependent now on the blood shed by innumerable others.

Another of the three foot soldiers, however, Michael Williams, has already bluntly pointed out that the king is not like other soldiers, and that his blood is not like other soldiers' blood. The fraternity Williams describes could not be more different from the blessed community imagined by Henry:

if the cause be not good, the King himself hath a heavy reckoning to make, when all those legs and arms and heads chopped off in a battle shall join together at the latter day, and cry all, "We died at such a place"—some swearing, some crying for a surgeon, some upon their wives left poor behind them, some upon the debts they owe, some upon their children rawly left. I am afeard there are few die well that die in a battle, for how can they charitably dispose of anything, when blood is their argument? (4.1.129–38)

Williams holds a different kind of "copy" up to the king's conscience, which he describes as heavy with chaotic, desperate, unprepared-for deaths. At first Williams grafts responsibility onto the king only "if the cause be not good." But by the end of this speech, his point is different and more uncompromising: soldiers' souls are not saved because they are not salvageable: "how can they charitably dispose of anything, when blood is their argument?" Williams offers a telling rejoinder to Henry's attempt to define (and discipline) the inward lives of unlettered soldiers by pressing them into unanimously cheerful surrender. For while Henry's contented self-image rests on the blood brotherhood he imagines sharing with his social inferiors, the commoners imagine their blood as determinedly different from the king's—and, perhaps more significantly, from each other. Williams describes a brotherhood of casualties all "join[ed] together"—but they do not return "at the latter day" as a troop of acquiescent shadows. For Williams, at least, the prospect of "communing" noble and common blood together into a gloriously victorious company remains hollow. His disturbing sketch of the king's "heavy reckoning" indeed tears apart the assumption that had underpinned Henry's promise of victory: that common blood is communal blood, indistinguishable from the blood of the nobility. Instead the common soldiers reappear as a noisy troop of pieces or fragments, defiantly and terribly separated from each other and from themselves.

Perhaps we may describe the indescribable Pistol himself as just such a noisy fragment. Pistols were not yet the sleek, sinister firearm of today, but were instead known at this time for their deafening volume and alarming unpredictability. Shakespeare surely knew that pistols were a relatively new and untested part of the English military arsenal, prone to fire without warning—or, indeed, to fail altogether.[34] According to the strategist Sir John Smythe,

> Pistolettiers are not to worke any effect against squadrons or troupes of horsemen or footmen above 10. or 15. yards off at the furdest, and if it be enemie to enemie single, then they are not to discharge their peeces above 4. or 5. yards off; unless they wil faile 5. times, before they hit once, so uncertain are those weapons of fire.[35]

An even blunter admonition was offered by Shakespeare's probable prototype for Fluellen, the professional soldier and military theorist Roger Williams: "Pistolls faile to goe off."[36] Offering only an alarmingly "perilous shot," pistols were particularly unreliable as a weapon used en masse by groups of soldiers—as Francois de La Noue makes clear:

> it is so assured a principle that a troope of Speares should beate and overthrowe a troope of Pistols, that who so seemeth to doubt thereof is taken to be but a meanly practised souldier.[37]

Since each pistol was unreliable, there was scant opportunity for a troop of pistolettiers to join forces as a cohort of blood brothers serving a common

Sorting Pistol's Blood

purpose. Pistol's very name therefore resonates with (Shakespeare's own) Williams's account of war's terrible risk and unpredictability, as well as his suggestion that combat—for those without quality or degree—involved trial and separation rather than togetherness.

In this way, as in others, Pistol exposes the conjuring trick that had proposed that plebeian blood, once shed, becomes noble and exemplary. Pistol finds an unlikely ally in Montjoy, who speaks to Henry in the "bloody field" (4.7.67) after Agincourt. Montjoy has one particular responsibility in mind, namely

> To sort our nobles from our common men—
> For many of our princes, woe the while,
> Lie drowned and soaked in mercenary blood.
> So do our vulgar drench their peasant limbs
> In blood of princes
>
> (4.7.69–73)

Here Montjoy describes the French defeat not so much in terms of the loss of gentle blood, but instead through the fearful mingling of the blood of nobility and commoners. Unlike York and Suffolk, who die together as noble "yokefellows" in each other's company, the French drown—humiliatingly—in mixed blood. The vision is a nightmarish one involving the confusion of blood-degrees. The only comfort left for Montjoy lies in "sorting" the gentles from the peasants and mercenaries. Now the process of separating one class of soldier from another becomes a desperate and belated one: princes may recover the respect and integrity afforded by their rank only if they can be pulled from "common men" whose vulgarity threatens to bleed terribly onto and into them.

Williams, Pistol, and Montjoy all resist Henry's suggestion that aristocratic and plebeian blood may be seamlessly worked together in the theater of war. In different ways, they draw attention to the class resentments that war gives rise to and expose the evasions that the aristocracy needed in order to get around them.[38] Most of all, Pistol gives the *fico* to the cultural practice (defended by Doll) of sorting people into recognizable, class-based categories according to fixed ideas of "place, degree, and form" (4.1.234). Pistol's own choleric "quick blood" seems at first to determine his place—but his unfixable title, borrowed rhetoric, and indeterminable rank all resist such ready sorting, affording him instead a social circularity quite different from the blood-based hierarchy sketched out by thinkers such as Markham. Pistol's indeterminacy indeed allows Shakespeare to reflect skeptically on Henry's famous historical decision to fuse monarch and military into what Jonathan Dollimore and Alan Sinfield have called a "single popular archetype," exposing instead how the king was obliged to smooth over class differences for political ends.[39] Pistol's name (like the names of Shallow, Silence, Mouldy, Shadow, and Feeble) resists familiar ideas of the self as bounded and fixed, suggesting instead that personhood may be sorted, circulated, and shared. At the same time, however, Pistol exposes the cold-bloodedness behind the habit of fixing degreeless people into expendable compounds and points up the feebleness of Feeble's conviction that workaday soldiers must extinguish themselves quietly for the sake of their noble-blooded betters. At times Pistol appears stubbornly singular, a hyperbolic man-weapon who remains resolutely and egregiously self-defined. At other moments he is a recognizable choleric type, or a composite of other people's words and actions, whose most notable characteristic is his vanished originality. Both aggressive and vulnerable, Pistol cannot be contained by blood-based rules for conferring social worth. He stands defiantly on the margins of represented personhood on the early modern stage.

PART II

Wounds

Chapter 4

Mantled in Blood

Shakespeare's Bloodstains and Early Modern Textile Culture

HESTER LEES-JEFFRIES

Toward the end of the stage adaptation of Hilary Mantel's *Bring Up the Bodies*, the courtiers found guilty of adultery with Anne Boleyn have been executed. A rough cart carrying their bodies is wheeled on, followed by this exchange between Cromwell's son Gregory, his servant Christophe, and Kingston, the lieutenant of the Tower:

> *Gregory.* Why have they stripped the bodies?
> *Kingston.* A traitor's clothes are the perquisite of the headsman and his assistants. The blood will wash out.
> *Christophe.* I doubt that.
> *Kingston.* Most of it will. But now the corpses are without their badges of rank.... Well, there is some confusion ...
> *Gregory.* Do you mean ... you can't tell which head goes with which body?
> *Christophe.* Oho!
> *Kingston.* It's difficult.[1]

At Cromwell's prompting, his man Rafe Sadler goes to identify the bodies by their hands—calluses, slender fingers, bitten nails—so that heads and bodies can be reunited for burial. This episode, only briefly reported in Mantel's novel but chillingly amplified on stage, brings together a number of issues. Despite the initial stage direction ("GUARDS *and* GRAVEDIGGERS *dump five bodies and five heads in bags in a heap*") these are not, of course, real bodies or body parts, but neither are they actors "playing dead." This unacknowledged blurring between the real, the realistic, and the fake is important. That the bodies are to be left in their shirts is part of their lack of differentiation: their shirts make them as good as naked, anonymous everymen, but that shirts were also exempted from the hangman's traditional perquisite makes them almost inseparable from the bodies. And the question of bloodstains and their removal is central to this chapter.

As Susan Baker puts it, "Drama is the fleshly genre, and the central dramaturgical fact is *embodiment*," but the succinct truth of this observation can obscure some of the messier aspects of that embodiment, not least the blurring of boundaries between fake and "real" when a character's body must do or suffer something that an actor's cannot.[2] Thomas Nashe's account of Talbot in *1 Henry VI* neatly demonstrates this conjunction and its potential for slippage: when the audience "in the Tragedian that represents [Talbot's] person, imagine they behold him fresh bleeding," the work of both personation and imagination is explicitly tied to (stage) blood, and "him" can refer both to the character of Talbot and the actor playing him.[3] Patricia Cahill's observation that theater represents "a world in which bodies are uncanny and time and space are out of joint" is a useful one; she suggests that such theatrical bodies "[register] the traumatic impact of the era's preoccupation with war."[4] But what does it mean, for instance, to describe "the blood flowing from [Beatrice's] wounded body" (at the denouement of Middleton and Rowley's *The Changeling*) as "*a theatrical reality*," as Maurizio Calbi does?[5] More persuasive is Katharine Eisaman Maus's suggestion that "in a culture . . . in which playwrights seem perversely to insist upon parading the shortcomings of their art, theatrical representation becomes subject to profound and fascinating crises of authenticity."[6] Yet even Maus's wide-ranging discussion at times overlooks illuminating distinctions in the matter of blood. In her account of *Doctor Faustus*, she discusses two moments "in which the facts of the body seem most vividly present" but which are also "possibly but not necessarily moments of delusion: when Faustus's blood clots on his arm, and he momentarily sees '*homo fuge*' written there, and then again when Christ's blood streams in the firmament, apparently forever out of reach."[7] These moments are different kinds of theatrical artifice and experience, however: there *will* probably be some kind of fake blood used in the first episode, which *will probably not* form the words of a Latin injunction, but the only blood streaming in the firmament is that which streaks, however vividly, across the mind's eye.

This discussion is particularly focused on the theatrical event and suggests some ways in which the practicalities of performance, especially in the early modern context, might have larger ramifications for thinking about blood. In performance, blood is very often not blood as such, but rather a blood*stain*, usually a bloodstain on cloth. Bloody cloths, especially in drama, are almost their own category,[8] but this discussion largely sets their particular symbolism aside, focusing rather on the textile nature of bloodstains and how that might shape and express larger ideas about bodies, blood, and cloth in early modern literature and culture. Especially in a theatrical context, the bloodstain necessarily becomes a means of staging and visualizing the wound, with the bloodied garment becoming both a surrogate for the wound and, on occasion, a way of imagining and defining the body itself. The bloodied body is sometimes described as *wearing* blood, and the language and techniques of early modern dress are often strikingly bloody, fleshly, bodily; the role of red cloth in particular is notable here. But where does cloth stop and body begin? Or does "I" only stop where the world, in textile form, begins? As is so often the case with the bloodstain itself, this chapter begins with clean linen.

The shirt, the ruff, and the cuff mark the margins of the body; they are points at which, literally as much as metaphorically, the individual bleeds into the world. In early modern culture, such margins were a locus of dependency, especially for the male subject. The integrity of clean and proper body depended on the laundress, herself a marginal figure: as Wendy Wall describes her, "the early modern laundress was a target of social condescension, often labelled as a prostitute and associated metonymically with the dirt she was charged to expel. Both laundresses and wanton women 'took up linen' or stripped gentlemen of clothes."[9] But the laundress was also in some respects privileged, in part because of this intimacy with the chambers and the bodies of her social superiors, and also through her ability to shape the very textile contours of what is now, almost unthinkingly, termed *self-fashioning*. A gentleman had to remain onside with his laundress to guarantee his supply of clean shirts, not to mention the finesse of his ruff.

In the household manuals of the period, the laundry techniques recommended to early modern housewives are surprisingly limited, especially to an imagination shaped by the Victorian mangles, coppers, and flat-irons on display in National Trust properties. Such manuals are mostly not concerned with the laundering of household linens or even shirts, but with "spot removal," garment care, and the laundering of delicate linens (such as bands, coifs, and collars). In Hannah Woolley's manual, for example, there are no particular instructions for the laundering of shirts or sheets, and the specific stains dealt with are made by ink or fruit, not blood.[10] On the evidence of such manuals, the object of such laundry was to avoid having to do laundry, which was strenuous and unpleasant work (largely depending on alkaline lye solutions made from wood ash or urine) and hard on clothes in terms of wear and tear. That which was soilable, visible—cuff, ruff, shirt—was also detachable, washable, and replaceable. Especially in towns and cities, shirts, smocks, sheets, and other household linens were often sent out to professional laundresses, who had access to the water supply (for example, a river) and the open spaces needed for the drying and bleaching of linen, as in the famous details on the "Agas Map" of London showing laundry laid out in Moorfields.[11] In *The Merry Wives of Windsor*, it seems obvious to connect Falstaff's escape in a "buck basket" with the horns of cuckoldry, but it is a buck basket because it is used to convey away the household linens, "foul shirts and smocks, socks, foul stockings, greasy napkins" (3.5.83–4), to be washed and "bucked," bleached, elsewhere (in the case of Shakespeare's Windsor, at Datchet Mead, by the "whitsters").[12] The shirt, however it was soiled, could mark the limits of the household, as much as the margins of the body.

As a number of critics have pointed out, the early modern professional theater had to manage its bloodletting carefully, because the substances used as stage blood—whether animal blood, vinegar, wine, or paint—would be likely to stain expensive costumes that were difficult, if not impossible, to clean. While the washing machine and tumble dryer are standard wardrobe equipment in theaters now,[13] this was, of course, very far from being the case in the early modern theater.[14] Once the anachronistic washing machine in the Globe is unplumbed, however, it is notable how few really necessary, really bloody scenes there are in Shakespeare's plays; in particular there are very few in which blood *must* be shed on stage in view of the audience, rather than in the tiring house, as Lucy Munro and Andrea Stevens have both recently shown.[15] To take one example, the final scene of *Hamlet*, probably the most famous duel in all Renaissance drama, is set up as a fencing competition rather than a mortal combat. As a display of skill rather than a fight to the death, there are not meant to be wounds at all, but rather "hits," technicalities, and what is meant to bring about Hamlet's death is not a fatal wound but, through Claudius's plotting, a deadly poison on the unguarded point of the weapon, so that even a scratch will be deadly. Despite the racks of bladed weapons to hand, no one is meant to be stabbed to death in this scene. There will be no wounds unless actors and directors choose to stage them; shirts or fencing jackets will probably remain unsullied, and the laundry (and the laundry bills) will not be extreme. Even if, as is often still the case, Shakespeare's actors stripped to their shirts for a fight scene, the laundering of linen remained labor-intensive and a charge on company finances that reasonably might be minimized. In an age of biological detergents and tumble dryers, fight directors and actors can more or less be as bloody as they like,[16] but on the early modern stage, where verisimilitude was not expected, the lure of getting a really realistic arterial spray and to hell with the consequences in the laundry was much less attractive or likely. (*Titus Andronicus* is, if not quite exceptional, then not the rule either; *onstage* bloodshed becomes rarer as Shakespeare's career develops, which may not necessarily correlate with his own financial interests in the company accounts, but could.)

To be in one's shirt was as good as being naked, having lost all the signifiers of rank and identity that other garments might afford, as *Bring Up the Bodies* attests. It was an intimate garment, worn in bed by those who did not sleep naked, and the shirt (or smock, for women) was the universal undergarment. It could be knee-length or longer, with men perhaps tucking the tail through their legs; men's under-drawers were uncommon and women's were centuries away. Although they might be sent out for laundering, the making of shirts was largely a household task in early modern England. It was noted that even in their estrangement, Catherine of Aragon still made her husband's shirts ("If I were her, I'd leave the needle in them," Mantel has her Liz Cromwell, wife of Thomas, say).[17] As its manufacture and laundering marked some of the defining limits of the early modern household and its relationships, the shirt also marked, or even constituted, the boundaries of the early modern body. It is therefore unsurprising that a linen layer could stand for and in a sense *was* nakedness on the early modern stage just as was apparently the case in early modern culture. And therefore, especially on the stage, the bloody shirt *was* the bloody skin; it wasn't simply a form of sleight of hand or a pragmatic theatrical solution, although it was those things too. Recognizing this might productively reshape responses to moments involving both bloodstained and unspotted linen in early modern texts.

In modern productions of *Coriolanus*, for example, whatever their notional setting, it has become the norm for Coriolanus to appear stripped to the waist, covered in glistening, viscous blood no doubt topped up backstage every time he goes into the wings. In the 2013 production of the play at London's Donmar Warehouse, Tom Hiddleston even showered on stage to wash away the blood. But that Coriolanus is described as "mantled" in blood (1.7.29) suggests a garment, one that is a metaphor *and* a theatrical practicality, and also a vivid expression of that early modern interchangeability between shirt and skin.[18] While it would be possible, and indeed likely, for the actor playing Coriolanus at the Globe to sport some bloody makeup, it seems likely, too, that he wore a garment—a shirt, perhaps—saturated in blood, less a costume than a prop. It wouldn't ever be washed. Mantel/Poulton again:

> *Rafe.* You have to feel sorry for Queen Katherine.
> *Thomas.* Do you? Henry went to France to have a little war—as Englishmen do—and left her as Regent. Down came the Scots. They were well beaten at Flodden and their King had his head cut off. Katherine—angelic Katherine—was going to send the head to her husband in his camp. But they advised her that such a gesture was "un-English." She sent instead the surcoat in which the Scottish king had died—stiffened, black and cracking with his pumped-out royal blood.[19]

The king's surcoat is no longer a garment but a thing, a trophy, but it is also a body or at least a skin, substituting the severed head (still familiar on the modern stage, although most successful when it is replaced with the synecdochic bloodstain, the dead weight in the cloth bag) with the flayed skin, now less familiar but surely well known to an early modern audience. In the battle that earns Coriolanus his name (he is originally Caius Martius), he emerges from the city of Corioles, described in the folio's stage directions as "*bleeding*" and "*bloody.*" The stage directions here must suggest not only his appearance, but record instructions to actor and stage keeper: keep topping up the blood. He must be so blood-soaked that Cominius can describe him as one "that does appear as he were flayed" (1.7.22), and, a few lines later, as "mantled" in blood.

As many have pointed out, this recalls the story of the satyr Marsyas in Ovid's *Metamorphoses*, who, in Golding's translation, "nought else he was than one whole wound."[20] In visual representations of Marsyas and his Christian counterpart, St. Bartholomew, the bloodied body, stripped to its musculature, is inseparable from its skin, which often hangs, garment-like, from the exposed flesh or, casually beside it (see Figure 4.1). Like the shirt, the skin becomes just another layer, one that emphasizes the layeredness of the rest of the body, and this perhaps accounts for the extraordinary (if now often very familiar) images of sixteenth-century "self-displaying" anatomies, who lift or unfold their own skin. Jonathan Sawday is one of many critics who have commented on the early seventeenth-century depictions, in engravings, of the anatomy theater at Leiden:

> A fashionably dressed woman is being shown what, at first glance, appears to be a piece of fabric. Looking more closely at the image, we see that what she is smilingly contemplating is not fabric at all. It is, rather, the flayed skin of a corpse.[21]

Flayed, as an adjective, can be applied to both body and skin; as both process and result, it would have been familiar to Shakespeare the leatherworker's son, and to many in early modern London, not least those who lived or worked in the vicinity of St. Bartholomew the Great, in the livestock-markets of Smithfield. The flayed skin, the mantle of blood, is still part of the body yet on occasion, like a terrible shirt, separable from it.

Figure 4.1 Apollo flaying Marsyas. Engraving by Melchior Meyer (1581). Wellcome Image Library, London.

In a twenty-first-century context, garments described as "flesh-colored" or "nude" often promise invisibility, something that will not show through the white shirt or the lace dress.[22] But in the sixteenth century, flesh-colored ("carnation" or "incarnate") was just that, the color of meat, a bloody, bodily pink as well as a more pink-and-white skin tone. "Horse-flesh" was a dark orange-red, and "sanguine" a proper blood-red; all three terms were particularly applied to textiles. The clothes of early moderns, especially the well-off, could mirror the interior of the body itself, perhaps even expressed in these vivid, visceral names. Although "ox-blood"-colored leather is still available, the more palatable, domesticated "cherry," "burgundy," and "claret" are far more common, and even Farrow and Ball, notoriously purveyors of "Dead Salmon" and "Elephant's Breath" and many other esoterically named "heritage" paint colors, offer only the reassuringly Shakespearean "Incarnadine" among their various reds.

Scarlet cloth had its own particular ceremonial valency in early modern culture, especially in London, as it still does in ecclesiastical, legal, and academic circles. "Scarlet" usually referred to high-grade woollen cloth, well finished and dyed. It might be described as dyed "in grain," that is, either using the expensive kermes or cochineal, both red dyes derived from insects, or, in more general usage, fast-dyed, or dyed in the fiber, before weaving, rather than as finished cloth (hence "ingrained," meaning "indelible"). Scarlet was not necessarily sanguinary in its associations, but on occasion such garments could indeed be bloody, bodily, properly visceral. In his vivid biography of Mary, Queen of Scots, John Guy makes much of her wearing red to the scaffold in the form of an underdress concealed by sober black until she was undressed at the block by her attendants. Guy plausibly makes the case that Mary's "tawny" was a deliberate claiming of the aesthetic of martyrdom, red being proper in the Catholic Church for the feasts of martyrs.[23] Yet the undeniably Protestant earl of Essex also wore a scarlet waistcoat to the block in February 1601, a waistcoat at this time being not a formal piece of outerwear but rather an informal extra layer usually reserved for domestic settings; not quite a shirt, but almost. Essex's red, and Mary's, could be interpreted as bringing the interior of the body to its surface in a vividly, unsettlingly anticipatory way: this is flesh and blood, sir, the propriety and integrity of which are about to be irreversibly ruptured. Mary's alleged smock is retained and displayed at Coughton Court in Warwickshire, but it was the red petticoat, the scarlet waistcoat, that made the point. Not every red garment was a bloody mantle, but some of them might well have been.

The treatment of the textile surface in early modern clothing could also reflect this sense of the body's layeredness and vulnerability. As is abundantly clear from surviving garments and portrait evidence, it was very common to draw attention to the layering of garments, through panes and panels, by turning back a sleeve or collar to display a rich contrasting lining, and especially through decorative cutting, slashing, or pinking, whereby an undergarment or lining became selectively visible, an effect that complicated the sense of what was outside and what in, what was surface and what interior, as in the miniature self-portrait by Isaac Oliver, or the author portrait in Andreas Vesalius's *De humani corporis fabrica* (see Figures 4.2 and 4.3). A modern analogy can perhaps be found in notorious dresses held together by safety pins, or more mundanely seen in elaborately "distressed" jeans or punk laddered tights: the flesh thus displayed is both what lies beneath and part of the garment, both body and its covering. The razor was as much a tool of the tailor in the sixteenth century as shears or scissors remain today, essential for the fine patterns of slashing that so often decorated the clothes of the elite. *Pink*, *cut*, and *slash* could equally be applied to stab wounds or punctures in the skin in early modern usage. Stephen Greenblatt quotes a passage from John Bulwer's *Anthropometamorphosis* (1653), which avows that "The slashing, pinking, and cutting of our Doublets, is but the same phansie and affectation with those barbarous Gallants who slash and carbonado their bodies, and who pinke and raze their Sattin, Damaske, and Duretto skins" (see Figure 4.4).[24] An illustration makes clear that the "Gallants" are native peoples practicing body modification such as scarification, their skins explicitly imagined in textile terms; that "bodies" and "bodice" are cognate in early modern usage adds emphasis to the parallel.[25] Thomas Nashe's Jack Wilton, sentenced to execution *and dissection* for a crime he has not committed, laments:

> Oh, the cold sweating cares which I conceived after I knew I should be cut like a French summer doublet! . . . Not a drop of sweat trickled down my breast and my sides, but I dreamt it was a smooth-edged razor tenderly slicing down my breast and sides.[26]

This connection between fabric, skin, and flesh, decorative slashing and dissection has been made, among others, by Luke Wilson, discussing the title page of Vesalius's *Fabrica*, which depicts a dissection: "the figure standing at the far right . . . wears hose the designs of which suggest, in context, surgical incisions or crude representations of the muscles dissected" (see Figure 4.5).[27] It is a horrible irony that Adriaen Adriaenszoon, the subject of both dissection and painting in Rembrandt's *Anatomy Lesson of Dr Nicolaes Tulp* (1632) was executed on January 31 in that year *for stealing a coat.*[28] In all of these examples, from the Oliver self-portrait to Nashe's Jack Wilton, from the anatomy books to Coriolanus, where does fabric stop and flesh begin?

For even once his blood is washed away and his bloody garment exchanged for a different costume, Coriolanus's wounds remain central to his character and to the play, as many critics have explored: in Cynthia Marshall's terms, "The play ... turns not simply on the matter of his having wounds but on the semiotic issues of showing and interpreting them."[29] No character in the play is more obsessed with them than his mother, Volumnia. After his victory at Corioles, she and Menenius discuss them:

Figure 4.2 Isaac Oliver. "The doublet is black, its lining crimson." Miniature painting by Isaac Oliver (ca. 1590).
© National Portrait Gallery, London.

Figure 4.3 Author portrait. Andrea Vesalius, *De humani corporis fabrica* (1555). N*.1.1(A). Reproduced by kind permission of the Syndics of Cambridge University Library.

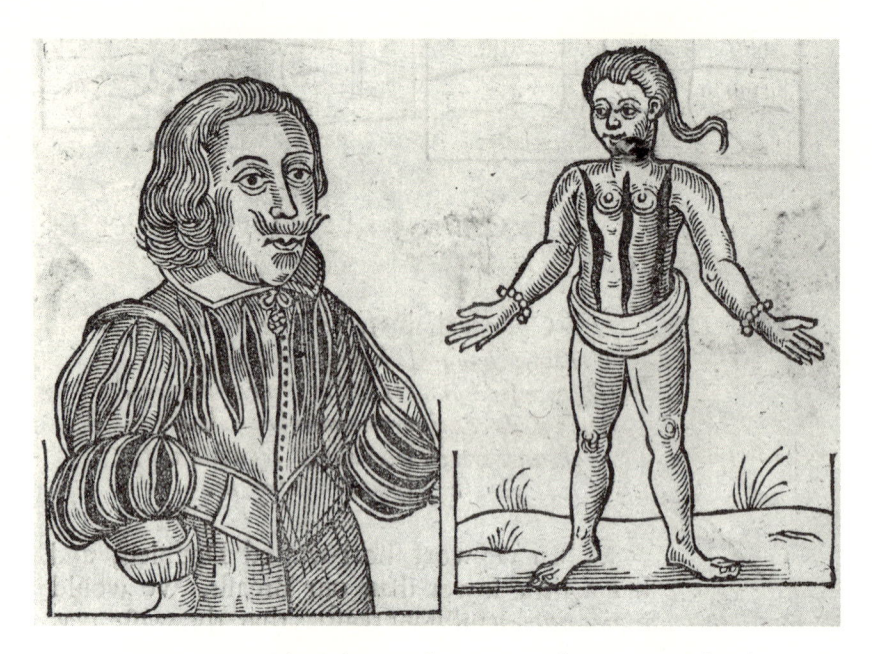

Figure 4.4 From John Bulwer, *Anthropometamorphosis: man transform'd; or, The artificiall changling* (1653). Hunter.d.65.13. Reproduced by kind permission of the Syndics of Cambridge University Library.

> *Menenius.* Where is he wounded?
> *Volumnia.* I'th' shoulder, and i'th' left arm. There will be large cicatrices to show the people when he shall stand for his place. He received in the repulse of Tarquin seven hurts i'th' body.
> *Menenius.* One i'th' neck and two i'th' thigh—there's nine that I know.
> *Volumnia.* He had before this last expedition twenty-five wounds upon him.
> *Menenius.* Now it's twenty-seven. (2.1.143–52)

The effect can be (and is perhaps meant to be) comic, the bloodthirsty mother rejoicing in the physical signs of her son's valor. These are the most specific wounds in Shakespeare, carefully enumerated and located on the body. But Coriolanus himself has no desire to show his wounds. They mark and even define his body and his identity, yet he prefers to conceal them. This is, like the ready-made bloodied garment, the off-stage death, theatrically expedient;

Figure 4.5 Frontispiece. Andrea Vesalius, *De humani corporis fabrica* (1555). N*.1.1(A). Reproduced by kind permission of the Syndics of Cambridge University Library.

there is no need to construct fake wounds or scars, but despite their anatomical specificity, their precise locations, the wounds are concealed.

Marshall borrows from W. B. Worthen the suggestion of 'character' in the Renaissance theater as "a more collaborative or even collusive activity, one in which the *seam* between actor and character may well have been visible," herself suggesting that "Coriolanus' wounds, testifying at once to the artifice of the stage and to the felt subjectivity of the character, present such a *seam*; they require collusion of several sorts from an audience."[30] The imagining of such a visible or at least apprehensible join in textile terms resonates in the wider context of this play. As a ritual part of his campaign, Coriolanus must stand in the forum, wearing what is referred to as a "vesture of humility," to allow his scars to be seen. In Plutarch this is the toga worn without a tunic underneath; in North, this becomes "a poore gowne . . . without any coate underneath." (That "toga" was mostly an unfamiliar term in early seventeenth-century English is suggested by the compositors' setting of "toge" as "tongue" in the Folio text.) Shakespeare seems to equate it with a sheet or shift worn by those doing public penance, or, again, a kind of undress, like the shirt Coriolanus may have been wearing when he was covered with blood. It might even be equated with a surplice: although the vestiarian controversy had peaked in the 1560s, the surplice was still a controversial garment in the early seventeenth-century church. There may be another clue as to what Coriolanus could wear in *All's Well That Ends Well*, in which the clown Lavatch suggests that "though honesty be no puritan, yet it will do no hurt: it will wear the surplice of humility over the black gown of a big heart" (1.3.91–3). That "toga" was usually glossed as "gown" could also identify it with the gowns worn formally or professionally by many in early modern England. For London's aldermen, sometimes Romanized as "senators," those gowns were scarlet. A triangular relationship could therefore be constructed between Coriolanus's bloody mantle, the scarlet of a London alderman or other authority figure, and the gown of humility or the bright white garment associated in imperial Rome with the seeking of political office: a candidate is *candidatus*, wearing white.[31] "Candidate" does not appear in *Coriolanus*, but it does in the opening scene of *Titus Andronicus*, when the victorious Titus is sent a "palliament of white and spotless hue" and exhorted to "be *candidatus* then" (1.1.182, 185).

But whatever its form, the garment worn by Coriolanus here is as much a surrogate skin as his previous bloody mantle. Like skin, it is both a covering and itself on display; as a white or undyed garment, and like skin, it must also encompass the possibility of wounding and staining. It becomes a surrogate for the wounds that will not be displayed and that cannot be revealed, because they do not, in fact, exist. As seen in countless advertisements for laundry detergents, the white textile is all about the *possibility* of stains. To be immaculate, unspotted, whole, entails the potential of being stained, disfigured, wounded. It is also a profoundly human state, and one might pause, briefly, on the role of textiles as signifiers of personhood in Christian iconography: the swaddling bands and winding sheet that frame the life, and emphasise the humanity, of Christ, and the *sudarium* that wiped away the sweat of his brow, Adam's sweat, on the road to Calvary. The Gospel narrative of the woman with the issue of blood, healed when she touches the hem of Christ's garment, is most easily interpreted as being concerned not simply with a miraculous healing, but with the repudiation of pollution taboos and the giving way of the old law to the new. Yet Christ's garment is itself a sign of wholeness (it is made without a seam) and humanity, incarnational love at its most fleshly. The bloodstained cloths implicit in the story, shameful and hidden, are transformed both by and into the seamless garment of the body of Christ.[32] Coriolanus's gown of humility is therefore a transitional, neutral state. It canvasses the possibility of a new identity, political rather than military, one that might even, to a seventeenth-century Londoner, connote a scarlet gown (especially if such garments are being worn by other political leaders in the play, such as Menenius). But it also looks back to the bloody mantle and reifies the potential for further bloodshed, Coriolanus's bloodshed, in the play: here is the *vulnerable* body.

There is also, perhaps, a gesture back at *Julius Caesar*. Caesar's death is staged as the climactic event of that play's first half. It has been bloodily anticipated, in ghastly prophetic visions of statues running with blood, and it is probably the most bloody of all Shakespeare's onstage deaths although, as Lucy Munro has pointed out, "the spread of blood through the play's language has perhaps encouraged critics to imagine it flowing too freely in the assassination scene itself."[33] The stage direction in the Folio is straightforward: "They stab Caesar," then, following the now famous "Et tu Brute?", simply, "Dyes"; this is in stark contrast to the violence of Shakespeare's source, in Plutarch, where the murder is described in some detail as a "horrible sight" with Caesar's body left "hacked and mangled" by a total of twenty-three wounds. In the play there is no immediate description of the wounds; instead, the conspirators smear their hands and blades with blood, in effect displacing the wounds and staging them at one remove. Brutus's instruction is clear:

> Stoop, Romans, stoop,
> And let us bathe our hands in Caesar's blood
> Up to the elbows, and besmear our swords.
> (3.1.106–8)

Caesar's wounds are displaced again later in the play in Antony's funeral oration, in which he largely uses Caesar's mantle as a substitute for the body:

> You all do know this mantle . . .
> Look, in this place ran Cassius' dagger through:
> See what a rent the envious Casca made.
> Through this the well-belovèd Brutus stabbed.
> (3.2.168, 172–74)

Although he later gestures at the "real" wounds, the emphasis is on the cloak. As would be the case with Coriolanus's bloody garment, Caesar's bloody mantle can be reused for every performance; there is no need for the actor, or the character, to be seen to bleed, and the real gashes in the cloak can evoke the nonexistent bleeding wounds.[34] When Shakespeare returns to the wounded Roman body in *Coriolanus*, it is perhaps unsurprising that he again employs the mantle or gown as a substitute for the body itself. Yet, as has already been seen, he develops the trope in crucial ways.

In relation to these ideas of blood seen and unseen, connections can also be made between *Coriolanus* and a slightly earlier, even bloodier tragedy, *Macbeth*, which looks a little different if it too is approached in these textile terms. *Macbeth* is a play soaked in blood, yet it also, on occasion, manifests a knowing playfulness in the ways in which it approaches the staging and imagining of blood, preparing the way for how blood and textiles work together in *Coriolanus*. *Macbeth* contains explicit references to washing blood away ("A little water clears us of this deed," 2.2.65) but the play is the *locus classicus* of the invisible, indelible bloodstain: "Yet here's a spot" (5.1.30). It is in *Macbeth*, in contrast to *Julius Caesar*, that it is explicitly established that neither the bloody wounds nor the moment of assassination need be shown. Instead Duncan is imagined, "his silver skin laced with his golden blood" (2.3.112), a complex textile image: here "lace" means string or tie, such as would fasten a shirt, but in this instance the blood marks "gashed stabs" (113), signs of rupture, not integrity. In the sleepwalking scene, Lady Macbeth's smock in a sense makes the invisible blood possible, a screen on to which it can be projected. It is a surrogate skin; she is in effect naked, a soul to be judged and in anguish, and the blood that she smells is her own mortality, her own maimed and vulnerable humanity, as much as the ineradicable stain of her crime. Perhaps Othello *must* explicitly announce "Yet I'll *not* shed her blood" (5.2.3), because the red and white textile context (handkerchief, sheets) has been so clearly established earlier in the play and reinforced in the final scene by his description of Desdemona as "pale as thy smock" (280): the possibility of staining and the condition of unspottedness have, after all, been central to this most color-*seeing* play.

As Elaine Scarry and others have shown,[35] the description of pain is heavily dependent on metaphor. In "real life," blood and wounds enable if not the transcendence of language, then at least its temporary evasion: they have an evidentiary force that is nonsemantic. However much Coriolanus protests, wounds, scars, and blood *can* speak, as Antony well knows; wounds are mouths with an eloquent, bloody language of their own. On stage, however, there are no wounds and that imagined bloody eloquence must be both displaced into costumes and props and also re-transformed into language, compensating in its copiousness (and also, often, its animation: blood pools and seeps as it is transformed from noun to verbs, adverbs, adjectives) for the unavoidable theatrical artifice. As the conspirators stand over the body of Caesar, Cassius reiterates Brutus's command: "Stoop, then, and wash" (3.1.112). But it's not simply another implicit stage direction, for he goes on to speculate,

> How many ages hence
> Shall this our lofty scene be acted over
> In states unborn and accents yet unknown!
> (112–14)

And Brutus adds, "How many times shall Caesar bleed in sport . . . ?" (115). It is this moment of theatrical fakery, as the bloody, invisible, impossible wounds are "staged" as lavishly smeared weapons and hands, that occasions this metatheatrical musing. "Stage blood" is a reminder that you're in a play, or watching one, in which Caesar will only ever be able to bleed in sport. What is perhaps less noticeable, because taken for granted, is the way in which such blood is almost always staged (and experienced in "real life") as bloodstained textile. And the richness of early modern textile culture, its linguistic and experiential density, give a peculiar force to these moments in Shakespeare's plays, moments that are often theatrically precarious and thin. A bloodstain destabilizes the boundary between self and world, inside and outside, play and not-play. And the characteristically early modern layeredness of that boundary, the apparent interchangeability of body and mantle, skin and shirt, slash and wound, sanguine and scarlet, even of white and red, is inseparable from and even most intelligible through the necessary artifice of the stage.

Chapter 5

Rethinking Nosebleeds

Gendering Spontaneous Bleedings in Medieval and Early Modern Medicine

GABRIELLA ZUCCOLIN AND HELEN KING

Introduction

In the mid-sixteenth century, Amatus Lusitanus described the case of a puerperal woman who menstruated from her mouth and nostrils after having given birth to a baby after a mere seven months' gestation. The physician ordered a number of bloodletting treatments, including the application of cupping glasses with scarification on the shoulders, the opening of a vein in the foot and the heating and purging remedy of "Byzantine syrup" to divert the menstrual flow back toward the "right pathway." He finally succeeded, at least for the mother, although not for the premature child, who did not survive.[1]

In this case, as was typical of bloodletting practices in premodern medicine, blood that should have come from one part of the body was removed through a range of other, created orifices, but the intention remained to return it to its proper place of exit. "Bleeding wounds" were generated in the body, to some extent as a substitute for loss from the correct outlet, but more importantly to restore the body's natural processes of evacuation. This was a common pattern in early modern medicine, but in this case there is something more that challenges our views of blood; namely, the status of bleeding from the mouth and, even more, from the nose. The patient here is a woman, and one who is expected to "purge" after giving birth. In her case, the assumption that a nosebleed is menstrual does at least have a certain logic, even to us with our very different views of the organs and fluids of the body. But, more generally, how far was bleeding from the nose gendered, and how should this affect our more general understanding of the late medieval and early modern body?

Bleeding from this particular site could in general be understood as therapeutic or as noxious, or as being triggered by a morbid condition. Among the many stories available, we have chosen this particular case by Lusitanus as the starting point for our more general analysis of theories of menstruation, nosebleeds (epistaxis), other spontaneous bleedings, and the therapeutic practices tied to them, because it encapsulates and merges together issues that have long been at the forefront of studies of the body, such as the menstruating body, alongside topics that have thus far eluded scholarly debates, such as the full range of possibilities for vicarious bleeding. This case blurs the lines between menstrual bleeding, postpartum bleeding, and nosebleed, as this nosebleed is explicitly characterized as "menstrual," *sanguis menstruus*. In a similar case, ps.-Albertus Magnus stated that a nosebleed in a woman about to give birth to a stillborn child was "really menstrual blood," and a commentator added that this was the result of the blood that was no longer needed for its nourishment traveling upward. The commentator noted that nosebleeds in early pregnancy were of no concern because they, too, were formed of blood that the child did not need.[2]

In Lusitanus's description, we see displayed almost the entire spectrum of cures available for nosebleeds, which, significantly, here do not include the use of local remedies applied to the nose. Menstruation theories, including ideas about vicarious and supplementary menstruation, are closely linked to phlebotomy practices in premodern medicine. Elsewhere, there is an acknowledgment of the potentially ambiguous relationship between nosebleeds and pregnancy, because a massive nosebleed toward the end of pregnancy could turn out to be either providential or lethal.[3]

This chapter aims to address nosebleeds in terms of their potential to challenge a still-dominant model of the premodern body: what has become known as the "one-sex" model. It is now more than two decades since Thomas Laqueur published his influential book *Making Sex: Body and Gender from the Greeks to Freud*, arguing that a two-sex model of the body only came to dominate Western medical theory in the late eighteenth century. Prior to this, he claimed, the Aristotelian and Galenic one-sex model conceptualized the bodies of men and women in pretty much the same way, according to a hierarchical pattern in which the female was merely seen as an inverted version of the male, a missed or defective male (*mas occasionatus*). In the one-sex body, men and women were thus thought to have the same sexual organs, differing only in their location: inside, or outside, the body according to that body's greater (male) or lesser (female) "heat." More recent scholarship has challenged Laqueur's assumption of a linear progression from a one-sex to a two-sex model and has recognized that he also fails to account for alternative concepts of bodies and sex-specific functions that were strongly emphasized already in the Hippocratic corpus.[4]

It is our contention that nosebleeds can reveal the gendered assumptions lying behind medical writers' descriptions of, and diagnoses in, female and male bodies, thus providing further refutation of the one-sex model. Here, we shall locate discussions of male and female nosebleeds within primary medical sources and attempt to understand the relationship between these, menstrual, and other bleedings in the context of ancient, medieval, and Renaissance phlebotomy theories. In the wider framework of considering blood flows from particular sites of the body, of which this chapter forms a part, the questions we are asking include: What were thought to be the causes of nosebleeds in general? Did the remedies used vary between men and women, or between bleeding that is described in terms that relate it to the menses, and "other" bleeding? When did nosebleeding move from being a symptom to a therapy, and was this the case for amenorrhea or only for conditions unrelated to menstruation? We hope that this study will act as a test case when studying gendered medical theories and practices in the Middle Ages and the early modern period.

The link between the presence of nosebleeds or other chronic bleeding and the absence of menstruation, or its irregular flow, continued to puzzle both physicians and their patients until the beginning of the twentieth century, if not beyond. Case histories recorded and published years after the British Gynecological Society reacted against the widespread theory of "vicarious menstruation" in 1887, as well as a recent Web survey, provide evidence in support of this link.[5] Cases of compensatory epistaxis are indeed so common in historical medical literature that a comprehensive list is impossible. Such cases cannot be explained by modern medical theories: this is just one of many places where attempts at retrospective diagnosis completely miss the point.[6] And the list of cases does not end, as one might expect, when a clear link between menstruation and ovulation was finally made in the first half of the nineteenth century, a time when the ancient theory of menstruation as having primarily a cleansing and purifying function was finally dismissed in favor of a straightforward connection between menstrual flow and reproduction. Only the identification of the gynecological disorder called endometriosis, where endometrial tissue is found in abnormal locations outside the uterine cavity—including the nasal mucosa—finally transformed the theory of vicarious menstruation into popular folklore in the thirties.[7]

Reviewing the whole of ancient, medieval and Renaissance literature devoted to the theory of menstruation's unusual pathways—whether "vicarious" or "supplementary" menstruation—would thus be a titanic task. The most extensive review of this literature on unusual hemorrhages, presenting them as a means by which nature seeks to relieve the body in cases of suppressed or insufficient menstruation, was provided by the eighteenth-century physician Martin Schurig in his *Parthenologia historico-medica*, a substantial part of which was devoted to *De insolitis menstruationis viis*. At the very end of the nineteenth century this section was echoed, updated, and somewhat internationalized by a similar one within the much-reprinted book *Anomalies and Curiosities of Medicine* by George Gould and Walter Pyle.[8]

Noses were not the only bodily parts involved in the menses' quest to find alternative ways out of the body: Schurig explains that menstrual blood could equally ooze out of the lungs, skin, wounds and scars, fingers and nails, eyes, ears, gums, and breasts, from the stomach, the navel, the bladder, and from virtually any place other than the womb. The medical theory that the blood is diverted upward if the normal way out is closed is far from being a ghostly remnant of ancient Hippocratic theory.[9]

The Lack of Secondary Literature and the Conceptual Framework

In the last twenty years or so, many studies have elaborated new conceptual frameworks to interpret the relationship between sex, gendered bodies, the role of menstruation, and medical attitudes toward the menstruating body in the premodern period. Yet the topic of vicarious menstruation in women and its theoretical framework has, with some notable exceptions, been largely neglected. This contrasts with scholarly interest in menstruating men, bleeding hermaphrodites, and "leaky males."[10] The understanding of the etiology of nosebleeds, and menstrual nosebleeds in particular, has never been assessed by modern historiographical studies.

In addition, we have little idea of how practitioners' theories regarding their patients' bodies played out in daily practice. How did physicians manage the similarities and differences between the sexes? Were male and female patients prescribed identical treatments for the same illnesses and/or symptoms?[11] To take a symptom with a neutral manifestation, such as a nosebleed, rather than one associated with the genitalia, thus provides a perfect litmus test to evaluate the "practicality" of the one-sex theory. If there is supposedly only one sex, with the organs in different places, would we not expect a nosebleed to be seen in very similar terms regardless of the sex of the patient experiencing it? We will demonstrate here that, despite assuming a number of similarities in diagnosing and treating female and male patients, physicians were well aware that women possessed unique physiological functions that had effects on the body far beyond the sexual organs and that their treatment—for many disorders—had to be prescribed accordingly. Medieval and Renaissance gendered medical practices thus entailed a much greater complexity than the theory of a one-sex/one-flesh model suggests.

But before coming to the difficult question of treatment, we must ask ourselves how the vicarious menstruation theory could have persisted for so long, even after the humoral system was abandoned. There are a number of possibilities: the dominant concepts of crisis, plethora, evacuation, and the idea of the healing power of Nature; phlebotomy theory considered as the artificial mimicking of this natural healing power; the centrality of menstruation in the health economy of women;[12] and the assumed direct physiological and anatomical connection between the genitals and the brain/eyes/nose,[13] also evident both in theories of generation and—especially from the Middle Ages onward—physiognomic theories.[14] While we cannot discuss all of these here, a brief overview of the first two is nevertheless needed because they represent the unavoidable cultural, theoretical, and conceptual framework upon which medical practitioners relied for nearly two millennia.

The importance of the concepts of crisis (a positive turning point in the disease course) and plethora (a periodical and pathological excess of blood in the body, seen as caused by an excessive or a poorly digested intake of nourishment) in ancient, medieval, and early modern medicine perfectly explains the success of the theory of vicarious menstruation until the Renaissance. Some kind of evacuation was needed to get rid of the bad matter accumulated in the body because the plethora was considered to fuel fevers and inflammation. From Hippocrates and Galen onward, if sick people did not naturally experience a kind of drastic event, they were thought more likely to die, so that the physician had to intervene to induce a crisis, mimicking the power of Nature. Purging, bloodletting, cupping, and leeching as well as inducing sweating, vomiting, and the expulsion of semen were all considered good ways to prevent illnesses. Natural crises like hemorrhages, skin eruptions, vomiting, diarrhea, and nocturnal pollutions were all considered to be ways "of taking care" of the surfeit of the body.[15] When reading medical treatises of the past, we must always keep in mind this theoretical framework, which interpreted spontaneous bleeding as normally being a good sign and thus urged the reader not to attempt to staunch those unprovoked hemorrhages considered "favorable," such as hemorrhoids, bleeding from the anus, nosebleeds (but not all kinds of nosebleeds, as we shall see), and even expectoration or vomiting of blood. The underlying rationale was that one must not interfere with Nature, even when she takes an extraordinary course. In short, these spontaneous bleedings support a theory that doctors found persuasive and stringent.

The very same framework explains the medical analogy and functional equivalence between menstruation, hemorrhoids, and nosebleeds, and the positive assessment of chronic hemorrhoids or nosebleeds in male patients as a "*morbus salutaris.*" It must be said that the theory of plethora was highly ambiguous with regard to the difference between the sexes. Why do most men not need to menstruate? The traditional explanation was the Hippocratic one: men are stronger and hotter than women; their tissues are more firm, less spongy, and therefore they better evacuate their excessive humors through sweat and urine and insensible perspiration, whereas the woman retains bad humors as a result of her natural weakness and coldness.[16] As for nosebleeds, they could be perceived as a good "purification tool" for both women and men; despite the perfection of the male body and its superior capacity for sweating, men were also at risk of plethora. But women had an advantage here; according to Aristotle, women who regularly menstruate are rarely affected by nosebleeds or hemorrhoids, as he explains in the third and seventh books of *De historia animalium* and in the first book of *De generatione*.[17]

Also important is the providential notion of Nature, the innate healing power of Nature (*vis medicatrix naturae*) to which we have already referred. This fundamental concept underpinned the whole of the Western therapeutic tradition, in terms of both theory and practice. Indeed, it was so persuasive and commonplace that it survived even the decline of Galenism.[18] Nature's healing power is not only demonstrated by discharges of blood but also through evacuation in general (for example, vomiting). Here, therapeutic intervention is simply the mimicry of nature. If for any reason the body is unable to perform evacuation by itself, the task of the healer is to help provoke a crisis by using artificial remedies. And again, as menstruation stands as the prototype of all critical evacuations, the model of the healing power of nature is the woman's body and its expulsive powers.

Bloodletting can therefore be presented as simply an imitation of menstruation. Galen himself, in his merciless attack upon Erasistratus (well known for his belief in a straightforward association between unregulated bloodletting and murder), clearly argues for the prescriptive value of menstruation in bloodletting.[19] Bloodletting was not only the chief remedy for the cure of any retention of blood but also the most common remedy to draw a flow of blood back to its "usual path," as in the case of Lusitanus with which we began. This was therefore one of the curative canons for menstrual nosebleed. The final, and related, reason for the endurance and historical success of the theory of vicarious menstruation is the early modern increase in interest in the marvellous, the exceptional, and the bizarre. But of course this does not apply to this theory alone, given the great role of "exceptionality" in the new early modern approach to the investigation of nature.[20]

When Is a Nosebleed Not a Nosebleed? Etiology and Treatment

So what was the origin of vicarious and supplementary menstruation theories? The Hippocratic *Aphorism* V.33 states that "in a woman when there is a stoppage of the menses, a discharge of blood from the nose is good." Many other *Aphorisms* deal with nosebleeds and more generally with bleedings; another suggests a hierarchy of direction, as "Blood discharged upward, whatever be its character, is a bad symptom, but downward it is favourable."[21] Not all nosebleeds and other kinds of unprovoked bleedings were perceived as menstrual or hemorrhoid-related, and thus as cleansing and desirable, nor were they always seen as vicarious of something else.[22] Within the Hippocratic corpus, *Prognostics*, *Epidemics* and *On Regimen in Acute Diseases* also give plenty of instances of both male and female nosebleeds, both beneficial and lethal, especially affecting young people who, in the humoral model of the body, were considered more likely to be dominated by blood.[23]

In the "problem" literature, however, ps.-Aristotle stated that not every nosebleed was menstrual. Within the animal kingdom, it is only man who suffers from nosebleeds, chiefly because of the moist nature of the human brain.[24]

Nevertheless, as we have seen, the connection between menstruation, nosebleeds, and hemorrhoids was already strongly asserted by Aristotle in many of his naturalistic works.[25]

Of the ancient medical authorities, both Celsus and Galen supported nosebleeds as a healthy substitute for menstruation, but Galen went further, trying for the first time to systematize the whole spectrum of hemorrhages and to differentiate between natural bleedings, such as menstruation in women, and bleedings "in the whole class contrary to nature."[26] For him both male and female nosebleeds should always belong in the latter group, together with hemorrhoids, but a subtler distinction follows:

> There are some things in the whole class "contrary to nature,"
> like haemorrhage through the nose, vomiting, bloody excretions, haemorrhoids, or some other such thing, which are nevertheless not yet contrary to nature if they occur at an appropriate time. It is clear that this is "in an appropriate time" if what is harmful is cleared out. The accord then remains, which we agreed on at the outset, i.e. that damages of functions are symptoms, and that none of those things occurring for the purpose of benefit is of this class of symptoms. For each of these is an action of nature rather than an injury.[27]

In the same work, Galen also identified three main causes of haemorrhage—the natural opening up of a vessel, changes in the blood itself, and damage to blood vessels. A fourth cause, *diapedesis*, is mentioned, which Galen particularly identifies with passing bloody serum in the urine due to hepatic or renal disease, but later authors extended this to many other phenomena.[28]

These various strands of the Hippocratic and Galenic traditions were widely adopted in Arabic and Western European medicine during the Middle Ages and the early modern period, although not of course in the same way by every author. In order to gain a deeper understanding of what nosebleeds might tell us about gender and medicine in the late Middle Ages and the Renaissance more broadly, we need to look across different literary genres and times. The types of sources that have proven most valuable here are the *Practicae*, medical handbooks that list a number of diseases from head to toe, and scholastic commentaries (chiefly on Avicenna's *Canon*)[29] and *Consilia* and their early modern evolution, *Observationes*. While commentaries and *Practicae* help us to discern the multiple causes of nosebleeds, *Consilia* and *Observationes* enable us to look for treatments.[30] As for early modern casebooks, for example the ones created by the most popular astrologers in early modern England, Simon Forman and Richard Napier at the turn of the seventeenth century, in these a clear connection is made between nosebleeds and amenorrhea or menstrual disorders in general, with some of the cases providing some rare and thus valuable information on treatments.[31]

Practicae, commentaries, and early modern *Dissertationes* teach us far more. Within these texts, references to nosebleeds affecting both men and women are primarily to be found in the sections on the diseases of the nose, but are also found in sections on brain diseases, womb diseases, liver and spleen diseases, and diseases of the anus. All of them stress the threat to life posed by massive loss of blood from the nose, but also praise the usefulness of critical nosebleeds, seen as created by the prudent Nature in healing the whole body. Some of them also praised Nature for the choice of the nostrils as the best exit point for the blood, since passage out of the body by means of the eyes, ears, and lungs was considered far more dangerous.[32]

In summary, scholastic and Renaissance authors attest to an increasingly complex differentiation of the causes (and treatment) of nosebleeds and to an increasing stress being placed on menstrual nosebleeds, which were not even mentioned, for example, in the section on nosebleeds in Avicenna's *Canon*.[33] After Avicenna's synthesis, critical nosebleeds—always good—were carefully distinguished from symptomatic nosebleeds—not always bad. Nosebleeds can be continuous or intermittent; they can originate from veins or (less frequently) from arteries. Not surprisingly, venous nosebleeds were considered easier to stop and cure than arterial nosebleeds. Choleric and sanguine people were most often affected by nosebleeds, although it was not seen as a problematic issue for them. Phlegmatic and melancholic people were thought to be the most damaged by such a loss.

Avicenna also introduces the topic of the therapeutic induction of nosebleed, practiced since antiquity to cure acute affections of the brain with the help of specific sharp tools or stinging herbs. This is a very important issue for our research on gendered medical practices. As we shall see, it seems that artificially induced nosebleeds only involve male patients supposedly suffering from brain diseases, and never females suffering from amenorrhea or other menstrual disorders. Another trope repeated by the entire later tradition consists in the belief that a nosebleed from the left nostril means a defective spleen, while one from the right nostril indicates a defective liver.

The section on nosebleeds of the *Compendium medicinae* by Gilbert the Englishman (ca. 1230–1250) quotes the Hippocratic *Aphorism* V.33 (on menstrual nosebleeds) and lists the Greek terms *anastomosis*, *diapedesis* (which he confusingly refers to as *rixis*) and *dieresis* to introduce the three humoral causes of hemorrhages that the later tradition would always distinguish: blood's *acuitas*, that is, its erosive and acrid quality, causes corrosion; its *subtilitas*, that is, rarefaction, causes exudation/oozing out; its *multitudo*, that is, quantity, causes rupture.[34] These terms refer to qualities of the blood itself (intensity, fineness, quantity) as assessed by the examining physician. But the problem may also lie in the organs (a weakness of the tissues of the nose) or in the natural faculties or virtues (a weakness of the retentive force or an overwhelming strength of the expulsive virtue). Scholastic authors also discussed secondary causes, which could be related to brain, liver, or spleen disorders, to womb conditions, and to hemorrhoids (only the last two cases involve a retention of blood). External causes, beyond falls, hits, and blows, often include seeing or thinking about red things. Other external causes include hot or steamy moist air; hot baths; hot, moist and "smoky" food; and "hot illnesses" (such as acute fever). Signs of secondary causes are often listed: these include headache, liver heaviness, red urine, pain in the spleen or in the left hypochondrium, and of course menstrual retention and retention of hemorrhoids.

The huge scholastic effort to differentiate between conditions and to match issues of the quality and quantity of blood to different bleedings formed part of the enterprise of medicine at this period to explain away apparent inconsistencies within Hippocrates and Galen in favor of "conciliation," in which a position was found in which all the authorities' views could somehow be contained. But it also led to the question of whether venesection could be useful in every nosebleed, or not,[35] and to the subtle differentiation between a universally applicable and a relative sense of "good" and "bad" when dealing with issues of bleeding.[36] Some medieval and Renaissance authors also attempted to sketch a kind of double hierarchy of bleedings, one in which menstruation is the healthiest form, and generally speaking bleeding downward is better than bleeding upward, alongside a second hierarchy in which spontaneous bleedings are generally more debilitating than artificial bloodletting. Medical practitioners all agreed in linking menstrual nosebleed to issues of plethora—that is, an excessive quantity of blood—and, as a general rule, they considered that such nosebleeds must not be stopped. Nevertheless, it was still important to divert the menstrual flow back toward the womb.

As for the treatment, physicians, after having explained that most nosebleeds must not be stopped, went on to list many curative canons. At the bottom of the list, we always find the artificial plugging of the nose, which is considered the last resort, generally not to be recommended. What comes first, in contrast, is dietetic advice on how to thicken up the blood; this is followed by evacuation, including bloodletting (but this must be practiced only if the causative agent is quantity, i.e., blood surplus to requirements); and this in turn is closely followed by advice on how to divert the blood by applying cupping glasses almost everywhere or by light phlebotomy at the opposite side of the body. Other means of blood diversion included testicle and/or breast ligatures; finger, hand, foot, armpit, and inguinal ligatures; and, finally, one may resort to "stopping administration," performed through the use of medical substances but also via cauterization. Some authors added here "as merchants do with horses," thus inadvertently contradicting the initial assertion of the uniqueness of nosebleed for humans. Simple cold water was also used, alongside stones, amulets, and prayers. The drugs used to stop bleeding, given in detail in Avicenna's *Canon*, included substances like spider webs, egg white, hare hair, sponges soaked in vinegar, leek juice, juice of stinging nettle, dried donkey dung, *terra sigillata*, or powder of burned frogs to be blown into the nostrils, to quote only a few of them.

Interestingly, instructions on how to *provoke* a nosebleed are also included. This was done, mainly with boar bristles or leeches, for some brain diseases, in particular lethargy, liver diseases, and spleen disorders.[37] In one male-related *consilium* by Bartolomeo Montagnana on the predisposition to phthisis, *fluxum sanguinis a narium provocatio* is listed, together with phlebotomy and inducing vomiting. A clear example of gender-differentiated treatment is found in Ugo Benzi's *Consilia*. The physician advises provoking a nosebleed for a male patient affected by hemorrhoids and headache whereas, a few lines below, he significantly recommends neither phlebotomy nor induced nosebleed in a woman suffering headache and superfluous menstruation. This is the same physician, in the same work, even talking about what are in a way the same diseases (if we take for granted the functional, theoretical, and practical analogy between them), yet there is a different treatment prescribed.

A Case Study: Nosebleed in Pieter van Foreest's *Observationes*

We will finish by illustrating the gendering of the nosebleed in one text: the *Observationes* of Pieter van Foreest (born in 1521). This collection of 1180 cases clearly differentiates between treatments according to gender. Roughly 50 cases of nosebleed, eight of them taken from the accounts of other physicians, are included. The location of these cases is itself illuminating; they are mainly to be found within the first ten books, on fevers and diseases of the brain, in Book 13, devoted to affections of the nose; in Book 19 on liver diseases; and in Book 28, with 82 cases, on women's diseases.[38]

A total of 21 cases of nosebleed concern women. In approximately 14 of these, the nosebleed is due not to menstrual suppression or menstrual disorders but instead to acute fever, hepatic dysfunction, plague, measles, or the temporary neglect of customary venesection, or to no identified cause. Seven of the cases are, however, clearly explained as cases of vicarious menstruation and not all of these are found (as one might have expected) in Book 28, dedicated to *morbi muliebrium*.[39]

Van Foreest shares the view that, as a general rule, menstrual nosebleeds must not be stopped, and he gives phlebotomy (from the saphena vein of either foot) as the chief remedy to divert the blood back to the womb; interestingly, he states that this kind of venesection should be performed in these cases alone, and he does not advise cutting veins in the feet in any cases given of male nosebleed. Moreover, nosebleeds in male patients are said to be caused not only by the diseases already mentioned (acute illnesses, fevers, liver malfunction, plague, etc.), but also by brain diseases.

It is therefore no coincidence that Book 10, on diseases of the brain, lists male nosebleeds only. Elsewhere, in dealing with the maximum loss of blood that the average man can sustain without endangering his life (in Book 13, *De nasi affectibus*), van Foreest uses on two occasions a case history mentioned by Johannes Arculanus of a woman who survived the uterine loss of 25 pounds of blood over three days. Arculanus himself placed this case in the chapter on affections of the nose, rather than the one on those of the womb, as we may perhaps have expected.[40] This proves that the link between menstrual blood and nosebleed was implicit for medieval and early modern medical practitioners and was so obvious to them that they did not feel any need to explain why cases of severe blood loss from the womb could be found within the sections of their works dedicated to the nose.

Conclusion

Nosebleeds were a highly unusual form of blood loss in premodern medicine. They could be found in a range of possible locations within an early modern medical text. Like menstruation, nosebleeds were a feature setting humans apart from the other animals. They could be spontaneous and therapeutic, best left to heal on their own, or they could be something requiring treatment. Indeed, they could themselves be a form of therapy to be induced for the benefit of the patient; but while this was true for men with hemorrhoids, it was not the case for menstrual suppression. For this was not a one-sex body. In a woman, an extra range of possibilities for the source of the blood existed in addition to the brain, the spleen, and the liver, and the physician needed to decide whether bleeding from the nose was vicarious menstruation or due to another cause. Scholastic medicine sought to classify all possible causes and types of nosebleeds, and nosebleeds defined as menstrual were not to be stopped by physicians.

While the artificial induction of nosebleeds could be recommended to relieve hemorrhoids, we have found no examples of therapeutically induced nosebleeds in women, even though we may expect to find them in cases of menstrual suppression in particular. Instead, for the female body, the main interest lies in restoring the natural, the normal, route of travel for the blood. We would argue that, for all the physicians discussed here, the analogical couple formed by menstruation and hemorrhoids should more correctly be seen as a trio, one in which the nosebleed was the third player. Renaissance physicians tended to agree with Galen that any bleeding, apart from menstruation, was contrary to nature in the whole class, which does not mean they believed other bleedings to be automatically nonbeneficial: if the evacuated matter is noxious, then this is not to be considered a preternatural bleeding. Therefore menstrual bleedings, menstrual nosebleeds, and women themselves clearly had a different status.

The characters of this trio had different life stories. Bleeding hemorrhoids (in both men and women) were increasingly pathologized, while regular menstruation continued to be seen as healthy (although menstrual disorders too became increasingly pathologized). Nosebleeds were acknowledged to have many possible causes, both local and more general, of which plethora was only one option. Despite the overall shared framework provided by the humoral economy of the bodies of the past, the distinct treatments for—or the different reasons for not treating—nosebleeds clearly emphasize the specificity of menstruation to women's conditions and the medical awareness of sex-specific diseases manifesting beyond the genitalia.

Chapter 6

Screaming Bleeding Trees

Textual Wounding and the Epic Tradition

JOE MOSHENSKA

At the end of the introduction to her 1866 novel *Felix Holt, the Radical*, George Eliot writes:

> The poets have told us of a dolorous enchanted forest in the under world. The thorn-bushes there, and the thick-barked stems, have human histories hidden in them; the power of unuttered cries dwells in the passionless-seeming branches, and the red warm blood is darkly feeding the quivering nerves of a sleepless memory that watches through all dreams. These things are a parable.[1]

A parable of what, we might ask? For Eliot, the figure of a plant or tree that suddenly, shockingly, emits screams and spurts blood, thereby revealing itself to be not mutely inanimate but capable of sense and suffering, is emblematic of the effects that a properly responsive and attentive writing can have. In Eliot's view it is the duty of the writer, as Adrian Poole observes, to give voice to "the suffering that goes unnoticed, unheard, unrecorded," and the figure of the screaming, bleeding tree captures the potential for this suffering to burst forth from the most shocking and unexpected of places, and for the presumptively voiceless suddenly to assume a voice.[2] Given Eliot's location of this scene in "the under world," Poole is surely right to suggest that she has Virgil and Dante principally in mind. While human-tree hybrids and trees that bleed are present in a range of mythological and folkloric traditions, the scene to which she alludes, in which a figure twists or plucks the branch of a tree only for anguished cries to burst shockingly forth, originates in Book III of Virgil's *Aeneid*, where Aeneas tugs at a myrtle bush that emits drops of blood and speaks with the agonized voice of the murdered Polydorus.[3] The scene was rewritten and relocated to the underworld by Dante in the thirteenth canto of the *Inferno*, where one of the metamorphosed figures in the wood of suicides also bleeds and speaks. Eliot would also have known, however, that these were only the most famous versions of a *topos* that became a privileged site of rewriting for those wishing to place themselves in a self-consciously Virgilian epic tradition. Long before Dante, Ovid already echoed Virgil's Polydorus episode in his depictions of Phaeton and Erysichthon in the second and eighth books of the *Metamorphoses* respectively, and, most closely, with the transformation of Lotis into a lotus tree in Book 9. In the wake of the *Inferno*, formulating their own versions of the scene became one of the ways that Italian poets could assert their own epic credentials, with similar episodes accordingly appearing in subtly varying forms in Giovanni Boccaccio's *Filocolo*, Ludovico Ariosto's *Orlando Furioso*, and Torquato Tasso's *Gerusalleme Liberata*. Finally, as part of his self-conscious emulating and superseding of Ariostan and Virgilian traditions, a screaming bleeding tree appeared near the beginning of the first book of Edmund Spenser's *Faerie Queene*.

The literary-historical fortunes of the screaming bleeding tree as a *topos* have been thoroughly traced.[4] The prominent appearance of a screaming bleeding tree in the *Aeneid*, however, has typically been taken as reason enough for the story to be told and retold as a node of epic self-consciousness. I want instead to argue that we must consider the nature of the bleeding wound itself that is opened up in the tree's surface, in order adequately to account for the recurrence of this scene. The bleeding wound inflicted upon each of these trees, I suggest, become a sort of textual wound or fissure: the breaking of the tree's surface is also potentially a rupture in the surface of the work in question. There is a connection here with arboreal grafting, which has received much discussion in light of Virgil's metapoetical discussion of the practice in *Georgics* 2.69–82; but whereas grafting opens a violent rift in one plant in order that a new growth might flourish, the bleeding wound in the plant or tree offers no guarantee of new growth.[5] Blood and words bubble forth, but this is a much more equivocal, much less comforting figure for the interplay between novelty and tradition than the Virgilian graft. The appearance of a screaming bleeding tree signals not only an encounter with poetic tradition, but a moment at which the poet confronts the forms of violence, wounding, and rupture that might be implicit within poetic representation itself. Reading the *topos* in this way means rethinking Eliot's interpretation: the screaming bleeding tree might not only reflect literature's ability to grant otherwise mute suffering a voice, but reveal deep anxieties that this revelation of hidden suffering might only occur at the cost of a further wrenching and a wounding in which the poet is complicit, and which is often suppressed in turn.

The simple fact that a screaming bleeding tree appeared prominently in the *Aeneid*, then, is not enough to account for its haunting recurrence. When a character in a work or the reader of a work meets a screaming bleeding tree, I will argue, he (it is, in fact, a man in every version of the story) does not simply encounter a meme from epic tradition, but confronts a particularly complex and volatile form of ontological enigma. The screaming bleeding tree involves a horrifying and captivating series of conflations—of the human and the inhuman, the vegetable and the animal, the living and the dead—and it is these mixtures that are exploited to tellingly different effect by the poets who availed themselves of the *topos*. This enigmatic ontological status is, I will suggest, reflected and encapsulated in the changing nature of the blood that is shed in each case. It is the labile and ambiguous nature of blood itself as a physical entity that partly facilitates the telling ontological confusions of the scene. In this specific context, the "red warm blood" that Eliot describes gushing from these wounded trees is not the marker of animal as opposed to vegetable life, but belongs to a being that hovers on the threshold between animal and vegetable, sentient and nonsentient, human and mere object. Blood is particularly suited to play this role because its appearance at a moment of rupture marks both the overwhelming presence of life and vitality, and the beginning of their entropic dissipation. Blood that appears, that is rendered visible and tangible, is simultaneously redolent of life and presages death: it is a form of sudden appearance that signals an imminent disappearance. Living death or deathly life is present both in the figure that is at once human and tree, and in the manifestation of blood itself.

Thomas M. Greene, in an important essay, argues that Maurice Scève's description of a "paradoxical 'féconde blessure,' the wound whose blood is a sign of fertility and power, can serve to emblematize the character of poetry.... The text wins its privileged status as a poem, as *literary* text, partly because it accepts a beneficent incision."[6] In this chapter I argue that the textual wound of the screaming tree starkly questions whether or not this bleeding—or the poetry within which it is represented—is indeed fecund or beneficent. I will focus on the origins of the *topos* in the *Aeneid* and its last substantial realization in *The Faerie Queene*. In my account of Virgil, I seek to trouble the status of this depiction of Polydorus as a privileged point of origin by arguing that it is already allusive and rooted in earlier tradition: not only does it look back to Eurpides's *Hecuba*, as has previously been noted, but to Lucretius's *De rerum natura*. Virgil's depiction of the sensate tree, I argue, is one of the various points at which he engages with the attempt by his predecessor in Latin epic to demarcate the boundaries between sentient and nonsentient beings. The transformed Polydorus, though, is a figure who thwarts these distinctions, and it is in this sense that his wounding becomes a textual wound, marking Virgil's violent break with his epic predecessor. Virgil, I argue, bequeathed these ontological concerns to his predecessors who made their own trees bleed. For Spenser, the figure of Fradubio allows him to conduct a self-reflexive interrogation of his own allegorical mode, in which all significant figures hover between fleshly personhood and mute thingliness: the status of the screaming bleeding tree as a textual wound is transformed by its location with Spenser's allegorical cosmos. The blood that trickles down the bark of the wounded Fradubio traces a line between the living and the dead, and the significant and the insignificant, that Spenser's own poetics will obsessively traverse and complicate.

* * *

In the third book of the *Aeneid*, the eponymous hero recounts to Dido his exiled band's flight from Troy to nearby Thrace, where he searched for foliage with which to festoon the altar of Venus and other gods:

> forte fuit iuxta tumulus, quo cornea summo
> uirgulta et densis hastilibus horrida myrtus.
> accessi uiridemque ab humo conuellere siluam
> conatus, ramis tegerem ut frondentibus aras,
> horrendum et dictu uideo mirabile monstrum.
> nam quae prima solo ruptis radicibus arbos
> uellitur, huic atro liquuntur sanguine guttae
> et terram tabo maculant. mihi frigidus horror
> membra quatit gelidusque coit formidine sanguis.

> It happened that there was a mound close by, topped with brushwood and bristling spears of myrtle. I approached, and, trying to tear some green shoots from the earth, so as to cover the altar with leafy boughs, I saw a monstrous sight, wonderful to tell. For from the first tree ripped from the earth with broken roots, drops of dark blood trickle forth and stain the soil with filth. Icy shudders shake my limbs, and my blood chills with terror.[7]

While the blood trickling from the tree horrifies Aeneas, his own blood rendered icy in response, he grimly continues to wrench at the bush with increasing force. The horror that he feels at the tree dripping blood does not halt his damaging actions, but causes him to redouble his efforts, assailing the bleeding shrub not only a second but a third time: "rursus et alterius lentum conuellere uimen / insequor et causas penitus temptare latentis; / ater et alterius sequitur de cortice sanguis . . . tertia sed postquam maiore hastilia nisu / adgredior genibusque aduersae obluctor harenae . . . gemitus lacrimabilis imo / auditor tumulo" (Once more, from a second also I go to pluck a tough shoot and probe deep the hidden cause; from the bark of the second also follows black blood. . . . But when with a greater effort I assail the third shafts, and with my knees wrestle against the shifting sands . . . a piteous groan is heard from the depths of the mound) (*Aeneid*, 3.31–32, 37–38, 39–40). Aeneas's wrenching of the bloody fronds only ends when a moaning floats to his ears from within the mound:

> quid miserum, Aenea, laceras? iam parce sepulto,
> parce pias scelerare manus. non me tibi Troia
> externum tulit, aut cruor hic de stipite manat.
> heu! fuge crudelis terras, fuge litus avarum:
> nam Polydorus ego. hic confixum ferrea texit
> telorum seges et iaculis increvit acutis.
>
> Why, Aeneas, do you tear me? Spare me in the tomb at last; spare the pollution of your poor hands! I, born of Troy, am no stranger to you; not from a lifeless stock oozes this blood. For I am Polydorus. Here an iron harvest of spears covered my pierced body, and grew up into sharp javelins. (*Aeneid*, 3.41–46).

The loaded language in which Aeneas frames his encounter with the transformed Polydorus—"horrendum et dictu uideo mirabile monstrum"—ensured that this episode assumed an important role in Renaissance debates surrounding the value and the proper role of the marvellous and the monstrous in epic and romance: Giraldi Cinthio, for example, listed "the changing of men into trees" as an example of the pleasurable feigning that comprised the wonderful.[8] In many ways, however, Virgil's depiction is more complex than the screaming, bleeding trees created in his wake by later writers. In most of the later versions, as we shall see, an individual has been transformed into a single tree, and this reflects one apparent attraction of the *topos*. It is partly because a tree seems so temptingly anthropomorphic that tales of arboreal transformation are ubiquitous in myth and folklore: hence the frequency of terms like "trunk" and "limb" that can refer interchangeably to human and woody bodies; and Joseph Pucci claims generally that "[w]ords, like trees, harbour much that cannot be seen."[9] Carl Jung wrote that "[t]he tree is as it were an intermediate form of man," while Maurice Bloch describes the tree as the quintessential "natural symbol" in the sense developed by Mary Douglas: "the symbolic power of trees comes from the fact that they are good substitutes for humans. Their substitutability is due to their being different, yet continuous with humans, in that they both share 'life.'"[10] If this linguistic and conceptual overlap is true of English and of various mythological traditions, both were particularly prominent in Roman literary culture, as Robin Nisbet powerfully stresses: "Trees are like people. They have a head (*vertex*), a trunk (*truncus*), arms (*bracchia*). . . . Their life moves in human rhythms, which in their case may be repeated: sap rises and falls, hair (*coma*) luxuriates, withers, drops off."[11] Virgil, though, eschews this direct substitutability of human and tree with his creation of a much more ambiguously humanoid bushy mound. The entity that Aeneas encounters in fact possesses a remarkable degree of opacity, accentuating the ontological fuzziness of the transformation that has transpired.

Polydorus has not simply been transformed into a tree: it seems instead that he has been treacherously and impiously buried beneath the mound, his body still transfixed with the spears that caused his death, and it is this iron crop of spears that has been metamorphosed into the myrtle that Aeneas grasps. These spears have themselves become part of this new composite being—part suffering body, part iron weapons, part earthy mound, part feeling fronds. The ambiguity of animate and inanimate is exacerbated by the fact that the plants that make up the bush—cornel and myrtle—were themselves used to make spear shafts (see *Georgics* 2.447–48), so the spears have in a sense reverted to their animate origins; furthermore, the metaphor of the "iron harvest of spears," rendering them both deathly and vegetable, and the earlier description of the fronds as "hastilibus," spear-like, at l.23, cause the distinction between animate and inanimate to waver even on the level of linguistic texture.[12] Voice and blood are separated—the tree bleeds for some time before the moan issues from the mound—but this serves only to accentuate the peculiar horror of the composite entity that Aeneas encounters and its form of muddled ontological integration. Scholars have disputed what exactly is involved in this transformation: Lyndsay Coo argues specifically that "the spears are *still connected* to Polydorus's body" and are "flowing with, and nourished by, his blood," whereas Marco Fucecchi emphasises "the reticence of the text" in refusing to make the details clear, such that "the hero and his audience can only rely on their imagination to surmise what has happened."[13] Whether or not the reader reaches a firm conclusion, the very need imaginatively to unpick the nature of the transformation blurs the boundaries in this moment between animate and inanimate, between feeling, woundable body, and mutely insensate thing. The plant that screams and bleeds seems to embody Sigmund Freud's suggestion that effects of uncanniness can be produced by "doubts whether an apparently animate being is really alive; or conversely, whether a lifeless object might not be in fact animate."[14] When the tree-crested mound in the *Aeneid* emits blood and cries, an object that seems to be inanimate becomes horribly alive, but in a fashion that seems further to provoke and intensify, rather than interrupt, the hero's violent grasp.

The lack of distinction between animate and inanimate may be even more baffling in this case than Freud's account suggests, however, and this is specifically due to the presence of the blood that trickles from the myrtle fronds. As has often been noted, the status of blood has a tendency to change markedly once it has been spilled: the same substance seems to undergo a transformation or even a reversal of meaning as soon as it is rendered visible and tangible. This means that blood is a substance whose physical nature and perceived significance is not intrinsic but unusually determined by its *place*. It is redolent of life and vitality so long as it remains invisible: as soon as it appears, the very fact of its appearance betokens wounding, the possible dissipation of life, and the specter of imminent death. René Girard puts this point in starkly baroque terms: "Spilt blood of any origin . . . is considered impure. . . . When men are enjoying peace and security, blood is a rare sight. When violence is unloosed, however, blood appears everywhere—on the ground, under foot, forming great pools. Its very fluidity gives form to the contagious nature of violence. Its presence proclaims murder and announces new upheavals to come. Blood stains everything it touches the color of violence and death."[15] In this sense, we might say that Virgil's Polydorus is not simply a form of troubling ontological muddle that happens to bleed: rather, blood, in this specific context, acts as a microcosm of the unstable oscillations that characterize the scene as a whole. Aeneas is presented with an entity that thwarts any attempt at categorization: it is neither human (Polydorus), mineral (iron spears transfixing the body), nor vegetable (myrtle), but rather combines and conflates these varied forms of life and lifelessness, just as the blood itself hovers between vitality and mortality. Polydorus appears, unexpectedly and horrendously, to Aeneas: but at the moment that he does so, his apparent surplus of life only proclaims the full horror of his treacherous death. Like the blood that this new and horrifying entity sheds, the mode of Polydorus's transformed appearance is that of life giving way to death.[16]

Before moving on to consider the way in which Spenser adopts and adapts Virgil's nightmarish technique in this episode, I would like to suggest that this scene in the *Aeneid* is itself already a moment of retrospection and allusion—and not only to Euripides, whose *Hecuba* provided a canonical account of Polydorus's slaughter, though lacking a transformation into a tree or bush.[17] I would like to build upon and adapt Philip Hardie's brief and compelling argument that, as he so often did, Virgil had Lucretius in mind when he formulated Aeneas's encounter with the screaming, bleeding tree.[18] I would like to suggest here that the problem of distinguishing animate from inanimate objects and the attendant difficulty of how to comport oneself toward objects whose degree of animation or sensitivity is difficult to determine were for Virgil primarily Lucretian problems. By advancing an Epicurean account of a cosmos consisting only of material entities comprised of atoms moving in a void, Lucretius offered a powerfully unified and comprehensive account of reality: but he also made it difficult to account for living phenomena, or to explain why atoms gave rise to life in certain configurations and not in others. Lucretius's attempt to develop an atomist physiology had a long and complicated afterlife in Renaissance discussions, but Virgil, I would suggest, already presented Polydorus's transformation in part as a riposte to the Lucretian claim that, having presented an ontologically unified account of the world, it was nonetheless possible to divide living from nonliving absolutely.[19] For Virgil, the reduction of the world to atoms does not only unsettlingly blur the bounds between human and mortal, but between animate and inanimate—again emblematized for Virgil in the form of the blood that wavers between these two states as soon as it appears. For Lucretius, the difficulty of distinguishing living from nonliving objects was ultimately no obstacle to the attainment of the calm, distanced, Epicurean repose that he ultimately advocates. Aeneas's continued violence toward the entity that he causes implicitly refutes this claim, as it shows the difficulty of comporting oneself properly in a world of blurred and bloody ontology. It is in this sense that we might productively think of the wound inflicted on the transformed Polydorus as a textual wound: its wrenching violence also marks a point of emphatic separation from Virgil's predecessor in Latin epic and captures a form of violence whose avoidance the atomistic account makes troublingly difficult.

These wider claims for Virgil's engagement with Lucretius in this moment can be substantiated on a more minute level of verbal choices. The word that signals Virgil's Lucretian engagement here is "conuellere," from which we derive the verb "convulse" and its cognates, and which is employed twice, with notable emphasis, to describe Aeneas's actions: "accessi uiridemque ab humo conuellere siluam/conatus"; "rursus et alterius lentum conuellere uimen/insequor."[20] This verb suggests a destructive tearing, wrenching, or rending, and it is well chosen for the plucking of a tree that turns out to be horrendously human, as it referred routinely to the ripping out of both plants and hair by the roots and the snapping off of the limbs of both people and trees.[21] Its prominence and dubious importance in the *Aeneid* is confirmed by its use in Book 6 to describe the way in which the golden bough cannot and should not be plucked: "aliter non viribus ullis / vincere nec duro poteris convellere ferro."[22] In this earlier, anticipatory instance from Book 3 the verb captures the essence of Aeneas's inexplicably continued violence—the extraordinary physicality with which his third attempt to pluck the myrtle f=ond is described, and the sense of his body bracing itself to wrench and pull as the ground shifts beneath him. As Michael Putnam says of Aeneas, "what strikes the reader is the persistence of his violence, even after the appearance of blood . . . as if the preliminary sight of blood aroused in the perpetrator a desperate need for understanding, even at the cost of further hurt."[23] Blood seems to spur violence rather than making a claim against it. The problematic nature of Aeneas's actions is accentuated by the Lucretian resonances of the verb "conuellere." For Lucretius, the meanings of this verb represent the violent opposite of the detached Epicurean repose that his poem advocates. In Book III of the *De rerum natura*, for example, the process by which the soul drifts free from the body after death is discussed. This is not, Lucretius writes, like boiling water, which emits heat without being diminished: "non, inquam, sic animai / discidium possunt artus perferre relicti,/sed penitus pereunt convulsi conque putrescunt" ("not thus, I say, can the frame endure disruption apart from the spirit which has left it; but it is utterly undone, torn to pieces, and rots away").[24] The verb "conuellere" here amplifies the contrast between the supple fluidity of water and the vulnerability of the body, subject to a rending and tearing that sets the soul free. Aeneas, by contrast, encounters a body that has died, but from which the soul has not flown free, and it is precisely for this reason that he has lain his hands upon a *monstrum*, hovering between the human and the vegetable, and the living and the dead.

Hardie has argued compellingly that, when Aeneas tries to justify his convulsive violence by explaining that he acts in order "causas penitus temptare latentis," "to probe deep the hidden cause," he "takes on the role of the active Lucretian enquirer," determined to penetrate into the hidden truths of at atomistic cosmos: but, whereas the Epicurean account produces in Lucretius *divina uoluptas . . . atque horror*, "a divine pleasure and shudder," Virgil's scene provides "abundant *horror*, but no *uoluptas*."[25] Virgil, I would argue, is here turning Lucretian tenets against Lucretius, arguing that there is no active enquiry without the risk of violence, no final position of calm repose from which the possibility of newly erupting horrors has been definitively banished. Lucretius is always aware of the burning urge to achieve certainty and its risks, and there are limits to the enquiry that he encourages: it is better even to suggest faulty explanations for sensory illusions, he suggests,

> quam manibus manifesta suis emittere quoquam
> et violare fidem primam et convellere tota
> fundamenta quibus nixatur vita salusque.

> rather than anywhere to let slip from your hands the holdfast of
> the obvious, and to break the faith from which all begins, and
> to tear up all the foundations upon which life and existence rest.
> (*De Rerum Natura*, 4.504–6)

To doubt the senses is, for Lucretius, not only a conceptual error: it is a tearing up of life by the roots, a brutal attack on the very foundations of human existence and happiness. Lucretius instead encourages his readers to retain their grip on "manifesta"—the obvious, or the ordinary. As Hardie notes, Virgil's account of Polydorus also resonates with Lucretius's description of a "counterfactual Anaxagorean cosmos, where plants could drip blood," in the opening book of his poem: corns crushed by a millstone would bleed, stones rubbed by stones would ooze gore, and this is patently absurd. By creating his ambiguously animate, bleeding entity, Virgil does more than just relocate this possibility to "a world of supernatural causation."[26] He may not endorse an entirely animate Anaxagorean cosmos, but he does insist that we remain terrifyingly uncertain as to precisely where animation begins and ends.[27] By insisting instead upon the nightmarish indistinction of the various parts and the kinds of being that make up the screaming bleeding tree, Virgil's textual wound forces his reader into a context in which the calm security that is the ultimate goal of the Epicurean stance no longer obtains. Instead, horror at gushing blood in its deathly manifestation seemingly compels a form of continued violence that perpetuates the very suffering it seeks to comprehend.

* * *

In emphasizing the significance of the blood in Virgil's scene, I am following the practice of later poets, for this is the aspect of the *topos*—the extent to and manner in which the tree bleeds—that they varied most subtly and extensively. When Dante's poetic alter-ego snaps a twig from the tree in the wood of suicides, "della scheggia rota usciva inseme / parole e sangue" ("from the broken splinter came forth words and blood together").[28] Dante focuses the more diffuse ontological muddling of Virgil's tree-topped mound into a tight and tortured space, as the gap left by the broken twig becomes a sort of multifunctional orifice—it is splintered wood, wounded and fleshy gash, and speaking mouth all at once.[29] Boccaccio's tree is wounded not with a grasping hand but by an arrow gone awry, and his tree, like Dante's, bleeds and speaks simultaneously.[30] In Ariosto's version, the overall seriocomic tone is assisted by the fact that his tree is neither violently assaulted with the hand in the manner of Virgil's or Dante's, nor, uniquely, does it bleed at all: Ruggiero ties his hippogriff to a myrtle tree, and the steed "crollar fa 'l Mirto, e fa cader la foglia" ("tugged at the myrtle, and caused a shower of leaves to fall").[31] The tree speaks, revealing itself to be the transformed Astolfo and complaining of the violence to which it is subjected, but does not bleed a drop. Responding in part to Ariosto, in this respect as in many others, Torquato Tasso set his tree in a much more nightmarish landscape—an enchanted wood, which the Christian knights must brave in order to prove that the trees can be transformed back into mere objects through acts of faith. When Tancredi assaults the tree, unlike Ariosto's, it positively gushes with blood: as it is rendered in Edward Fairfax's Elizabethan translation, the knight creates a "gaping wound" from which pour "red streams . . . That all bebled the verdant plain around."[32] This is revealed, though, to be a horrible illusion that must be seen through: Tasso's is the bloodiest tree of all those created by Italian poets, but it is also the only tree whose bleeding and suffering is not real.

As even this brief survey suggests, when Spenser inherited this *topos* he was exposed to a wide variety of ways in which a tree might bleed. I have suggested that the ontological indistinction of the screaming bleeding tree is a crucial feature of Virgil's account, and that it represented an implicit and horrendous riposte to Lucretius's faith in atomism as an adequate basis on which to distinguish the animate from the inanimate, and to his ethical insistence on "manifesta" as a sufficient grounding for human experience. I would now like to suggest that Spenser's version of the scene reveals his particular sensitivity to Virgil's deliberate muddling of categories. In the second canto of the first book of *Faerie Queene*, the "Book of Holiness," its hero, the Redcrosse Knight, having been separated from the pure and fair Una and taken up with the wicked and seductive Duessa, settles down to rest in a shady grove. Aiming to make a garland for his new paramour,

> He pluckt a bough; out of whose rift there came
> Small drops of gory bloud, that trickled downe the same.
>
> Therewith a piteous yelling voyce was heard,
> Crying, O spare with guilty hands to teare
> My tender sides in this rough rynd embard[33]

The tree identifies itself as Fradubio and explains that his fate arose from errors that exactly echo the Redcrosse Knight's own—forsaking his virtuous betrothed for the temptations of Duessa. Spenser's attempt to emulate the foundational epic scene involving Polydorus is obvious, but he is particularly like Virgil, I would suggest, both in the full extent to which he blurs man and tree, which permeates down into the careful choice of individual words, and in the role of the blood that is shed in this blurring. The narrator describes Fradubio as "Wretched man, wretched tree" (I.ii.33.4); so when Redcrosse bids him "Say on *Fradubio* then, or man, or tree" (I.ii.34.1) it is not necessarily an indication of his failure to assess the nature of the being that confronts him, but a suggestion that Fradubio resists such categorization. The fact that Redcrosse opens a "rifte" in the bark of the tree is of particular significance. While the word can denote any gap or tear, the OED notes a sense of the term particular to a crack in the *skin*, which seems to have been used only in the

Renaissance. One example cited, from a description of indigenous peoples in Richard Eden's *A treatyse of the newe India* of 1553, reads "Theyr skinne is very rowghe & full of chappes & riftes like the bark of a tree."[34] In this word, then, skin and bark are potentially indistinguishable. The very same might be said of the word "rynd," which refers primarily to the skin of a fruit or vegetable, but was also used to refer to the skin in the sixteenth century and before. It is not clear either to the Redcrosse Knight or to a reader of the poem just what manner of surface has had this wound inflicted upon it—the vocabulary employed is itself metamorphic, shimmering between vegetable and animal.

In describing the "Smal drops of gory bloud" that emerge from the tree, Spenser also addresses with particular directness the ambiguity of shed blood as a sign of life giving way to death. Spenser in fact uses the terms "gore" and "gory" throughout the poem to emphasize this dichotomy. Gore is almost always a pollutant in *Faerie Queene*, shed by the monstrous and wicked characters, such as the "filthy gore" that stains the "gay garments" (I.viii.16.7) of Duessa and the "fowle bloody gore" (I.viii.24.4) of the giant Orgoglio.[35] Of the twenty-seven occurrences of the nominal form "gore" in the poem, nineteen appear in conjunction with some word connoting contamination, such as "filthy," "fowle," or "poyson."[36] The fact that the tree sheds gore identifies it most obviously as a monstrous rather than a sacred image: but, I would suggest, it also identifies it—even as its bleeding grants it a strange vitality—as a being whose very mode of life tends toward death. The appearance of blood marks the tree as an entity with a startling form and degree of sentience, but as its blood clots into gore this very appearance intimates Fradubio's deathliness and stasis.

While Spenser's blurring of human and tree, and of life and death, signals his deep understanding of the Virgilian original, it is through being subsumed into the sustainedly allegorical universe of *Faerie Queene* that the trope undergoes its most decisive transformation.[37] Spenser's allegory is notably bloody from the outset: in the Redcrosse Knight's first encounter, when he beheads the monstrous Errour, "A streame of cole black blood forth gushed from her corse" (1.i.24.9). Her blood is unusual in that its appearance portends death in more than one way: not only Errour's own, but that of her monstrous brood, which "flocked all about her bleeding wound, / And sucked up their dying mothers bloud" until "Their bellies swolne he saw with fulnesse burst" (I.i.25.7–8, 26.5). This scene is much more frenetic and visceral than the subsequent encounter with the static Fradubio, but raises the same fundamental questions. Spenser's technique of allegorical personification involves the creation of persons who are also things: each individual in the poem is, at least potentially, a disposable vessel for a higher form of significance. As I have argued elsewhere, however, reading *The Faerie Queene* is characterized by an experience of ceaseless oscillation, as given characters can seem at successive moments like mere things valuable only for the meanings that they bear and as vivid, flesh-and-blood individuals with warmly pliant, woundable bodies and idiosyncratic personal histories.[38] Gordon Teskey has suggested in his compelling account of a similar dynamic in the poem that the imperative to be both object and subject sets up within Spenser's personifications an interplay between life and death. Teskey describes Guyon, the Knight of Temperance, as existing in a "paradoxical state . . . at once dead and alive. The boundary within him between the living and the dead is not so much a boundary as a rift between his meaning as a pure allegorical sign and his vitality as a narrative figure."[39] Teskey here is both building upon and adapting Walter Benjamin's seminal account of allegory as an intrinsically deathly form, its fragmented repertoire of images forming a "grim store which signifies death and damnation."[40] For later accounts of allegory, however, what characterizes the form is not the pure deathliness captured for Benjamin in the figure of the skull, but the more unsettling form of life in death or death in life that Teskey identifies. It is telling that modern writers have reached for the realm of science fiction in order to describe this state: Angus Fletcher's description of driven, single-minded allegorical agency as demonic may draw upon archaic modes of thought, but he also states that "[t]he perfect allegorical agent is not a man possessed by a daemon but a robot," while Teskey himself invokes zombies and Frankenstein monsters: "The very liveliness of the allegorical figures, their frenetic, jerky, galvanic life, makes us think of dead bodies through which an electric current is passed. The figures move with something that is less than life but also with a force, with a single-mindedness, that is greater than the living can achieve."[41] In all these accounts, the life of allegory becomes scarcely more than a living death.

Fradubio, though, presents a very different and no less unsettling version of the collision between life and death implicit within allegorical agency. He does not present movement in the absence of life, but a shocking abundance of life in the total absence of movement. As with Virgil, this deathly life is encapsulated and made manifest in the drops of blood as they coagulate into gore. In Spenser's poem, though, the tree's bleeding does not simply add to the horror and ontological indistinction of the scene. The wound inflicted upon the transformed Fradubio becomes another textual wound, making him a self-reflexive figure for the operations and the costs of Spenser's own allegorical procedure. Spenser can create life only if it verges on death: all of his allegorical figures are, in a sense, like blood, that emerges resplendent with life only to begin clotting immediately into gore. It is deeply significant, from this point of view, that Fradubio is never freed from his arboreal prison—even though, uniquely among screaming bleeding trees, he knows exactly how he might be freed. As he explains to the Redcrosse Knight: "We may not chaunge (quoth he) this euill plight, / Till we be bathed in a liuing well" (I.ii.43.3–4). At the end of the Book of Holiness, the Redcrosse Knight will himself be restored during the fight with the Dragon when he falls into "*The well of life*," which "vnto life the dead it could restore" (I.xi.29.9, 30.1). There is no mention, though, of Fradubio: no suggestion that the knight will return with a beaker of water scooped from the well and free his unfortunate alter-ego from his arboreal prison. This lack of rescue would have been particularly notable due to the stark contrast with Ariosto's Astolfo, Spenser's most immediate source, who not only does not bleed but is eventually liberated from his myrtle to travel farther than any other character in the poem, taking his griffin as far as the moon, where he meets John the Baptist. This renders Fradubio's perpetual stasis all the more emphatic by contrast. It is a contrast that brings to the fore the perpetual tendency toward stasis, toward death-in-life, that haunts so many of Spenser's allegorical creations.

It is not only Redcrosse's eventual and conspicuous failure to return to and liberate Fradubio that makes the latter a figure for allegorical self-reflection: this becomes clear immediately after he has spoken, in the way that Redcrosse responds to the wound he has inflicted. The process by which Fradubio is forgotten begins before the reader's eyes immediately after he finishes his speech. In a telling and unique addition to the *topos*, Spenser wonders what his knight should do with the bloody twig that he has snapped from the tree, and decides the following: Redcrosse,

> When all this speech the liuing tree had spent,
> The bleeding bough did thrust into the ground,
> That from the bloud he might be innocent,
> And with fresh clay did close the wooden wound.
> (I.ii.44.5–8)

This is a deeply equivocal act. The closing of the wound with clay could seem like an act of mercy, an attempt to heal the damage that the knight has inadvertently caused—if we think of the rift in the tree only as a wound. This reading is central to the most recent account of the screaming bleeding tree, by Joseph Campana, which locates it within the theological topography of Spenser's poem, whose landscape Campana reads as "one in which literary compensations replace lost sacramental forms or religious emphases in the wake of the Reformation." Campana sees Spenser as racked with "hunger . . . for the corporeal and affective resources adumbrated by the suffering, bleeding body of Christ," and claims that "[t]he encounter with Fradubio represents another attempt to reintroduce the texture of suffering to a landscape denuded of corporeal and affective experience by heroic, iconoclastic violence."[42] It is important to note that, since Virgil's *topos* was first brought into a Christian context by Dante, the screaming bleeding tree had appealed to poets in part as a grotesque and distorted image of the Crucifixion, since the cross was often described simply as a tree.[43] Campana's reading, though, relies on seeing the Redcrosse Knight's actions as themselves recuperative, a proper response to the suffering that Reformation culture was at risk of forgetting: "However naïve, Redcrosse's gesture is one of reparation and repair, as violated organic matter returns to a nurturing earth."[44] This seems highly debatable and works only if we see the rift opened in Fradubio solely as a wound. If, as with other versions of the *topos*, it is here implied that blood and words emerge together from the same rupture or rift, then in stopping Fradubio's blood the knight also quells his speech, returning him to muteness.

Redcrosse's motive in thrusting the branch into the ground is made explicit: it is to make himself innocent, not to ease or acknowledge the macabre suffering that he has encountered or to appeal to the earth's nurturing abilities. If the perennially static Fradubio and his coagulating gore are emblematic of Spenser's allegorical agents, as I have suggested, then the Redcrosse Knight here echoes the ambivalent stance of the allegorical poet at work: compelled to give voice to bloody suffering as it emerges startlingly from what seems an inanimate object, but equally compelled to begin forgetting this suffering as soon as it claims a voice and to absolve himself of the bloody mutilations involved in its apprehension.[45] It is in this sense that the wound inflicted upon Fradubio becomes a textual wound: it is not only a mark of the knight's blithe inadvertence as he seeks gifts for his false beloved, but a form of the violence through which Spenser himself compels objects to speak as people, to bear the burden of a higher significance. It may be even more vexed a moment of self-reflection for, if the poet is aligned with the knight here—since both inflict wounds whose costs they would prefer swiftly to forget—the poet is also implicitly aligned with the enchantress who effected the transformation into the sentient tree. No less than Duessa, the poet is engaged in reducing persons to things: things that can speak and feel, but that are often frozen in place and forced timelessly to bear a particular significance; things that are achingly alive but tending always toward death, just as the appearance of their blood begins to coagulate swiftly into gore.

* * *

Reading the screaming bleeding tree not only as a wounded being within a text but as a form of self-reflexive textual wound necessitates a reappraisal of George Eliot's striking invocation of this poetic trope. As Poole observes, in this moment Eliot "is urging a new attention to historical process, and to the pain that is 'noiseless,' 'unuttered'—until the artist gives it a voice. She appeals for attention, a kind of silence that will allow the cries of those who have *seemed* silent to be heard."[46] This is a beautiful plea, but it is also a radical departure from the trope as Eliot encountered it. What Eliot omits is the fact that, in the *topos* of the screaming bleeding tree, the pain toward which she urges attention becomes apparent only through moments of inadvertent and horrific violence on the part of those who break the branches. Blood and speech emerge together, hissing forth indistinguishably. Without this bloody violence there is only silence, no matter how hard we listen. Without the broken branch there is only a tree—if we want to make the object speak, we must make it bleed. This is the awful possibility that Virgil glimpsed when refuting Lucretius's reluctance to convulse the ordinary world of our senses by encountering marvels and horrors. The same conviction underpins Spenser's self-incriminating awareness of the violence implicit within his own poetic mode. He recognizes that he, not Duessa, has imprisoned a man in bark and forced him to bear a particular meaning: he, with the Redcrosse Knight, has forced him to speak and to bleed. This history of the screaming bleeding tree as a *topos* does not only reveal a series of poets who would urge us to attend to silent suffering, confident in the ability and propriety of their own art as a form of revelation and a form of testimony. Rather, it bespeaks a much more troubling anxiety that the desire to give voice might itself become a form of wounding: testifying to suffering might perpetuate suffering and become indistinguishable from the shedding of blood.

PART III

Corruption

Chapter 7

Corruption, Generation, and the Problem of *Menstrua* in Early Modern Alchemy

TARA NUMMEDAL

Alchemical texts are full of blood. Reading through the alchemical corpus, a reader might encounter not only distillations of human blood, but also the blood of red and green lions, the blood of kings, or even the "menstrual blood of our whore."[1] Not surprisingly, this striking imagery has drawn the attention of historians of alchemy, who have tended to focus on whether and how the allegorical language of bloods, lions, and hermaphrodites was intended to convey information about alchemical ideas, techniques, and practices. For the psychiatrist Carl Jung, one of the first modern scholars to write about the history of alchemy (albeit not as a historian), the florid imagery we find in alchemical texts primarily documented projections of alchemists' own psychic states, not any kind of transferable instructions that might be useful in the laboratory. More recently, specialists in the history of alchemy have demonstrated that knowledgeable readers could (and still can) in fact "translate" these images into physical materials. Seemingly fantastic descriptions of hermaphroditic royals and ravenous animals, it turns out, are encoded directions for the alchemist's manipulation of substances in the laboratory. The use of these coded "cover names" for material substances, or alchemical *Decknamen*, offered authors a surprisingly effective way to communicate alchemical ideas and practices, making alien substances and their reactions with one another comprehensible in familiar cultural terms.[2] For scholars who seek to understand historical alchemy as a material practice, this imagery has served as a valuable source for reconstructing what alchemists actually did in their workspaces.[3]

Alchemical bloods also point in a different direction, however, inviting us to grapple with questions of culture. For the selection of *Decknamen* was never self-evident and always involved choices on the part of the author; there was no consistency in the alchemical corpus, in other words, about which images should represent particular alchemical materials or concepts (indeed, this is in large part what makes so alchemical texts so confusing).[4] Given any number of images that alchemists potentially could have used to represent their materials, then, why did so many choose blood or *menstrua*? This chapter will suggest that one of the reasons that blood figured so prominently in late medieval and early modern alchemy is that it allowed alchemists to probe the unstable boundary between corruption and generation, or destruction and creation. In exploring blood, some alchemists made their art a place to work out—and perhaps even resolve—one of the most vexing and difficult questions at the heart of early modern culture, namely the tangle of reproduction, sin, and gender embedded in early modern Christianity.

* * *

Alchemical blood was as polysemous as any other kind of blood. Blood often appeared in alchemical texts as some form of menstrual blood, for instance, sharing the deep ambivalence about menses found elsewhere in medieval and early modern culture. On the one hand, menstrual blood was understood to play a crucial role both in maintaining women's bodily health and in generation. While medical authors rooted in the Aristotelian or Galenic tradition disagreed about whether only fathers or also mothers contributed seed in the process of generation, all nonetheless agreed that the mother's uterine or menstrual blood played a positive role by nourishing the fetus during gestation. Furthermore, menstruation itself was thought to be a normal, healthy occurrence that purged the female body of excess. On the other hand, an equally ancient and venerable tradition, most notoriously encapsulated and disseminated in the late thirteenth-century Latin treatise *De secretis mulierum* (*On the secrets of women*), viewed menstrual blood as a poisonous and corrupting substance, potentially even one that could cause leprosy if it contaminated the organs during pregnancy.[5] This ambivalence toward menstrual blood—as something with the potential to both create and destroy—persisted well into the early modern period in lay and learned medicine alike.[6]

Like menstrual blood in medical, magical, or popular discourses, alchemical *menstrua*, too, could be figured simultaneously as corrupt/corrupting and as generative. Writing as Eirenaeus Philalethes, for example, the seventeenth-century alchemist George Starkey offered his readers the following striking images in discussing the philosophers' stone. In his *Introitus,* Philalethes tells his readers, "our matter undergoes various states before our Regal Diadem is extracted from the menstrual blood of our whore." In his *Ripley Reviv'd*, Philalethes again refers to the production of a "pure milky Virgin like Nature, drawn from the Menstruum of our sordid Whore."[7] This arresting imagery may at first seem opaque, but in his exegesis of these passages, William Newman used clues in other parts of the Philalethean corpus to decipher Philalethes's menstrual blood as impure antimony, a silvery, brittle semi-metal that fascinated seventeenth-century alchemists because of its curious properties. In essence, Newman explains, Philalethes is telling his readers that, by using iron to refine impure antimony ore ("menstrual blood" or "Menstruum"), alchemists could extract from it extraordinary things: a crystalline star pattern in the metallic antimony known as the "star regulus" (the "regal diadem") or philosophical mercury (the "pure milky Virgin like Nature"), both of which Philalethes understood to be crucial ingredients in the production of the philosophers' stone. While the "menstrual blood" or "Menstruum" of a whore here signifies impurity, then, it is still a productive impurity; in fact, it is a crucial ingredient in the creation of the most generative substance of all, the philosophers' stone.[8]

Not all alchemical bloods were *menstrua*, however. Indeed, one of the most famous (and elusive) "bloods" in alchemical texts is the "blood of the green lion." In the late medieval alchemical traditions associated with George Ripley and Raymond Llull, for example, this substance often signifies a type of mineral acid, a solvent capable of dissolving metals. These powerful solvents played an important role in the creation of the philosophers' stone, since they dissolved the alchemist's starting materials into the formless *prima materia* and thus prepared them for their elevation as a more refined form of matter.[9] If Philalethean menstrual blood represented impurity generally, the Llullian and Riplean "blood of the green lion" captures the notion of blood as powerfully corrosive—but again, this destruction is a crucial step in creating the philosophers' stone. This sense appears in the alchemical recipe literature as well, where one can find blood (in this case, blood from animals, rather than a mineral alchemical substance) used to make diamonds or other hard gemstones soft enough to engrave or otherwise fashion.[10] This use of blood to break down matter in the production of both the philosophers' stone and gemstones came together in a book of recipes that the Saxon alchemist Anna Zieglerin gave to her patron, Duke Julius of Braunschweig-Wolfenbüttel, in 1571. After making the philosophers' stone, she advised, one should put it in a glass with the blood of a slaughtered suckling lamb and keep it warm in the gentle heat of decaying horse manure for nine weeks. Once the blood had softened the stone, she concluded, "then cast it into the shape of a lion, lindworm, dragon's head, or whatever similar thing pleases you."[11] Only then, once the philosophers' stone had been shaped, could it be used for further operations.

If some alchemical authors emphasized blood's powers to break down or corrupt substances, others underscored blood's fecundity, its power to generate matter, if not life itself. Although alchemy is more often associated with transmutation, generation—of metals, plants, and even animals or homunculi—was in fact a major preoccupation among practitioners. Unsurprisingly, alchemists often turned to human sexual reproduction as a way to understand these processes, and this, in turn, highlighted the need for blood in generative alchemical processes. They often expressed the generative potential of their art as a series of binaries (king/queen, sulfur/mercury, hot/cold, dry/wet, semen/menstrual blood, form/matter, etc.) that, when combined, would produce something new, just as a mother and father produced a child. For example, writing of the Mercury-Sulfur theory of the composition of metals, Albertus Magnus explained, "Sulfur is like the father and Mercury like the mother, although it is more aptly to be expressed that in the commixture of metals the Sulfur is like the substance of the paternal seed, and the Mercury like the menstrual blood which is coagulated into the substance of embryos."[12] Attempting to explain how a sulfuric principle (hot, dry) could act with a mercurial principle (cold, moist) to produce metals, in other words, Albertus turned to the conventions of human reproduction.

Alchemists did not only use human reproduction as a metaphor; at their most ambitious, alchemists moved beyond metaphor and actually sought to produce life itself. In the Middle Ages, a handful of authors writing in Islamic, Jewish, and Latin Christian traditions took up the theme of the homunculus, a small artificial human that embodied alchemists' loftiest aims. The project really took off, however, in the sixteenth century in the hands of Paracelsus and his followers.[13] The Paracelsian homunculus appeared in two texts: the possibly pseudo-Paracelsian text *De natura rerum* (On the nature of things), which appeared in print in 1572, and the authentically Paracelsian *De homunculis* (On the homunculus, ca. 1529–1532). Together, these two texts explored the production of the homunculus and offered an ambivalent assessment of its moral meaning. The author of *De natura rerum* addresses the homunculus following a discussion of how to create an artificial bird through putrefaction. "You must also know," he continues, "that people can be born without natural fathers and mothers. In other words, they are born not from a female body in a natural way as other children are born, but rather a person may be born and grow by art and by the skill of an experienced spagyrist, as will shortly be shown."[14] The text then goes on to describe how to make a homunculus:

> But how such a thing may be approached and come about is a process, namely that the sperm of a man be putrefied by itself in a sealed cucurbit with the highest putrefaction in a horse's womb [i.e., warm, decaying dung] for forty days or long enough for it to come to life and move itself and stirs, all of which is easy to see. After this time it will appear in many ways just like a person, but transparent and without a body. If, after this, he is be fed and nourished daily and entirely wisely with the arcanum of human blood for up to forty weeks and kept in a constant warmth of a horse's womb, then a living human child will appear as a result, with all of its limbs just like a child born from a woman, but much smaller. This we call a homunculus and it should be raised just like any other child, with great effort and care, until it comes into its own and possesses its own understanding [*bis es zu seinen tagen und verstant kompt*].[15]

Here the generative potential of alchemy used blood to reach the art's ultimate potential: the creation of human life.

Several elements of this recipe are worth underscoring. First, the process parallels early modern European understandings of ordinary sexual generation insofar as it requires both sperm and blood. In this instance, however, it is not menstrual blood that gives the homunculus its body, but rather an alchemically manipulated blood, the *arcanum* of human blood. This harkens back to a host of medieval alchemical elixirs that used human blood as their starting point. Roger Bacon, for example, proposed that the alchemist could use distillation to separate out the four elements or humors that blood contained, then recombine them with other calxes and mercury to create healing elixirs and to transmute metals; a work attributed to Arnald of Villanova also proposed a blood-based elixir. The Franciscan alchemist John of Rupescissa developed this tradition farther, attributing to his blood-based alchemical quintessence the power to regenerate human flesh.[16] Two centuries later, the Paracelsian homunculus tradition extended the potential of the blood-based alchemical elixirs farther yet by claiming that alchemically manipulated blood could be substituted for menstrual blood in the creation of life itself. In this context, alchemical techniques purportedly allowed the practitioner not merely to replicate ordinary human generation, but to perfect it, to create something better than a regular human child, for the homunculus was born with unparalleled knowledge of the arts.

The second notable feature of this recipe, however, is that the alchemist can only reach this lofty goal by eliminating the female principle that is typically present in both human reproduction and alchemical processes. For the author of *De natura rerum*, the homunculus was remarkable not least because it "may be born outside of a female body and a natural mother."[17] In fact, the text suggested, if one begins the process with menstrual blood, rather than male sperm, one will instead produced a basilisk, able to kill with a glance, "not entirely unlike a woman in her time of month, who also has a hidden poison in her eyes."[18] As Newman has pointed out, the author of *De natura rerum* presents the homunculus as a sort of "masculine twin" to the female basilisk; the homunculus derives its purity from an *absence* of menses, just as the basilisk owed its venomous qualities to its origins in menstrual blood. This Paracelsian tradition, in other words, proposed alchemy as a means to eliminate ordinary menstrual blood, with its risk of corruption, from the generation of life, substituting instead a purer, more powerful, alchemically processed form of blood. Indeed, the author of *De natura rerum* figures this generative alchemical knowledge as a divine secret, "one of the highest and greatest secrets that God has revealed to mortal and sinful humanity. It is a miracle and great work [*magnale*] of God and a secret above all other secrets, and it should remain a secret until the last days, when nothing more will remain hidden and all will be revealed."[19]

Discussions around the Paracelsian homunculus, therefore, also make visible the extent to which the fault line between generative alchemical blood and poisonous human bloods could also be gendered. Male sperm combined with an alchemical blood elixir could produce a homunculus with near divine insights into the workings of nature; ordinary female menstrual blood, however, risked producing a basilisk. The alchemical homunculus thus embodied not only the ultimate generative and perfective potential of alchemy, but also a way that the art could triumph over the poisonous potential of menstrual blood in human reproduction. Like the author of *De natura rerum*, Anna

Zieglerin shared the ambitious goal of extending alchemy's powers into the creation of human life, as her recipes suggest. She also shared the Paracelsian concern about the poisonous potential of menses and looked to alchemy as a potential solution. Unlike the author of *De natura rerum*, however, these concerns did not lead Zieglerin to reject categorically female participation in the alchemical generation of life, as we shall see, but rather to use alchemy to preserve a role for women (at least some women) in generation, while eliminating the risk of corruption that they necessarily carried.

Zieglerin's alchemical calling card was a golden oil called the lion's blood. As she described it in the book of recipes she gave to her Wolfenbüttel patron in 1571, the lion's blood, produced by repeated distillation of lead and alchemically prepared gold, promoted fertility across the natural world, generating vegetable, mineral, and animal life alike. Dropped into water, for example, the lion's blood could work as a plant fertilizer, spurring a branch of a fruit tree to bloom and produce even in winter. It also could be used to produce gemstones, and, as the starting point for one of her two recipes for the philosophers' stone, the lion's blood could ultimately produce gold as well. Taken by both members of a barren couple, Zieglerin explained, it could cure infertility, and if the woman continued to take it throughout her pregnancy, it could also nourish the fetus *in utero*. Fed to the infant once born, the lion's blood alone, without any additional food or drink, could nourish the child for an astounding twelve years.[20]

The lion's blood recalls the arcanum of blood that *De natura rerum* called for in the production of the homunculus, insofar as it alchemically stimulated the generation of human life and then nourished the fetus (and ultimately the infant) as it grew. Zieglerin complicated the Paracelsian homunculus tradition, however, with respect to the role of the female body in producing life. Zieglerin and her fellow alchemists appear to have shared the Paracelsian belief in the destructive powers of menstrual blood, as the records from their work at Duke Julius's court in Wolfenbüttel suggest.[21] Mere proximity to a menstruating woman, they reported, could corrupt both living things and inanimate objects. When Anna's alchemical collaborator Philipp Sömmering was asked about menstrual blood, "he gave an example of a rose. When a man and a menstrual woman each pluck a rose, and each puts it in front of or near a window, the man's rose will wither slowly, and the woman's will be putrid on the third day" because of the corrosive power of her menses.[22] Even Anna appears to have shared this view of menstrual blood as toxic. Asked about a dispute she had with Philipp's wife when "Philipp's wife said that she [Anna] was a whore," Anna reported that she retaliated by giving Philipp's wife "some of her menses in warm wine that she sent over to her house, because she bore her a grudge."[23] Anna confirmed Philipp's view of the corroding powers of menses: "When someone ingests that," Philipp explained, "he becomes . . . ill."[24]

When Anna Zieglerin and her collaborator Philipp Sömmering attributed noxious powers to menstrual blood, therefore, they drew on the age-old tradition that continued to thrive in sixteenth-century central Europe. But they also spelled out some of the problematic implications of this view of menses for practicing alchemists. After relating the example of the flower, Philipp added a second story that suggested a connection to alchemy: "Once, a female dog was brought into Theophrastus's [i.e., Paracelsus's] *Laboratorium*," Philipp continued, "and all of the glassware cracked open."[25] Although Philipp did not say so explicitly, clearly he had a menstrual dog in mind, since he related the story about Paracelsus's laboratory in answer to a question about menses. Anna also apparently thought menstrual blood could jeopardize alchemical work. Philipp reported that Anna "said to him that he should not go to his wife because of the *menstrua*."[26] Anna confirmed this in her own testimony to the Wolfenbüttel court, stating that she "told Philipp that he must abstain from women, otherwise he will not be able to accomplish anything in alchemy."[27]

Such comments from Wolfenbüttel point to the belief that menstruation could interfere with alchemy; it caused decay, illness, and corruption, and it could spoil alchemical processes, presenting a risk to alchemists, their laboratories, and the materials they sought to create. And yet, the alchemical generation of human life outside of the womb did not appear to be a good solution, for it posed dangers as well. Zieglerin may have shared the concerns outlined in Paracelsus's *De homunculis*, where, as William Newman has pointed out, the homunculus became "a potent image of sin," rather than a supremely knowledgeable creature. In fact, in this text Paracelsus described a much more monstrous homunculus, claiming that it would lack a soul because it originated in human seed expelled outside of the proper context of marital reproductive sex. Perhaps responding to the frightening possibility of a monstrous homunculus without a soul, or perhaps simply rejecting a distinctly masculine fantasy of creating human life *without* a woman's body, Anna Zieglerin put her own twist on the homunculus tradition by putting the female womb back at the center of alchemical reproduction. Unlike the arcanum of human blood in *De natura rerum*, after all, the lion's blood was to be taken internally by the mother, preparing her body alchemically to host the creation of life in her own body, rather than in a sealed cucurbit. This approach had many advantages, not the least of which was that it ensured that, unlike the homunculus, alchemical infants made in the womb with the lion's blood would have a soul. But, for Zieglerin, who clearly worried about menstrual blood's power to corrupt alchemical processes, locating the reproductive work of the lion's blood in the female body still contained risks. It could expose the lion's blood to a polluted womb, possibly preventing the intended growth of alchemical "fruits" or, worse, producing a basilisk instead.

Fortunately, alchemy offered a solution here as well, for alchemists touted not only the generative powers of their art, but its power to purify and "redeem" bodies—whether of metals, minerals, or humans—as well. Some alchemists advocated using alchemical techniques to separate the poisonous or impure parts of matter in order to recombine them and produce powerfully effective medicines (a process that Paracelsus and his followers called *spagyria*). Others used their art to purify metals and minerals, of course, separating impurities from samples of ore, as did their fellow refiners and smelters.[28] More abstractly, the philosophers' stone's power to transform metals into silver or gold was frequently likened to redemption via the analogy between the philosophers' stone and Christ. Just as Christ had to be crucified in order to redeem humanity, the logic went, so too must the alchemist subject matter to similar torments, even death and resurrection, in order enable it to "redeem" base metals as the philosophers' stone.[29] It is perhaps unsurprising, therefore, that Zieglerin's lion's blood, too, promised to purify and redeem bodies. It could cleanse the body of leprosy, for example, causing the disease to leave through an incision "like grains of sand." Zieglerin equated the lion's blood with Christ's blood as well in her discussion of the philosophers' stone, made according to her recipe for feeding the lion's blood to a small bird, then roasting it and grinding it into a transmutative powder: "on the timber of the holy cross the son of God tinged all of us poor sinners with his most holy rose-colored blood and took part [in earthly affairs], just as this small bird will take part in the earthly tincture."[30]

Zieglerin's written recipes, therefore, took up fairly standard alchemical themes of generation and redemption of matter. More informally, however, she circulated a much more ambitious vision at the Wolfenbüttel court, using her own body to posit alchemy as a way to resolve the dilemma of menstrual blood. Her infant body, she claimed, had been treated alchemically at birth with a tincture, with the result that her adult body was unusually pure. For one thing, as Zieglerin's fellow alchemists in Wolfenbüttel evidently knew, she did not menstruate. Given her fears about the power of menstrual blood to corrupt alchemical processes, this was an advantage and an important part of Zieglerin's claim, as a young woman in her twenties, to be able to contribute to her patron's alchemical projects. Moreover, whereas in a different context a lack of menstruation might have been understood as an obstacle to reproduction, Anna Zieglerin turned it into an opportunity to pursue a superior method of generating life. Following in the tradition of the homunculus and her own recipe for using the lion's blood to treat infertility, Zieglerin described a process whereby she would use the lion's blood to gestate fetuses in her own spotless womb, uncorrupted by menstrual blood. Once born, Zieglerin claimed, these infants would be nourished by the lion's blood, which not only would accelerate their growth, but also would ensure that they were as long-lived as the patriarchs, that their bodies remained free of illness, and, in the case of the females, that they, like Zieglerin herself, "were not to be burdened with the flux."[31] The alchemical lion's blood, in short, purified Zieglerin's own womb so that it could host the generation of the extraordinary bodies who also could evade the corruption of the world.

Like the homunculus, Zieglerin's extraordinary reproduction was framed in an apocalyptic context; it was privileged knowledge, a secret whose very revelation signaled that the end times were at hand. For one thing, it would fulfill a prophecy. Zieglerin's fellow alchemist Philipp Sömmering claimed, in fact, that none other than Paracelsus, the early sixteenth-century medical reformer, had prophesied that "a maiden would be born who was free from the monthly flux, and [she] was to have children who would live until the final days."[32] Evoking some kind of millennium populated by alchemical progeny, Zieglerin's husband Heinrich Schombach added to the prophecy, "From such children would arise a new world."[33] Situating Zieglerin's lion's blood as an instrument for the last days conjured another extraordinary moment of artificial reproduction, the birth of Christ. Indeed, Anna and her fellow alchemists did not miss this connection. Schombach reported, "that she did not have the flux [*Fluß*] and [that she had] many other virtues, and that she was like the angels."[34] Philipp Sömmering agreed. He said that he "praised Fraw Anna a great deal concerning her purity [*Reinigkeit*], and compared her to the Mother of God, just as she herself did. . . . He . . . praised Anna greatly, and that he perceived her to be equal to the Virgin Mary."[35] This was no ordinary reproduction, in other words, but situated the exceptional generative powers of the alchemical lion's blood—working at once within and beyond nature—within the framework of sacred time. Where the Virgin Mary had achieved an exceptional form of generation through a miracle, Anna Zieglerin could do so with the aid of an alchemical blood, which could bypass the cluster of sin, corruption, and potential monstrosity associated with menstrual blood, while still keeping the generation of human life in the female body.

* * *

Zieglerin's vision of alchemy's potential at the end of time, not to mention the role she imagined for herself in the unfolding of the Last Days, was ambitious, to be sure. The problem she attempted to resolve, however, was a longstanding one in both alchemy and late medieval and early modern culture, namely, the vexing contradictions of blood. Late medieval and early modern alchemists found it difficult to imagine the generation of anything—plants, the philosophers' stone, or human life—without some form of blood, especially menstrual blood. And yet at the same time, the very presence of menstrual blood threatened to corrupt, dissolve, and pervert the very generative processes that required it in the first place. The prevalence of blood in alchemical texts suggests that alchemists clearly were drawn to this problem, and some proposed alchemy as a solution. For Paracelsians, alchemically prepared blood could substitute for the more problematic menstrual blood required to create life; for Anna Zieglerin, alchemy could purify both blood and bodies, making both more suitable for the production of life.

These authors made it clear, moreover, that alchemically generated lives, whether Paracelsian homunculi or Zieglerin's children, would be extraordinary. Indeed, the apocalyptic framing of these techniques as secrets to be revealed at the end of time underscores their potential as a resolution to the entire arc of human existence. Fertility, and female fertility in particular, had been associated with sin ever since Adam and Eve ate from the Tree of Knowledge and God said to Eve, "I will greatly multiply your pain in childbirth, in pain you will bring forth children; yet your desire will be for your husband, and he will rule over you."[36] Until the sixteenth century, only one woman, the Virgin Mary, had managed to generate life without the stain of sin.[37] What Anna Zieglerin suggested, however, was that alchemy might have the power to achieve something similar by retaining, even enhancing, the generative power of blood while eliminating its associations with sin and corruption. This was a far more precious secret than the recipe for the philosophers' stone, for it proposed that alchemy could have a role to play in unfolding sacred time that was as pivotal as the Virgin Mary's.

Not all alchemists imbued blood with such importance, of course. Sometimes "the menstrual blood of our sordid Whore" was just raw antimony ore, as it was for Philalethes. Even when it represented material substances in a straightforward way, however, blood simultaneously contained powers of both corruption and generation. This made blood a compelling concept for alchemists and can help explain why it appears so often in alchemical texts. Blood, in sum, offered alchemists a distinctive opportunity to make a case for their art's ability to reverse corruption and to generate matter, even to generate life itself.

Chapter 8

Bloody Students

Youth, Corruption, and Discipline in the Medieval Classroom

BEN PARSONS

At some point in the mid-fifteenth century, an amateur poet by the name of Edmund Fulmerston recorded his one surviving text in a manuscript now held at Cambridge University Library. This is a quatrain in elementary but efficient Latin, imparting the following piece of wisdom:

> Whoever drinks well, sleeps well,
> Sleeps well, and thinks no evil;
> Whoever thinks no evil will be healthy:
> Therefore, whoever drinks well will be healthy.[1]

Although Fulmerston was sufficiently proud of this brief snatch to set not only his signature by it but also his place of residence, inscribing "Edmvnd ffvlmerston" in its margin and "Braken Ashe" beneath its final line, his work is in no sense an original composition. The contents of the verse seem to be derived from popular tradition rather than its author's imagination: numerous analogues survive from the sixteenth century onward, not only in English and Latin but Dutch, Danish, and German.[2] Yet despite its unoriginality, the piece has some suggestive ties to the context in which it was produced. Its manuscript is squarely rooted in the late medieval classroom. It preserves the only extant copies of the work of John Drury, schoolmaster at Beccles in Suffolk in the 1430s: the texts in the manuscript include a treatise on grammar, a *regulum* for teachers, a Latin wordlist with specimen phrases, and a lecture on confession in which Drury explicitly describes himself as "mays*ter* at þis tyme . . . here in Becclis schole."[3] What little can be determined about Fulmerston himself also places him in the same orbit. The Fulmerstons were an East Anglian family based in Thetford and Ipswich, just over the county line from Suffolk, with connections to the dukes of Norfolk from at least the 1460s.[4] Likewise, Fulmerston's reference to "Braken Ashe" locates him at Bracon Ash, a village only twelve miles east of Beccles. Fulmerston therefore seems to have been a pupil taught by Drury or one of his successors, scribbling his text into a spare page of his teacher's handbook. Even his preservation of the poem reinforces this point: the obvious delight he takes in this modest composition, proudly inscribing his name beside it, seems unmistakably schoolboyish.

Yet despite its intrusive, even disruptive appearance in Drury's manuscript, Fulmerston's text is deeply embedded in medieval education and reveals some important points about it. Even at first glance, it is clear that the composition has arisen from the general matrix of instruction. The adage Fulmerston is quoting was clearly part of the bloodstream of pedagogic discourse, as later sources often use it to demonstrate a principle of one or other of the liberal arts. In Augustinus Hunnaeus's handbook on logic, for instance, the phrase "whoever drinks well will be blessed" is presented as a model syllogism, "a silly example that is commonly recited, which nevertheless applies."[5] Along the same lines, Juan Luis Vives uses a similar saying to illustrate the rhetorical figure *transitus*, observing that the formula "whoever drinks well, sleeps well" performs a "trick" by "crossing over to another tense, for no-one can drink and sleep at the same time."[6] Fulmerston's verse also conforms to a wider sense of what teachers thought would best appeal to their students. Its general theme and tone accord with the humorous "down-to-earth approach" most schoolmasters showed in selecting their illustrative material, as they often drew on popular and proverbial verse when formulating tasks for pupils, as Joanna Bellis and Venetia Bridges have most recently emphasized.[7] The piece, in short, is consistent with the sort of text medieval pedagogues would customarily use for translation exercises or to demonstrate the arts of the trivium, and it is probably the result of such activities.

But more significantly still, it also resonates with its setting in further and more complex ways, articulating a number of important assumptions about the nature of learning in the period. It is difficult to ignore that the main focus of the piece is educative, at least in a broad sense. It addresses the measures that can be taken to ensure that one "thinks no evil," to condition the mind to overcome its tendency to temptation and immorality, and to make it operate fully and properly. What is interesting, however, is the manner in which this conditioning proceeds, as the verse conceives improvement of the mind largely in biological terms. Thought is placed at the end-point of a causal chain, being shaped by a whole battery of physiological processes and requirements: it is informed most immediately by sleep, although this in turn is seen as a consequence of other, more directly controllable factors, specifically the food and drink taken into the body and the influence diet holds over the constitution. The text therefore merges the pedagogic with the medical, or at least the dietary. It sees the mind of the learner as intrinsically bound up with the body, to the extent that the manipulation of the latter can be used to access and mold the former.

Even though Fulmerston's quatrain steers this logic in a purposefully absurd direction, the reasoning that underpins the snippet is detectible throughout medieval pedagogy. The movement presented here between proper management of the body as well as the mind plays out on a larger scale in other manuscripts associated with teaching, where medicine is often a conspicuous element. Thus a miscellany of ca. 1490 held at Lincoln Cathedral and probably originating from the grammar school housed there cuts across the same boundaries. As well as containing several works obviously tied to elementary instruction, such as grammatical and mathematical problems, and the wordlist *Medulla grammaticae* (ca. 1425), it assembles a series of formulas for ailments likely to impair study: its prescriptions tackle both general disorders such as "þe pestilence" and "þe fallyng euel" and complaints related to excessive reading, such as eyestrain and cataracts, described as "rede eyen" and "þe webbe."[8] At points these concerns even enter into teaching materials themselves. This can be clearly witnessed in a series of *latinitates* or brief translation exercises compiled in 1520 by Robert Whittinton, a master at Lichfield.[9] At a number of points Whittinton's text delivers advice on health as it inducts students into latinity, asking students to render such phrases as "if thou fere sekenesse / beware of euyll dyet" and "I fere myselfe of the ague / for I fele a grudgynge euery seconde daye."[10] What is more, these sentences were evidently used by at least one early teacher, as they are among the twenty or so marked with marginal insignia in a copy once held at Sion College.[11]

More significantly still, rather than having a merely cosmetic or incidental relevance, this thinking often seems bound up with medieval pedagogy at a deep-seated theoretical level, insinuating its way into its basic preconceptions. From at least the thirteenth century adolescence is often seen as an anatomical and medical problem as much as a disciplinary one, a point at which the body is temporarily corrupted and corrupts mind and morals in turn.[12] One witness to this thinking is the work of the physician and teacher Bernard of Gordon, writing in Montpellier in ca. 1308.[13] Bernard explicitly conceives youth itself as a diseased state, referring at several points to its *morbi* or "infirmities": at one stage he even advises that the teacher "ought to appraise the infirmities of boys like a good doctor, establishing whether any sign of goodness can be seen, and then keeping not that which will decay but that which is wholesome."[14] Bernard's language is more than purely figurative, as other commentators also see a physiological basis for the perceived disorders of youth, at times anticipating ideas of greensickness in subsequent centuries. In the early thirteenth century, Thomas of Cantimpré imputes the wild behavior of the adolescent to his newfound capacity for procreation, the fact that "the seminal virtue naturally grows stronger" in him, "loosening the bridle of lust and causing desire to dominate the body." In Thomas's eyes the preponderance of this "virtue" and its continual demand for "expulsion of the flow of desire" directs both the behavior and mentality of the young. On the one hand it generates a lack of reason, depleting the power of both mind and body, as continual "discharge debilitates the boy to the point of weariness," expelling "the strength that ought to be possessed in body and soul."[15] On the other hand, it also leads to the unruliness characteristic of adolescents: the fact that their internal processes are always directed outward predisposes youths to act in an uncontained, uncontrolled manner, "resisting their duty, staying awake complaining about food, disturbing the household ... wandering in the rain and watching the violence of tempests, all of which is their youth at work discharging itself."[16] A different but comparable set of ideas is given by the Benedictine encyclopedist Pierre Bersuire in his *Repertorium morale* (1355). Bersuire begins his account of *adolescentia* by outlining the "delinquency" of this stage of life, listing "ignorance, caprice, and an unstable condition" among the difficulties it presents.[17] This again is laid at the door of the body, as "the flesh of young animals is moist, changeable, and flexible, and therefore easily manipulated. Yet when they reach this state, they start to harden, and then it is largely futile to influence and convert them ... then bad inclinations towards vice are fixed."[18] Adolescents are therefore dangerous because of their impressionability, their ability to receive corruptive as well as beneficial influences, an absorbency that is at once physical and psychological: they are "like soft wax that indifferently receives a beautiful or grotesque imprint."[19] Again, the behavioral problems of the young are given a biological origin, as their imperfect reasoning and general disorderliness both emerge from their compromised physiologies.

These convictions are not only confined to the rarefied world of medical theory, as they have a direct influence on pedagogy, both in terms of the expectations surrounding the young and the practical measures needed to train them. Just as childcare in the household often veers toward nutritive and digestive considerations, as Bonnie Lander Johnson discusses in the current volume, so the medieval school makes the body a point of focus for its own projects. This can be witnessed in Vincent of Beauvais's influential teaching handbook *De eruditione filiorum nobilium* (ca. 1261). When outlining the peculiarities of youngsters for the benefit of prospective tutors, Vincent shuttles between the physiological and mental: he specifically defines the adolescent as "weak in bodily strength" as well as "infirm in judgement, obstinate in pleasure-seeking, heated in vices," spelling out a close association between habit, body, and mind.[20] The same concerns take more elaborate form in the regimen written by Pedro Fagarola in 1315 for his sons studying at Toulouse. Pedro situates learning among a formidable array of environmental and bodily factors, giving the impression that the adolescent body needs to be precisely regulated and guarded in order to receive tuition. Among his many pieces of advice are proscriptions against eating uncooked onions in the evening because they may "dull the intellect and senses," against wearing slippers to bed "because they generate vapors which are very bad for the brain," and against eating too heavily before going to sleep, since this will cause vapors to "rise to the head and fill it with rheum and steal away and cut short memory."[21] Therefore, whatever can be said about the literary value of Fulmerston's efforts, his verse brings to light a vital strand of materialism in medieval pedagogy. By casually drawing together nutrition and psychology, his quatrain lays bare two pervasive assumptions about teaching in the period: a sense that schooling must take the body of the learner into account, and the idea that it redresses faults that are situated in the degraded anatomy of the adolescent.

As might be expected, given its close association with the troublesome "seminal virtue," blood plays a pivotal role in this medicalization of learning.[22] A range of authors single it out as a vital factor in the instruction of the young, citing it as part of the students' physiology that requires special attention, even at times blaming it for larger shortcomings in their minds and bodies. What motivates this approach is the belief that blood is a crucial element in the constitution of youngsters, being more abundant during youth than at other times.[23] Such thinking is already in evidence in the early medieval period, where the complex field of analogies surrounding the body tends to associate blood with the earlier stages of life.[24] In a tenth-century gloss on Boethius, for instance, the interlocking schemata of elements, humors, seasons, and ages is used to fasten blood to childhood: drawing on the commonplace that "the world is composed of four elements and four seasons, and the same is true of man," the gloss argues that children "correspond" to blood, "the air, and the time of spring" in the same way that "during the age of decrepitude man resembles water and winter and phlegm, which possess coldness and moisture, for it is true that old men are cold."[25] This association received its strongest impetus, however, from Avicenna's *Canons* (1025), where it gained a newly rationalized form. Avicenna not only notes that youths are ruled by hot and moist humors necessary for growth, but asserts that "their blood is much more plentiful and thicker" than at other stages, something apparently proven by their frequent nosebleeds, their efficient digestive systems, and their rapid bodily movements.[26] Thanks in large part to Avicenna's observations, this view was absorbed into general medical opinion during the High Middle Ages, and from there crossed into pedagogic theory. Thus in his great encyclopedia, compiled in the 1240s at Madgeburg for student friars under his care, Bartholomew of England looks to blood to explain both the behavior of the young and the overall function of schooling.[27] His entry for *pueritia* ("boyhood") sees a profound connection between blood and the need for education:

> The childish age is hot and moist, on account of the overburdened blood-vessels, which do not strengthen until the time of puberty is reached.... Boys are soft in body, pliant in flesh, rapid and swift in motion, with easily-taught mind, without any concern or anxiety or thought for a prudent life, only valuing amusing things, and fearing nothing more than beating with the rod.[28]

For Bartholomew, blood is firmly implicated in the general frailty and imperfection that Bersuire and the other commentators find in the young. The characteristic heat and moisture of youth and the impetuosity and impressionability that come with these properties all stem from the large quantity of blood in the developing anatomy. The "overburdened blood-vessels" create a body that is itself like blood in its fluidity and plasticity, giving the child an erratic and unstable character that requires containment. Blood, in effect, is seen as a problem that needs resolving: while its dominance might make children receptive to instruction, giving them a "yielding mind" along with "pliant flesh," it also creates the need for this discipline in the first place, conferring on them a dangerous lack of regularity that must be stringently curtailed.

Bartholomew is not alone in this valuation of blood, as other writers follow a similar path. Hence Jacopo of Forli, a philosopher-physician active at Padua in the late fourteenth century, gives a similar account, arguing that the heightened level of blood during youth adversely affects the intellect.[29] According to Jacopo, the brain is unable to work at its optimum strength when saturated with blood: as he writes, "such operations require the departure of superfluous humidity from the organs, in order that they can be fully perfected; therefore it appears that the animal operations of consciousness can only be most perfect in the adult."[30] In his view, the presence of blood in the adolescent anatomy creates the lack of reason that is the entire reason for schooling. The conditions that necessitate education in the first place arise out of the proliferation of blood in the biology of the young, as the abundance of fluidity and heat that growth requires also leads to flux in the mind. Again, blood is a necessary but corruptive humor, its warmth and fluidity running directly counter to the exercise of reason.

However, while accounts such as these suggest that blood is primarily an obstacle to be overcome, rendering students volatile and unreasonable, other medieval authorities regard it in more positive terms. One such work is the *Glosae in Iuvenalem* (ca. 1130), sometimes attributed to William of Conches.[31] The *Glosae* itself is clearly rooted in the medieval schoolroom: it consists of long explanatory glosses for one of the key texts on the curriculum, the satires of Juvenal, and is preceded by a brief *accessus* that refers to its author as "magister." What makes the text especially notable is its occasional tendency to interpret its source as an allegory of the learning process itself: thus Juvenal's references to *marmora* ("marble statues") and *platani* ("plane-trees") are taken as symbols of "obstinate pupils" and "teachers harassed by thickly-pressed queries."[32] This approach turns at length to the role of blood in the learning process, which the author regards in a markedly productive light:

> The master therefore, seeing the sluggishness of intellect proceeding from the blood congealing around the heart, strikes the boys on the left hand, which is closest to the heart, with the instrument made from wood for this purpose. And thus the blood from the hand travels and is driven elsewhere . . . and in this way the intellect is excited.[33]

Blood is again understood as a fluid with psychological as well as physiological properties, as it is bound up with the student's "intellect" or *ingenium*. Although this term carries a wide range of meanings in medieval philosophy, here it seems to mean something like alertness or concentration, since lethargy and inattention will overcome any pupil whose blood lies too heavily on the heart.[34] However, the author also sees blood as a solution as much as a hindrance: by striking boys on the hand supposedly closest to the heart, he claims that a master can stir the blood and so rekindle *ingenium* when it threatens to stall. His attitude is therefore quite different from that of Jacopo or Bartholomew, as blood is the teacher's ally as much as his opponent. While it has the potential to disrupt thought, it does not merely represent a dangerous excess of heat or moisture. Its circulation within the body and its movement between surface and interior means that it can be used by the master to access the internal architecture of his students: it transports stimuli into parts of the body that would otherwise prove unreachable, providing a means of crossing the threshold between body and mind. It is therefore conducive to the central projects of education, transmitting the master's influence to processes housed within the pupil's anatomy.

Other sources take this point of view further, assigning further educational functions to blood and developing intricate networks of ideas around it. In some discussions, blood even offers a means of systematizing teaching, helping to adapt the general precepts of the classroom to meet the requirements and abilities of individual students. One of the foundational texts in this enterprise is *De disciplina scolarium*, a brief treatise accepted as the work of Boethius from the time of its composition, although in fact written at Paris in the 1230s.[35] The text attained a high degree of popularity throughout the Middle Ages and beyond, surviving in over 130 manuscripts and early printed editions.[36] Its unknown author addresses blood almost as soon as his attention turns to the practicalities of instruction. After outlining some of the fundamental geographical and astronomical knowledge a master ought to know, he goes on to list the different factors teachers should consider in order to "inculcate wisdom" among their students. From the first he shackles this system to the four humors, stating that "everything important for facilitating the instruction of scholars" can be extrapolated from the fact that "the human body is supported by a union of phlegm, blood, bile, and black bile," and the inevitability that "a particular one of the foresaid should attain preeminence."[37] In the discussion that follows, these points develop into a full-blown classificatory system for students, a means of determining how their bodies should be managed in order to ensure the fullest possible absorption of knowledge. The point throughout is either to compensate for the peculiar impediments each humor brings with it, or to exploit these same features for the ends of learning. Thus melancholic students are described as "subject to timidity and idleness" and needing to "drink moderately to enliven their nature," while choleric students "should always be placed in solitude, so that hearing too great a ruckus does not cause an excess of bile to burst out against the entire cohort."[38] When the author addresses bodies in which blood is the ruling humor, his remarks take on an interesting inflection. While he agrees that instability is the main property of blood, he regards this as advantageous rather than detrimental, seeing in it a vital adaptability. He thus claims that sanguine students can adjust themselves to any physical environment and "digest even the finest food and liveliest drink"; by contrast, their melancholic or phlegmatic colleagues can only eat very particular types of food and are limited to quiet and shadowy places or spacious, bright dwellings respectively.[39] It is for this reason that the author claims that sanguine students are "best suited to study."[40] Nevertheless, he does not regard blood as wholly unproblematic. He also notes that sanguine students cannot be relied on to behave in any consistent way: they are, for instance, prone to lapses in concentration, as "the corners of their eyes are always twisting towards the walls."[41] The best way to teach them is therefore to exploit their fickleness and ensure that teaching appeals to the mobility of their bodies and minds: they should be "encouraged to take pleasure in the weightiest questions."[42] For the treatise, then, blood is again an aid to teaching rather than an impediment. Even when its liquidity brings inconstancy, this can still serve the ends of instruction, as it also promotes mental athleticism. But blood also supports teaching in another respect. In the hands of this author, it develops into an index of competency, even a category of student. The humors themselves become a framework by which the teacher can diagnose the aptitudes of his pupils, providing a key to their behavior by which he can learn "many intimate facts about the mind."[43] Sanguinity is then not merely an inconvenient fact the master must confront but a means of directing and facilitating his teaching, signaling how he can best guarantee that his pupils assimilate knowledge.

As befits a text that attained such an impressive level of influence, the schema worked out in *De disciplina* was echoed by several later commentators, even if it was not upheld to the letter. For example, Pier Paolo Vegerio, teacher of logic and canon law at Florence and Padua in the late fourteenth century, also uses humoral theory to classify the potential of students: however, in his system, "those in whom black bile preponderates" are favored over sanguine students, since pupils with this complexion are "most suited to carry out judgment and to enjoy intellectual freedom."[44] But one of the most thorough engagements with these ideas is that of William Whetyly, schoolmaster at Stamford and Lincoln, who composed a series of lectures on *De disciplina* in 1309.[45] While Whetyly is fairly even-handed when expanding on his base text, producing a commentary some seventeen times longer than the original, he paid particular attention to its chapter on the humors. A signal of its importance is his inclusion of brief mnemonic verses, mostly culled from Giovanni of Milan, condensing his remarks on the complexions: for instance, he summarizes phlegmatic boys with the couplet "sleepy, slow, full of spittle, / Dull in senses, thick in form, pale in colour."[46] In fact, physicality proves to be a central concern throughout Whetyly's pedagogy, as he frequently steers the focus of the text toward the proper management of the body.[47] This preoccupation is most visible in his remarks on deformed or disabled students: he urges that masters do not attempt to teach any boy with "a hunched back or defect in any other members" on the grounds that "nature is founded in the body, and an unsteady foundation always threatens disaster and degeneration of condition; from such defects at the beginning great error is liable to appear at the end."[48] This focus on the body leads Whetyly to place particular emphasis on the role of blood in learning. He extends a point only sketched out in his source text, stressing not only the elasticity of blood but its vigor and vitality. The fluid is thus defined as "a certain humour in the body, which is so called because it restores to man that which is crucial for health and pleasantness," while sanguinity itself is defined as the "complexion that is most favourable among all the complexions."[49] The connection between blood and well-being becomes especially important when Whetyly sets out to explain why sanguine students can adapt themselves to all environments. Their versatility is seen as both an inherent goodness and the power to derive goodness from every situation. He asserts that "the sanguine man can in practice study in all places indifferently . . . in places both dark and light, narrow and large" because "goodness always transmits itself to itself, communicating itself to the good of good things, since it is similar to those things." The ability of sanguine students to study in any location is the result of this quasi-magnetic property, as the innate vigor of their blood draws toward it whatever benefit can be found in their immediate surroundings: it is, he states, "in this way that the sanguine complexion is best and healthiest among all the complexions."[50] In Whetyly's work, therefore, blood takes on an even greater importance. In effect, it comes to symbolize the very potential to be educated, representing in bodily form the scope for improvement all pupils require to be effective learners. Here blood is not merely conducive to study, but is indispensable to it.

Taken collectively, these remarks show blood to be a site of profound ambivalence within the medieval classroom. Like the other discourses examined in this volume, especially alchemy and childcare, with their similarly transformative and metaphoric understanding of blood, pedagogy sees both productive and disruptive energies at work in the fluid. On the one hand, there is a clear sense that it has a corruptive influence on mind and body. Not only is it associated with the fraught condition of youth itself, with its lack of reason, consistency, and restraint, but it is thought to be the direct cause of such qualities, its heat and fluidity unbalancing thought and behavior at this point in the life cycle. As a result many pedagogues encounter it as a problem, something that generates the very unruliness and unreason education seeks to overcome. Yet on the other hand the same features that render blood objectionable also align it with the central projects of schooling. Blood's liquidity renders pupils malleable in the first place, and it can even be used to convey instruction into the internal structures of the child. It might be said that these remarks on blood, conceiving it as equal parts obstacle and instrument, equally corruptive and beneficial, provide a focus for larger concerns around the adolescent body—a sense that it too is both a resource and a danger, both a dashboard by which the teacher can manipulate the student's mind and a locus of counterproductive forces ruled by perilous appetites. It is perhaps, then, not surprising that some of the largest questions in education also coalesce around blood: how to tailor lessons to meet the varying needs of students, on what basis to rank pupils, and how to manage disruptive or inattentive children. These are questions that remain at the heart of pedagogy; moreover, even now solutions often take the same course as medieval discussions, veering toward the medical and pharmaceutical.[51]

Chapter 9

Blood, Milk, Poison

Romeo and Juliet's Tragedy of "Green" Desire and Corrupted Blood

BONNIE LANDER JOHNSON

Natural affection, without doubt cannot be so earnest, either from the mother toward the child, or from the child toward the mother, if she have not nursed him and given him suck. For if she nurse him, he sucks and draws her own blood.
—Jacques Guillemeau, 1612

Without doubt the child will be much alienated in his affections by sucking of strange Milk, and that may be one great cause of Children's proving so undutiful to their Parents.
—Jane Sharp, 1671

One of the key premises of this book is that in the Renaissance "blood" denoted far more than the fluid in human veins. And yet the vast proportion of Shakespeare's uses of the word refer simply to the red stuff. In *Romeo and Juliet*, we might expect to find blood signifying the division between Capulet and Montague, the various passions of violence, civil unrest, thwarted adolescent love, murder and suicide, or even the idolatry of the lovers' excessive desire for each other. In fact, of the thirty or so references to blood or bleeding in *Romeo and Juliet*, only one is figurative: the Prince's reference to Mercutio as his kin ("my blood for your rude brawls doth lie a-bleeding").[1] And yet this play is subtly but crucially concerned with the problem of corrupted blood and its effect on the lovers' appetites: it is concerned with the lovers' greensickness.

Considerable ink has been spilled over the question of Juliet's greensickness.[2] Not so for Romeo, whom we first meet augmenting the morning dew with his tears, wandering under the sycamores at night, and locking himself up all day to pen bad verse: behavior that more readily suggests his melancholic disposition or, perhaps, a tendency to lovesickness.[3] However, I think *Romeo and Juliet* is far more invested in the "virgins' disease" than has been recognized, or than could be recognized by attempting to diagnose the lovers' humoral imbalances. Diagnosing greensickness in fictional characters is not only hindered by insufficient clues to their symptoms but also by the fact that descriptions of the disease in early modern medical guidebooks are far from consistent. And yet in one sense the exploration of greensickness is uniquely suited to literary analysis because the early modern understanding of the disease was, to a certain extent, metaphorical. As Helen King has suggested, few sufferers seem to have presented as green in hue, yet the rich metaphoric significance of "green" articulated the disorder most comprehensively to those who sought treatment: in the second half of the sixteenth century, King argues, the label "greensickness" remained the one to which potential patients would most often respond.[4] Something in the popular early modern understanding of green and its figurative reverberations articulated a set of cultural fears about youth, desire, and the dangers attending sexual maturation; it is this interest in green that, I think, lent itself readily to the narrative of thwarted love that Shakespeare inherited from his sources.

Ecocriticism has for some decades turned its attention to the early modern period. Together with a more general historicist interest in "green" cultures, ecocritical scholarship has posed questions about the way early moderns related to the natural world; how the various medical, pharmaceutical, botanical, and agricultural sciences interacted with each other; how pastoral poetry and gardening literature emerged out of particular cultural and religious paradigms; and the various semiotic patterns at work in early modern writing on paradise, gardens, trees, and the politics of land ownership.[5] My interest in *Romeo and Juliet*'s distinctive green vision is indebted to this rich scholarly field but also emerges out of a concern that the vast majority of this work describes early modern human beings as engaged in various forms of conflict with the natural world around them. However, a recent collection, *The Indistinct Human in Renaissance Literature*, has begun to overturn this view. Its essays instead explore the early modern awareness of the impossibility of separating humans from their animal, vegetable, and mineral environment.

I find this model of indistinct humanness more useful when attempting to discern Shakespeare's vision of "green." In fact, I think Shakespeare was very invested in the Genesis model of human beings as clay, earth, or "dust"; in his corpus I find a deep sensitivity to the created world as a phenomenon in which man, as much as beast, vegetation, and the elements, emerges from the same material expression of divine will. I don't want to suggest that a definitive philosophy of creation can be located in and behind the plays and poetry, but for the purposes of this chapter I will say that in the 1590s especially Shakespeare was interested in figurative descriptions of the earth as a body as much as he was interested in the actual earth-ness of men and women.[6]

The early modern perception of green with which I think *Romeo and Juliet* is concerned drew on a similar belief that humans were only ever partially removed from the rest of the created world and would eventually return (at least bodily) to the earth. It is true that Shakespeare renders this vision quite differently across his dramatic corpus (and it is a vision that alters significantly depending on the genre in question). But even when, as in *Romeo and Juliet*, characters fail to felicitously make the transition from earth to flesh and back to earth, the ideal form of such a life cycle is still presented as possible, desirable, as right and proper to human experience, and thus in itself as "natural." The lovers' failure to make this transition is presented in *Romeo and Juliet* as both a social and physiological reality: their "greensickness" is a direct result of the social conditions governing their appetitive development, but it is expressed throughout the play in the figurative language that collapses their bodies and desires with the vegetative life of the earth from which they emerged.

My reading of *Romeo and Juliet*'s interest in greensickness locates the lovers' erroneous appetites, their desire for bad medicine and for each other, within early modern thinking about the weaning of infants and its effect on the purity of blood. The play's concern with bad weaning (explicit in Juliet's narrative and implicit in the characterization of Romeo) describes the lovers' errant appetitive formation at adolescence as a direct result of their failure to successfully make it through the crucial infant stages of blood, milk, and food nourishment: a failure determined both by Galenic understandings of weaning and early modern cultural perceptions of wet-nursing cultures. In this way, the lovers' ultimate demise in the bloody "womb" of the earth, sucking on the poison they believe is their last source of comfort, is the inevitable but tragic conclusion of their early appetitive corruption, of their greensickness.

My exploration of *Romeo and Juliet*'s interest in greensickness is therefore less concerned with the play's specific references to the disease (Capulet's diagnosis of his daughter's rebellion is in any case unreliable since he doesn't know all the facts of her sexual and marital situation) and more concerned with the figurative reverberations of green as newness, perverted appetites, corrupted blood, and fertile earth. The play places its characters on a metaphoric plane in which they are bound to the earth, whose "womb" blood they have never quite shaken off; part of the lovers' "green" suffering stems from the fact that their emergence out of the earth has gone wrong in some way. As a result, their trajectory back to the bloody tomb, the "womb of death" (5.3.45), becomes a logical extension of their corrupted blood and "green" appetites. By tracing the medically alarming trajectory of the lovers' extreme passion, my reading follows early modern Galenic thought on sexual diseases and the blood, but it also offers a historicist adjustment to the critical tradition that interprets the inevitability of the lovers' trajectory as a neo-Classical or psychoanalytic death wish.[7]

The symptoms usually ascribed to greensickness in the early modern period included psychological distress (anger, sorrow, sometimes love), pale skin color, abnormal appetites, digestive disorders, and an absence of menses. From a humoral perspective, the retention of menses was the most significant symptom: it could itself be the cause of other symptoms associated with the disease. The failure to purge menstrual blood was thought to cause a dangerous buildup of unclean matter in the body, which in turn blocked the healthy flow of humoral movement and poisoned the sufferer. Primarily, early modern greensickness was a disease of the blood, just as it was a disease of the womb. It was a disease of (female) virgins (although Shakespeare attributes green desire to men too) and was cured by sex, marriage, and childbirth. While the commencement of sexual activity was thought to offer a functional solution to the problem of blockages in the womb, such "medicine" also indicates how the disease emerged out of broader social imperatives surrounding the regulation of female sexual desire.[8]

It is out of these imperatives that some of the metaphorical implications of green can be said to emerge. Green signified sexuality, fertility, youth, desire, and appetite (all definitions for which the OED provides ample early modern examples). It also signified earthly or vegetative ripeness as well as unripeness, and it is around the convergence of these two opposing views of a young woman's readiness or unreadiness for "plucking" or "harvesting" that the social anxieties articulated by greensickness seem to hover. Shakespeare's Juliet is precisely the age when early modern parents began to watch for signs of ripeness. But, as Juliet's father evidences, guardians of adolescent girls were equally attuned to the perils of unripeness: Capulet worries that his daughter may be "marred" if made a mother before she is "ripe" (1.2.11–13). Faced with her grief and rebelliousness later in the play, however, he is quick to assume she is "greensickness carrion" and sends her off to take a husband (3.5.156).

"Green" signified earthly fertility but "greensickness" signified the failure to exploit a narrow window of fertility in young women for whom lateness, as much as earliness, could equal death. It is this capacity for green to signify both life and death that finds expression in more general early modern moral concerns about sexuality, with which *Romeo and Juliet* is particularly interested. Friar Lawrence asserts in his meditation on plants as both medicine ("grace") and poison ("rude will") that sexuality is as fertile and productive as it is deadly. More specifically, early modern thinking on the "greenness" of the womb targeted the organ's duplicity (as the source of both life and "deadly poison"[9])—a duplicity it shared with nature. Women who failed to menstruate and women who had recently given birth were both considered "green." One important explanation for this view is that menstrual and postpartum bloods were thought to be both corrupted and fertile. A pseudo-Aristotelian tract warns that menstrual blood will kill any plant life it touches or send mad any dog that consumes it.[10] And yet menses were consistently called "flowers" and, despite their Galenic role as waste, were nonetheless signs of a woman's healthy fertility. The delicate state of fertility and potential corruption thought to attend the postnatal "green" mother was similarly informed by anxieties over the health of birth blood, but her greenness could also be attributed to the newness of her situation. So too for "green" maids whose new desires and new anatomical capacities placed them in a vulnerable position both humorally and morally. The capacity for green to signify newness is central to *Romeo and Juliet* (the freshness of naïve love or gullibility but also the newly buried body: Tybalt's bones are "yet but green in earth" [4.3.42]).

According to Jacques Guillemeau, newly pregnant women could also suffer greensickness. His understanding of the disease emphasizes the relationship between corrupted blood and corrupted appetites: the pregnant woman didn't menstruate, therefore her body did not expel waste blood, therefore she suffered a "depraved and disordinate appetite."[11] Guillemeau is referring to what we would call morning sickness (the desire for unlikely, and especially alkaline, foods in the first trimester of pregnancy), but his description of the condition utilizes the same language frequently applied to the womb in the early modern period: the source of both life and poison, the womb itself had a dangerous appetite.[12] Early modern thinking on the duplicity and appetite of the womb dovetails with similar views of the maternal breast: both were perceived as both generative and corrupting.[13] In Nicholas Culpepper's opinion, the "fondness" of breast-feeding mothers or wet nurses for their children could "do more mischief then the Devil himself."[14] The perceived duplicity of both womb and breast articulated a nexus of early modern anxieties about the maternal body and its influence on the vulnerable infant.

These anxieties were central to thinking on greensickness because the maternal appetite (for unnatural food and for excessive intimacy) influenced in turn the infant appetites being formed at the maternal body. The womb (and its blood) was a form of infant sustenance that preceded the breast (and its milk). But the lactating breast was also the bleeding womb under a different guise. The duplication of the two fluid-producing maternal organs had a functional premise (breast milk was simply womb blood transformed through the action of maternal love), but it also had a moral and semiotic premise: both organs were subject to the early modern perception of "women's treachery in the feeding situation."[15] The victims of "feeding" treachery were infants, whose appetites were formed first in the womb and then at the breast—appetites that emerged again at adolescence and that (if they met with "unnatural food") would, Culpepper thought, "make a devil of a saint."[16] *Romeo and Juliet*'s green vision relies on the conceptual association between womb/blood and breast/milk: both are bound up in the play's concern with corrupted appetites and unnatural "foods."

Appetite was a crucial element of early modern perceptions of the virgins' disease, its corruption of the blood, and the cluster of ideas I am describing as "green." The OED's premodern examples of green as a signifier of desire include the desire for actions, food, and sex. Across the corpus, Shakespeare uses green widely and for different purposes, but he frequently uses the word to describe those desires and appetites (of both men and women) that are sickly or dangerous in some way. The full early modern meaning of green as dangerous desires and appetites is yet to be explored critically, but my reading of *Romeo and Juliet* goes some way in this direction. Early modern medical authorities understood greensickness, like melancholy, as a corruption of the blood and digestion, affecting the judgment and appetites. In his *Erotomania* (1623, 1640), Jacques Ferrand, following Hippocrates, describes love as "a kind of poison engendered within the body, and taken in at the eyes." Such "poison" "deprave[s] the judgement, and corrupt[s] the blood."[17] More recently, Gail Kern Paster reads the concern that early modern greensickness narratives express over erroneous appetites as indicative of "a cultural perception that the virgins' disease involves a skewed relation to the object world—a perverse misclassification and misuse of things."[18]

It might, perhaps, be helpful to think about early modern green desire as "bitter" or "sour": as that erroneous desire which turns back upon the subject like the poison of retained and corrupted blood. Sufferers of the virgins' disease did not yearn for bitter food, but their desire for alkaline food was thought to extend from the bitter humor accumulating in their stomach due to blocked menses. Certainly, *Romeo and Juliet* utilizes the bitterness of green desire in its thinking about poison and medicine as the fruits of the earth, the "foods" for which the "sick" lovers yearn.

* * *

Compared to the other plays, *Romeo and Juliet* contains many instances of "earth" as a sign for the human body. Capulet's revelation that Juliet is the last of his children alive is a primogenitary vision of fleshly descent that plays on the two meanings of earth: "earth hath swallowed all my hopes but she; / She's the hopeful lady of my earth" (1.2.14–15). Romeo thinks Juliet's beauty is too rich for her (and his) "earth" and that Juliet is now his "centre" or soul, to which his body, his "dull earth," must return (1.5.46; 2.1.2). And Juliet condemns her own body to death: "vile earth to earth resign" (3.2.59). But *Romeo and Juliet*'s investment in the earth/body figure is especially attuned to the image of the earth as a mother and the perilous process by which the earth's "children" enter and exit her womb. Friar Lawrence makes the point most elaborately:

> The earth that's nature's mother is her tomb;
> What is her burying grave, that is her womb;
> And from her womb children of diverse kind
> We sucking on her natural bosom find [both canker and grace].
> (2.3.9)

The Friar's analogy sees human beings as plants emerging out of the earth and returning to her womb/tomb, having spent a life feeding from her breast. The analogy is uneven since the "milk" that the plants/humans feed on is other plants, those "baleful weeds" and "precious-juiced flowers" he is collecting from his garden (2.3.8). But the ease with which his speech ranges across images of bloody wombs/tombs, feeding, plants, medicine and bitter poison (images in which the play is elsewhere steeped) does have an associative logic of its own. The four lines of the Friar's speech that I have quoted stand at the center of the play's green vision: the earth is a womb from which people emerge and to which they return, but it is also the breast that feeds us while we are here. Such an earth is nothing if not duplicitous. As in early modern thinking on "green" women's duplicitous blood and milk, the Friar's earth/womb gives life but also takes it away and its breast/milk feeds both medicine and poison.

The Friar's meditation works through numerous formulations of the human/plant analogy, but the application of his conclusions remains general: all humans, like all plants, are capable of good and evil, open to life and corruption. Their earthly capacities can be turned to medicine ("grace") or poison ("rude will") (2.3.23–28). With Romeo's entrance, however, the Friar's moralizing takes on a more particular application. In the Folio version of 2.3.22–23 Romeo enters the stage just as the Friar refers to a particular plant: "within the infant rind of this weak flower / Poison hath residence, and medicine power." The point is made even without such an explicit referent (Romeo's entrance after the lines are spoken invites comparison nonetheless), but the Folio's stage direction ensures the message is impossible to ignore: Romeo is the weak flower whose "infant rind" (both a youthful/attractive exterior and a soft or sour shell) hides the duplicitous effect he has on those who consume him. He is the flower that "being smelt, with that part cheers each part, / Being tasted, stays all senses with the heart" (2.3.24–25).

In the preceding balcony scene, Juliet has fallen into the very trap that Romeo-as-flower represents. Her assertion that "that which we call a rose / By any other name would smell as sweet" constitutes a failure to identify him correctly. Using language that echoes the Friar's, she enjoys Romeo's "sweet" "smell," which has, of course, "cheer[ed]" her. But she then proceeds to "dr[ink]" of his "tongue's uttering" (2.2.43–59). Juliet's wish that "this bud of love, by summer's ripening breath, / May prove a beauteous flower" (2.2.121–22) foreruns the play's assertion, some ninety-five lines later, that the rose she longs to taste and see blossom is in fact poison to her. The lovers' "sweet" first encounter will, in Tybalt's words, "convert to bitt'rest gall" (1.5.91).

Juliet's appetite for dangerous medicine has, however, already been suggested by the Nurse's account of her weaning. On the evening of the Capulet feast, Lady Capulet and the Nurse speak to Juliet about marriage to the Prince. Before Lady Capulet can raise the subject, the Nurse retells the story of Juliet's weaning eleven years prior: on the day of the earthquake, the Nurse sat down in the garden and put wormwood on her breast to deter the three-year-old Juliet from feeding. We are told that the Capulets were away in Mantua, that the day before Juliet had suffered a "perilous" fall and broken her brow, and that after the fall the Nurse's husband had lifted Juliet up, joking with her: "dost thou fall upon thy face? / Thou wilt fall backwards when thou hast more wit / Wilt thou not, Jule?" To the merriment of the Nurse and her husband, the child looked up through her "bitter" tears and replied "ay" (1.3.17–49).

The weaning narrative is a story of serious physical danger told in comic tones; it is an account of loss and separation remembered with affection and intimacy; it is a story of innocence lost told as though it were about innocence; it is, as Paster notes, a narrative loaded with "disjunction and rupture."[19] Early modern guidebooks recommended that infants be breastfed by their mothers (advice that aristocratic women seem to have largely ignored), that infants be weaned much earlier than three years old, and that weaning with wormwood be avoided except as a last resort.[20] Juliet's appetite has thus been formed by the very "unnatural food" that Culpepper fears is the product of "women's treachery in the feeding situation." By Culpepper's definition, both the Nurse and Lady Capulet fail Juliet: the one by feeding too much and the other not enough. Lady Capulet severed the humoral and relational thread connecting womb blood to breast milk when she sent Juliet off to the Nurse, and the Nurse's narrative provides ample evidence of what breast-feeding guides would describe as excessive fondness for her charge. We are told that the Nurse lost her own child: the girl of Juliet's age who initiated the Nurse's lactation and for whom Juliet became a surrogate. The fact that Juliet is still feeding at three years old could be attributed to the infant's own excessive appetite, her emotional "hunger" after removal from her mother.[21] Or it could be attributed to the Nurse's (emotional and economic) desire to feed. Both experiences of hunger would, of course, perpetuate each other in the feeding situation and exacerbate the trauma of separation at weaning.

The diseases that attended weaning were numerous, and Valerie Fildes has suggested that among them might be counted melancholia. Early modern aristocratic breast-feeding cultures with their double trauma of geographic and somatic separation (from birth mother and then from nurse) may themselves, Fildes suggests, have been a cause of the melancholia suffered by the social class that was wet-nursed in early modern societies.[22] Like the transition from blood to milk, the transition from milk to food was considered a dangerous period in an infant's life, attended by potential mortality, and yet Juliet's weaning takes place on the same day as an earthquake, on the day after her "perilous" knock to the brow, and while her parents are absent. At the narrative (and psychological) center of the trauma surrounding Juliet's weaning is the husband's rendering of the child's fall as a sexual event: "thou wilt fall backwards when thou hast more wit / Wilt thou not, Jule?" By soliciting Juliet's assent that the blood on her brow foreruns her impending sexual maturation, the Nurse's husband codes that sexual fall in the same painful terms as the child's injury—a pain further confirmed the following day by the "bitter" separation from the Nurse's dug and the trauma of the earthquake. The Nurse's retelling of this story just before Juliet's emotionally absent mother proposes marriage further confirms how collapsed the two key moments in Juliet's sexual and appetitive development are along the same psychological fault line of loss and separation. Juliet's emerging sexual appetite is thus already "bitter": a fact further evidenced by the subtle but definite point made by the Nurse's wormwood-poisoned dug.

The image of the Nurse's "bitter" dug stands alongside the Friar's earth/womb/breast image at the center of the play's green vision. Both are built from the speakers' very different capacities: the Friar's reasoned rhyming couplets are shaped by the "learning" that the garrulous Nurse later wishes she too had received (3.3.160), while the Nurse's account is comic, meandering, emotional, and illogical. But from the Nurse's stream-of-consciousness comes those details (of Juliet's weaning) that not only articulate the figurative truth that structures and gives meaning to the play but which offer an astonishing version of the Friar's same thought: both speakers think in the analogous terms of body/earth, food/plants, milk/medicine.

Why was Juliet weaned on the day of the earthquake? The event is almost absurdly portentous. The Nurse may, as Barbara Everett has suggested, be too addled to remember her dates correctly, in which case the telescoping of events that her story sets up emerges from a psychological rather than actual truth.[23] Both ways of reading the conjunction between earthquake and weaning are just as portentous and both share the same earth/body vision upon which the Friar's plant/human analogy rests. We could say that through the play's green vision, Juliet's "bitter" passage from milk to poison is echoed in the earthquake: the earthiness of the infant Juliet's body "falls," "stint[s]," and "shakes" when her milk source turns to poison, and in sympathy the earth itself shudders (1.3.34; 1.3.49). Or, conversely (and therefore in keeping with the duplicity of breast/womb/earth), Juliet "fall[s] out wi'th'dug": both the Nurse's dug and the earth's dug (1.3.33). In this way, the Nurse's account brings an arresting emotional and pathological force to the Friar's more philosophical and measured depiction of the earth as womb, as a source of human sustenance (the plant/breast we feed on) and the matter from which humans-as-plants are formed. At the very least, the earthquake serves to deepen the play's awareness of how integrated the earth is in the appetitive formation human beings undergo as they emerge through the stages of bodily maturation: blood, milk, food.

Wormwood oil is a green and bitter ointment; from an early modern point of view, Juliet's consumption of it is an unfortunate introduction to her food-only diet. The weaning story sets up an economy of bodily fluids in which blood, milk, and poison are transmuted into each other, not by the maternal love that was thought to heat and distill womb-blood into breast-milk, but instead by bitterness and separation. The presence of blood (from Juliet's broken brow) at the moment of weaning might also be read as a sign of the wet-nursed child's retrograde motion through the fluids: the poison of wormwood (her first food) recalls the poisoned, "unnatural," or bitter state of her earlier sustenance (both milk and blood). But the economy of fluids can also be read forward: the poisoned matter on which Juliet's appetite was formed signals that the blood of Juliet's impending sexual "fall" will also be poisonous.

Crucially, I think the weaning story functions as a greensickness narrative: it not only anticipates the corruption of Juliet's sexual maturation but is itself constructed out of the same anxieties. Juliet's weaning, like her subsequent "plucking," is bitter, traumatic, recorded in earthly and vegetative terms, and "perilous." Her weaning is focused around the fraught relationship between her appetitive development and that blood (in the form of both blood and milk) that ought to sustain her infant body and ensure she makes it through the difficult passage of sexual, humoral, and moral maturation. I hope to show that in the same way her "plucking" is focused around corrupted appetites and the dangerous foods to which they turn.

* * *

As a greensickness narrative, a narrative of sexual and appetitive development, Juliet's story of weaning and pre-sexual "fall" is offered as a sign of danger: to readers and audience members already attuned to the perils of "green," Juliet's subsequent readiness to fall passionately and dangerously in love with the son of the rival dynasty is perhaps only to be expected. The play's green vision invites such expectation by having Lady Capulet and the Nurse follow directly upon the weaning narrative with repeated descriptions of Paris as a "flower." The duplicitousness of flowers, articulated so clearly by the Friar in the following act, is first established through the Nurse's wormwood and Juliet's willingness to see both her suitors as flowers. Only one of these flowers (the "rose") is the one for whom Juliet will feel the green desire that is both passionate longing and bitterness. That is, only one flower is the kind for which Juliet's bitter weaning has prepared her. By following the lovers' hunger for what they believe to be medicine or "comfort," but what is actually poison to them, it becomes clear that the economy of fluids set up in the Nurse's story is one to which Romeo is also subject. Both Romeo and Juliet suffer from the same corrupted appetite and "skewed relation to the object world" that early moderns attributed to sufferers of greensickness.

Through her work on breastfeeding cultures, Gail Kern Paster articulates the oppositions between "blood" parents and "milk" parents. Paster and Fildes both describe these relationships as marked by separation and loss; detachment and reattachment; the seeking, provision, and removal of food and comfort; and, ultimately, the failure to provide infants with consistent sources of sustenance and emotional security.[24] The Nurse is Juliet's milk parent, and the Friar is Romeo's. Like Juliet with her blood parents (the Capulets), Romeo shares with Lord and Lady Montague the emotional remove of a wet-nursed infant. The Friar, however, is Romeo's confidant and advisor and his source of "comfort": "I'll give thee armour . . . Adversity's sweet *milk*, philosophy, / To comfort thee" (3.3.54–55, emphasis mine). However, I think a third category needs to be added to those provided by Paster: the "food" parent. Arriving as it did after weaning, this source of sustenance was not embodied by one person or one parental couple (as were blood and milk). Instead, I think the "food" parent can be identified in *Romeo and Juliet* as that absent source of nourishment for which early modern wet-nursed infants longed once they were weaned and which reemerged at adolescents in the form of a lover or passionate longing.

One could, of course, posit a similar role (and through established Freudian idiom) in more modern societies, but early modern wet-nursing cultures were so beset by repeated acts of separation and reattachment that they can be said to have created distinct appetitive patterns that combined longing and bitterness over a long period of development. I think Fildes's observation on wet-nursing cultures as a potential cause of melancholy deserves greater attention here: one way of understanding the greensickness explored by *Romeo and Juliet* is as a bitter appetite for a source of comfort that is always already removed and which turns instead on the subject who, in longing for a love or passion that is thwarted or unrequited, instead embraces death. Just as the greensick virgin's blocked menses poison her body and corrupt her appetite, so the badly weaned adolescent lovers form "an unnatural longing for such things as are noxious, and unfit for food."[25] Romeo and Juliet see each other as medicine, comfort, and good "food" when in fact their fraught social and familial environment has already determined that they are each the other's poison. In this way, the greensickness narratives of both lovers can be traced through their ongoing search for food and comfort, poison and medicine—from the Nurse, the Friar, the impoverished Apothecary and, ultimately, from each other.

The Friar's meditation on the duplicity of plants articulates the risks attending a "green" subject's longing for sustenance: "comfort" will come in the form of both medicine and poison. But the successive nature of this longing and of the relationships that feed it is suggested by Benvolio when he advises Romeo to "take thou some new infection to thy eye, / And the rank poison of the old will die" (1.2.48–49). Benvolio's description of lovers as poison is figurative, just as the play's many descriptions of Juliet's suitors as flowers are figurative, but both sets of signifiers establish the lovers' mutual desire for their not-yet-encountered other as yearnings for medicinal or poisonous food. Once the lovers meet and the crisis of their situation makes the greenness of their longing both a pathological and a social reality, their quest for "comfort" escalates. Romeo is twice called to "comfort" Juliet, first by the Nurse and then by the Friar (3.3.139; 3.3.147). And Romeo is himself given "comfort" by the nurse when she brings him Juliet's ring (3.3.165).

Juliet's search for comfort and her movement through the various "food" relationships available to her is given special emphasis and realizes a particularly affecting tragedy in light of her weaning story. Until Juliet marries Romeo, the Nurse inhabits the place of "food"-giver: Juliet turns to her for all forms of comfort and sustenance. But when Romeo is banished and the Capulets demand that their daughter marry the Prince or be disowned, the successive losses of the "green" subject's blood, milk, and food relationships are again rehearsed in the span of a single scene. Emphatically rejected by her blood parents and their command to "hang, beg, starve, die in the streets" (3.5.192), Juliet cries desperately and repeatedly to the Nurse for "comfort" (3.5.208–212). The Nurse comforts her charge by suggesting she instead marry the Prince. Having once again "fall[en] out wi'th'dug," Juliet registers the Nurse's betrayal quietly. She ends the conversation by thanking her, with no little irony: "thou hast comforted me marvellous much" (3.5.230). Once alone,

Juliet vocalizes her new separation from the Nurse (her milk-parent and her more recent food-parent): "Go, counsellor! / Thou and my bosom henceforth shall be twain." Juliet vows to either reattach to Romeo's food-parent, the Friar, or to die: "I'll to the friar to know his remedy / If all else fail, myself have power to die" (3.5.239–242).

Capulet's concern in this scene that his daughter is "greensickness carrion" is therefore laden with tragic irony: by disowning her he initiates the repetition of those "bitter" separations that characterize the weaning culture to which Juliet has been victim and from which Juliet's greensickness may have emerged. Juliet's green desire for the forbidden Romeo may already be irrevocable, but this one short scene ensures her desire realizes its most poisonous potential. Juliet will now have Romeo or die; but for the Friar's brief remaining service as provider of medicine, Romeo has come to inhabit the place of Juliet's food-giver. The succeeding narrative of the sleep-potion takes on a relevance to Juliet's greenness that is both ironic and terribly apt. Alone in her bedroom with the poison vial, she falters and thinks again—briefly—of her blood and milk parents: "I'll call them back again to comfort me. / Nurse!'—What should she do here? My dismal scene I needs must act alone" (4.3.17–19). Even in the tomb, Juliet still seeks comfort from someone other than her poisoned "rose." When waking from sleep, she cries: "O comfortable friar! Where is my lord?" (5.3.148). Finding Romeo dead, Juliet fulfils the "unnatural" trajectory of her green desire: the "cup" of "poison" that has killed him becomes her "friendly drop" and the poison on his lips enables her "to die with a restorative" (5.3.161–66).

Romeo's narrative moves through a similar succession of estrangements, and his final appeal to the impoverished Apothecary provides him with that medicine which the Friar could never give: "Come, cordial and not poison, go with me / To Juliet's grave; for there must I use thee" (5.1.85–86). In the final scenes, with Juliet asleep, it falls to Romeo to acknowledge the earth's role in the lovers' demise. Entering the tomb, Romeo curses the earth for having swallowed his love and promises to medicine it further with his own poison-"steep'd" flesh:

> Thou detestable maw, thou womb of death,
> Gorg'd with the dearest morsel of the earth,
> Thus I enforce thy rotten jaws to open,
> And in despite I'll cram thee with more food.
>   [*Romeo opens the tomb*]

The earth has now lost all trace of its life-giving, nurturing capacity; it is a devouring monster feeding on its own progeny. The earth-as-mother, a figure established by the Friar's and the Nurse's respective breastfeeding images, has continued to operate through the play's use of various medicines, poisons, and comforts: those earthly fruits that should nurture the needs of developing appetites but which (via the greenness caused by early modern failures to properly nurture infants) instead become poisonous.

Romeo's bitter observation at the end of the play that the earth has finally succeeded in eating its own children encapsulates the tragedy of his "green" love: it is Romeo's own corrupted appetites that have drawn him to this end, not the earth's appetites. Were we to read Romeo's words as an acknowledgment of the metaphorical truth articulated throughout the play (that he is himself part of the earth and must choose how best to consume the earth's gifts before returning to dust), then we might rightly expect from his speech a greater degree of self-admonishment and penitence. Instead Romeo continues to seek a source of "comfort" or food and find it lacking: this time the earth itself, which ought to have provided Romeo with the object of his desire, has instead devoured Juliet. But Romeo's figuring of the earth as a "womb of death" perhaps also signals his latent acknowledgment of the deathly "womb," the corrupted nourishment, on which the two wet-nursed and badly weaned infants were reared. He may know something has gone wrong at the appetitive level of his and Juliet's narrative, but he cannot pinpoint the real source of that mistake. His partial vision and his final desire to die epitomize the tragedy of those green appetites that "suck" on the earth's "bosom," looking for "sweet" blood and milk but finding only wormwood and "gall." The final and somewhat redemptive image provided by the play is of the lovers' golden statues, but behind this image hovers one that fulfils the play's green and tragic vision: the young lovers, "yet but green in earth," daubed in blood and poison, embracing in the belly of the earth.

PART IV

Proof

Chapter 10

"In Every Wound There is a Bloody Tongue"

Cruentation in Early Modern Literature and Psychology

LESEL DAWSON

Near the end of the anonymous play *Arden of Faversham* (1592), Alice and her lover Mosby have finally managed to kill Thomas Arden, Alice's husband, with the help of two hired murderers, Black Will and Shakebag. Although a number of seemingly chance occurrences suggest that providence will ensure that the guilty will be caught, it is only at the moment that Alice is made to confront her husband's body that she admits to her part in the crime. The Mayor directs Alice's gaze toward Arden's corpse and awaits her response to his accusation of guilt:

> *Mayor.* See, Mistress Arden, where your husband lies.
>   Confess this foul fault and be penitent.
> *Alice.* Arden, sweet husband, what shall I say?
>   The more I sound his name the more he bleeds.
>   This blood condemns me and in gushing forth
>   Speaks as it falls and asks me why I did it.
>   Forgive me, Arden; I repent me now;
>   And would my death save thine thou shouldst not die.[1]

Alice recognizes that the game is up; it is not just the circumstantial evidence but Arden's blood itself that condemns her. Alice's proximity to her husband's body makes his wounds bleed afresh, and this occurrence identifies her as the killer.

Cruentation, also known as the ordeal of touch or bier rite, in which the victim's wounds bleed spontaneously in the presence of the murderer, was seen as a vital form of evidence in early modern Europe; Malcolm Gaskill, in his study of early modern English depositions, has demonstrated that bier rite was often used to identify the murderer and secure a conviction.[2] A similar pattern can be found in murder pamphlets and domestic plays about crime and punishment. As Subha Mukherji observes, within these narratives "God is not merely the omniscient spectator, but also a maker of theatrical shows" uncovering "His own intention—through 'manifest tokens.'"[3] Like ghostly apparitions and bizarre coincidences, cruentation reveals God's hand in uncovering sin; as one pamphlet puts it, it engineers "Gods revenge, against the crying and execrable sinne of murther."[4]

Traditionally seen as a heaven-sent miracle, cruentation was also given a variety of natural and magical explanations by medieval and early modern theologians and natural philosophers.[5] While these did not necessarily challenge the providential nature of cruentation (God could be seen as acting through secondary natural causes as well as directly through miracles), they articulate different assumptions about the physiology of the dead, about the spiritual and psychic consequences of murder, and about the nature of the material world. While some writers suggest that cruentation is caused by corpses retaining some form of consciousness or vitality, others held that it was caused by the murderer's presence through guilty rays emanating from the eyes, which heat up the wounds, causing them to flow. Another model attributes the postmortem bleeding to an exchange of *spiritus* between the murderer and victim during the act of violence, a phenomenon that makes it analogous to Neoplatonic models of lovesickness. In each of these theories blood provides proof not only of the suspect's guilt, but also of wider beliefs behind the process itself: it offers, alternatively, proof of God's providence, proof of the corpse's lingering vitality, or proof of the relationship created between the murder and victim at the moment of violence.

In this chapter, I will offer an overview of explanations for cruentation and explore their psychological implications, supporting Lucy Munro's observation that early modern stage blood is "both corporeal and symbolic, appealing to spectators' eyes, emotions and intelligence simultaneously."[6] I will argue that explanations for cruentation frequently provide a material basis for complex psychological processes and structures, offering insight into the operation of guilt on the psyche and its impact on subjectivity. Although the legal function of cruentation is to identify the killer, literary texts also highlight its profound emotional and psychological impact, in which the murderer reexperiences the act of wounding from the position of spectator rather than actor. This shift in vantage point can be transformative: callous individuals whose sole aim is murder are frequently flooded with guilt and remorse. Whereas in legal history cruentation provides vital evidence, in literary texts it becomes the means through which murderers come to see and understand their own sin: the function of cruentation thus moves from being an identification of guilt to a profound apprehension of what it means to be guilty. If Michael Schoenfeldt has highlighted the closed, self-contained Stoical self as an early modern ideal, here the subject's redemption depends on his or her receptive openness to the powerful affective force of the mutilated corpse.[7]

* * *

Although cruentation is sometimes traced to ancient times by early modern writers, it probably has medieval origins and is related to the trial by ordeal, in which suspects were asked to undergo a dangerous trial to establish their innocence.[8] Robert P. Brittain describes the practice:

> The usual procedure was as follows: the suspect was placed at a certain distance from the victim who had been laid naked on his back. He approached the body, repeatedly calling on it by name, then walked round it two or three times. He next lightly stroked the wounds with his hand. If during this time fresh bleeding occurred, or if the body moved, or if foam appeared at the mouth, the suspect was considered to be guilty of murder; if not, further evidence was sought. Sometimes the whole local population was made to pass in front of the corpse. A positive result was considered as evidence of divine intervention.[9]

Gaskill has demonstrated that bier rite "was actually performed, often on official orders," at times providing a key piece of evidence to prove a suspect's guilt.[10] For example, when William Sherwood denies having killed Richard Hobsen, despite being "embrued in his fellowes blood," Sherwood is confirmed as the murderer when "he beeing brought to the slaine bodie, the blood which was settled, issued out a freshe."[11] In another source, the murderer's presence is discovered through cruentation. Although Arnold Cosby initially avoids capture after stabbing Lord Bourgh multiple times, when he inadvertently nears the house where his victim lay dying in his attempt to escape, Lord Bourgh's "wounds bled more freshlie then when the[y] were first giuen, whereby the people in the house beeing agast at that suddaine and straunge spectacle made forthe to search, for surelie they supposed the murtherer was not farre off."[12] Their hunch proves right and Crosby is apprehended.

Frequently cruentation prompts the murderer's confession, highlighting the bleeding body's power to move the passions and stir the soul. Gail Kern Paster's claims for the porous and labile early modern humoral body "with its faulty borders and penetrable stuff" can here be extended to corpses, which appear highly reactive to the murderer's presence, gaze, and voice.[13] The anonymous *Sundrye Strange and Inhumaine Murthers* (1591), for example, tells a particularly grisly story about a father who hires a man to kill his three youngest children in the hopes that he will gain the hand of a wealthy widow, who has refused his offer of marriage because of his children. Initially the murderer gets away and the father buries the children in a hole under the floorboards. Eventually, however, the hired killer is apprehended and taken back to the house where the bodies are dug up. Although there is a spring under the ground, which causes the children's bodies and wounds to become "clear and white," they change when in the presence of the murderer:

> the father being there also, the woundes began to bleede afresh, which when the Crowner sawe, hee commanded the partie apprehended to looke upon the children, which hee did, and called them by their names, whereupon, behold the wonderfull works of God, for the fact being still denied, the bodies of the children, which seemed white like unto soaked flesh laid in water, sodainely received their former colour of bloude, and had such a lively countenance flushing in theyr faces, as if they had been living creatures lying asleepe, which indeede blushed on the murthers—when they wanted grace to blush and bee ashamed of theyr owne wickedness. Which wonderfull miracle caused the murderer there present not onely to confesse and acknowledge himself giltie of that damnable deede, but also to accuse the father of the children as principal procurer of their untimely deaths.[14]

The dead children respond vividly to the presence of the murderer: their bodies bleed and their faces flush, blushing with shame "on the murthers." The murderer too is changed: he is overcome with guilt and speaks on his victims' behalf, accusing himself and their father of the "damnable deede." The murderer's change of heart in the presence of his victims and his mirroring of their behavior suggests the visual and physiological component to sympathy, supporting Eric Langley's claims that the early modern "vocabulary of sympathy" is "increasingly tainted—infected even—by medically informed connotations of contagion."[15] In this example, however, the process happens in reverse; if early modern contagion depends upon an underlying likeness between individuals, here the mirroring is the consequence of the physiological exchange rather than its precondition.

The wealth of testimonies to individuals seeing cruentation and the widespread belief in it as a real phenomenon prompts a number of questions: did people actually believe that they saw corpses bleeding, or was this just a convenient means of making an accusation of someone suspected of the crime? Gaskill argues that in early modern testimonies miraculous phenomena (such as cruentation, ghosts, and dreams) can "be interpreted as fictions enabling witnesses not just to testify with conviction, but to distance themselves from the origin of their evidence."[16] In referring to "fictions," however, Gaskill is not suggesting that these stories are deliberately falsified. Rather, Gaskill daws on Natalie Zemon Davis's analysis of the fabricated elements of testimony from those appealing for mercy in sixteenth-century France, in which fiction refers not to "their feigned elements, but rather . . . their forming, shaping, and molding elements: the crafting of a narrative"; such fictions, according to Zemon Davis, "did not necessarily lend falsity to an account; it might well bring verisimilitude or a moral truth."[17] In cases when there is someone the local community already suspects, cruentation can secure a conviction of murder that might otherwise go unproved. When, for example, the local women who lay out Sarah Langhorne's body testify that her body bleeds at her husband's touch, their claim corroborates a widely held view that she died as the result of the violent beatings her husband was known to give her.[18] As Gaskill observes, cruentation is here not "the occasion when his guilt was laid bare before his astonished neighbours, but as a public display which vocalized a firmly entrenched belief that this beating had caused her death."[19]

Even those who were skeptical about the validity and origin of the phenomenon recognized that the arrangement and performance of the trial nevertheless often revealed a great deal. As the anonymous writer of *Five*

Philosophical Questions Most Eloquently and Substantially Disputed (1650) observed: "dead bodies being removed doe often bleed, and then he whose conscience is tainted with the Synteresis of the fact, is troubled in such sort, that by his mouth or gesture he often bewrayes his owne guiltinesse." Suspects thus had to be watched closely to see if their facial expression or body language suggested their guilt; Michael Dalton in *The Countrey Justice* (1618) instructs magistrates to look for a suspect's "change of . . . countenance, his blushing, looking downewards, silence, trembling."[20] A refusal to participate could be seen as a sign of guilt, and sometimes the very thought of having to undergo the trial led to the guilty confessing before they could be tested.[21] However, as Lynn Alison Robson demonstrates, there does not appear to be a straightforward shift within the period from superstitious belief to a more rational approach to criminal cases based on empirical evidence; as she writes, "The pamphlet accounts of the influence of apparitions all come from the second half of the century, while the importance of what we would now term 'forensic' evidence is clear in pamphlets from the first half."[22]

The origin of cruentation could be explained via divine, occult, or natural causes. At times, these ideas overlapped; as Francesco Paolo de Ceglia suggests, "for some the phenomenon was natural, for others supernatural, for still others, the one and other at the same time."[23] Most commonly, cruentation was regarded as a divine miracle and part of a wider providential design in which the murderer is punished; or, as one murder pamphlet puts it, "Against this sin of Murther, the wrath of God hath been revealed from heaven, by his just and daily revengings of innocent blood upon Murtherers."[24] Texts frequently depict the blood itself as crying for vengeance, probably alluding to God's words to Cain that "The voice of thy brothers bloud crieth unto me out of the ground" (Genesis, 4.10). Describing the phenomenon in *Daemonologie* (1597), for example, King James writes:

> in a secret murther, if the deade carcase be at any time thereafter handled by the murtherer, it wil gush out of bloud, as if the blud wer crying to the heaven for revenge of the murtherer, God having appoynted that secret super-naturall signe, for tryall of that secrete unnaturall crime.[25]

Robson has argued persuasively that murder pamphlets follow a "distinctive chain-link structure which began with original sin, [and] progressed through sinfulness to murder, condemnation, death and salvation through

God's divine grace," a narrative pattern that "had its foundations in Calvinist theology and ideas of providence and predestination."[26] These texts, as Randall Martin writes, thus "reconstructed murderers' lives as allegorical narratives of transgression and redemption to advance a Calvinist agenda of spiritual and social reform."[27] Although literary texts are rarely this formulaic in their construction, plays (such as *Arden of Faversham*) frequently depict cruentation as a divinely authored event that triggers the murderer's confession and repentance. In the anonymous *A Warning to Fair Women* (1599), John Beane's cruentation is perceived by the onlookers as the workings of God's providence; as one observer remarks, "in the case of blood / God's justice hath been still miraculous."[28] The exception to such a pattern appears to be the Duke of Gloucester in Shakespeare's *Richard III*. Unmoved by Lady Anne's claims that it is God's outrage at the murder of Henry VI that causes his wounds to "Ope their congealed mouths and bleed afresh" in his presence, Richard proceeds to seduce Anne over the body of her dead husband.[29] Moreover, while Richard does eventually have a crisis of conscience that, I will argue, appropriates the discourse of cruentation, even here what is so striking is his conscious rejection of this ethical insight.

In some accounts, cruentation was caused by the soul remaining in the body for a period of time after the person was killed.[30] The sense that there was a liminal period during which the dead retained some vitality could be accounted for in several ways; while a few writers held that the soul itself remained alive for a brief period after the body's death, more suggested that one of the lesser parts of the soul (such as the animal soul) would retain life for a short period. As Katharine Park has argued with regard to the late medieval period, early modern northern Europeans also saw death as "an extended and gradual process, corresponding to the slow decomposition of the corpse," in which recently dead bodies were, for a liminal period, seen as "active, sensitive, or semianimate, possessed of a gradually fading life."[31] In George Chapman's *The Revenge of Bussy D'Ambois* (>1613), for example, Clermont draws on this view to explain the presence of ghosts of the Guise, Monsieur, Cardinal Guise, and Chatillon, who appear in order to celebrate Clermont's successful revenge:

>   learned'st men hold that our sensitive spirits
> A little time abide about the graves
> Of their deceased bodies, and can take
> In cold condensed air the same forms they had
> When they were shut up in this body's shade.[32]

The dead victim could also be seen as causing the spontaneous bleeding through a "*post-mortem imagination*, able to produce effects within its own body or in the bodies of others."[33] Here the murdered victim's fury causes the blood to heat and flow, either because there remains some vestige of consciousness or because the victim's thoughts and feelings are imprinted on the body and blood. As Lemnius explains in *The Secret Miracles of Nature* (1658), because "in dead people for a time there remains a vegetable force, whereby their hair and nails increase,"

> blood will run forth of the wound, though it be bound over with swathbands, if he that did the murder stand by. For so great is the force of secret Nature, and so powerful is Imagination, that if there be any life left, or the dead body be warm, the blood will boyl, and wax hot by choler kindled in the dead body.[34]

In many accounts, the victim's hatred of the murderer is encoded in the blood through *spiritus*, a highly refined and invisible vapor of blood that connects the body and soul. Francis Bacon accepts this view, suggesting that a strong imagination can operate on "Things Living, Or that have, been Living" via *spiritus*, so that if the cause of cruentation "be *Naturall*, it must be referred to *Imagination*."[35] And Cornelius Gemma argues in *De naturae divinis characterismis* (1575) that "images or ideas etched and represented in the thickened blood would persist until the third day, and, in the presence of the murderer, would activate the residue of the spirit."[36] A similar idea is advocated by Walter Charleton, whose emotive language sits interestingly beside his mechanical account of the phenomenon:

> we may conceive, that the Phansy of the Person assaulted by an Assassine, having formed an Idea of Hatred, Opposition, and Revenge, and the same being Characterized upon the Spirits, and by them diffused through the blood; though the blood become much less Fluid in the veins after death, by reason the vital influence and Pulsifick Faculty of the Heart, which Animated and Circulated it, is extinct: yet, because at the praesence of the Murderer, there issue from the pores of his body such subtile Emanations, as are Consimilar to those, which were emitted from him, at the time He strove with overcame, and killed the Patient; and those Emanations entering the Dead Body, doe cause a fresh Commotion in

> the blood remaining yet somewhat Fluid in its veins, and as it were renew the former Colluctation or Duell betwixt the yet wholly uncondensed Spirits of the slain, and those of the Homicide: therefore is it, that the Blood, suffering an Estuation, flows up and down in the veins, to seek some vent, or salley-port; and finding none so open as in that part, wherein the wound was made, it issues forth from thence.[37]

In the presence of the murderer, the corpse's blood bubbles and boils, reacting to the "subtile Emanations" that issue from the murderer's pores. Keen to "renew the former Colluction or Duell," the fight carries on after death though physiological reactions that, although mechanical, capture something of the crackling electricity and jolt of uncanny recognition that a confrontation between murderer and victim could entail.[38]

From the skeleton of Hoffman's father in *The Tragedy of Hoffman* (1602) to the Lady's ghost in Middleton's *The Second Maiden's Tragedy* (1611), the dead in early modern literature also display a "lingering liveliness" and are capable of inciting action and bearing grudges.[39] In revenge plays, in particular, bloodthirsty ghosts demand retribution no matter what the cost to their living survivors. In Shakespeare's *Titus Andronicus* (1594), for example, Titus claims that the sacrifice of Alarbus be enacted "T'appease their groaning shadows that are gone."[40] And in Jasper Heywood's *Troas* (1559), a translation of Seneca's *The Trojan Women*, the ghost of Achilles demands the death of Polyxina, the woman he was promised in marriage: "Vengeance he craves with blood his death to quit." As if satisfying the ghost's vampiric appetite, when Polyxina is killed, "Her blood the tomb up drunk."[41] A similar moment occurs in Marston's *Antonio's Revenge* after the protagonist achieves revenge for his dead father by murdering his enemy's innocent son, Julio, and sprinkling the child's blood on his father's tomb. The ghost of Antonio's father appears to be pleased: "From under the stage a groan" is heard (sd 5.3). Antonio then speaks directly to his father:

> Ghost of my poisoned sire, suck this fume;
> To sweet revenge perfume thy circling air
> With smoke of blood. I sprinkle round his gore,
> And dew thy hearse with these fresh reeking drops.
> Lo, thus I heave my blood-dyed hands to heaven:
> Even like insatiate hell, still crying: more.

> My heart that thirsting dropsies after gore.
> Sound peace and rest to church, night ghosts, and graves;
> Blood cries for blood, and murder murder craves.[42]

The sheer brutality of this scene, in which Antonio murders an innocent child to appease his father's ghost, foregrounds the maliciousness of the dead and their ability to bend the will of the living. Antonio may hold up his "blood-dyed hands to heaven," but they seem more like the product of hell. Thirsting after blood, Antonio's final words suggest that revengers not only reenact crimes, but also replicate venomous psychological states.

The belief in *spiritus* and its ability to act directly on bodies external to the self was also the source of another explanation of cruentation, which suggests that it is the murderer who instigates the spontaneous bleeding. In this account, the corpse's bleeding is caused by rays of *spiritus* emitted from the eyes of the murderer, whose imagination is fired by guilty anguish. *The Problemes of Aristotle* (1595), for example, describes how the murderer

> is in anguish of mind, and in a great heat, through the strong imagination which he hath conceiued, and by that meanes all his spirits doe stirre and boyle and repaire vnto the instruments of the sight, and so goe out by the beames of the sight of the eies vnto the wounds which are made, the which if they bee fresh, doe presently fall a bleeding.[43]

If Charleton's account describes cruentation as the product of pressure building up in the victim's body, here it is the murderer's body that becomes heated and overflows. This explanation clearly has some correlation with the evil eye and other kinds of occult activity in which the imagination of one party impacts the body of another.

Mary Floyd-Wilson focuses on this explanation in her discussion of *Arden of Faversham*, arguing that it gives us in miniature a sense of the wider way that Alice's presence acts on the bodies, minds, and constitutions of those around. Discussing Alice's words to her dead husband, she observes: "Without a narrator . . . to insist that God directs the bleeding of Arden's corpse, the audience may believe that as Alice speaks her husband's name her passions and eye-beams provide the heat that causes his blood to flow."[44] Cruentation, for Floyd-Wilson, is another instance of sympathetic contagion, which highlights the dangerous and corrupting power of Alice's magnetic attractiveness.

Floyd-Wilson's reading gives a powerful sense not only of Alice's ability to captivate others, but also of Arden's culpability in the play: for Arden to be susceptible to Alice's influence he must also have an underlying sympathy with her.[45] However, if Alice's presence can be seen to act upon her husband's corpse causing it to bleed, we can also see the way in which the corpse works on Alice. It is only when confronting her husband's body that Alice fully understands what she has done.

There is a further explanation for cruentation that might provide a material basis for Alice's shift in perspective. This theory also attributes cruentation to vital spirits emitted from the eyes, but here the murderer and victim are seen to exchange *spiritus* at the moment of murder. It is an idea that the medieval theologian Giles of Rome puts forward and rejects in question 25 of *Quodlibet V*. As Steven P. Marrone describes:

> the explanation ran that in the violence of the act certain material spirits or vapors were generated in both the murderer and victim. Parts of these spirits or vapors were exchanged through eyes on the occasion of a mutual glance at the instant of the murder, so that when murderer and corpse were brought together again, the parts sought to return to the source whence they came, following the presumed rule that the part seeks to go back to the whole.[46]

Although this explanation is the least popular among early modern natural philosophers, it is in many ways the most evocative, in that it not only suggests that there is an oddly intimate aspect to violent crime, but also provides a physiological explanation for the rapidity with which murderers move from wrongdoing to remorse. Whereas the second set of theories focuses on the anger of the victim, and the third focuses on the guilt of the murderer, the fourth theory focuses on the interaction of the two.

Although Marrone suggests that this account could be regarded as "a purely mechanistic explanation" of cruentation as it is caused by "a perfectly routine operation involving material bodies, local motion and contact between agent and acted-upon," if one considers how the exchange of *spiritus* is regarded in Neoplatonic theory, this explanation can also be read as open to having a psychological significance in early modern literature. Within this framework, the material exchange described resembles less the one-way phenomenon of the evil eye, than the reciprocal gaze of lovers, who are also said to exchange *spiritus* when looking into one another's eyes.[47] According to Marsilio Ficino, the exchange of *spiritus* happens in lovesickness, in which the sufferer's hungry gaze acts as a magnet, drawing a thin vapor of blood out of the eyes of the beloved and toward the image in the mind. When love is reciprocated, the lovers' interlocked gaze allows for the physical exchange of *spiritus*, as in John Donne's "The Ecstasy" where the lovers' eyes are twisted and threaded "upon one double string."[48] The consequence of this exchange is spiritual as well as material: lovers exchange subject positions and selves. It is partly for this reason that being in love is said to allow for a greater self-knowledge, as one is able to apprehend oneself through the subject position of the beloved (just as one is able to see a tiny image of the self reflected in the beloved's eyes). This apprehension of the self through the beloved other is thus triggered by a dislocation of subjectivity that grants a new knowledge of the self.

In murder, the exchange of *spiritus* is attributable to an emanation (caused by fear and hatred) rather than a magnetic draw (caused by desire), but the exchange of spirit is the same. And there are, at times, similar psychic consequences in the aftermath of murder, in which the murderer is suddenly able to apprehend the crime from the position of victim. This shift is often evident when murderers speak on behalf of their victims. When it comes to cruentation, although the wounds may communicate the individual's guilt, it is the guilty person who often articulates the accusing words. In *Arden*, for example, although Alice sees the blood as speaking ("This blood condemns me, and in gushing forth / Speaks as it falls and asks me why I did it"), it is of course Alice who says these words, interpreting and, in some sense, inhabiting the perspective of her dead husband. That Alice is Arden's wife as well as his murderer is also significant, in that cruentation here could be seen to reignite a physiological exchange found in lovesickness.

Given the relative obscurity in early modern natural philosophy of this explanation for cruentation, one must be cautious about making too strong a link between medical theory and literary representation in this instance. However, even if we disregard the final medical account of cruentation, blood nevertheless functions repeatedly in early modern texts as the means through which the murderer recognizes and acknowledges his or her guilt, suggesting the ways in which the early modern subject's ethical understanding can have a physiological and visual component. In the anonymous *A Warning to Fair Women*, for example, George Browne murders George Sanders, whose wife he has fallen in love with and hopes to marry, and also seriously wounds John Beane, who happens to be accompanying Sanders when Browne assaults him. Later in the play, Browne is brought before Beane, whose "wounds break out afresh in bleeding" (4.4.135). Although Beane's cruentation is ultimately irrelevant (Beane names Browne as his murderer with his last breath), Browne's asides demonstrate a new understanding of his actions:

> I gave him fifteen wounds,
> Which now be fifteen mouths that do accuse me.
> In every wound there is a bloody tongue
> Which will all speak, although he hold his peace;
> By a whole Jury I shall be accused.
>
> (4.4.138–42)

Browne reacts with horror to the sight of his victim's body, whose freshly bleeding wounds enable him to reexperience his violent act and understand its significance: if "In every wound there is a blood tongue," then Browne sees Beane's multiple wounds as a noisy, angry jury all proclaiming his guilt; they are, as Subha Mukherji suggests, "both a witness to, and sign of, the murder, at once accusing Browne and striking his conscience with all the power of a mnemonic token."[49] Overcome with remorse, Browne confesses his crime, later stating in court that "were it now to do / All the world's wealth could not entice me to't" (5.1.35–36).

In scenes such as these we can see the way in which blood on the early modern stage has a symbolic meaning. Just as the skull in the *memento mori* is both a physical reminder of death and a symbol for life's transitory nature, blood on the early modern stage physically identifies the murderer's guilt and is the means though which his sin is apprehended. In *The Witch of Edmonton* (1621), for example, although Frank's guilt is suggested by the odd behavior of Susan's corpse (she stares at Frank "With one broad open eye still in my face"), it is only when Old Carter confronts him with the murder weapon, "enamelled with the heart-blood of thy hated wife," that he breaks down; recognizing that Frank is profoundly troubled by the sight of the knife, Winnifride beseeches Old Carter, "Strike him no more; you see he's dead already."[50] Macbeth's understanding of what he has done is also precipitated by the sight of blood. Catching a glimpse of his bloodstained hands, he initially fails to recognize them; "What hands are here!" he exclaims, experiencing a moment of self-alienation that is also self-protective.[51] As Robert Miola suggests, it is this sight that "brings him to the painful perception of his guilt and brutality and of the permanence of his misdeed. . . . No ocean can cleanse such stains, no Thebes purify such defilement."[52]

At times, the blood that characters see is not real, but hallucinated. In killers with a conscience "blood cries out" in the imagination, accusing them of their hidden crimes. Lady Macbeth's sleepwalking and repetitive hand washing, for example, suggests that murderers are also sometimes trauma sufferers who endure psychic injuries of their own making.[53] In her somnolent state, Lady Macbeth reveals that the sight and smell of Duncan's blood remain: "Here's the smell of the blood still" (5.i.50). Similarly in Middleton and Rowley's *The Changeling*, DeFlores avoids Tomazo, the brother of the man he has murdered, remarking "this man's not for my company; / I smell his brother's blood when I come near him." Later in the play, when Tomazo strikes him, he declares "I cannot strike: I see his brother's wounds / Fresh bleeding in his eye, as in a crystal!"[54] And in Tourneur's *The Atheist's Tragedy* (1611), when D'Amville asks for a glass of wine to try to rouse his spirits, he sees the liquid as blood:

> *D'Amville*: —Why, thou uncharitable knave,
>   Dost bring me blood to drink? The very glass
>   Looks pale and trembles at it.
> *Servant*: 'Tis your hand, my lord.
> *D'Amville*: Canst blame me to be fearful, bearing still
>   The presence of a murderer about me?[55]

Although D'Amville tries to justify his fearfulness by suggesting that it results from his proximity to his nephew, Charlemont (falsely accused of the murders that his uncle has in fact committed), D'Amville's words are of course truer than he intends, capturing his own crisis of conscience and self-alienation. Appointing himself to act as his nephew's executioner, he lifts the axe and strikes his own head. D'Amville interprets the events as divinely authored and confesses his crimes; dying from his self-inflicted injury, as he remarks, "yond power that struck me knew / The judgement I deserved, and gave it" (5.2.263–64).

D'Amville's death not only gives the revenger's self-destructive aspect a providential design, but also violently literalizes his self-division. Conscience for the sinful intrudes as a radically alien voice, which simultaneously unhouses the self and makes it other. Richard III articulates this uncanny effect, finally feeling the bite of conscience after being confronted by the ghosts of everyone he has killed; he asks: "Is there a murderer here? No. Yes, I am. / Then fly! What, from myself? Great reason. Why? / Lest I revenge. Myself upon myself?" (5.5.138–40). Richard III's crisis of conscience, in which he contemplates the impossible task of fleeing from himself, sounds like a form of voice hearing.[56] It also appropriates the discourse of cruentation:

> My conscience hath a thousand several tongues,
> And every tongue brings in a several tale,
> And every tale condemns me for a villain.
> Perjury, perjury, in the high'st degree!
> Murder, stern murder, in the dir'st degree!
> All several sins, all used in each degree,
> Throng to the bar, crying all, "Guilty! guilty!"
> (5.5.147–53)

As if reacting to the ghosts' catalogue of wounds and their accusation that Richard is "Bloody and guilty," Richard draws on the language of cruentation, although here it is the conscience that speaks the wounds' words, accusing Richard of his sins and condemning him as a villain (5.5.108). The pricks of conscience are here attributable to a ghostly possession that splits the psyche and dislocates the self, allowing the murderer a flash of self-knowledge that renders the self its own antagonist. Richard, however, rejects this insight and the threat to the psyche this entails; mastering his fear and self-alienation, he declares: "Conscience is but a word that cowards use / Devised to keep the strong in awe" (5.6.39–40). Like Macbeth, Richard's ability to control his emotions and regain a manly fortitude is also his ethical undoing; as Katherine Rowe observes, it is such characters' very "sealing up of [their] passions" that allows them to commit murder.[57] Redemption instead depends upon allowing one's pity and fear to take hold, dissolving manly fortitude and awakening conscience.

Literary and medical accounts of cruentation offer vivid proof of a providentially ordered world, depicting it as a mechanism through which God penetrates the eyes and minds of the guilty. Although competing etiologies of cruentation advance different models as to the nature of human physiology and its relation to the material world, all locate meaning in the fabric and fluids of the body, in particular the blood, which is seen to encode a subject's experiences and embody some quintessence of the self. Early modern representations of cruentation also explore the phenomenology of guilt, depicting its physiological processes as working hand in hand with the conscience. The different accounts as to the cause of cruentation give a physiological basis to real or imagined psychological states, explaining the searing remorse of the perpetrator, the venomous anger of the dead, and the change in perspective of the murderer. In this last explanation, the exchange of *spiritus* allows murderers to see their crime from the position of victim; the murderer is able to speak the wounds' words, gaining moral insight at precisely the moment that that self is discovered to be irredeemably stained and lost. In explanations such as these we can see how the apprehension of sin is supported by physiological processes. For killers with a conscience, their violent acts are doomed—as early modern texts make clear, the consequence of murder is not to rid oneself of one's opponents, but to become more fully possessed by them.

Chapter 11

"In such abundance... that it fill a Bason"

Early Modern Bleeding Bowls

ELEANOR DECAMP

The differences between legitimate and unlawful bloodletting were highly legible to early moderns, especially those living in London. Such differences can be located in early modern understanding of the particular conditions that determined the success of bloodletting, such as diet, weather, season, and planetary influence. However, this chapter is concerned with the immediately available, visible evidence of good and malpractice embodied by bloodletting equipment. It will explore the commonplaces of language, symbol, and material through which early moderns understood proofs of unlawful or legitimate phlebotomy.

Bloodletting was practiced frequently in early modernity but the risks attending the practice were a well-catalogued source of anxiety. In the literature and drama of the period illegitimate bloodletting, communicated through the objects and terms associated with the practice, could signal a variety of associated moral, physiological, and even sexual failures. Unearthing these commonplaces enables a more precise interpretation of those literary and dramatic moments in which they occur and a better understanding of those signs that exerted attraction to audiences. This chapter poses a simple question for the dramaturges among us: why is there a basin to collect blood in the final retribution scenes of Shakespeare's *Titus Andronicus*? Critics have for some time been drawn to the semiology of the play—its inspired application of Ovid, Plutarch, and Livy (among others), its somatic, conceptual, and linguistic interest in tongues, wombs, hands, and heads, and its bold stagecraft.[1] But by locating Lavinia's basin within early modern discourses of bloodletting, a new reading of V.ii emerges and in turn opens up opportunities to revisit the play's overarching concerns with revenge and sexual corruption. To enable this reading, I will first identify those visual registers through which early moderns proved good and bad bloodletting: the figure of the medical practitioner who conducts the procedure; the mechanisms through which the practice was advertised; the types of receptacles in which blood was collected; and the incising instruments applied to patients' skin.

I am focusing on instances when blood is let directly from a vein or artery through a single incision (this was normally called phlebotomy, bloodletting, or breathing) rather than evacuations through leeching, scarification (multiple little cuts), or cupping (a suction technique also contemporarily known as "boxing"—hence cupping- and boxing-glasses—and as "ventosing" in the Middle Ages). This is because in cultural allusion to the practice of induced blood loss, the term phlebotomy is the most prolific. I also work on the assumption that to the early seventeenth-century population, bloodletting carried risks but was generally thought—at least in theory—to benefit a body suffering from humoral imbalance, putrefaction, or griefs of overactive organs that resulted in plethora (or *repletion*): to most, bloodletting could be therapeutic, preserving or restoring if conducted in a measured way by the right practitioner following the right instruction.[2] Bloodletting was prescribed in a vast range of cases too numerous here to reflect. The practice was not limited to the human body: read any contemporary companion to farming, grooming, farriery, and the like, and you will find detailed directions on bloodletting horses, for example.[3] It was not until later in the seventeenth century that the more formal attacks by medical authorities on the practice of bloodletting and an increasingly vehement rejection of Galenic physiology gained prominence.[4] William Harvey's treatise on the circulation of the blood had little immediate effect on bloodletting practices.

Practitioner

Although the early modern practice of bloodletting was routinely unlawfully carried out by untrained quacks, counterfeiters, tinkers, and vagabonds of all kinds, the main ground of contention between the regular and irregular practitioners of bloodletting was more closely fought between surgeons and physicians on the one side and barbers on the other. For the medical men writing in the period, surgeons and physicians were acceptable phlebotomists (although often a physician would prescribe phlebotomy by writing a bill and the procedure would be administered by a surgeon); but barbers were not. The distinctions that served the urban populations of early modern England between "surgeon," "barber," and "barber-surgeon" have been lost over time, and much of my early research has focused on clarifying what people would have understood by these names. Many critics assume barbers, surgeons, and barber-surgeons are one and the same: they are not. For the purposes of this chapter a brief summary of their differences will suffice, focusing on London as the epicenter of medical advances in the country and the location of the most prolific publication and staging of popular writing.

In 1540 the Company of Barbers in London merged with the Fellowship of Surgeons. This new company was given the royal stamp of approval by Henry VIII's Act of Parliament. Importantly, this unified city company was not for a group of practitioners who would collectively conjoin barbery and surgery and be practicing barber-surgeons, but for a group of practitioners who had a supervisory role in ensuring that the practices of barbery and surgery were discrete. The official title of their company was formally conjunctive, not hyphenated: The Mystery and Commonality of the Barbers *and* Surgeons of London (italics mine). Members could only legitimately be a practicing barber or surgeon. The title "barber-surgeon" had a competing meaning in the period: at once the name was given as a civic appellation to a member of the company (as a convenient shorthand) but also to the irregular practitioner who offered the services of both barbery and surgery to his paying subjects. We should always, therefore, be on guard to read the context in which a barber-surgeon/barber/surgeon is evoked or represented.

In separating the responsibilities of a barber and a surgeon, the company's decrees are, from the outset, specific about who was permitted to perform bloodlettings:

> Wherefore it is now enacted ordeyned and provided by thautoritye aforesaid that no maner of person within the cities of London . . . using any Barbary or shaving . . . shall occupy any surgery lettyng of bloud, or any other thynge belongyng to surgery drawing of yeeth only excepte.[5]

Dentistry was the only "medical" activity that a barber was allowed to employ. In William Clowes's sixteenth-century manual for trainee surgeons it is clear that his description of an "ignorant blood letter," who is scorned by the local physician and surgeon, leans on the fact that he is also the local dentist, the "tooth-drawer": this irregular bloodletter belongs to a group of counterfeit medical practitioners (most probably barbers) who "unadvisedly overshoot" themselves.[6] Simon Harward was a clergyman interested in the competency of surgeons. His treatise on letting of blood, *Harwards Phlebotomy* (1602), is written specifically as "an advertisement and remembrance to all well minded Chirurgians."[7]

In literature, the person who is called upon to oversee bloodletting is significant to our interpretation of the text. It is important that we understand how a practitioner is referred to in literature in terms of legitimate or illegitimate bloodletting. This is usefully illustrated through four vignettes: (1) Portia's plea to Shylock in *The Merchant of Venice* to "Have by some Surgeon . . . To stop his [Antonio's] wounds, lest he do bleed to death" (IV.i.254–55) acknowledges the authoritative figure, who was much associated with cautery, in acts of controlling extreme blood loss.[8] Shakespeare is specific—a surgeon, not a barber(-surgeon). Portia (as Dr. Balthazar) is seen to commit Bassanio to the supervision of a reliable practitioner, and Shylock's refusal to comply is means to heighten the invective against the Jew: it is another way for Portia to prove his diabolical intention. (2) In II.iii of Richard Brome's *The Sparagus Garden* (1635) Mony-lacks, Brittleware and Springe try to dupe Timothy Hoydens into spending huge sums of money on becoming a gentleman, which involves, they explain, removing his "foule ranke blood of Bacon and Pease-porridge . . . to the last dram." Timothy is worried that he will "bleed to death" (a valid concern), so the confederates reassure him that an "excellent Chyrurgeon" (i.e., not a barber or a barber-surgeon) will be his charge, and his "Mother vaine shall not be prickt."[9] They evoke the legitimate practitioner to reassure Timothy that he will be safe; and because safety is Timothy's sole concern, his dupers successfully distract him from questioning how the procedure will turn him into a gentleman at all and why he should spend any money in the first place. (3) The ballad of "The Catalogue of Contented Cuckolds" (1662–1692) relates how "A Surgeon which opens the vein" is two-timed:

Once I
Followed my Wife and her Spark to Horn fair,
Where I took them both napping as Moss catch his Mare,
He was letting her Blood near the Leg and the Loyn.[10]

The Surgeon proves that he is cuckolded because he points to the Spark's misappropriated role of the blood-letter to the Wife. This misappropriation acts as a proxy for usurping his role as the Wife's carnal partner. The Spark is not the husband and he is not the Surgeon: and he therefore performs sex and bloodletting illegitimately. (4) Using the same idea of a bloodletting by an illegitimate practitioner to signal an inappropriate sexual pricking, the female subject in "The Northern Ladd" (1670–1696) complains of the impertinence of a barber-surgeon:

> A *Barber-Surgeon* came to me,
>   whom I did take in great disdain,
> He said his art I soon should see,
>   for he would prick my master-Vein.[11]

The barber-surgeon is not supposed to prick bodies and the Northern Lass's reservation is clear. His bawdiness is misplaced and proof that he is not the man for her to wed.

Despite the formal distinctions asserted (and ruled upon) between who should and should not undertake bloodletting, unlawful practice (as well as malpractice) was a daily occurrence. No doubt this was partly because there was some money in it: "a veine being commonly opened for twelve pence" (a shilling).[12] Thomas Middleton's satiric comment in *The Owl's Almanac* that *without* surgeons the "letting of blood will be common" (2032–2033) amuses a readership that knows it is already.[13] Quite simply it was an ongoing joke to suggest that only surgeons or physicians embarked on these delicate procedures. The point here is that the early modern population had an implicit sense of who was a licensed and unlicensed practitioner, and this provided a simple frame for more general commentary about legitimate practice, a means of instantly indicating what was proper and not proper in a given scenario.

Bloodletting by barbers (among others) was common partly because barbers resisted giving up all their competencies in surgery and had a long history of performing bloodlettings that preceded the Act of 1540; and partly because for most people a surgeon was an expense they could not afford. However, the barber was considered far from harmless. In his defense of "profitable" bloodletting called *The English Phlebotomy*, Nicholas Gyer warns that only highly able practitioners, namely physicians and skilled surgeons, could successfully perform phlebotomies, and he attacks barbers several times for their lack of expertise:

Ignorant Barbers doo great hurt herein, taking that which comes to hand first, or which appeareth greatest (perhaps a sinew for a veyne) so letting out the vitall spirits, and killing many: and when it is done, this is all their defence, to say the signe was there, and he would needs be let bloud.[14]

Indeed, any mention of "Barbers" in Gyer's treatise is premodified by "ignorant." When confronted with a practitioner who had flouted the rules, the company would take note in their Court Minutes and fine the offender. On July 3, 1599, one "Watson confessed before the Maisters that he used Flebotomey beinge not Surgeon."[15]

Of course surgeons were also quite capable of botching the procedure, making the distinctions between good and bad practitioners fairly wishful. Gail Kern Paster reflects that phlebotomy "was, at least in theory, a *controlled* opening and closing of the bodily container, a deliberate invitation to that body to bleed where, when, and for how long the phlebotomist and his patient chose." She concludes, "We cannot be surprised that phlebotomies often went disastrously wrong" and those performing them easily gain the reputation of being sanguinary.[16] Thomas Gale at the time warns how "easely [a chirurgeon] shall fall into intollerable errours, especiallye in phlebotomye."[17]

Indeed, in their role as regulators of practice, senior company members made it obligatory for surgeons to present before them any of their patients in mortal danger—by all accounts a somewhat impractical expectation. On March 31, 1573, "Here was Edwarde Saunders warned because he . . . had let one bloude at Blackwell and that he dyed, his arme fallynge to Gangrena and no p[re]senta[cio]n therof."[18] In his pamphlet, *Have With you to Saffron-Walden*, Thomas Nashe satirises by making vulgar the practitioner's legitimate training in blood-letting. Of surgeon Richard Lichfield's patients, Nashe orders, "Phlebothomize them, sting them, tutch them Dick, tutch them, play the valiant man at *Armes* and let them bloud and spare not; the Lawe allowes thee to doe it."[19] In other words, proof of lawful, good practice in literature and drama was not just a matter of *who* was carrying out the procedure but also of how it was done.

Advertising

Before we think about the equipment that could denote regular and irregular bloodletting, let us consider briefly how the practice was improperly advertised to get a sense of its visibility in early modern London and of its cultural currency, which is important for the next section on material signifiers. An ordinance in a Letter-Book of ca. 1307 from Guildhall reads:

> Concerning Barbers. And that no barbers shall be so bold or so hardy as to put blood in their windows, openly or in view of folks, but let them have it privily carried unto the Thames, under pain of paying two shillings to the use of the Sheriffs.[20]

After hundreds of years of acting as phlebotomists it is not surprising that barbers persisted in letting blood despite the new laws that made it irregular for them to do so: it was part of their tradition. But I am also interested in the suggestion that blood was put to use by these practitioners—against the authorities—as an advertisement. To their revised Ordinances in 1566 the company added something very similar to the rule of 1307: "An order that none let any bloud stand to the annoyaunce of the people":

> no p[er]sonne of the said mysterye exercysinge fleabothomye or bloudlettinge at any time hereafter shall sett his measures or vesselles w[i]th bloude out or within his shoppe windowe but to hange or set his measures or vesselles cleane one [*sic*] the out syde of the shoppe windowe.[21]

These precepts give us a sense of how conspicuous bloodletting receptacles—and human blood—were on the streets of London. Ironically the proof of bloodletting, the public displaying of blood in receptacles, was also a proof of irregular practice. Clean, empty receptacles, by comparison, are more ambiguous in their function in advertising: for one thing, a basin could simply be a barber's shaving or washing bowl.

Why was it objectionable for bloodletters to exhibit blood in this way? For some who may have complained to the company, most phlebotomized blood was noisome (polluted and poisonous) and entirely different from an encounter with, for example, the fresh animal bloodbaths of the domestic kitchen that Wendy Wall imagines so vividly in *Staging Domesticity* (2002), or the blood that butchers collected for culinary purposes, the image with which Dolly Jørgensen opens her chapter later in this collection.[22] While bloodletting was prescribed to bodies deemed to have overabundant blood, the most common or popular layman understanding was that one had his or her blood let to combat bodily putrefaction. The chapters on corruption in this book explore further contemporary perceptions of blood as a contaminant. But people's reaction to blood could be purely sensory as well. Gyer observes that "when blood commeth forth, it appeareth simple & of one forme: but in the porringer it loseth his colour, & every part thereof congeleth severally. The watrie humor swimmeth above, not farre unlike urine": it is a disconcerting sight and no doubt could smell too.[23] Certainly, as William Turner finds in Cambridge, the noisome street smell of "a stinking butcherie" was in part caused by "stinking bloud."[24] The great French surgeon Ambroise Paré describes how he "drew out some seaven or eight ounces of putrified and stinking blood" when evacuating congealed blood from the midriff of a soldier whose wound had been sewn up too tightly by another surgeon.[25] Lady Macbeth, of course, becomes obsessed with trying to sweeten her hands, hallucinating that that they are still covered in blood and specifically still "smell of blood" (*Macbeth*, V.i.47). Moreover, the blood in these receptacles could be mixed—proverbially "there is no difference of blood in a basin"—and contribute to the early modern anxiety, explored by Katharine Craik, that your blood "type" was not legible outside the body.[26]

If blood-filled receptacles were stacked along the sides of poky London alleyways or within crowded shops, one hazard and cause of annoyance may simply have been spillage. Lucy Munro, and Hester Lees Jeffries and Elisabeth Dutton in this volume, point out that were actors to have splashed blood about very liberally on the early modern stage, there would have been costly repercussions for those preparing the actors' costumes for the next performance—blood stains so well.[27]

So blood displayed in vessels on the streets could be corrupting, unsightly, smelly, an object of disquiet, and could spill and stain. Given this, one wonders why it was deemed an effective means of advertising the practice. Perhaps the very fact that the evacuated blood caused revulsion was an enticement to individuals to seek phlebotomy in the realization that they too did not want such rank fluids to remain inside them. The rancid, stagnant blood that lined streets could have acted as a type of proof that being phlebotomized was a wise decision.

Receptacle

In an extended set of the company's bylaws drawn up in 1606, the terms of the measures and vessels that the practitioners were supposed to exhibit *blood-free* are spelled out: "porringers, saucers or basons."[28] Porringers and saucers were smaller than basins, were designed specifically as measures, and were used by surgeons to calculate how much blood they should (or had) let. Porringers were deeper than saucers and saucers broader than porringers. Of the "*Blood Porrenger*" Randle Holme writes, "These are small little things, that will hold about an ounce, some two, of Blood, by which the Chirurgion guesteth what quantity of Blood (at one Breathing of a Vein) he taketh from his Patient."[29] The eminent surgeon John Woodall reckons that his porringers hold "just three ounces" when full, and stipulates that from a good candidate for phlebotomy, "never take . . . more then two poringers, and a half at the most, but often lesse."[30] In many of the medical textbooks from the period the authors stipulate between seven and eight ounces maximum as a guide for a single bloodletting. Harward explains that if the body suffers from considerable putrefaction or phlethora, the surgeon should let blood several times but not all at once.[31] Even Lanfranc of Milan writes in his seminal thirteenth-century work on surgery, *Chirgia Magna*, which was circulating in translation throughout the sixteenth century: "The consyderation of quantity shall muche farther knowledge, in avoidynge of daungers."[32] Helkiah Cooke refers to "a saser" for bloodletting in which, because of its shallowness, blood becomes "caked" (coagulated) if left.[33] Similarly, Gyer observes blood that "congeleth" in a porringer. Harward refers to "the little basins" in which they compare the blood of their patients: he does not use the technical terms for the receptacles, but size still clearly matters.[34]

The nonmedical or commonplace receptacle in which blood was collected in this period was a basin. Basins, which were both broad and deep, were not suitable objects in which to collect blood in a measured way. In receipt books basins were, for example, large saucers (like saucepans) in which to simmer concoctions. On several occasions in his *Golden Practice of Physick* (translated into English in 1664), Felix Plater, an early seventeenth-century Swiss professor of medicine in Basel, refers to a basin as a means of expressing a sense of copious matter, particularly matter that "gushes forth violently": basins simply stand for a large amount rather than specific quantities. Describing patients spitting out bloody effusions when suffering from inflamed lungs, Plater notes that there is danger of death if the spitting "be sent forth in such abundance . . . that it fill a Bason."[35] The modifiers generally applied to basins in the period are telling: "large," "great," "deep," "broad" (rarely "little," as in Haward's description of a saucer). Advising young apprentices and warning of the dangers of using a basin in bloodletting, Woodall writes:

> German Surgeons doe ever let blood into a Bason, which I hold not good for the Surgeons Mate to imitate . . . except he be of good judgement indeed to judge of the quantity.[36]

And Woodall is also fairly dismissive of the brass basin, explaining to the surgeon's mate, "I Have nothing to write concerning it," playfully suggesting surgeons should sell whatever ones they possess in exchange for good liquor.[37] As in many of Woodall's comments about surgeons' instruments, here he calls for a shift from crude and nontechnical equipment to more refined and specialist kinds, implicitly advocating that objects do and should reflect skill sets.

The basin's association with barbery was entrenched in the early modern period, and indeed the "barber's basin" was an exclusively modified noun: it was both a fundamental piece of barbery equipment and also a cornerstone of the trade's entire lexicon in popular culture. It generally represents the receptacle that would be filled with water, soap, suds, and razored hair—in other words, a washing basin. The barber's basin is referenced and stipulated as barbers' standard appurtenance in several early modern plays: Cocledemoy borrows a "basin" as part of his barber disguise (*The Dutch Courtesan*, II.i.186); Barber Secco's equipment includes a "*Bason*" (*The Fancies Chast and Noble*, s.d. I4r); one of Barbaroso's prisoners emerges from a cave (aka a barber's shop) "*with a basin under his chin*" (*The Knight of the Burning Pestle*, s.d. III.366); and the object outside Barbaroso's dwelling, which likely merits a prop, is a "basin" (III.239).[38] To a contemporary audience, the basin on stage is a stereotype of barbery in general. Early modern descriptions of the barber's basin give us a sense of its volume. Randle Holme describes "A *Bason* or *Barbers Bason*, having a circle in the brim to compass the Mans Throat, and a place like a little Dish to put the Ball in after Lathering"—a small receptacle (probably saucer-sized) could fit inside the basin.[39]

If the barber's washing basin always had the potential to double up as a receptacle for bloodletting, then the very size of the object means that the barber or barber-surgeon is readily associated with copious, unregulated bloodletting. This correlates with definitions of barbers in terms of their practice of removing excessive hair—enough to stuff pillows with, according to some descriptions. In popular culture the barber is associated with plethora because they remove what is superfluous. On the one hand this association with plethora can become a joke—an elaboration of their basic function to trim back rather than cure. On the other, it is cautionary of commentators to point out that the barber can be without technical skill and is inclined to judge his own work by the mantra "the more removed, the better," whether that be hair, ear-wax, teeth, or blood. In Middleton's *The Meeting of Gallants at an Ordinary*, Famine challenges his interlocutor: "What art thou, War, that so want'st thy good? / But like a barber-surgeon that lets blood" (lines 116–17).[40] He suggests that War poses as a means to resolve extreme complications but measures success in terms of immense blood-loss.

The size and the type of a blood-collecting receptacle matter in contemporaries' efforts to define the appropriateness of phlebotomy.

Instrument

The correct instrument with which to make incisions for bloodletting was a lancet or fleam. Thin and like a penknife, the lancet was designed to incise only shallowly and make a small orifice. Publications for surgeons in the period dictate that practitioners should have access to a range of differently sized lancets for different cases.[41] Back to Gyer:

> There is a newe kinde of instrument to let bloud withall nowe a daies: as the Rapier, Sword, and long Dagger; which bring the bloud letters sometime to the Gallowes, because they strike too deepe. These instruments are the Ruffians weapons . . . veyne[s] must be opened with a fine Launcet.[42]

Gyer terms the instruments "newe" either perversely to make the point that these are actually crude, outdated objects of medical works, or to suggest the increasing pervasiveness of people taking to bloodletting by any means possible. Woodall also insists on the use of a well-formed lancet in phlebotomy. He remarks, "it is not amisse to advise [the apprentice surgeon] that he cary . . . at least six of the best sort [of lancet], besides six more common ones," and he advocates the German example of surgeons practicing their tool-making capabilities by fashioning the perfect lancet.[43]

Patricia Parker examines in detail the significance of the lancet in relation to the character "Launcelot" (Lancelot) and forms of conversion in *The Merchant of Venice*.[44] My two main points here are first, that there was a specific instrument for incision-making, and second, that this instrument was not so technical as to be known only to men of science. A lancet is probably as technical in the period as a scalpel or a needle is today.

Lavinia's Bason

So why does Lavinia carry a basin and Titus carry a knife on stage in V.ii of *Titus Andronicus*? There is straightforward answer, of course: father (and daughter) are going to kill the Goth brothers for raping and dismembering Lavinia, and then feed them to their mother, Tamora, in a pasty. The knife will make a fatal wound in each brother. The basin will catch the blood necessary to form a paste for pie-making.

But there is signifying potential in the entire configuration of the scene beyond the basic need to kill and bake Chiron and Demetrius—as an act of butchery and preparation to play the cook. The theme is also irregular bloodletting in V.ii because the Goth brothers' bleeding has a therapeutic imperative; the instruments are "ruffians weapons" but essentially the nontechnical equipment of an irregular phlebotomist; heinous crimes against Lavinia in the play are contextualized by diabolic barbery, and so Titus's act of retribution is apposite reprisal; and there are implicit references in the play/scene to "those" practitioners (barbers and surgeons) that are central to commentaries on bloodletting. The final paragraphs of this chapter therefore explore—in a notorious but not yet fully comprehended scene of Shakespeare—the signs of bloodletting that underpin the dramaturgy and bring meaning to this revenge sequence: by focusing on these signs we will find evidence of Shakespeare's embedded conceptual (as well as dramaturgical) design, which draws on hazardous phlebotomy and the darkly satirical commentary of contemporary "medical" practice.[45]

We know that in order to make an incision, practitioners of bloodletting regard—either truthfully or spuriously—a subject's blood as rank or overabundant. To Titus, Chiron and Demetrius's blood is "guilty" (V.ii.183), and therefore the brothers are suitable candidates for bloodletting because their blood is corrupt and corrupting—an expression of their true selves.[46] Significantly, Titus goes for the brothers' throats. One of several reasons for opening "these veines of the necke or throat," Gyer explains, was for "griefs of the Splene" as well as for "hot bloud," something from which we are told the Goth brothers are suffering.[47] Demetrius refers to "this heat" (I.i.634) that overwhelms him, and the brother's "lust" is mentioned three times in II.ii. Aaron encounters them "*braving*," ready to spill each other's blood because they are brimful of passion. Lust is described by Jean Baptiste Helmont as a condition of the spleen: "carnal lust hath respect unto the spleen," he writes, and observes that "very many who from a Quatana Ague had retained their spleen ill affected . . . have been very much curtail'd in the provocation to leachery."[48] Crooke writes of the spleen's "great helpe to the Liver" (which is, according to Crooke, the seat of the body's desire) and its function in purging and defecating blood "to make it more pure and bright": it could purify half-concocted blood.[49] When the audience must imagine that Chiron and Demetrius are raping Lavinia offstage, Tamora refers to her "spleenful sons" (II.ii.191).[50] As well as a punitive action, bloodletting in *Titus* is also strangely curative: Titus draws from his patients the over-concocted blood that gave them the vigour to enact their heinous deeds.

"*Enter Titus Andronicus, with a knife, and Lavinia, with a Bason*" (s.d. V.ii.165).

We know that the basin and the knife in V.ii signal that the amount of blood being let will be too much for anything other than a cataclysmic bloodletting. By this moment in the play, a fair amount of blood has already been spilled. But Shakespeare resists repeating the sudden violence of Titus's arm amputation or Aaron's quick dispatch of the nurse. The basin and knife signal murder before the murder takes place. But more than this, they signal murder through the particular context of irregular phlebotomy, which instills Shakespeare's medical commentary in the scene.[51]

The basin prop is crucial in our reading of the scene and it imbues the knife with signifying potential. A basin is a material and linguistic prop, stipulated in stage directions and also in dialogue when Titus refers to the "Basin that receives your guilty blood" (V.ii.83).[52] As we have discovered, blood in a basin was a potent signifier (an advertisement, even) of bloodletting practice, common to the streets of London. But it was also a sign of irregular practice by an untrained practitioner who will "let the bloud to runne . . . so long as they see it to be grosse and corrupt": in other words, someone who is likely to fill with blood a large receptacle in one sitting and overthrow the strength of their subject.[53] The very presence of Lavinia's basin means that there will be blood: lots of it, and it is there for display. Similarly, in William Davenant's *The Cruell Brother* when Foreste dispatches his sister, Corsa, by bleeding her out, it is into a basin ("Here in this Bason bleed") that he collects her blood.[54] In part because of the basin we know that Corsa's fate is inevitable. By comparison, when Roderigo Borgia in Barnabe Barnes's *The Divils Charter* (1607) signs his satanic blood contract with Astaroth (the demon prince of hell), his blood is collected in a "*saucer*" that acts as an inkwell: this bloodletting will not of itself kill Roderigo. Further, this technical procedure is administered by a devil-surgeon with "*a box of Lancets.*"⁵⁵ That there is a collection of specific tools for the procedure suggests that bloodletting *can* be enacted with precision, which is necessary for this satanic contract to take effect. In other words, it is possible for phlebotomy to be represented in a highly controlled, nonlethal fashion on the stage by a different set of objects.

Titus's knife is not the right instrument with which to let blood: it fits within the category of general cutting implements used by irregular bloodletters: it will lance too deep and create an orifice too wide for any body to sustain life. Phlebotomists commonly slit veins in patients' necks, but it was vital that in this procedure they used a very fine lancet, "a launcer *cum pilo*," writes Thomas Geminus, "that hath a pyn over-thwart about the ende of the lau[n]cer, to kepe it for goying to depe in the [necke] veyne."⁵⁶ In his *Government of Health*, William Bullein cautions, "Veins called Originales, open not without great counsaile of a learned Physicion, or cutting Chirurgion. They be in the necke, and have a great course of bloud, that governeth the head, and the whole body."⁵⁷

We know that barbers are not supposed to perform phlebotomies. Earlier events and dialogue in the play shape our response to Lavinia's basin as a barbery prop and therefore an irregular apparatus of bloodletting. As we found in examples (particularly in ballads) earlier in this chapter, sex that is unwanted can be analogized by irregular, crude, and forced phlebotomy. For one thing, Lavinia's raped and mutilated body is at first conceptualized as all bleeding: "a conduit with three issuing spouts" (II.iv.29).⁵⁸ But crucially, it is *barbery* metaphor earlier in the play that underlines the basin and bloodletting's thematic importance as a trope of revenge. When Lucius confronts Aaron about Chiron and Demetrius's abominable acts, Aaron jeers at Lavinia's rape and dismemberment. Literal and figurative meanings clash uncomfortably in his description and the lively punning is manifold.

> *Aaron.* They cut thy sister's tongue and ravished her
> And cut her hands and trimmed her as thou sawest.
> Lucius. O detestable villain, call'st thou that trimming?
> Aaron. *Why, she was washed and cut and trimmed*, and 'twas
> Trim sport for them which had the doing of it.
> (V.i.92–96, italics mine)

Aaron uses the common language and sexual provocativeness of barbery: the figure of speech "to wash, cut, and trim" was specific to barbery, not surgery (and not even butchery as some editors have glossed). Lucius responds to

Aaron's description: "O barbarous, beastly villains, like thyself!" (V.i.97). Q1's spelling is "barbarous" (*Titus* (1594), I1v). But graphemic variations do not alter the effect of this word in performance: whether spelled with an "a" or an "e," when uttered—especially in this context—"barbarous" to an audience puns on "barber."[59] The fact that Lavinia's rape is contextualized by barbery and its associative cleaning habits comes to bear on our interpretation of her later appearance with a basin.

We know that names are important in officially designating a regular practitioner. In *Titus*, the names of Lavinia and Chiron are particularly significant. Lavinia is from the Latin, *lavare,* meaning to wash.[60] In *The Taming of the Shrew* Gremio boasts to Baptista that one of the enticements of his city home for Bianca are "Basons and ewers to lave her dainty hands" (II.i.344). The Goth brothers taunt Lavinia after her rape, suggesting that she "Go home, call for sweet water" and "wash [her] hands" (II.iii.6): they evoke a basin and make a painful irony of her name. Given the puns on barbery I outline above, Lavinia's basin is also logically a barber's large washing basin.[61] Tellingly, within the milieu of barbery and washing, the basin also explicitly represents the vagina. From *The Taunton Maids Delight*:

> But I made to him [the barber] this reply,
>   I will not be married yet,
> Your Rayzer and Washing-balls truly
>   for my Bason is not fit.[62]

And from *Age Renewed by Wedlock*:

> My Husband is a Barbar
>   His Washbals are admir'd,
> And I have got a Bason
>   Where he Ladders whilst he's tyr'd.[63]

The basin in these examples is an emblem of licentious lathering and in *Titus* Lavinia is cast as the subject of these atrocities. So when her basin is later reified as a receptacle for Chiron and Demetrius's blood, it is as a transformed article (from washing basin to blood basin) and reverses the symbolism of her as the victim of a perverted lavation. Lavinia's name and her prop come together in V.ii in a strange moment of empowerment, and the condition of irregular barbery comes back to bite the Goth brothers.

Do we have a surgeon in this scene? Yes, but he is one of the subjects of the bloodletting: Chiron. Mythological Chiron was a harmless centaur, a specialist in herbs and the teacher of the medical arts to Achilles and Asclepius; he was regarded for his justice and virtue. Galen writes of him:

> The most auncient of all the Grecians, I supposed to
> bee *Apollo,* who dyd cure many great and wonderfull diseases,
> by the helpe of the forenamed *Chiron Centaurus,* and some suppose . . . that the name of the Arte of *Chirurgia,* was first derived
> from *Chiron,* for that hee dyd minister medicamentes with his
> hands, and so cured the people, and being the first that practised
> with medicines by the use of the hande, it is supposed that hee gave
> it that name.[64]

Critics have acknowledged the relentless punning on "hands" in *Titus,* which draws us to the idea of *craft,* which is the surgeon's jurisdiction; but the embedded, onomastic reference in Chiron as the satyr-come-surgeon is not cited.[65] The figure of mythological Chiron in *Titus* relapses to the stereotypical satyr; and at the same time his association with surgery is turned upside-down. Ultimately, irregular bloodletting in *Titus* disposes of corrupt barber-surgery behaviors, and the stakes at the end of the tragedy are reset. By taking on the role of the hazardous barber-surgeon and evacuating the blood of Chiron and Demetrius, Titus revenges, quid pro quo, the rape and disfigurement of his daughter. The interwoven proofs of irregularity that contextualize the Goth brothers' emblematic bloodletting in *Titus* imbue one of the play's systems of abuse—which centers on Lavinia and her basin—with a series of provocative signifiers. These signifiers give semantic richness and thematic coherence to the enactment of revenge and mucky sexual politics as well as contribute to the play's uncomfortable humour, punning, onomastics, and outrageous drama of incidents.

Chapter 12

Macbeth and the Croxton *Play of the Sacrament*

Blood and Belief in Early English Stagecraft

ELISABETH DUTTON

Blood and the Jews

Throughout its ugly history, anti-Semitism has repeatedly asserted perverse and pervasive connections between Jews and blood. Most obviously, there is the blood libel, which asserts the existence of a secret Jewish ritual in which a Christian child's body is tortured and killed, often in a manner perceived to imitate Christ's Passion, and its blood collected, usually for baking in the unleavened bread eaten at Passover. The first blood libel in England related to the death of a twelve-year-old boy, William, in Norwich, in 1144: the story was recounted by Thomas of Monmouth to create a prestigious local cult, but numerous other examples followed, of which the most renowned was the "martyrdom" of Hugh of Lincoln, reputedly victim of Jewish child murder in 1255. The story lies behind Geoffrey Chaucer's blood libel narrative, *The Prioress's Tale*, but it was earlier recorded in the chronicles of Matthew Paris:[1] Paris echoes the language of Christ's passion as he describes the scourging, piercing, and crucifixion of eight-year-old Hugh in insult to Jesus Christ. The blood libel is of course entirely historically unconvincing—ritual bleedings are a nonsense for Jews, who are rendered ritually unclean by contact with blood—the blood libel was, in fact, primarily a tool for persecution of the Jews by the authorities.²

Thomas of Monmouth, in creating the blood libel, contributed also to a second bizarre connection made between Jews and blood. According to Thomas, a sheriff who tried to protect the Jews of Norwich was punished by a flow of blood from his anus. This curious divine punishment seems to have been inspired by Psalm 77:66, "He smote His enemies in their posteriors," a passage that Hugh of St. Victor interpreted as showing God afflicting the Jews with tumors that protrude from their anuses and are nibbled by mice. Medically, menstruation and hemorrhoidal bleeding were understood to serve the same function: purging. "Many men are purged [of bad humours] via these small veins (just as women are by their menses) and preserved from diverse illnessses when they flow in the appropriate amount."³ Scriptural scholars argued that menstruation was part of Eve's punishment for her disobedience in Eden, and the spilling of Judas's guts, after his betrayal of Christ, was thought to have been through his anus. As the image of the cursed Jew evolved in medieval Europe, these elements combined in the myth of Jewish male menstruation, perhaps the weirdest manifestation of an association of Jews with blood found also in the Passion narratives: "When Pilate saw that he could prevail nothing, but *that* rather a tumult was made, he took water, and washed *his* hands before the multitude, saying, I am innocent of the blood of this just person: see ye *to it*. Then answered all the people, and said, His blood *be* on us, and on our children" (Matthew 27:23–25).

However, the myth that is most relevant to the play that will be the focus of this chapter, the Croxton *Play of the Sacrament*, is a bloody myth that has, in origin at least, nothing to do with the Jews. According to the eighth-century biography of Gregory I, as the pope was celebrating Mass, a woman in the congregation remarked that the host could not possibly be the body of Christ, since it was bread that she had baked herself: the Eucharistic host was then transformed into a bleeding finger. Later versions of the story have not a finger but the whole body of Christ appear: what all the host miracles have in common, however, is blood. In 1263, in the Italian city of Bolsena, a Bohemian priest who did not believe in the Real Presence of God in the host was convinced when the host started to bleed: the church at Bolsena still displays the stones stained with blood, and the neighboring cathedral of Orvieto preserves the bloodstained cloth in which the host was wrapped. It is now in a chapel surrounded by frescoes of related host miracles—many of which involve Jews. This is odd, since Jews do not feature in either the miracle at Bolsena or the Mass of St. Gregory. But since they were already understood to torture and bleed little Christian boys, they were soon also to be found torturing Christ in the form of the Eucharistic host. The miracle of Bolsena led to the institution of the feast of Corpus Christi, celebrated across Europe. In 1320, Jews were banned from the streets of Barcelona on Corpus Christi day.[4]

Staging Croxton's Blood

This chapter will discuss blood as "proof" in the late fifteenth-century Croxton *Play of the Sacrament*, a miracle play in which a group of Jews bribe a Christian merchant to steal the Eucharistic host for them; they then stab the host and it bleeds and sticks to the hand of Jonathas, the chief Jew; the Jews resort to increasingly violent methods to destroy the host, symbolically reenacting Christ's passion; in the process they sever Jonathas's hand, but he rejects the medicine offered by a drunken doctor, Master Brundyche. The host then becomes a vision of the bleeding Christ and the Jews are converted and Jonathas healed, while the Christian merchant repents and is absolved.[5] The present discussion of the *Play of the Sacrament* will demonstrate that its use of blood as proof, its exploitation of the possibilities of stage blood, and its attention to bloodied cloths and bloodied limbs anticipate much of what scholars have found remarkable about blood a century later in the early modern playhouse;[6] this chapter will briefly consider how *Macbeth* may be illuminated by being read alongside the Croxton play.

Croxton has attracted considerable scholarly attention; it is significant for those engaged in the study of Jewish history, for those interested in sacramental theology, and also for those interested in theater history. It gives us an early example of the stage Jew—a precursor of Marlowe's Barabbas and Shakespeare's Shylock. The establishment of the Jew as a figure on the early English stage follows from anti-Semitic mythologizing and from the fact that, throughout medieval and early modern Europe, Jews were forced to wear distinguishing clothes—usually red hats—which made Jewishness, conveniently for an acting company, a matter of costume. The Croxton play also gives us some intriguing evidence about just what a late fifteenth-century or sixteenth-century acting troupe could achieve onstage. The play requires an onstage amputation, then reversed onstage; a cauldron of over-boiling oil; an oven that can crack, leak blood, and explode; and an apparition of the bleeding Christ. It is clear that, in the words of the celebrated sixteenth-century French miracle play stage direction, "There must be blood."

The Croxton *Play of the Sacrament* includes, for a fifteenth-century play, an unusual number of stage directions. Blood is explicit in these three:

Here the Host must blede

Here shall the cawdron byle, apperyng to be as bloode

Here the ovyn must ryve asunder and blede owt at the cranys, and an image appere owt with woundys bledyng[7]

And blood is perhaps implicit in this stage direction, which indicates the amputation of Jonathas's arm:

Here shall thay pluke the arme, and the hand shall hang styll with the Sacrament[8]

As I have discussed elsewhere in relation to the play's performance locations, the language of these stage directions apparently shifts in and out of recognition of the play's fictionality.[9] Croxton asserts that it reenacts real events (a miracle that occurred in Eraclea, in Aragon—Banns, 11–12) and that those events were first represented in Rome in 1461 (Banns, 57–58); the stage directions sometimes refer to stage phenomena as if they were real—"Here goeth the Jewys away, and the preste commyth home" (255, s.d.), and sometimes use frankly theatrical language—"Jonatas (shall) goo down off his stage" (148, s.d.). The stage directions for blood indicate that the Host "must bleed," and the oven must "bleed out at the cracks," and the image's wounds must be "bleeding," but although the cauldron "shall boil" and the oven "must rive asunder," the boiling oil must only "*appear* to be as blood." The conventions for stage directions are far from fixed in the medieval and early modern periods, so it is possible that this variation is purely by chance: however, "appearing to be as blood" draws attention to an illusion within the story that the play presents, not simply a theatrical illusion within that presentation. Croxton claims that the original, historical events that it depicts included a host that actually bled, but the oil in which it was boiled did not, of course, bleed or even turn into blood, but rather was turned to the appearance, the color, of blood by the bleeding host placed in it.

Stage directions might be for readers rather than those producing a play, and they were not necessarily authorial but might also be based on an actor or audience member's memory of a production, for example.[10] The modal verbs "shall" and "must" do suggest that these are instructions for a company staging the play, and it is perhaps useful to an acting troupe to know that their cauldron still contains oil, that they do not have to stage an additional miracle of oil turning to blood; when they place the bleeding host and hand in the exploding oven, the oven presumably "bleeds out at the cracks" with the blood of the wounded figure inside it.

Nonetheless, the stage directions seem to present any acting troupe with a huge challenge and hardly any help: there is no practical guidance as to the type of trick by which a host can be made to bleed, an oven to explode, or a bleeding image to appear miraculously. Again, this is not untypical: the approximately contemporary *Mary Magdalene* play, for example, includes such challenges as "Here shall come a cloud from heaven and set the temple on fire,"[11] and the *Conversion of St. Paul* requires that Belial and Mercury "shall vanish away with a fiery flame, and a tempest."[12] Fireworks might well have been used for these effects and to make the Croxton oven explode, for all that there was perhaps a child playing the image of Christ inside: a stage direction for the *Castle of Perseverance* instructs "he that shall play Belial" to "look that he have gunpowder burning in pipes in his hands and in his ears and in his arse when he goes to battle," so there seems to have been limited concern about putting actors at risk. Perhaps the boiling cauldron was given a blood-red color using colored smoke, which, as Philip Butterworth has noted, was used on the medieval stage.[13] But to understand the technology for blood that might have been used in early productions of Croxton, we need to look either to the medieval French drama, or to the early modern English professional stage. There is much more blood in medieval French drama than in medieval English drama, probably because the bloodiest plays are always saints' plays, of which many survive in French but very few in English.[14] Early French theater especially depended on spectacular visual effects, often bloody, and civic presentations of saints' plays would employ a highly skilled technician to manage these *fainctes*. So we know, for example, that in order to make Christ sweat blood there were at least two techniques used. In Provence:

> Jesus must wear a wig and when he puts it on he must put underneath it two or three carefully positioned sponges, full of vermilion well diluted and . . . when he prostrates himself on the ground he must put his hand on his head and press firmly so that the sponges spout forth the vermilion that they have absorbed.[15]

And at Revello:

> Then he (Christ) shall stretch out on the stage (*zafaldo*) on his face, and underneath there shall be someone who shall paint his face and hands with crimson paint as if he were sweating. And when he has been like this for a time he shall rise. And one of the angels shall come and without speaking wipe away the sweat.[16]

The Provencal Director's Notebook also gives practical advice as to how to make the blood flow when staging the nailing of Christ to the cross, a technique that might well have been duplicated by the Croxton players:

> a large wooden nail should be made, hollow and filled with vermilion, and there should be a small hole at the end so that the blood flows over the hand.[17]

On the other hand (so to speak), since the hand that the Croxton Jews are nailing to a post subsequently has to be torn off, which implies that Jonathas has at some point to be wearing a prosthetic hand, it is possible that the dummy hand was already in use at the moment of nailing: the dummy hand could itself be filled with sponges soaked in vermilion of the type used for Christ's bloody sweat, so that when it was nailed to the post it would then inevitably "bleed" as the sponges were pierced.

What is noticeable about all of these instructions is that they are concerned with how to get blood on to the stage, or specifically on to the body of the actor, and in the case of Revello also how to get it off the stage, or off the actor, again. There is thus something fascinatingly parallel about stage blood and the "real" blood it represents in host miracles, and perhaps in Christ's sweating blood: the point of host miracles is that blood, while itself natural, is seen to flow where it does not naturally flow—from bread. Illuminating comparisons might be drawn here with the screaming, bleeding tree of epic tradition, discussed by Joe Moshenska: the blood from the bread, like that from the tree, "is not the marker of animal as opposed to vegetable life, but belongs to a being that hovers on the threshold between animal and vegetable, sentient and nonsentient, human and mere object."[18] Precisely because this is unnatural, it is a miraculous proof—and a challenge to the actors who must work out how to make it appear to happen.

These stage directions all indicate the use of paint, crimson or vermilion, rather than real blood taken from an animal, for example. There is some evidence suggesting the use of sheep's blood on the early modern professional stage in Peele's *Battle of Alcazar*,[19] and also in conjuring tricks: Reginald Scot describes how a juggler might appear to stab himself using a false belly filled with calf or sheep blood.[20] But there are more references indicating the use of other substitute liquids: Lucy Munro cites stage directions calling for vinegar and red ink, as well as paint, on the English professional stage and in the Lucerne passion plays, in which Christ was made to "bleed" when a painter inside a mound splashed him with paint.[21] Scot's caution to his juggler that he should "in no wise" try to use ox or cow blood, "for that will be too thicke,"[22] has an almost comically solicitous tone, as if from the stage manager who has had a bad experience with a belly that failed to bleed: it is no mean trick to make blood flow convincingly, and it appears that paradoxically real blood (albeit animal) is harder to manage than paint.

Blood as Proof

Host miracles all involve an unbeliever and a bloody proof. The Jews, who did not recognize Christ as the fulfillment of their own prophecies, were, for the medieval church, the ultimate unbelievers: "the Jew" acquired a symbolism in Christian culture that was increasingly divorced from social or religious realities, and this play, written two centuries after the Jews had officially been expelled from England, is perhaps not really about Jews at all. The Jews here swear by Muhammad, but the play is not about Muslims either: this play is about the sacrament and the doctrine of transubstantiation. The "Jews" stand for all those who do not believe that Christ is, as the Jew Jonathas puts it, "in a cake"[23]—really present in the Eucharistic host. In England in the fifteenth century the "Jews" are the "unbelieving" proto-Protestant Lollards. But Jews are also mythically "bloody," and blood is what proves guilt in the unbeliever: blood is what proves truth and creates belief. In Croxton, there is both a bleeding host and an apparition of a bleeding body, which appears to be Christ—the Bishop apparently addresses it as "fili dei" (734)—but which is also described by Jonathas as "a chyld . . . with wondys blody" (724). The Christian child tortured by Jews in imitation of Christ appears actually to have become Christ, contained in the Eucharistic host: a number of different bloody miracles have been combined to bring about the conversion of the unbeliever to faith in the Real Presence.

The Jews in the play explicitly discuss blood as proof. In a rather puzzling passage (362–68) the chief Jew, Jonathas, alludes to Isaiah's prophecy of a hero coming *tinctis Bosra vestibus* ("with dyed garments from Bozrah"). Isaiah's hero speaks righteous words and has salvific power, and his garments are stained as if he has been pressing grapes:

> I have trodden the winepress alone; and of the people *there was* none with me: for I will tread them in mine anger, and trample them in my fury; and their blood shall be sprinkled upon my garments, and I will stain all my raiment. . . .
>
> And I will tread down the people in mine anger, and make them drunk in my fury, and I will bring down their strength to the earth. (Isaiah 63:3–6)

The garments from Bosra, dyed splendidly red, are a symbol of strength and power, but their color is then linked to the red of grapes and wine, and the red of blood. The apparently bloodstained garment identifies Isaiah's hero; it is proof of messianic status. It is easy to see why this passage was attractive to Christian exegetes establishing the connection between the Eucharistic wine and the blood of Christ.[24] Jonathas, who as a Jew is conveniently familiar with Old Testament prophecy, suggests that they must test the Eucharistic host to see whether it is, in fact, the hero who comes from Bosra with stained garments—to test whether or not Christ is the fulfillment of the prophets. Malchus, in a loaded pun, declares that they will discover the truth through "clowtys" (372): *clowtys* here are both the blows which the Croxton Jews inflict on the host, and the cloth in which the host is wrapped—and by extension the bloodstained Bosran clothes of Isaiah's hero. Iconographically the cloth in which Jonathas wraps the host and which, presumably, becomes bloody when the host bleeds (though no stage direction mentions the fact) suggests the bloody cloth displayed in Orvieto Cathedral, proof of the Real Presence to medieval Christians.[25]

That some acting troupes managed their blood to great effect is indicated in the following account of a French host miracle play very similar to Croxton:

> The treacherous Jew, wishing to find out if the Host were God . . . struck it with a knife then by a secret (*feincte*) great abundance of

blood came forth and soared up high from the said Host as if it had been a child pissing, and the Jew was all blood spattered and stained by it.[26]

Here it may be observed not only that considerable skill is needed to make bread bleed so forcefully,[27] but also that the Jew is splashed and stained with the blood of the miraculous host. This perhaps indicates that the blood is a proof not only of the Real Presence in the host, but also of the guilt of the Jew as torturer of the host and thus, as a representative of the Jewish race to the medieval mind, as murderer of Christ.

Blood cannot, in the ordinary run of things, be found outside the body; once it is outside the body, it demands attention and explanation.[28] The blood that comes from the host is a proof *because it comes from the host*; it proves that the bread is not what it seems, but a body, and it proves that that body has been tortured and bloodied not just by the Jews' stabbing of the wafer but also because of the Crucifixion of Christ commemorated in the Mass, which the Jews parody. Blood is a proof not only of life, injury, and death, but also of guilt: blood is transferable, splashing and staining bodies from which it does *not* come, and so indicating a murderer. But blood is an unstable proof because it is so readily transferred. It is impossible to tell, from the appearance of blood, from which body it came or who made it flow. Lady Macbeth, for example, "guilds the faces of the grooms" with Duncan's blood so that they appear to be his killers.

Blood as Theater

Theatrical illusions depend on the deployment of material realities—actors' bodies, costumes, props—in such a way that the audience will accept that they are at once real and fictionalized: a prop handkerchief is materially a handkerchief, but it is only fictionally the handkerchief Othello gave to Desdemona, and the fiction is only maintained while it is on stage. A stage crown may look like a real monarch's crown, but even if it were materially valuable, decorated with real gold and gems, it could only be a crown fictionally, onstage, since it is not invested with real political power. The audience must also accept a fictional narrative about where the actor's bodies and their props came from and where they will go: Andrea Stevens argues that, just as bodies and props move on and off the stage through "entrance doors or stage hangings whose movements help create impressions of unseen interior spaces," so "paint, when applied to or removed from a body, fosters effects of depth, gestures towards 'hidden' passions, and constructs and dismantles identities."[29] Stevens points out also that paint was used elsewhere in the theater to create props and sets, not only blood, and she argues that for early modern writers paint even embodied "the essence of theatricality."[30] Whether paint or real blood is used, stage blood is at once material and fictional; it is a prop, but one that is transferable, and it cannot travel endlessly like other props, but can only be very physically transferred. Nonetheless, blood has inherently huge theatrical potential. When made visible, it implies a narrative that commands attention. Its materiality is indisputable, and its significance in one sense instantly recognizable; on the other hand, its fluidity and transferability ensure that there are numerous potential narratives behind its appearance.

In a discussion of blood on the early modern professional stage, Munro argues that the material quality of blood, most importantly its staining power, was a reason it was in fact used with care by professional companies: perhaps unlike spectacular civic productions like Lucerne, which were by their nature occasional and lavishly funded, professional productions had to ensure that blood did not stain costumes, which had to be reused day after day. She discusses *Julius Caesar* and *Coriolanus*, and I would like here to add a brief consideration of *Macbeth*, a play that suggestively draws attention itself to the staining powers of blood, although the stains are not on clothes but on hands.[31] "Out, damned spot" (5.1.33)—in one of the best-known lines in Shakespeare, Lady Macbeth tells us that her hands are stained with blood, which she cannot wash away. In every production I have seen, Lady Macbeth's hands are clean when she declares that the color and smell of blood remain on them: "all the perfumes of Arabia will not sweeten this little hand" (5.1.47–48). Her words are taken as the product of delusion. But they echo Macbeth's anxious words after the murder of Duncan:

> Will all great Neptune's ocean wash this blood
> Clean from my hand? No, this my hand will rather
> The multitudinous seas incarnadine,
> Making the green one red.
>
> (2.2.59–62)

And Macbeth's hands at this point are literally bloody.[32] The hyperbole of the conceit, with its notoriously erudite coining "incarnadine," invites an interpretation of the literal blood as symbolic of Macbeth's guilt. But nonetheless there is literal blood, and Macbeth's conceit might also serve metatheatrically—even comically so—as a moment of anxiety about the practicalities of staging that involves painted blood. How can an actor get rid of a "blood" stain? How might the play be affected if these lines, along with "Out, damned spot!" are taken as implicit stage directions, and the hands of both Macbeths are actually stained with blood—as might indeed have been the case given the difficulty for actors of quickly ridding their hands of stage blood between scenes? It is true that Lady Macbeth declares that "a little water rids us of this deed"—clearly the Macbeths, and the Macbeth actors, attempt to wash their hands after the murder of Duncan and his grooms. But perhaps Lady Macbeth's words are too optimistic: the actors might not have been able, with a little water, to rid their hands of every last spot of blood as quickly as the scenes would require, and indeed a "damned spot" or two might remain as proof of the protagonists' guilt. The murderers' stained hands would then be a theatrical necessity of which the playwright makes a virtue.

If the Macbeths' damned spots are indeed traces of stage blood, why would the characters around the Macbeths apparently fail to notice the bloodstains on their hands? Three possible explanations might be considered. One is that they actually *do* see the stains and ignore them either because they do not wish to upset Macbeth, the rising star, or because they do not know how to interpret them. After all, Macbeth achieves his promotion through gory violence on the battlefield, so the question within war-torn Scotland is not whether he has blood on his hands, but whose blood, and whether it was shed in the "legitimate" context of battle. We first learn of Macbeth as the violent killer of the rebel Macdonwald: "For brave Macbeth . . . with bloody execution . . . unseam'd him from the nave to the chaps" (1.2.16–22). However, we do not at this point see Macbeth, but rather hear of his actions through the words of the "bleeding Sergeant" (1.2.1 s.d.) who is in some sense the visual substitute here for the protagonist whom we will not meet fresh from the battlefield. The practical reason for this is clear: were the Macbeth actor to appear at this point covered in stage-paint battle gore, it would be impossible for him to clean himself up in time for his encounter with the witches in the next scene, or indeed perhaps for the rest of the play. The stage direction also emphasizes, however, the rich ambiguity of blood as a stage signifier: that the Sergeant is "bleeding" implies that the blood is his, but the audience will not have access to this stage direction and so will perhaps be uncertain whether the blood on the Sergeant indicates his wounds or the wounds he has inflicted on others with a "bloody execution" like Macbeth's. After all, when Macbeth later talks of Malcolm and Donalbain as their father's killers, he calls them "our bloody cousins" (3.1.29), just as here Duncan calls the Sergeant "this bloody man" (1.2.1). Of course, Duncan refers literally to the presence of stage gore, and at the end of the scene it becomes clear that the Sergeant bleeds from gashes on his body, but later stage blood is worn by the killer, rather than the victim:

Macbeth. . . . There's blood on thy face.
First Murderer. 'Tis Banquo's then.
(3.4.14–15)

There is another possible reason that, if the Macbeths' hands have stains of (stage) blood on them, those around them do not appear to notice, and it concerns the selective and/or subjective nature of ocular proofs. Just as the bearing of blood on hands or clothes can be a sign of guilt, so also the *seeing* of blood can be the sign of a guilty conscience. At a banquet Macbeth sees the bloody ghost of Banquo, whose murder he has ordered, but the other dinner guests, innocent of Banquo's blood, apparently do not. Interestingly, it appears that the audience is situated with the guilty, if the stage direction for the appearance of Banquo's ghost is authentic (3.4.41 s.d.). So also in the host miracles it is the party that is in some sense "guilty" who sees the bloody apparition of finger, hand, or whole body of Christ—the skeptical priest, the mocking baker, or the host-torturing (and, in medieval thought, Christ-murdering) Jew. In Croxton, the whole audience sees the child appear with wounds bloody, and indeed the (presumably faithful) Bishop can see it, too: in a sense, this is appropriate, since the audience and the Bishop will have seen the host, which is merely a prop, unconsecrated, and have interpreted it as a prop, not as the sacramental symbol but as a substitute for that symbol. The "belief" of theatrical audiences is not like the "belief" of the faithful: the former is a willed belief in what is seen, the latter a willed belief in what is not seen.

So if we believe that the consecrated host in a church is Christ but the prop-host in Croxton is not Christ, we can enjoy, within the fictional world of the play, the spectacle of Christ's bloody wounds with which the church would present the unbeliever. This brings us to a third reason that those onstage with the Macbeths might not comment on the (stage) blood on their hands. Stage convention is very potent and audiences are sophisticated in their ability to distinguish between what they should and should not "see." If Macbeth tells the audience that it is a foul night, then they will willfully not "see" that it is a sunny afternoon; so also the Banquo actor, on stage with Macbeth, must see only what he is told to see. Sometimes an actor's lines, or those of characters around him, imply "seeing" different things, as when Macbeth sees Banquo's ghost in his seat and Lennox asserts that the seat is empty (III.4, 45): the audience is then able to see two "realities" at once through the eyes of different actors. But the actors have no lines with which either to support or contradict the Macbeths' assertions that they have blood on their hands, and no stage directions to indicate reactions, either. Therefore their characters do not react, and the audience has no way to know whether to see or not see the bloodstains, no way of knowing whether they are within or without the play's fiction.

The transferability of blood as a prop marks its vital difference from severed heads or limbs, which can mark violence and murder by being apparently detached from one body, but which cannot then be attached to another. But if the Macbeths' comments on their bloodstained hands are actually metatheatrical moments in which the actor ruefully references the difficulty of washing off stage paint, then bloodstains would function a little like the severed body part that, left on stage, becomes "the focus of generic and tonal uncertainty"[33] marking a moment when a play may veer between comedy and tragedy. The severed limb does this because it is a prop, with a "real" existence within and without the play's fiction, and this existence is awkward. Special effects present challenges in the execution—how *did* the Croxton troupe sever Jonathas's hand?—but also sometimes in their aftermath—what does one do with the hand once severed? How does one clear the stage of fake limbs or fake blood?

The practical problem that the actors must face is in some way the same as the one that confronts the characters they present, as Shakespeare gleefully indicates in *Titus Andronicus*. At the end of 3.1, Titus is left on stage with Marcus, Lavinia, and the severed heads of two of his sons, as well as his own severed hand. They need to clear the stage, and, Lavinia having also had her hands cut off, they only have three functioning hands among them with which to do it. Titus improvises instructions to deal with this problem of stage management, including the macabre order to Lavinia that she carry his hand in her mouth: "Bear thou my hand, sweet wench, between thy teeth" (3.1.283).[34] In the 2013 RSC production directed by Michael Fentimen, Stephen Boxer as Titus played this to superb comic effect, presenting the exasperation and mild embarrassment of a stage manager caught short by an unanticipated practical problem. That this stage direction is, metatheatrically, an improvisation forced on the actors presenting mutilated characters apparently rendered it implausible to early printers: a variant reading in Q1 seems to indicate that "teeth" was altered to "arms" by an early corrector who could not believe that the hand was really supposed to be carried in the mouth. In fact, as Jonathan Bate notes, "*Pace* correctors and editors, the emblem of the hand between the teeth is perfectly appropriate: it accentuates Lavinia's role as *hand*maid of Revenge."[35] We could add that it accentuates Lavinia's momentary role as a—somewhat inadequate—stage*hand*. Shakespeare the man of the theater makes a potent theatrical symbol out of a stage management contingency.

So also in the Croxton *Play of the Sacrament*, when Jonathas loses his hand, his fellow Jews have to deal with the severed hand and a bleeding host both nailed to a post. The post, with its bloody load, apparently remains on stage during the scene between Master Brundyche and his sidekick Colle, whose promises of diagnosis through uroscopy and healing through herbs are patently inadequate for the situation: their absurdity is emphasized by the onstage presence of the severed hand, since Jonathas clearly does not need to "piss in a pot" for medical analysis.[36] His complaint is material and obvious. Equally material and obvious is the "image" that appears "with woundys bledyng" when the Jews' oven bursts, but the material difficulties of stage management that both image and severed hand present can, in the Croxton narrative, be miraculously resolved. Jonathas's severed hand, exceptionally for severed body parts on stage, can be miraculously reattached to its owner though the intervention of Christ, the Real Presence behind the Eucharistic host, represented onstage by the bleeding image that emerges from the prop host. As the stage directions have it, "Here shall Ser Jonathas put hys hand into the cawdron, and yt shalbe hole agayn" (697 s.d.); and "the image" shall then "change agayn into brede" (745 s.d.): these stage directions at once assert the fictional narrative, stating that the hand "shall be whole" and referring to an image and bread, not to Christ and a host, and also offer a fictional resolution to the stage management problem—although no advice is given as to how these theatrical illusions are to be achieved, the reattached hand will not be difficult to get off stage, and neither will the bread. The Bishop simply picks up the bread and lays it on the altar, at which point even the stage directions refer to it as "the Host" (785, s.d.). The Eucharistic symbolism has been reasserted, and for the audience this prop is once again theatrically unremarkable.

The severed hand and the bleeding image, for all their potency as proofs, are objects that can be readily removed from the audience's sight—though perhaps not their memory[37]—through tricks of theater craft. However, blood, or even paint used to represent it, can only be transferred and is not readily washed away. The bleeding host of Bolsena left its mark on the stones of a church floor and the cloth of a church altar as a witness to the Real Presence. The theatrical blood of the Croxton stage effects is likely to make its mark on the costumes of the Jews; it is also likely to leave traces in the playing area of the *Play of the Sacrament*.[38] How may these traces be interpreted; of what are they proof? Blood in the playing area marks the theatrical nature of the violence that has been enacted: comfortingly, it is unreal; discomfortingly, the play insists on its imitation of reality, and the very fictionality of the stage blood ensures that it is not miraculously absorbed or cleared up, but nor can it shine as proof of any Real Presence, since it was always only theater. Blood on the hands and clothes of Jonathas may be the proof of his "murder" of Christ, but may also indicate his own wounded hand, nailed like Christ's: Jonathas the Jew and Christ, the victim of his violence, are curiously connected through the blood proof, which, as we have seen, cannot always distinguish between perpetrator and victim.

Chapter 13

Simular Proof, Tragicomic Turns, and *Cymbeline*'s Bloody Cloth

PATRICIA PARKER

Shakespeare's late romance *Cymbeline* has been famously called "much ado about everything." And that can be said with a vengeance about its relation to blood. It begins with "blood" and ends with "blood"—from its opening echo of medical and cosmological discourses ("Our bloods / No more obey the heavens than our courtiers / Still seem as does the King," [1.1.1–3]) to its concluding "Never was a war did cease, / Ere bloody hands were washed, with such a peace" (5.4.482–83).[1] It repeatedly raises the issue of "royal blood" (4.2.173)—from Cymbeline's accusation against Posthumus ("thou'rt poison to my blood," [1.1.128]) after his daughter has married this "baser" man (for which her punishment will be to "languish / A drop of blood a day" [1.1.156–57]) to the "princely blood" (3.3.93) of his stolen sons in Wales, who had never "looked on blood" (4.4.36) before the Roman invasion but whose "blood" shows them to be "princes born" (4.4.53–54), even before they are discovered to be "blood" of the King's own "begetting" (5.4.331). Its iterated evocations of "bloody" death (1.2.4) include the "bloody affirmation" (1.4.47) of the zero-sum game of dueling to which both Posthumus and Cloten are addicted and the description of the "paper" of Posthumus's letter as having "cut" Innogen's "throat" with "slander" ("Whose edge is sharper than the sword" [3.4.31–32]). It dramatically foregrounds stage blood in the simultaneously gruesome and comically incongruous scene in which Innogen (disguised as the boy Fidele) smears herself with the blood of the headless body (or "bloody man" [4.2.296]) she thinks to be Posthumus but the audience knows is Cloten, in a visual display that evokes what Simon Palfrey has called a "post-coital tableau of bloody dehymenization."[2] It explicitly invokes bloodletting in Arviragus's "I'd let a parish of such Clotens blood" (4.2.167) to regain the "color" of the boy Fidele he wrongly earlier assumes to be dead, a line that gains an ironic resonance when the apparently resurrected Innogen/Fidele smears herself in "blood" she doesn't know is Cloten's, in order to "give colour to my pale cheek" (4.2.329). And it foregrounds the relation of blood and genre in its reprise of the revenge tradition of the *lex talionis* or "blood for blood" and the "bloody cloth" (5.1.1) that ultimately effects a tragicomic turn from revenge to forgiveness.

* * *

At the same time, blood in *Cymbeline* is inseparable from the problem of proof, including ocular proof, even apart from the "bloody cloth" that Posthumus demands his servant Pisanio provide from a distance as a definitive "bloody sign" (3.4.124) of Innogen's death. The issue of hymeneal blood is not only central to the question of whether or not the marriage of Posthumus and Innogen has ever been consummated but is directly conflated with "testimonies" (the major issue in a play obsessed with what is credited as reliable testimony and proof), in the letter in which Posthumus gives Pisanio the order to shed Innogen's blood as revenge for her assumed infidelity, in lines where Posthumus himself is figured as a bleeding female body:

> Thy mistress, Pisanio, hath played the strumpet in my bed, the *testimonies* whereof lie bleeding in me. I speak not out of weak surmises, but from *proof* as strong as my grief and as certain as I expect my revenge: That part thou, Pisanio, must act for me, if thy faith be not tainted with the breach of hers. Let thine own hands take away her life. (3.4.21–26, italics mine)

This speech has traditionally been read in relation to Francis Beaumont and John Fletcher's play *Philaster, or Love Lies A-Bleeding*, now usually thought to have predated *Cymbeline*.[3] But—on its own terms—the pun here on bleeding "testimonies" and testicles (noted by Janet Adelman, Ruth Nevo, and others) conflates a bloody emasculation or castration with an image of hymeneal blood (as proof of the loss of virginity), strangely transferred from female to male.[4] Adelman reads these lines as a kind of sex change, in which "The vivid physicality" of Posthumus's response to Innogen's assumed strumpetry—"the testimonies whereof lie bleeding in me"—not only "conflates the two acts," the "supposed act of adultery" and "the act of marital consummation," but makes it not Innogen but rather the husband Posthumus who is "left bleeding in bed."[5] And she goes on to observe that the "bloody cloth" that will later become the "bloody sign" of his revenge not only alludes, like Othello's handkerchief, to the bloodied wedding sheets, but "reverses the act that left Posthumus's testimonies bleeding there," signaling "the excision of the woman's part in him" and reassuring him ("through its allusion to menstrual blood") that "she—not he—is the bearer of the woman's part."[6]

We will return to *Cymbeline*'s bloody cloth in relation to the central issue of what is credited or believed (including what Iachimo calls "simular proof"), but it is important to note first that its echoing of the spotted handkerchief of *Othello* (the play it famously rewrites) not only connects it to the problem of blood as evidence, testimony, or proof of Innogen's death but also to the problem of whether the marriage of Innogen and Posthumus has ever been consummated—a crucial issue in a play that harps on penetration (2.3.11, 12, 24) and carnal "knowledge" (2.4.51, 79), but that remains enshrouded in what Ellen Spolsky has called "cognitive impenetrability,"[7] even though this radical uncertainty also ups the stakes of the wager plot and the assumed infidelity of Innogen herself.

Critics and editors of *Cymbeline* have come down on differing sides of this question, marshaling evidence or proof from the text to buttress their position.[8] But in the absence of any certain evidence (a cognitive impenetrability that *Cymbeline* shares with *Othello*), this critical and editorial history stands as a double or mirror of the problems of proof foregrounded by the play itself.[9] As Karen Cunningham has observed, "The clearest thing about evidence in *Cymbeline* . . . is that it is neither stable nor self-pronouncing, its meanings open to resistance and reformulation."[10] And the evidential problem of hymeneal blood is even further compounded in a Shakespeare canon in which, as Heather James has observed, "Arguments that stress the status of a Shakespearean marital contract by consummation run up against Shakespeare's delight in having his heroines both ways: Desdemona, Imogen, and Lavinia 'are and are not' virgins. When Lavinia is raped the day *after* her marriage, Shakespeare uses images of defloration."[11]

* * *

The bloody cloth of *Cymbeline*'s final act, which Posthumus assumes to be definitive proof of Innogen's death, is itself surrounded by ambiguity in the lines in which Posthumus addresses it as that act begins:

Yea, bloody cloth, I'll keep thee, for I wished
Thou shouldst be coloured thus. You married ones,
If each of you should take this course, how many
Must murder wives much better than themselves,
For wrying but a little!
                                                    (5.1.1-5)

"Yea, bloody cloth, I'll keep thee, for I wished / Thou shouldst be coloured thus" ambiguously conflates the "bloody sign" of his desired revenge with the other consummation devoutly to be wished, the (displaced) ocular proof of hymeneal blood that aligns it with the spotted "handkerchief" of *Othello*. But it is also crucial to the play's own tragicomic turn—as the sight of it transforms Posthumus from murderous revenge to repentance and forgiveness, including forgiving Innogen for what he still (falsely) believes was her "wrying" or infidelity.

As almost the definition of an overdetermined signifier, *Cymbeline*'s bloody cloth is capable of very different readings, including in relation to the turn from tragedy to comedy it effects. For Janet Adelman, it stands as a sign of the female sacrifice that is necessary for this very turn to take place: "Posthumus's return to Imogen is in fact thoroughly mediated by her victimization, as though that victimization were its precondition: he returns to her in imagination only when he thinks her dead, only when he is given safe passage by the bloody cloth that ambiguously signifies both her wounded sexuality and his punishment of her." And it echoes the "self-abnegation" of Innogen's own earlier self-sacrifice—in the scene in which she turns from "the righteous indignation of 'False to his bed? What is it to be false?'" (3.4.38) to "When thou seest him, / A little witness my obedience. Look, / I draw the sword myself'" (3.4.63–64).[12]

Valerie Wayne also points to the bloody cloth's "enigmatic significance," noting that it provides yet "another sign of the woman's part," since it evokes not only the "supposed stain of Innogen's blood . . . designed to confirm her murder" and "the bloodstained sheets of a marriage bed—like the handkerchief spotted with strawberries in *Othello*"—but also "associations . . . with menstruation."[13] And it simultaneously evokes "the stain of womankind associated with Eve and original sin in the second wager scene," where Innogen's mole, described as having five spots ("cinque-spotted, like the crimson drops / I'th' bottom of a cowslip" [2.2.38–39]), becomes a moral "stain when Iachimo sullies it to entrap Posthumus," a "stain" whose "associations of the erotic body and sexual guilt migrate to the bloody cloth" of the play's final act.[14]

Wayne notes that this bloody cloth is linked to sacrifice and the blood of a lamb through one of the play's own acknowledged sources—the anonymous *Frederyke of Jennen*, where the character who corresponds to Pisanio (who has been "commanded to deliver his mistress's tongue and a lock of her hair") instead "kills a lamb that has accompanied her, uses the lamb's tongue and a lock of his mistress's hair, then anoints her clothes with the blood of the lamb and presents all three objects to his master"[15]—a detail that she relates to the scene in *Cymbeline* where "Innogen encourages Pisanio to dispatch her quickly and invites his knife with the words, 'The lamb entreats the butcher' (3.4.96)," so that "The bloody cloth is associated with sacrifice," and hence "more like a martyr's relic or a memento mori than a commodity." But in a reading very different from Adelman's, Wayne sees this enigmatic bloody cloth—and its putting on by Posthumus[16]—as Posthumus's acceptance (and even cherishing) of "this sign of women's sexuality, a visual stain associated with the sex that bleeds at the loss of virginity and has a bloody discharge as part of the process of generation." Wayne argues that "for Posthumus the cloth replaces the diamond ring that had belonged to Innogen's mother," functioning as "a sign of women's role in establishing lineage, as a token of Innogen's body, and evidence of Posthumus's guilt"; and that "Through this stage property, the play provides some alternative to Janet Adelman's opinion that 'the fantasy solution of *Cymbeline* was to do away with the female body altogether.'" She adds that "Through the bloody cloth, Posthumus's acceptance of the stain of womankind, his incorporation of it on his own body and admission of his greater guilt, are presented as resolutions to sexual and marital discord" in a final act where the "theatrical display of the cloth animates this accommodation and manifests it through performance." And she concludes that by the end of the play, where Cymbeline refers to "bloody hands" not yet washed, all

Simular Proof, Tragicomic Turns, and *Cymbeline's* Bloody Cloth 203

of the figures on stage are "so stained with the blood of war that the stain of womankind on the bloody cloth is no longer a visual exception to the scene but in keeping with the larger spectacle."[17]

* * *

What I would like to do is not to contest earlier descriptions of the bloody cloth's complex overdetermination, but rather to complicate it still further by adding another cultural subtext it simultaneously evokes and transforms, including in relation to the crucial issue of proof—not just the bloody wounds of the stigmata (cited by Marion Lomax in a now-classic study[18]), but also the bloody cloth that was a bloody sign of Christ's resurrection, familiar not only from earlier religious drama but also from the "Redcrosse" of Spenser's *Faerie Queene*. *The Faerie Queene* has been cited as an important source for *Cymbeline*—but not (curiously) its biblical First Book, even though Redcrosse, its error-prone protagonist, like Posthumus, falls into despair and is ultimately ministered to by Fidelia, the female figure evocative of the "faith" of 1 Corinthians 13, whose name is recalled in *Cymbeline*'s "Fidele."[19] And both Spenser's Redcrosse knight and Posthumus come to doubt the fidelity of the principal female figure on the basis of specious, counterfeit, or "simular proof."

Blood and the biblical iconography of blood figure prominently in Redcrosse's romance journey—from reminders of baptism as being washed in the blood of the Lamb to the sacramental flow of blood from the lancing of Christ's side, the blood-red clothing worn by the treader of the wine-press in Isaiah 63 (alluded to in the Croxton Play and other biblically inspired earlier works), and the figure of Christ as the knight "Faithful and True" in Revelation 19 (11–16).[20] But even more central to this biblical and religious iconography is a bloody cloth—the "red cross" of whose meaning Spenser's erring protagonist is ignorant but that stands as the bloody sign of the death and resurrection of this knight "faithful and true," a sign (also requiring faith or belief) that was a visual commonplace in the iconography of the resurrection of Christ as the sacrificed Lamb of God (recalled in the comparison of Innogen to a lamb) as well as the red and white of St. George and the Tudor iconography that appropriated it.[21]

Readings that align *Cymbeline* with Spenser's romance frequently see this play as endorsing a similarly biblical orientation,[22] a "transcendental" turn in its final act that its New Cambridge editor Martin Butler relates to the "play's hidden awareness of the 'fact' that Christ was born in Cymbeline's reign."[23] But in arguing for the bloody cloth of Act 5 as a reminder of this resurrectional iconography (among its other significations), what I want to suggest is something quite different—namely that Shakespeare's late tragicomic romance simultaneously evokes this religious tradition and gives it a perverse early modern theatrical twist. The bloody cloth of Act 5 is undeniably instrumental in effecting the turn from tragedy to comedy that has led some critics to a "transcendental" reading, one that often stresses the biblical echoes of Act 5 itself. But *Cymbeline*'s last act (and final "recognition scene") simultaneously underscore that by the end of the play that revelation has not yet occurred. The ultimate recognition scene of the Apocalypse (with its separation, at last, of counterfeit or "simular" sign and true) may be foreshadowed, but even the coming of Christ remains an epiphany, blood sacrifice, and redemption still in the future. The extended speech of Iachimo that purports to be a sincere confession and repentance for his having led Posthumus astray, by what he calls "simular proof enough" (5.4.200), is in the play's final scene a consummate theatrical performance. There is in the play itself no ultimate "Faithful and True."[24] Even "Fidele" (whose name evokes faith and Fidelia as well as fidelity to the truth) is revealed in this "recognition scene" to be part of the counterfeit or simular, in the metatheatrical moment in which the "woman's part" is revealed to be a theatrical "part" performed by a boy player (5.4.228–29) in an English transvestite theater that traffics in such simulations. And the "bloody cloth" (or "bloody sign") that effectively turns Posthumus from revenge to forgiveness is itself only "simular proof," recalling the falsely assumed death (and empty tomb) of *Much Ado About Nothing* that has a similar effect on Claudio but is (in Barbara Everett's wonderful phrase) not the empty tomb of the Resurrection but only a theatrically effective "tomb trick."[25]

Spenser's Redcrosse knight carries a bloody sign of whose transcendent meaning he is ignorant (unlike Posthumus who wrongly thinks he *knows* what is signified by *his* "bloody sign"), but that is ultimately (and transcendentally) aligned with the bloody sign of the death and resurrection of the figure the Book of Revelation calls "Faithful and True," as well as the stigmata or bloody wounds of the Lamb of God. By contrast, the "bloody sign" sent to Posthumus as (false) ocular proof of the death of the woman who has been compared to a sacrificed lamb is a simular or counterfeit sign of a death that has not taken place, and hence is not in need of any resurrection, though it seems to be one to the characters on stage who are surprised to see Innogen/Fidele alive on stage in the final recognition scene.

The faith that Posthumus places in this bloody cloth or bloody sign is ironically not unlike the faith or belief he had accorded earlier in the play to other false signs, like the bracelet or "manacle" that initially convinced him that Innogen had "wryed" or been unfaithful or the "simular proof" of the "mole" as a five-spotted (or "cinque-spotted") stain, among the so-called "natural notes" (2.2.28) on Innogen's body, a "note" that itself may provide an echo of the stigmata (another well-known meaning of *nota* or "note" in the period).[26] The bloody cloth (or "bloody sign") that Posthumus credits as evidence in Act 5 is thus part of the complex issue of false or misleading evidence (or ocular proof) in this late Shakespearean play. But at the same time, this false sign effects a change in Posthumus *as if* it were true.

* * *

There is one other twist the play gives to the "sign" of this bloody cloth, not from its biblical but from its Ovidian context, the *Metamorphoses* of Ovid from which Innogen has been reading in Act 2. The most striking Ovidian instance of a *false* bloody sign or proof is the bloody cloth of the Pyramus and Thisbe story, already used in both tragic and comic contexts in Shakespeare before a bloody cloth becomes in *Cymbeline* the pivotal symbol of its tragicomic turn. The blood of this Ovidian story had itself already been connected to the blood of Christ through the tradition of Ovid moralized,[27] which Shakespeare comically recalls in *A Midsummer Night's Dream* in the scenes involving Bottom as the Pyramus who (like Christ) exits the stage but is to "come again" (3.1.92).[28] In this "moralized" tradition, the blood of Pyramus that turns the mulberry from white to purple or blood-red is the counterpart of the shedding of Christ's blood on the cross. But in Ovid's *unmoralized* story of lovers separated by their families (as Posthumus and Innogen have been), the bloody cloth famously functions as a misleading sign that is tragically misread. When Pyramus in Ovid sees the cloth stained with blood, like Posthumus he wrongly assumes that his love is dead and offers his own blood in return, in a suicide echoed in Posthumus's suicidal death wish in Act 5, after he enters with the bloody cloth that convinces him that Innogen is dead.

Though we usually associate this Ovidian story with the tragedy of *Romeo and Juliet*, reprised in burlesque comic fashion in the Pyramus and Thisbe play of *A Midsummer Night's Dream*, Shakespeare in fact returned to it again and again in the plays before *Cymbeline*, including grotesquely in relation to both murder and hymeneal blood in *Titus Andronicus*, where the "blood-stained hole" (2.3.210) in which the bloody murder of Bassanius is discovered becomes linked with the sign of a vaginal deflowering, in the reference soon after to Pyramus bathed in "maiden blood" ("So pale did shine the moon on Pyramus / When he by night lay bath'd in maiden blood" [2.3.231–32]). As Jonathan Bate comments in his edition of that play, the image of "maiden blood," with its "hint of hymeneal blood, evokes the simultaneous offstage action in which Lavinia is being deflowered (as if for the second time in a few hours, with the difference that on the wedding-night it was consensual)." And even more grotesquely, in the immediately following scene, the blood streaming from the limbs of the raped and mutilated Lavinia (in lines that simultaneously evoke the rape of Philomel, the Ovidian story that Innogen is reading) recalls the image in Ovid of Pyramus's blood spouting as if from a conduit pipe (or as Arthur Golding rendered it, Pyramus's "bloud did spin on hie / As when a conduit pipe is cract") in "all this loss of blood. / As from a conduit with three issuing spouts" (2.4.29–30).[29]

Ovid's bloody cloth is recalled yet again in *As You Like It*, where a "bloody napkin" (4.3.93, 138) or "handkerchief" (4.3.97) functions as a (true) sign of Orlando's fidelity to his "Rosalind" (or Ganymede) and of his wounding by the "lioness" (4.3.114). And it returns once again in *Othello*, where the reference to the "worms" that did breed the "silk" of the handkerchief itself (3.4.73) recalls the silk-producing mulberry tree of the Pyramus and Thisbe story, in a tragedy that racializes its plot of doomed love.[30] In the most famous comic reprise of the story, in *A Midsummer Night's Dream*, the bloody cloth is not only taken as a false sign or proof of a tragic death but is also identified with hymeneal blood or deflowering—in lines that conflate both kinds of consummation—as the "mantle" of Thisbe "Which Lion vile with bloody mouth did stain" (5.1.142–43) is assumed by Pyramus/Bottom to be a sign of her death ("Thy mantle good, / What, stain'd with blood?" [5.1.282–83]) in lines where he goes on to ask "O, wherefore, Nature, didst thou lions frame? / Since lion vile hath here *deflow'r'd* my dear" (5.1.291–92). Strikingly, in the plot of separated lovers in *Cymbeline*, a play that traces Posthumus Leonatus to his etymological "root" (as a "lion's whelp," or the "fit and apt construction" of his name as "*leo-natus*," [5.4.442–43]), Posthumus himself is tragicomically cast as *both* the Pyramus figure and the "Lion" he (mistakenly) thinks has killed his "deer," in lines on a bloody cloth whose enigmatic "coloured" simultaneously evokes hymeneal blood.

* * *

Andrew Sofer, in *The Stage Life of Props*, argues that the bloody cloth of Thomas Kyd's influential *Spanish Tragedy* simultaneously recalls earlier dramatic cloths on the English stage that provided "ocular proof of Christ's resurrection" and transforms them into a theatrical sign of bloody revenge, exploiting "the medieval association between holy cloth and sacred blood" for commercial purposes and implying "that the power of the theater is the power of surrogation: the ability to spin out a potentially infinite chain of metonymic displacements."[31] Shakespeare's late romance simultaneously recalls and transforms through its "bloody cloth" the familiar iconographic sign of a religious form of "ocular proof," in a false "bloody sign" that paradoxically effects a major transformation, turning the plot from tragic to comic and recalling the paradox articulated by its sender Pisanio himself ("Where I am false, I am honest; not true, to be true" [4.3.42]).

Sujata Iyengar has surveyed what she calls the "Passion Plays" in Shakespeare that feature bloody cloths, from the cloth steeped in the blood of York's murdered child in *3 Henry VI* that recalls "Christ's Passion and Crucifixion" and the Pyramus and Thisbe play of *A Midsummer Night's Dream* that suggests "a monstrous parody of the Passion" to the evocation of "the sacrificial Biblical passion" in the "bloody napkin" that is "dyed" in Orlando's blood in *As You Like It* and the spotted "handkerchief" of *Othello*, where the word "passion" is insistently repeated. And she concludes of *Cymbeline*, where the bloody cloth provides "(faked) evidence of Innogen's death," that it "lacks passion."[32] What I would suggest instead is that the "bloody cloth" of this late play simultaneously and strikingly recalls the Passion (and proofs) of the biblical context its final act so insistently evokes, the "moralized" tradition that enabled its conflation with the Ovidian, and the unmoralized "bloody cloth" of the Ovidian subtext in which its status as proof is tragically undermined. And that it transforms all three into a false "bloody sign" that has an ironically transformative effect, not only recalling the "tomb trick" of *Much Ado About Nothing*, but ultimately turning tragedy into comedy via a cloth that is no less a "simular proof" than the material signs that had led to the tragedy to begin with.

PART V

Signs and Substance

Chapter 14

Blood of the Grape

FRANCES E. DOLAN

This chapter examines the associations between blood and wine that are so central to the Christian Eucharist in a different context: arguments that the English should grow their own grapes and make their own wine. As we will see, these arguments link wine to blood in order to add urgency and prestige to economic and medical incentives, to demonize the widespread tampering required to make most wines palatable, and to characterize wine as, like the blood it resembles, equivocal, unstable, necessary yet dangerous.

In early modern England, blood and wine were associated at the most basic level by their appearance: the wine most widely drunk and discussed usually seems to have been red—because red wine did a somewhat better job of disguising the effects of time and decay. Even wines we might now think of as white, including sack or sherry, Rhenish, and canary, were sometimes made from red grapes, raisins, or a mixture of grapes. These "white" wines were sometimes associated with urine, as the red wine on which I will focus here was associated with blood. Wine was, for the most part, oxidized, dark, and sticky.[1]

Blood and wine were also assumed to have analogous functions in human and plant bodies and to be compatible, even interchangeable. As we will see, promoters of growing grapes and making wine in England and its colonies drew on the association between blood and wine to justify their enterprise. The frequent analogies between these two fluids reveal the perceived affinities among plant, animal, and human bodies; the overlaps between agricultural and medical discourses; the practical consequences and material manifestations of figuration; the complex entanglements of past and present; and the challenges of "drinking local."

Communion in both kinds, experienced physically or mystically, modeled the ingestion of blood and reinforced the association of wine with blood. Genesis prohibits the consumption of blood because it is the manifestation of vitality itself—"But flesh with the life thereof, which is the blood thereof, shall ye not eat."[2] Yet, elsewhere in Genesis and in Deuteronomy, we also find wine described as having a privileged and purifying status because it is the "blood of the grape."[3] We see here a double view of blood and by extension wine. The association with the essence of life that makes the ingestion of blood prohibited also elevates wine as especially powerful and salvific. The medieval tradition of depicting "Christ in the winepress" imagined Jesus as both a winemaker and a "pressed grape." He is "crushed like a grape in a winepress" to yield the sacrificial blood that will redeem the faithful. In popular woodcuts of Christ in the winepress from the twelfth century through the fifteenth, the Western-style press, in which a screw or lever presses a weight down on the grapes, replaces the crucifix as the mechanism by which Jesus's sacrifice becomes sustenance. Through these representations, "belief in the symbolic unity of blood and wine trickled down to every level of society."[4] This imagery also informed religious poetry from Lydgate through Milton. Following the Reformation, debate focused on whether wine figured or became Jesus's blood. But this debate did not rupture the perceived connection between these two ubiquitous fluids.

Despite widespread consumption of beer in England, wine was a favored beverage for most of the seventeenth century, until coffee, tea, chocolate, and distilled spirits diversified beverage options and challenged its monopoly. Most people drank fermented beverages of one kind or another rather than water. Valueless at best, contaminated at worst, water was only considered potable if it was amended with honey, sugar, or wine or boiled.[5] Water was so disparaged that one English prisoner of war complained in his account of his captivity by the French that he and his fellow sufferers had "no other Drink but Water."[6] He recounts the improvement in their circumstances in terms of their upgrade from water to wine. One kind of evidence about the ubiquity of wine as a generic beverage in early modern England is its presence on stage where, according to Alan Dessen and Leslie Thompson's *Dictionary of Stage Directions*, wine is "the most common item in tavern or banquet scenes or at other times when figures drink," appearing in about sixty-five stage directions.

Blood of the Grape

This stage wine is undifferentiated by grape or region.[7] Wine, then, stands as daily "drink" in palaces and public houses even as it has particular significance in part because of its biblical and sacramental precedents and its visual resemblance to and conceptual resonance with blood.

Just as wine was ubiquitous, blood, too, was a familiar sight and smell, as other contributors to this volume attest. Public punishments and executions; blood sports such as bear baiting; butchery, often conducted at home, and its concomitant blood and guts; the use of blood as an ingredient in food and medicine; and bloodletting in medical practice all conspired to make the sight and smell of blood almost certainly more common then than now.[8] Everyone consumed blood—in repurposed form as breast milk, in the communion cup, in various foods and medicines. Yet, at the same time, blood consumption was demonized in representations of cannibalism or of witches suckling their familiars.

The biblical characterization of wine or juice as the blood of the grape suggests the ways that an understanding of human anatomy, however flawed, served as the model for understanding plant anatomy by analogy. As the circulation of blood was gradually understood, so the sap in trees and vines and the juice in fruits came to be understood as circulating through plants and essential to their vitality.[9] The analogy between blood and wine both holds and breaks down in equally interesting ways. At the most basic level, the analogy obscures the distinction between the sap of a tree or vine and the juice of its fruit. It also ignores the fact that juice is not wine in the grape but requires time and intervention to become wine. Yet most early modern discussions of wine are acutely, uncomfortably aware that what was in the glass was not just what had been pressed out of the grape and that wine changed over time. Even before the operations of yeast and bacteria in wine were understood, wine was recognized as dynamic, for ill and for good.

William Harvey used the resemblance between blood and wine to explain what he saw as the loss in vitality that occurred when blood left the body:

> in their different ways blood and spirit . . . mean one and the same thing. For, as wine with all its bouquet gone is no longer wine but a flat vinegary fluid, so also is blood without spirit no longer blood but the equivocal gore. As a stone hand or a hand that is dead is no longer a hand, so blood without the spirit of life is no longer blood, but is to be regarded as spoiled immediately it has been deprived of spirit.[10]

Harvey compares shed blood to flat wine; both have lost their spirit. In her important study of humoral medicine and the early modern body, Gail Kern Paster points to the proverb "There is no difference of bloods in a basin" to demonstrate that blood could only do its job of asserting social distinctions when it was inside the body. Once out of the body, Paster argues, blood lost its "spirit or driving force" to become "waste matter to be disposed of."[11] Yet Harvey's description of "equivocal" gore suggests that blood as it leaves the body is both in and out, living and dead. It is the sap of life in the process of coagulating into a thing.

Blood's "equivocal" status outside the human body and the analogy between blood and wine informed even the most practical early modern agricultural advice. With regard to pruning, for example, one treatise advises that vines will bleed "themselves to Death" if they are pruned too late in the season.[12] In agricultural manuals, we find both a lingering association of blood with pollution and blight—in the advisory, for example, that a menstruating woman who walks among plantings will wither them[13]—and a particular value placed on blood as a soil enrichment, especially for vines. In several of his texts, Sir Hugh Plat reports that "Blood laide at the roots of old Vines, hath bin commended for an excelent substance to harten them," although he advises care in the use of so rich and hot a compost.[14] Ralph Austen suggests that the "blood of Cattle, dead Dogges, Carrion, or the like, laid or put to the Roots of trees . . . [is] found very profitable unto fruit bearing."[15] John Evelyn advises that "*Blood* is excellent almost with any Soil where Fruit is planted, especially the Mural [by which he means trees grown against and fastened to walls], to improve the blood of the *Grape* of great advantage, being somewhat diluted, and pour'd about the Roots."[16] The figuration of wine as the "blood of the grape" allows Evelyn to rhyme soil amendment and outcome, suggesting a natural affinity between the two. Spent blood found value as a fertilizer precisely because it retained some of the vitality it supposedly lost when shed, enabling it to add the juice of life to grapevines.

Just as blood's analogy to wine distinguished it as especially beneficial compost, so wine's resemblance to blood underpinned its medicinal value. Some discussions of the benefits of wine defended it not just as a supplement to the blood but almost as a substitute for it. In his treatise *The Tree of Humane Life, or the Blood of the Grape, proving the possibilitie of maintaining human life from infancy to extreme old age without any sicknesse by the use of wine* (1638, 1654), Tobias Whitaker, physician in the household of Charles I, argues that wine has a vital heat, as if it were exuded by a living body, as if it had a soul. It therefore benefits the body and especially builds up the blood because, he writes, "wine, especialy red wine, is halfe blood before it be received"; it is already, he explains, "sanguinified." While "sanguinification" had a highly technical meaning, Whitaker's use suggests that he means that wine is always "equivocal," part itself and part blood, and poised for further transubstantiation. In his own experience as a physician, he claims to have witnessed wine drinkers' "consumptive and extenuate bodyes restored to a farcocity [which seems to mean fullness or plenitude as if restuffed], and from withered Bodys to fresh, plumpe, fat and fleshie; and from old and infirme to young, and strong." Wine suits itself to different humors and persons, giving each what he or she needs. Whitaker's word for the affinity between blood and wine is "homogeneall": wine is "Homogeneall, pleasant and familiar to humane constitutions and tempers." Recounting that he himself was cured of consumption by wine, Whitaker concludes that wine "in purity . . . exceeds all spermatique humors, sucked either from women, or breasts [sic]."[17] Just as blood might fertilize vines, so wine is sometimes depicted as a kind of fertilizer for human health. For example, Falstaff attributes Prince Hal's "heat" to his diet: "for the cold blood he did naturally inherit of his father he hath, like lean, sterile, and bare land, manured, husbanded, and tilled, with excellent endeavour of drinking good, and good store of fertile sherry, that he is become very hot and valiant."[18]

It is as if discussions of the medical benefits and risks of wine are rehearsing in advance arguments about transfusion: receiving wine as a kind of blood supplement or replacement can restore and replenish. But it can also invade and infect. If wine's close association with blood constitutes its benefit for Whitaker, it is also what worries some other commentators. John Worlidge, in *Vinetum Britannicum: Or a Treatise of Cider* (1691), first follows Whitaker in explaining that "there is no Drink more homogeneal to the Blood than *Wine*, the Spirit thereof being the best Vehicle of any Medicine to the most remote parts that the Blood circulates in." But he goes on to explain that the "homogeneality" between blood and wine can also make wine dangerous: "therefore if any evil mixture be in it, the more it operates, and is soonest conveyed to the Heart and all other parts of the Body." In other words, because wine is so like blood, it will convey contamination all too efficiently. "If it be new, that is to say, under the age of a year, or be set into a new fermentation by the addition of new *Wine* or *Stum* [which is grape must], it purges, and puts the Blood into a fermentation, that it indangers the health of him that drinks it, and sometimes his life." Whereas relatively new wine that is being raised into a new fermentation is too busy for the blood, older wine poses the problem that it was usually spoiled. "If it be old *Wine*, which is commonly the best, then the Vintners cunning in preserving it, and making it palatable by his secret and concealed Mixtures, renders it dangerous to be drank either fasting, or in great quantity; many having died suddenly meerly by drinking of such Wine."[19] The problem with wine, then, is a problem that every English writer on wine in the early modern period discusses: deterioration and adulteration.

It was so difficult to stabilize wine in this period that virtually everyone doctored it in one way or another. This might be as benign as the addition of herbs and spices. Strategies for preserving and improving wines included variations on what have since become reliable methods: increasing its sugar level (with added sugar, honey, or raisins or spirit of wine—a kind of wine concentrate—or bastard—a blend of wine and honey); or using a preservative in the form of vitriol (a metal sulphate) or sulfur. Early moderns knew that the ancient Greeks had put sulfur in their wines to keep them from "fuming";[20] some experimented with this preservative, which is still widely used in winemaking, although early modern writers describe it as a purifier as much as a preservative. In addition, other attempts were made to clear cloudy wines or remove impurities. These included adding vinegar, wood shavings, powdered marble or alum (an astringent mineral salt), egg whites, parrel (a mixture of eggs, alum, and salt), and isinglass (a kind of fish gelatin), on the argument that it bonds with any foulness or filth in the wine and causes it to sink to the bottom. Pigeons' dung is even recommended to make wines sparkle.[21] This list itself should suggest the dangerous potential of such additions. Even housewives might righteously engage in vinous adulterations and bastardizings.[22] This ingenuity was required because most wine probably tasted pretty terrible. Making it tasty was as miraculous as turning it into blood or gold.

As a consequence, some discussions of the adulteration of wine, in the guise of amendment, assign to those who doctor wines a kind of priestly or alchemical presumption. Plat points out that coopers not only "hoop the vessels" in which wine was stored but blend and often amend wines, to the profit of merchants and vintners. How, he asks, do they learn the "great variety of jugling" they practice? How is it that "these plain fellows that never read their Grammer, nor scarcely know their A, B, C, should be able to run through Ovids Metamorphosis as they do at midnight"? Plat goes on to describe "these alterations, transmutations, and sometimes even real transubstantiations of white wine into Claret, and old lags of Sacks or Malmsies, with Malassoes [molasses] into Muskadels."[23] Evelyn, in his *Pomona* (1679), a treatise on cider making, reviews the various ways of amending wine in order to warn readers off wine and win them over to cider. He concludes: "If Health be more precious than Opinion, I wish our Admirers of Wines, to the prejudice of Cider, beheld but the Cheat themselves; the Sophistications, Transformations, Transmutations, Adulterations, Bastardizings, Brewings, Trickings, not to say, even Arsenical Compassings of the Sophisticated God they adore."[24] Evelyn's exposé casts wine itself as a sophisticated god and reminds us that these arcane mysteries take place in local taverns, where vintners freely blend and amend. In the satirical dialogue *In Vino Veritas*, Chip the Cooper presents the amendment of wine as a kind of alchemical transformation. "Wines in general are not only abominably Sophisticated, but lameutably [sic] metamorphiz'd; The very *Rosycrucians* themselves transmute not metals so much as you and we do Liquors."[25] These comparisons simultaneously elevate and disparage the amendment of wine, expressing distrust of all processes of "sophistication." Rather than turning wine into blood, these magicians turn wine into poison. What's worse, relatively humble yet presumptuous workers undertake these transubstantiations and metamorphoses—and while they may clarify wines, they muddy their origins. When transubstantiations occur in English wine shops rather than in French vineyards, at the hands of coopers, tavern keepers, and housewives rather than priests, is the wine that results domestic or foreign? Amendment both adulterates wine and, arguably, domesticates it. Whereas the very name of "bastard" associates wine doctoring with illegitimacy, inferiority, and impurity, wine amendment was so widespread that there was probably little wine available that was not bastardized or adulterated.

Those who believed in the "real transubstantiations" of Catholic ritual and the Rosicrucian transmutations of alchemy were widely ridiculed as gullible, colluding in their own deception. Descriptions of wine amendment as parallel to transubstantiation or alchemy placed wine drinkers in their ignominious company: wine drinkers, too, were simultaneously desirous and dumb. Plat scolds that "we are now grown so nice in tast, that almost no wines unless they be more pleasant than they can be of the grape wil content us, nay no color unless it be perfect fine and bright, wil satisfie our wanton eyes. . . . This makes the Vintners to trick or compass all their natural wines."[26] Whereas wine drinkers want something more than grapes can really offer, they also know too little about wine. Merchants can get away with adulteration because "not one in ten of our *Chapps* knows the difference, if it be but (thought) Wine, it goes down cleaverly, poor fools, they have not Wit enough to distinguish good from bad, except it be very plain indeed, dead or sowre." One vintner supposedly boasted "nothing was so easy, as to deceive Mens Palates, in Themselves various, uncertain, and often misled by fancy and humour; that a little supple-cringing, a few fair words, and a positive asserting it to be such or such Wine, neat and rare, carried it off cleverly."[27] In the epilogue to *As You Like It*, Rosalind reminds the audience of the proverb that a "good wine needs no bush," that is, that good wine needs no advertising.[28] But exposés of winemaking reveal that bad wine needs only "a few fair words" to pass it off as good. Like alchemists and priests, the logic goes, vintners cunningly deceive their marks.

The widespread awareness that imported wines were almost invariably adulterated motivated the claim that honest beverages of English manufacture would be better for English constitutions—despite the fact that much of the alteration of imported wine, as we have seen, probably took place in England. The quest to make English wine that can rival that of the continent continues today, receiving an assist from global warming. The desire to make wine in England in the seventeenth century emerged first from concerns about punitive import taxes, the costs of transport, and, before reliable ways of stabilizing wines, the inevitable loss in flavor with time and transit, as well as the risks of additives. But it gained urgency from what Mary Floyd-Wilson calls geohumoralism—the presumed relationship between body and place, health and location.[29] Sir Thomas Browne robustly refused this notion when he claimed, in *Religio Medici*, that "I am of a constitution so general, that it consorts and symphathizeth with all things. I have no antipathy—or rather idiosyncrasy—in diet, humour, air, anything. . . . I am no Plant that will not prosper out of a garden; all places, all airs, make unto me one country—I am in England everywhere, and under any meridian."[30] But many others persisted in the belief that sympathy bound body, birth, and diet (among other things) and that the foreign was antipathetic. By this logic, if blood and wine are analogous, even fungible, then it is perilous to infuse English bodies with foreign blood. At a time of agricultural innovation at home and colonial expansion abroad, defenders of English winemaking drew on the claim that wine was not just any food or beverage but had the potential for a more intimate relationship to the body—for good or ill—in order to argue that English wine would best suit English bodies.

One of the earliest and most influential articulations of this argument appears, ironically, in Richard Surflet's English translation of *Maison Rustique or the Country Farm* (first translated in 1600).

> But howsoever foraine wines, which are fetched from far countries may seeme pleasant unto our taste, yet indeede the truth is that we

are not to use them except it be with as great advise and judgement as may bee, because that besides their manifest outward qualities, they have also close and hidden ones, which indeed may become familiar and well agreeing through some sympathie, with the inhabitants of those countries, where the said wines grow: but unto us they are enemies, by an antipathie or contrarietie which is betwixt them and us, which are of a soile and countrie far unlike.[31]

Foreign wines keep secrets from their drinkers, chief of which is their own status as enemies rather than friends. In 1665, William Hughes's *The Compleat Vineyard* assures his English readers that English wine is "most natural to our constitutions" as part of a project to "advance our English wines."[32] At the end of the seventeenth century, *England's Happiness Improved . . . Containing the art of making wine of English grapes . . . equal to that of France and Spain*, later reissued as *Vinetum Angliae*, stakes its case on the health benefits of English wine for English drinkers: "those Liquores produced from our natural growth . . . are far more agreeable to the Constitution of *English* Bodies, contributing to Health and lively Vigor, and if not taken in excess, which indeed in all things is hurtful, they lengthen Years, and free Old Age from those Calamities that adulterated Wines and Foreign Liquors, make it obnoxious to, in the Pains Aches and many Diseases that their Sediments Entail, by corrupting the good, or creating Bad Humours in the Body."[33] The sympathetic beverage, then, is not local as much as national.[34]

There were counterarguments, often focused on substituting cider for wine, but these were also based on the idea that the locally produced would be most salubrious for English drinkers. Worlidge, in his treatise on beverage making in England, *Vinetum Britannicum*, argues that cider and juices of "English Fruits" are the best drinks for English bodies.[35] Not only will it spare expense to produce cider and perry, but these drinks "(being once accustomed) will be as proper and wholsome for our *English* bodies, as French wines, if not more."[36] Note that English bodies must become accustomed over time to this proper and wholesome beverage, as they have to French wines. This will be a process rather than a return to a given. But promoters of English beverages argue that imported wine renders the English slavishly dependent on other countries; it has suffered in transit; and it lacks some ineffable property that suits English-grown and -made drinks to English bodies. So even arguments for cider rather than wine depend on a subtle association of wine and blood, body, place, and drink.

Although geohumoralism underpins some of these arguments, whether in favor of making wine in England or replacing wine with other English-made beverages, the definitions of the English and the local remain pliant. To begin with, those who promote English winemaking argue that it is not new but rather a reclamation of a lost art, traces of which survive in English place names, histories, and gardens. What was once known has since, somehow, been forgotten. What's more, the history of grape growing and winemaking in England is a history of colonization of one kind or another. In his history of Britain, William Camden dwells on the legacy of the Romans in planting vines "rather for shade than fruit."[37] Camden also insists that the landscape itself reveals a past that might offer hope of a future: "wee have no cause to wonder, why many places in this countrey and else-where in England are called *Vine-yards*, seeing it hath affoorded wine."[38] John Parkinson adds that "manie Monasteries in this Kingdome having Vineyards, had as much wine made therefrom, as sufficed their co[n]vents yeare by yeare: but long since they have been destroyed, and the knowledge how to order a Vineyard is also utterly perished with them."[39] The history of English vines and winemaking that serves as precedent and inspiration is, then, a history of transplants, occupation, and decline.

If vines once grew in England, as various writers aver, then why doesn't England produce wines that can compete with French wines, already the gold standard? Sixteenth- and seventeenth-century writers acknowledge differences of soil and climate. Parkinson, for instance, argues that even those who have brought in French experts, "being skilfull in keeping and dressing of Vines," have failed to make drinkable wine. "And indeede the soile is a maine matter to bee chiefly considered to seate a Vineyard upon: for even in France and other hot countries, according to the nature of the soile, so is the rellish, strength, and durabilitie of the wine." Acknowledging what is now called the little ice age (ca. 1550–1750), Parkinson argues that it is hopeless to make good wine in England especially because "our years in these times do not fal out to be so kindly and hot, to ripen the grapes, to make anie good wine as formerly they have done."[40] But many writers counter all arguments against disadvantages of soil and climate. Plat, for example, accuses "the extreme negligence, and blockish ignorance of our people, who do most unjustly lay their wrongful accusations upon the soil, whereas the greatest, if not the whole fault justly may be removed upon themselves."[41] The English must overcome their ignorance—by learning from skilled winemakers elsewhere.

Thus, paradoxically, the solution to the problem of imports and the mismatch of foreign wine with English blood lies in different imports: importing plant starts and know-how from the continent. "Vines themselves have sometimes been Strangers as well in *Italy* as in *Britain*," one writer reminds his readers. Like other plants that have become stalwarts of English gardens, staples in the English diet, vines "in a few Years may become naturalized to our Soil."[42] Again. Once we introduce the idea of naturalizing plants—a crucial consideration in the many treatises on soil amendment and agricultural innovation in the period—then the difference between native and imported quickly collapses—at one level. At another, this distinction proves remarkably flexible and therefore durable. The local is not what comes from here but what has been localized, made to flourish here. If one problem is the dependence on foreign imports, then any wine made from grapes under English control, wherever those may grow, and made for an English market, can be considered English. This is one of the rationales behind attempts to create vineyards in Colonial Virginia. This effort included shipping guidebooks, seedlings, and experts to Virginia in the early seventeenth century.[43] Although Virginia is only now emerging as a winemaking region, the desire to plant vineyards in Virginia suggests that both Englishness and the local are adaptable, flexible concepts. Wine made in Virginia from imported vines by French experts might be English if the English control the colony and the plantings there. Wine made in England from imported vines that had been "naturalized" could become English enough to prove more wholesome for English bodies. But wines imported into England and doctored there are not English, no matter how they are transubstantiated. The local is an achievement rather than a given, a process as much as a place. It must be created and asserted through occupation and narration. The importance of English wine for English bodies was a story some promoters of an English wine industry told their readers, a story that drew on magical associations around blood that were simultaneously unravelling.

The early modern writers I've been discussing assert that one's blood and beverage should share the same country of origin. But then again they also reveal that wine, wherever it seems to be from, is ultimately from "foreign" stock, at the same time that its adulteration is as likely to be domestic as outlandish: it is as much the composition of the merchant or cooper as it is the blood of the grape. The visual resemblance so crucial to the assumed affinity of blood and wine might itself have been fabricated. Still, it remains a compelling myth that nature matches place, body, and plants, so that at our doorstep we find those foods, drinks, and medicines best suited to our needs, whose appearance providentially describes the "sympathy" between them and human bodies.

An article in *Woman's Day* magazine in 2012 argues that healthy foods resemble the body parts they benefit and is organized around paired images of comestibles and organs. Among its arresting juxtapositions of clam and testicle, sweet potato and pancreas, it includes red wine and blood. "Red wine, which is rich in antioxidants and polyphenols, including powerful resveratrol, looks like blood," the article points out.[44] This attempt to make recent scientific research readily accessible might seem at first to authorize and naturalize the venerable association of wine as "homogeneall" with blood. Early modern people sometimes claimed that resemblances between plants and bodily organs might indicate sympathy and thus be a guide to curative properties.[45] In Robert Turner's *Botanologia: The British Physician or the Nature and Vertues of English Plants* (1664), for example, he argues that "God hath imprinted upon the Plants, Herbs, and Flowers, as it were in Hieroglyphicks, the very signature of their Vertues; . . . as, the Nutmeg being cut, resembles the Brain."[46] Resemblance might still be a useful mnemonic, as it is in the *Woman's Day* story, but it is not proof of a relationship somehow both magical and natural. Indeed, resemblance can blind us to differences in substance.

Some foundational texts in what is sometimes called environmental humanities, or more narrowly, ecocriticism, focus on the persistence of outdated narratives and figurations, as well as their power to shape how we evaluate the past, ameliorate the present, and predict the future. Daniel Botkin, for example, exposes "the idea of a divinely ordered universe that is perfectly structured for life" as an "ironic" connection "between ancient beliefs and twentieth-century ecological assertions." Humans often work hard to create the symmetry and order they then value as "nature," Botkin argues. In *The Moon in a Nautilus Shell* (2012), Botkin revisits his influential but, he feels, misunderstood book, *Discordant Harmonies* (from 1981), in order to reiterate his argument that nature is neither stable nor orderly. Botkin blames ruinously inaccurate explanations of how nature works and should be managed on "inadvertent use of imagery, metaphor, and analogy." Despite widely used figurations, Nature, he argues, is not a "living creature" with a life course or a machine. It is, instead, a system, "dynamic, imperfect, powerful," and unpredictable. To move forward in addressing urgent environmental issues, he argues, "We need not only new knowledge but also new metaphors."[47] I share Botkin's sense that the past bears down on the present by means of tenacious "old metaphors" and that figurations have material effects. Like equivocal gore, they retain vitality even when discarded as waste. My goal, then, is to create new knowledge about persistent metaphors and the unpredictable cultural work they continue to do. In order to recognize the persistence and implications of "old" metaphors, such as the metaphor that is my chapter's title and topic, we might first explore the ways in which such metaphors were, from the start, internally fissured, problematic, and held in doubt. The early modern meanings of both blood and wine constantly moved back and forth from literal to figural, conjoining and separating as they did. Their resemblance can make it hard to see the ways in which their interrelation was debated in the early modern period, even as it was also relied upon and mobilized in highly interested ways. If, as Roland Greene argues, blood was a "concept under revision" in the period, wine was as well.[48]

Promoting a dream of English wine, the writers discussed here exploited the instability and figurative power of these two categories. In the process, they suggested, on the one hand, that blood and wine are markers of identity, rooting body, home, and dietary habit in one's native soil, and, on the other, that one's constitution, as fundamental as the blood in one's veins, might be remade by daily practices and dietary choices. Describing the transformations required to make imported wine drinkable as transubstantiations and alchemical transformations, they simultaneously exposed them as frauds and emphasized their remarkable power. They argued that blood is precious and, ultimately, another waste product to be fed back into that hungry cannibal, the earth. They vested practical advice with enormous consequence. In discussions of English wine, then, we see yet again how, long after the Reformation, blood remained both a substance available for practical uses and a sign freighted with figural meaning. Perhaps knowing this history will enable us to resist the story of nature as purposeful and human-centered, cunningly providing in the blood of the grape the perfect match for our own constitutions.

Chapter 15

Blood on the Butcher's Knife

Images of Pig Slaughter in Late Medieval Illustrated Calendars

DOLLY JØRGENSEN

A butcher straddles the pig on the building floor, holding its front leg safely out of the way. With his knife, he slits the pig's throat with precision so that the blood gushes into an awaiting basin. The precious blood, which is often collected by a woman holding a bowl or basin, will be transformed into culinary treats and hearty meals. The slaughter takes place late in the year, often in December, as a way of stocking the food stores and reducing the number of mouths to feed over the lean months. This pig butchery process, as depicted in manuscripts illustrated in the fifteenth and sixteenth centuries, highlights blood as the object of interest with squirting or dripping blood drawing the eye toward the pig and the bleeding incision (see Figure 15.1).

This is one of many images of pig slaughter found in medieval books as an illustration to accompany the month of December on calendar pages, which will be the focus of this chapter. The late medieval period has complex and contradictory developments in the thinking about animal blood from butchery. It is both a potential pollutant to watercourses and soil, as well as a valuable ingredient in food for human consumption as blood pudding. It is a practical necessity, but also infused with spiritual meaning. This chapter explores the acceptability and desirability of these blood-soaked butchery

Figure 15.1 December calendar image of draining the pig's blood in a manuscript from Bologna dated 1389–1404. The J. Paul Getty Museum, Los Angeles, Ms. 34, fol. 6v. Image in the public domain, courtesy of the Getty Open Content Program.

images in the late medieval period within the context of the calendar image as both devotional and practical. What are we to make of this emphasis on blood in the pig slaughter?

During the late medieval period, there was a shift in the way images of butchery are portrayed, particularly images for the month of December in calendars. They change from relatively sanitized images of a man with raised axe over a pig's head to scenes of bloodletting practices on freshly killed pigs to extract the desired blood. Images of the medieval pig slaughter in winter were not always as graphic as they would become in the late medieval period. Those from the thirteenth century are highly stylized—rather than showing the dead or dying pig, the images only signal intention to kill the animal (see Figure 15.2). Typically, a man stands with an axe raised over his head and will soon drop it on the unsuspecting pig below. The axe is positioned with the blunt end toward the pig to knock it unconscious rather than serving as a mode of beheading the beast. Sometimes, the axe is shown already striking the pig, but there is no visible effect of the blow. The animal is alive and unblemished in these images.[1]

Figure 15.2 Calendar page for December from a psalter made in the Netherlands in the mid-thirteenth century. British Library, Royal 2. B. III, fol. 7v. Image in the public domain, courtesy of British Library.

Blood on the Butcher's Knife

While the use of the raised axe scene continues in the later period in some manuscripts, images began to focus more on blood. In the fourteenth century, these innocuous pig slaughter images were supplemented by a few depictions of the butchery process. The December illumination in the Queen Mary Psalter dated between 1310 and 1320 includes both the standard raised axe scene and a pig hung up for butchering. A breviary made in Metz in 1302/3 illustrates December as a pig hanging with the intestines visible as a man cuts into it. In this case, unlike the Queen Mary Psalter, there is a pan to collect blood on the floor and blood droplets emanating from the pig (see Figure 15.3). This is the earliest medieval illumination I have found showing the collection of blood during pig slaughter.

The images under consideration in this chapter are illustrations in medieval calendars. These calendars were most often the beginning pages of psalters and books of hours. Wealthy aristocrats prayed with the help of extravagantly illustrated versions of these books during private devotion. The medieval calendar served as a guide to the church year by listing the major and minor feasts, like Christmas, and the veneration days of local and well-known saints. The calendar was organized according to months, January to December, with

Figure 15.3 An early depiction of pig slaughter and blood collection in the Breviary of Renaud de Bar from Metz, 1302–1303. British Library Yates Thompson 8, fol. 6v. Image in the public domain, courtesy of British Library.

the days of the month indicated by the Julian calendar system.² Unlike modern calendars printed specifically for one year, medieval ones could be used and reused indefinitely through the special numbering and lettering schemes.

Each month in a medieval calendar was often illustrated with an occupation of the month and/or the prevailing zodiac sign. Illuminated medieval calendars were firmly established by the twelfth century in Western Europe and continued in prominence throughout the Middle Ages.³ The compositions are linked to the liturgical year, as demonstrated by their common occurrence alongside Resurrection or baptism motifs in church decorative programs.⁴ Although there was some degree of flexibility in the iconography chosen for each month, the most typical series consisted of feasting (January); warming by the fire (February); pruning vines (March); gathering flowers (April); hunting with falcons (May); mowing (June); reaping (July); threshing (August); crushing grapes (September); sowing seeds (October); feeding pigs on acorns (November); and slaughtering pigs (December).⁵ The series stresses the cyclical passage of time from life to death, then back to life again at the start of a new year. The same illustrations would be seen year after year as the months passed by. The last month, December, is of interest here with its illustration of swine butchery.⁶ How might we interpret the scene both practically and spiritually?

On one level, these are practical images of the labor of the month: preparing the larder for winter. Pig blood was a substantive ingredient in food recipes. A household book from Paris at the end of the fourteenth century, *Le Ménagier de Paris*, explains that pigs are to be killed in November and December and gives the steps for making blood sausage. According to the recipe, the cook collected the blood in a suitable basin or pan, then removed the clots of blood that had accumulated on the bottom, then added minced onions, fat from around the intestines, and spices. Cleaned intestines were then stuffed with this mixture and pan-fried.⁷ Blood puddings, blood sausages, and other recipes calling for blood as an ingredient are found throughout medieval cuisine and are a continuing part of European culinary heritage.⁸

As a substance, blood could be transgressive if not properly collected. Butchery was a dirty business and by the late medieval period, royal and town governments highly regulated the profession and tried to control where activities happened within city walls.⁹ The butchers of Coventry, England, for example, were not permitted to slaughter animals in the street or tie up animals outside.¹⁰ Coventry was not alone in forbidding street slaughter. King Charles VI of France ordered the demolition of the meat market near his

Châtelet in Paris because of "the filth of the slaughtering and skinning of beasts" and ordered that those kind of activities must move to places "less dangerous to the public health."[11] According to the financial rolls, York fined three butchers in 1475 for slaughtering animals in the street contrary to city ordinances.[12] Blood was of particular concern. The Coventry council specifically ordered each butcher to "kepe his durre clene fro bloode and other fylthis."[13] In fourteenth-century Lucca, Italy, allowing animal blood to flow into a public space was punishable by a fine; officials who failed to stop animal blood discharges could also be fined.[14]

Pig butchery received special attention in a few cases. In Coventry, for example, a mayoral proclamation of 1421 required that all pig slaughter take place at the common scalding house. The process of scalding involved pouring boiling water over the pig carcass, which loosened the bristles, after which the hair was scraped off, the organs removed, and edible entrails cleaned of feces. This process needed water but also produced filth, thus the Coventry scalding house had been located along the local river next to a latrine house. The problem of scalding waste is evident in a complaint from 1370 against a butcher and his wife for having a scalding house in their London tenement because the water used in the scalding process, mixed with blood and hair, was ejected into a ditch, causing a vile stench. At least using a common scalding house avoided replicating the waste problem throughout town.[15]

In some of the calendar pig slaughter images, urban sanitation controls appear to be in force. The pig is sometimes being bled within a domestic room with some kind of tile or solid floor (see Figure 15.1). Although some images place the slaughter in the street of a rural town, others are more obviously a dedicated butchery space. A fifteenth-century Book of Hours contains a particularly interesting image of this sort with a pig lying on the floor while four individuals work on butchering it—one slits the throat while holding down the front leg, another holds the pan to catch the gushing blood, the third holds the head up, and the fourth holds down the back leg.[16] The two individuals we see most clearly are wearing aprons, and the slitter is wearing a mask covering his mouth and nose. A tub, presumably filled with hot water for scalding, and two other containers stand ready for use. The scene is clearly placed in a room with white walls and a timbered roof. An open door is visible behind the action. The scene is so rich in detail and different from other simpler depictions of the same activities that the artist must have previously observed the process being shown. The image thus confirms the indoor slaughter of pigs as a fifteenth-century practice.

During the later Middle Ages, at the exact time that butchery was coming under stricter urban controls and moving out of sight into dedicated scalding houses and courtyards, the calendar images reveal butchery practices in more and more detail. Late medieval artists are known for their growing interest in realistic depictions of nature, so some of the transition from representational killing to visual bleeding could be explained by those larger trends.[17] The fourteenth century witnessed a rise in drawing animals and birds as still-life zoological specimens embellishing the page.[18] The naturalistic impulse is evident in many of these scenes that show butchery in progress. The pig is shown in a natural pose during slaughter, the equipment stands ready, the butchers perform their tasks. However, even in the midst of all these practicalities, it was not a given that the bleeding of the pig would become the primary focus of this new naturalistic interest in butchery practice.

While there are practical reasons for bleeding—bleeding before cooking allows fresh meat to be kept longer—it is also a practice culturally situated in Mosaic tradition. In this tradition of bleeding at slaughter, blood poured out as part of the sacrifice is taboo for consumption yet can be used as a ritualistic purifying agent.[19] Medieval Europeans (and indeed modern European peoples) have continued to practice bleeding. Noëlie Vialles's remarkable anthropological study of French industrial slaughterhouses reveals how the process of separating blood from meat turns the animal's body from corpse into deanimated, usable products. Bleeding makes the flesh bloodless while making the blood visible. This creates a paradox since "all visible blood is an image of present life *and* a sign of potential death."[20] Vialles argues that butchers involved in the bleeding have thus historically been thought of as violent and brutal, as stained by the blood of their victims, even though they are making a product for wider consumption. Blood for later consumption required careful handling during the slaughtering process, something that is apparent even in the medieval images. The blood signifies a liminal object between life and death.

Significantly, a pig is always the animal being bled in the calendar images, even though blood from other animals was sometimes used in cooking and a few December illustrations show the killing of a cow (although never the bleeding of it). Within the framework of medieval Europe, pork was a distinctly Christian food—it is taboo in both Jewish and Muslim religious custom.[21] Because Jews rejected eating pork, the myth of the Jews' sow developed, which claimed that Jewish children were piglets who suckled milk from a female pig and thus would not consume one of their own.[22] On the other end of the religious spectrum, Christian holiday feasting at Christmas and Easter often involved eating pork. Pigs had both saintly and devilish iconographic connotations. On the saintly side, pigs were associated with Saint Anthony beginning in the eleventh century, giving them a place at the side of the holy hermit.[23] On the sinner side, pigs are often depicted in medieval texts and images as filthy, lusty, shameful, and gluttonous.[24] The pig thus signified a wide host of religious and social meanings, both good and bad. Claudine Fabre-Vassas has argued that "the singularity of the pig stands out" through its multifaceted nature as the incarnation of "the sins of lechery and gluttony" while also being "a Christian flesh, endowed with a soul of blood."[25]

The pig's blood takes center stage in the late-medieval images of the winter slaughter and as such it becomes not just a signifier of nature, but of culture. Although Bridget Ann Henisch, who has written the most extensive work on the medieval calendar year, has claimed that its agricultural images are devoid of religious significance, others like Colum Hourihane have stressed that although modern viewers see these as secular motifs, during the Middle Ages they "were religious symbols that used an immediate and forceful iconography, largely drawn from the surrounding natural world but intended to convey the meaning of man's place in the order of life and eternity."[26] These images are part of the program in a religious book, one intended for personal contemplation and prayer. Michael Camille advocated seeing the agricultural images of the *Luttrell Psalter* as part of *imagines verborum* (word-images) that couple image and text in the creation of meaning.[27] As equal partners, written word and agricultural image juxtapose sacred text and social work.[28] Such insight is useful for reading these images, which adorn pages listing the church's feasts for December.

December was one of the most important medieval feast months, with the Feast of the Immaculate Conception (8th), the Feast of the Nativity (25th), the Feast of the Slaughter of the Innocents (28th), and saint's day feasts for Nicholas of Myra (6th), Doubting Thomas (21st), Stephen the first martyr (26th), and John the Evangelist (27th). This list of feasts combines life and death. The conception and birth of Christ are intricately joined with his own death and resurrection as revealed to Thomas in Christ's wounds and the untimely death of innocents. The feasts of December, more so than other months of the year, look forward to the Crucifixion of Good Friday through sacrifice.

Although ostensibly about the birth and early years of Christ, the December celebrations directly tied those events to the Crucifixion. At the Nativity, the Christ Child is laid in the manger where animals usually eat, becoming the body and blood that would feed believers in the church according to medieval sermons and writings. This was more than just a metaphor—a popular medieval miracle was the transformation of the elevated host during Mass into the infant Christ who was subsequently dismembered and eaten in order to prove that the bread was indeed Christ's flesh.[29] The bleeding body of the child broken as the host confirmed its life-giving power. The Christ Child both prefigured and became the Calvary sacrifice.

The Slaughter of the Innocents commemorated the death of all the boys under two years old in Bethlehem ordered by Herod (per Matthew 2:13–18). Its celebration was infused with mourning, resulting in the exclusion of standard segments in the mass that were joyful (most notably the gloria and alleluia); yet at the same time it was one of the fool's feasts in which the choirboys and a boy bishop ran the show.[30] Medieval sermons and exegesis considered the Innocents to be the first Christian martyrs. As lambs led to slaughter, the Innocents died in order that the Christ Child might live, forging a connection between their sacrifice and Christ's later sacrifice as Lamb on the cross so that others might live.[31] Some texts and performed plays about the Innocents frame their deaths as child martyrs at the hands of Jews, linking them with circulating twelfth-century reports of children crucified by Jews.[32] Images of the martyrdom of the child Simon of Trent could explicitly link the child's murder with pig slaughter by showing the child being bled just like the pigs in December butchery images.[33]

The Feast of Innocents often featured plays related to St. Nicholas, whose feast was earlier in December, because of his boyhood ordination. St. Nicholas imagery, plays, and carols told the popular apocryphal story "The Three Clerks."[34] In the most widely circulated fifteenth-century version of "The Three Clerks" legend, a butcher murders three clerks who are lodging with him. When the butcher discovers they have no money, the butcher's wife suggests salting the bodies like pork: "pastis and pyus . . . for pork hy cholleth ben solde" (pasties and pies . . . they should be sold as pork).[35] Nicholas discovers the crime and reassembles and raises the clerks from a pickling tub. The clerks and pigs become interchangeable in this story. Their death at the hand of the butcher is the same as the pig's death. The difference is that St. Nicholas is able to redeem the clerks from their fate as meat.

The iconographic programs for December in sixteenth century Books of Hours reflect an emphasis on sacrifice through blood. Flemish works of the early sixteenth century such as Pierpont Morgan Library M.52 and M.1175 and

Blood on the Butcher's Knife

Figure 15.4 Illustrations on calendar page for December in the Spinola Hours, dated 1510–1520. The J. Paul Getty Museum, Los Angeles, Ms. Ludwig IX 18, fol. 7. Image in the public domain, courtesy of the Getty Open Content Program.

Getty Ms. Ludwig IX 18 (see Figure 15.4) feature the monthly task of draining pig blood as the largest image in the lower section with roundels of the important feasts, including the Slaughter of the Innocents, complementing the agricultural image. On these pages, we read the images of the deaths of martyrs and children alongside the death of the pig.

The similarity of these deaths might not have been lost on medieval readers. The medieval mystic Margery Kempe wrote that she thought of Christ beaten or wounded not only when she saw a crucifix but also whenever she "saw a man or a beast . . . [with] a wound or if a man beat a child before her or smote a horse or another beast with a whip . . . as well in the field as in the town. . ."[36] For Margery, a wound on a beast was a sign for the five wounds of Christ. Seeing a suffering animal could serve as a substitute for seeing the suffering Christ himself. The pig would be particularly appropriate for boundary-crossing between man and beast. Karl Steel has argued that pigs are the domestic animal most like man, especially anatomically which was recognized in both ancient and medieval texts, and as such they substituted for humans in medieval literature and art. Pork and human flesh are often interchangeable in stories, perhaps playing on the common word pun *porcus/corpus*.[37]

Caroline Walker Bynum has discussed the violence in medieval religion, particularly the prominence of motifs of body parts and blood.[38] Bleeding images of Christ including images of the five wounds without the whole Christ figure "actively encouraged devotion to Christ's blood" in the thirteenth to fifteenth centuries.[39] The fourteenth and fifteenth centuries in particular were a time of "a great welling up of blood piety".[40] Blood in these contexts is a metonym, a part which stands in for the whole; the blood is both separated from Christ or the saint and yet still part of him. Late medieval piety was characterized by paradox as embodied in metonymnity, in which the part is the whole and vice versa, and Christ's bleeding body, which symbolizes both life and death, salvation and sin. Seeing or reading of Christ's body on the cross encouraged empathising with his suffering on behalf of sinners; but more than empathy-inducing, it both signalled the presence of the divine and reproach of the guilty.[41] Blood encapsulated and enacted the paradox of life in death.[42]

December in the calendar has the same tensions. The year's cycle that started with feasting ends with the death of the pig. It ends the year as a cold winter month, indicated by snow on the ground and in the trees. Just as man's life cycle is likened to the seasons with winter coming at his end, the annual calendar ends with death. Yet at the same time, the viewer of the December image knows that in January the cycle will begin again. The pig that is slaughtered will be consumed at the feast. Death will bring life. The bloody image evokes empathy for the pig's sacrifice while the viewer can still revel in the life-giving food it provides.

With this in mind, if we look at the December image in the Book of Hours of Anne de Bretagne (BNF Latin 9474, fol. 15; see Figure 15.5), we see something entirely unexpected. The blood squirting from the butcher's fresh knife wound, which is collected in a pan and a jug as well as soils the ground, is not just for making blood sausage—it becomes a visual, palatable reminder of sacrifice and death at the hands of the sinner. The pig's carcass hangs upside down with blood running out of its mouth—the detail reminding us that this animal contained life not long before. The bleeding out allows us to experience the hidden suffering of the animal.[43] Its hanging position beneath the image of a church in the background reminds us of Christ and Christian martyrs who likewise were hung up to die. While medieval scholars have most often interpreted pigs in medieval art as the filthy, unclean or gluttonous other, often representing Jews, the pigs in this Book of Hours and in the other December images do not encourage such a reading.[44] The flowing blood is carefully

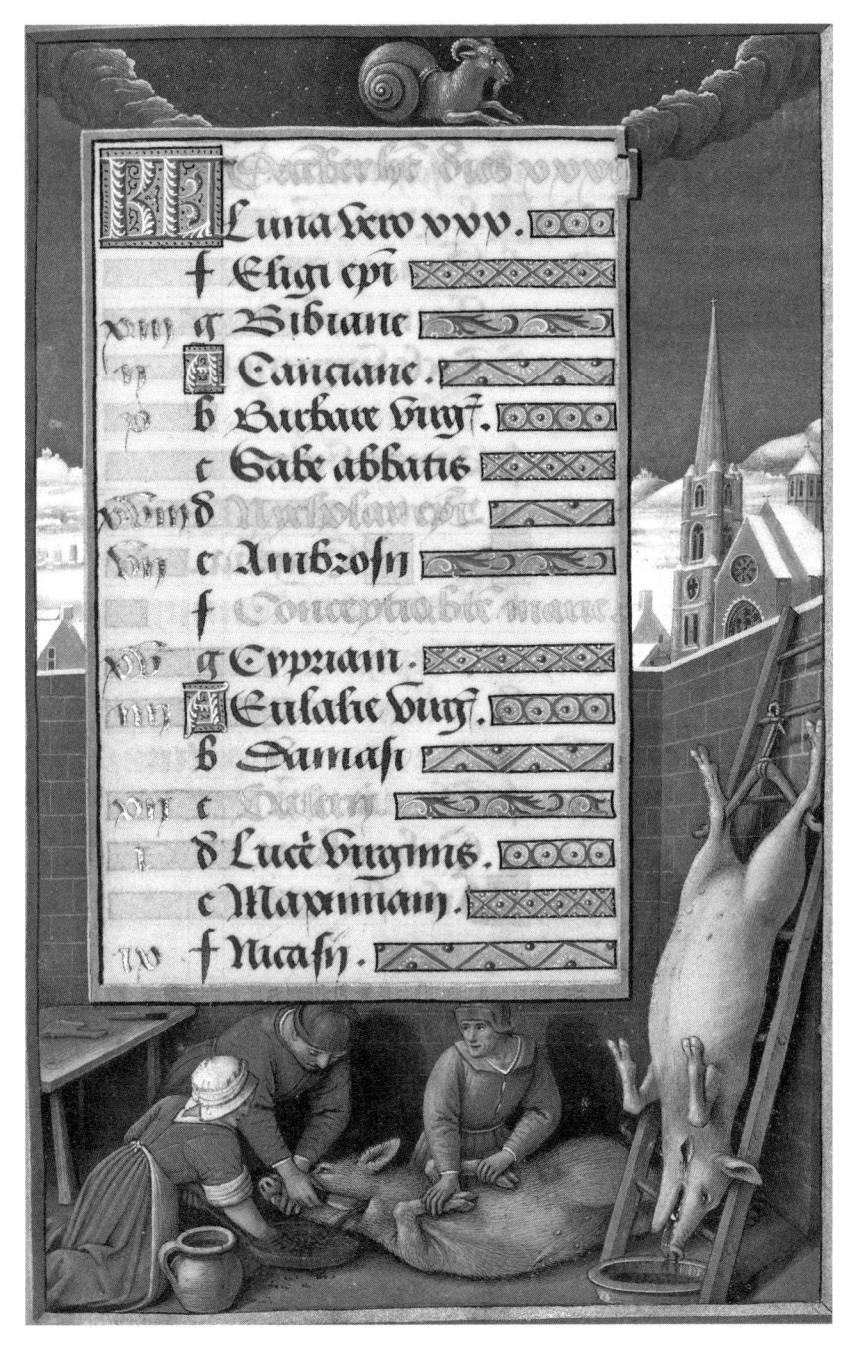

Figure 15.5 Image for December from Book of Hours of Anne de Bretagne, Tours, ca. 1503–1508. BNF Latin 9474 fol. 15. Used with permission from Bibliothèque nationale de France.

collected in a bowl, as a precious commodity. With their blood pouring out of them so that we see the inflicted wounds, these pigs evoke Christian empathy, just as Margery said they should. They die so that we will live through another winter. They have been sacrificed. It is fitting then that the image of the pig sacrifice appears in the month of December when the first sacrifices of the Innocents along with the foreshadowed sacrifice of the babe in the manger are celebrated. The blood that flows from the pig mirrors the wounds of Christ as well as the slain infants.

The visual representation of butchery thus took on new meaning. Before the fourteenth century, the December image of pig slaughter showed an agricultural task for the season. The man with an axe raised above his head in order to bludgeon the swine below was doing a job everyone knew well. The pig's death at the beginning of winter filled pantries and bellies. Butchery was a highly regulated craft because of its potential to corrupt bodies with bad food and streets and waters with noxious leftovers. Making sure that blood and entrails stayed in their proper places ensured wholesome and pure food and environments; yet the early images of pig butchery left those details to the imagination. While the butchery task did not change in the late medieval period, the images of it did. Manuscript illustrations of the labor of December made from the fourteenth century onward still show butchers at work, often in spaces mandated by up-to-date city regulations, yet the new representation stressed the death of the pig rather than the agricultural activity. Blood is shown gushing out of the pig and being carefully collected by the slaughterers. The blood itself, rather than the ultimate food products that it would become, is the key component of these images, focusing attention on the pig and its sacrifice. This moves the image's symbolism beyond the practical to the spiritual.[45]

The pig killing images are situated alongside the textual calendar with its listing of December feasts that join birth and death as well as illustrations of the slaughter of young boys at the hands of Herod's soldiers. Labors of the month like the December killing of the pig were infused with spiritual meaning because of their placement on the page together with these items. This juxtaposition merges the pig's blood with Christ's blood and the sacrifices of the Innocents celebrated in December. The blood—life-giving blood—pours out of the wounds. The pig substitutes for human sacrifice. Rather than being filthy or unclean, the pig is purified through its shedding of blood. Seeing the swine's bloody death reminded the viewer that the cycle of birth-death-rebirth continued, repeating year after year in the Christian calendar. The pig would die in December to feed us, but would reappear again the next year in the autumn to feed in the woods, only to die once again, just as Christ would do over the calendar year. Reading these images within their context enables modern readers to see the images as their medieval viewers would: as images embodying life and death, sacrifice and salvation, through blood on the butcher's knife.

Chapter 16

Queer Blood

HELEN BARR

Of all the wonderful accounts of medieval blood, none is more intriguing than a fifteenth-century response to Chaucer's *Canterbury Tales* known as *The Canterbury Interlude*.[1] Transgressive in more ways than one, this anonymous "Canterbury Tale" cross-matches the miraculous blood of Thomas Becket, the archbishop murdered in Canterbury cathedral on December 29, 1170, with the blood that belongs to a version of Chaucer's figure of the Pardoner. Pardoners are universally vilified in medieval literature for their practice of selling fake pardons that endanger the souls of their clients.[2] Chaucer's Pardoner traffics relics that may not be relics at all. And the description of his body and his sexual practices places him outside of normative discourses.[3] One fifteenth-century manuscript of *The Canterbury Tales* illustrates the Pardoner holding the jawbone of an ass.[4] The Pardoner is seen as Cain, the first murderer; the fratricide who made Abel's blood cry from the earth for God's vengeance.[5]

The Canterbury Interlude Pardoner is both an avatar of his Chaucerian predecessor and a figure of the holy martyr Thomas Becket. *The Interlude* conflates the sacrificial, healing, and sacred blood of a saint with the polluted and contaminated blood of a figure associated with murder, swindling, and sexual deviance. This commixture of unlikely bloods raises profound questions about the ontology of sacred blood and the figures with which it is associated. I argue in this chapter that *The Interlude* iterates and destabilizes the whole project of Becketian devotion at Canterbury Cathedral. The poem produces a reading of martyrdom that dramatizes crucial paradoxes of medieval religious blood:

blood as the sign of miraculous sanctity and the mark of unholy dissidence; blood that inspires heartfelt religious piety as the blood that swells the profits of the established church; blood as proof and pernicious fraud.[6] *The Interlude* presents us with blood that resists substantiation; queer blood that refuses identification and legibility.[7]

Almost before the body of Thomas Becket was cold (apparently), biographers were at work to record the miracles that occurred in response to his murder. Written texts and pictorial representations focus on the blow to his head that killed him. In illustrations, Becket is shown at his altar with knightly assailants raising their swords as he kneels in prayer. In some versions, a sword pierces the archbishop's tonsure, or slices his skull causing blood to spurt so copiously that it sends the archbishop's mitre flying. The iconography of the moment before the blow resembles a perverse version of the ceremony of dubbing a knight: the sword raised above the head as if to bestow a tap on the shoulders.[8]

Written accounts of the murder are steeped in blood. Early biographer William Fitzstephen describes how Becket's innocent blood cried out to God from the pavement of the church. Fitzstephen turns the knights into Cain and Becket into Abel, first shepherd of the church; the spilling of tonsured blood is a sacrilege that God is called to avenge.[9] Becket's assassination reenacts the passion of Christ. Edward Grim, an eyewitness, writes that when Becket's crown was severed, the blood, white from the brain, and the brain equally red from the blood, brightened the floor with the colors of the lily and the rose, the virgin and mother, and the life and death of the confessor and martyr.[10] The rose represents the blood of the passion of Christ, and white the blood of a living martyr and Marian purity. Benedict of Canterbury's description of Becket supine on the floor of the cathedral with a circle of blood around his head invests the archbishop with Christ's crown of thorns. A thin line of blood spreads down from his right temple to his left cheek.[11] While all the other accounts provide four knightly assailants, Grim adds a fifth; a clerk, "so that a fifth stroke was not lacking to the martyr who in other things, had imitated Christ."[12] Thomas's five blows become Christ's five wounds on the cross. As Becket lies dead on the floor, one of the murderers turns back, and with the point of his sword, pierces Becket's head, causing his brains to pour forth upon the pavement of the church; blood and water mixed.[13] The effusion from Becket's head recalls the blood and water that gushed out from Christ's side when he is wounded at his crucifixion by the spear of the soldier commanded to ascertain whether the King of the Jews is dead. Exegetical commentary names the soldier Longinus and records how the flow of blood and water pours onto the eyes of a blind torturer and restores his sight. Violent penetration produces a healing miracle and in turn, a long tradition of exegesis associating that blood and water with penance and with baptism, with repentance, and with the renewal of life.[14]

This Christomimetic emphasis on the properties of Becket's blood is pervasive. Benedict of Canterbury compares the bloodied water of Thomas, the lamb of Canterbury, with the blood of the lamb of Bethlehem.[15] The antiphon for the Feast of the Martyrdom of Becket in the Sarum Breviary sings of how the miraculous blood and water changes color five times: once into milk, four times into blood: "aquae Thomae quinquies varians colorem / in lac semel transit, quater in cruorem." The liturgy collates Becket's blood and water with Marian breast milk and Christ's redemptive cruor.[16] Christological resonance is built into the very fabric of Canterbury Cathedral. The pillars at the east end are made of rose and cream marble symbolizing the red and white of Becket's blood and brains. The floor tiles are ruddy, and the stones of the steps in the east end of the Cathedral blood red.[17] Pilgrims to the site of Becket's martyrdom stepped (and still do) among and upon the signs of his blood.

Almost as immediately as Becket's blood was shed, the healing miracles it performed were seen as signs of Thomas's martyrdom, and the stories were collected to provide evidence in support of his canonization. Fitzstephen recounts the first act of healing when a citizen of Canterbury dips a garment in Becket's blood, rinses it in water, and gives the fluid to his paralyzed wife. She drinks it and is immediately healed.[18] There are countless tales of people dipping clothing or rags into Becket's blood and then washing them. The liquid produced by these aspersions, known as the water of Canterbury, heals all kinds of infirmities, including blindness and leprosy, and even revivifies persons assumed to be dead.[19] The practice mimes the imagery of Revelation 7:14 in which robes are washed white in the blood of the lamb and sins are washed away with the blood of Christ.

The healing properties of Becket's blood turned Canterbury Cathedral into one of the most important pilgrimage sites on the international stage. On the night of the murder, the monks mopped the blood and water from the ground of the cathedral and stored it in ampullae. Garnier invests them with Eucharistic significance: "in semblance of wine and water did God cause his own blood to be used by the world to save souls: in water and in phials did God cause to be carried to the world the blood of the martyr to heal the sick. By healing and by sign he doubled the honour for him."[20] Unsurprisingly, given the Canterbury hype, these phials became a highly prized object of desire.[21] Pilgrims traveled far and wide to acquire one. They drank Thomas's blood, gargled it, and applied it topically. Becketian blood made sick people whole and purged noxious substances. Penitents who drink St Thomas's blood vomit a variety of surprising objects. They include fruit trees, a four-footed lizard, and a worm measuring half a cubit in length. The worm was hung up in the church as a trophy, visible sign of the curative powers of Becket's blood.[22] If pilgrims were unable to get hold of the blood itself in an ampulla, they could buy a little pilgrim badge in the shape of one to display on their return from pilgrimage: a souvenir simulacrum of the blood of Thomas Becket.[23]

The east end of the cathedral was rebuilt after a fire in 1174 as a theater of devotion to Thomas Becket. Trinity Chapel is still known today as the corona, shaped in the likeness of the severed crown of Becket's skull. Either side of its apex a series of ambulatory windows showcase his healing miracles. The stained glass gleams red with blood, both that of St. Thomas and of the penitents who sought its healing properties. William of Kellet had promised to go on a pilgrimage but postponed it. One panel shows how a piqued St. Thomas causes William to cut his shin open with the blade of an axe. Moved by William's prayer and penitence for his procrastination, however, Thomas heals him. The adjacent panel shows that when the bandages are removed from Kellet's leg all the blood spurted from the grievous wound has disappeared. There is not even a scar. Becket can cause bloody wounds but he can also cure them, leaving not a trace behind.

When Roger of Valognes promised to go on a pilgrimage but forgot, he injures his left foot. Only by making good his pledge by journeying to Canterbury and washing his leg in the holy blood of Thomas is he healed. The glass shows his foot in a huge bowl of blood. The Canterbury monks are shown mixing the blood and water that cures Richard of Sunieve's leprosy. Richard is depicted grabbling around in the holes of Thomas's tomb looking for the scabs of leprosy that have fallen off his face. Etheledreda of Canterbury was cured of malaria. The inscriptions on the panels record that she had grown pale through loss of red blood cells but when she imbibed the blood of St. Thomas mixed with water, she recovered. The glass depicts the bowl and the ampulla of blood with unfeasible prominence. Hugh of Jervaux was afflicted with an incurable malady beyond the wit of physicians to diagnose, let alone to remedy. But the inscription here reads, "hope remains for the hopeless in the blood of the saint." Drinking Becket's blood grants Hugh a graphically illustrated nosebleed, which restores his health.[24]

Stained over and over in the glass, built into the pillars, the floors, written about in pages and pages of hagiography, Becket's blood appears to have been as copious in supply as it was abundant in display. It diagnoses the source of all manner of illness and restores full health. Thomas's blood makes the pale face pink and the leper lose his spots. Miraculously fresh, unstintingly available to the penitent, Becket's blood and water is a highly prized object of desire. It replicates the restorative properties of the blood poured out from Christ's side and reenacts Eucharistic communion. The reiteration of the Christ-like qualities of Becket's blood in a variety of media made the "water of Canterbury" eminently po[r]table, as *The Canterbury Interlude* recognizes.

Unlike Chaucer's pilgrims, those of the *Interlude* do reach Canterbury. They take their lodgings in an inn across the road from the cathedral before performing their devotions at St. Thomas's shrine. Some of them gape at a stained glass window whose details they are unable to decipher, and some purchase, and some of them steal, pilgrim badges to sport on their return journey to show where they have been. We are not told whether any of those badges feature Becket's phial of blood; no pilgrim appears to be in quest of one of those prized ampulla or of a blood miracle. Neither Becket's blood nor any sign of it appear where we might expect them in the cathedral. Instead the archbishop's blood turns up on the head of the Pardoner—in the kitchen of the inn.

When the Pardoner arrives at the inn he sets up a nighttime assignation with Kit the tapster and gives her his pilgrim staff for safekeeping. Readers attuned to the well-attested figurative association between a pilgrim staff and a phallus will recognize that with this crude sexual invitation, the Pardoner castrates himself.[25] And he never gets his phallus back—at least not in the way that he expects. After supper, when he seeks Kit in her chamber to demand she return his staff, unbeknownst to him, the Tapster is dallying with her lover, a character named simply Paramour. Scraping and whining at the chamber door like a dog, the Pardoner pleads for his phallus in vain. Instead, Kit instructs Paramour to use it to thrash the Pardoner: "I pray yow dub hym knight" (456).[26] In a parody of the ceremony of a knight's investiture, Paramour whacks the Pardoner's shoulders with a pilgrim staff cum sword cum phallus: "and leyd it on his bak, / Right in the same plase as chapmen bereth hir pak / And so he did too mo" (523–25). The most grievous blow lands on the Pardoner's head: "And fond hym otherwhile redliche inowghe / With the staffs ende highe oppon his browe" (529–30). Knightly shoulder d[r]ubbing and a head wound recall the iconography of Becket's murder. Under the cover of darkness, in the midst of a botched sexual assignation in a hostelry, two scoundrels replay Becket's murder in the cathedral. The Pardoner becomes a version of Becket, and Paramour one of the knightly assailants. Becket's beaten crown becomes bathed in phallic bloodshed. The uproar wakes Jak the innkeeper. He joins Paramour in chasing the Pardoner through the kitchen. Jak has his own staff with which he intends to attack the Pardoner but is prevented because he falls over a saucepan in the dark and cuts open his shin.[27] Performed in a kitchen, with ladles and pans for swords and helmets, the sacrilegious bloodshed of the archbishop becomes a mock-knightly tournament positioned somewhere between a queer bashing and a sodomitical threesome.

Having survived further injury, the Pardoner ruminates on his ill-luck: "His chekes ron on blood / And he was right evil at ese al nyght in his hed" (620–21). *The Interlude* sustains a mischievous focus on the Pardoner's wounded head. These lines reprise the detail of the blood running from Becket's forehead down his cheek. But while the archbishop's head rested on the tiles of England's most famous cathedral, the Pardoner's battered head spends the night in the bed of a huge dog so violent that it is chained with a clog. "He coude noon other help, but leyd adoun his hede / In the dogges litter" (645–46). No holy crown of thorn blood for *this* Becket; only the abjection of laying his head in dog's litter. And yet, *The Interlude*, like all those early hagiographical accounts of Becket's martyrdom, invests the Pardoner's predicament with Christological significance. The growling mastiff bites the Pardoner viciously in the thigh: "The warrok was awaked and caught hym by the thy / And bote hym wonder spetously" (640–41).

This is the Pardoner's fifth and final wound. Longinus's spear has become the fangs of a dog. Christ's side wound with its purifying blood and water, and the thaumaturgical iconography of the wound to Becket's head, are become a dog bite close to the Pardoner's genitals.[28] This is not the first Christomimetic moment in *The Interlude*. When the Pardoner cowers in the kitchen, he reflects on the wounds he has received: "And thought that he had strokes right ynowghe / Witnes on his armes, his bak and browe" (597–98). He sounds as though he is speaking a Complaint of Christ lyric in which Christ called humankind to account by directing them to gaze on the bloody wounds he suffers for their sins.[29] So *The Canterbury Interlude* not only forges association between the Pardoner's blood and Becket's; it reprises the equation of Becket's blood with the blood of Christ and paints the Pardoner's body with them both.

What happens next is even more beguiling. Although Jak and Paramour have been unable to inflict further injury on the Pardoner, they believe they will easily pick him out from the pilgrim assembly the next morning because he bears "a redy mark of his own staff" (612). The Pardoner's head wound, like that of Becket's, is clearly visible. Only, when the pilgrims leave Canterbury the next day neither the Pardoner nor his head wound can be detected: "The hosteller of the house, for nothing he cowd pry / He coude nat knowe the Pardoner among the company" (665–66). For all the scanning and peering, the bloody mark that sets the Pardoner apart is invisible because of his early morning preparations:

> Yet or he cam in company, he wissh awey the blood,
> And bond the sores to his hede with the typet of his hood,
> And made lightsom chere for men shuld nat spy
> Nothing of his turment ne of his luxury.
>
> (661–64)

> And evermore he held hym amydward the route
> And was ever synging to make al thing good,
> But yit his notes were somwhat lowe, for akyng of his hede.
> So at that tyme he had no more grame,
> But held hym to his harmes to scape shame.
>
> (670–74)

In contrast to the public display of Becket's bleeding skull just across the street in the cathedral, Pardoner Becket's bloodied head remains under wraps. He plasters over the wounds with his hood. Whereas one of the first of Thomas's miracles was the citizen of Canterbury dipping his garment in the martyr's blood and washing it in water to heal his wife, Pardoner Becket's ablutions fail to cure his pounding headache. While the monks and the pilgrims in the cathedral mopped up Becket's blood to store it in precious phials, the Pardoner's private laundry recalls Pilate's washing the blood of Christ off his hands (Matthew 27:24). Pardoner Becket rinses himself not only of Becket's healing blood, but also the redemptive blood of Christ. Clothing that the pilgrims dipped in blood made their ailments disappear, but the Pardoner's tippet makes blood itself appear to have vanished. And in contrast to all the signs of blood on the pillars, on the steps, and in the stained glass of the cathedral, Pardoner Becket's signs of blood are not visible to the pilgrim company as they return to Southwark.

The choice of garment to hide the blood makes a significant substitution to the headgear that is sported by the Pardoner in Chaucer's *Canterbury Tales*. *The General Prologue* expressly states that the Pardoner does not wear a hood. Instead he sports with conspicuous display the pilgrim sign of St. Veronica's vernicle on his cap (A.680–81).[30] St. Veronica's highly prized relic features in two stories about healing blood. One version of the legend says Christ's face became imprinted on the handkerchief that St. Veronica used to wipe his bloody sweat as he carried his cross to Calvary. Another strand to the legend equated St. Veronica with the woman whom Christ healed of a flow of blood as she touched the hem of his garment (Matthew 9:20).[31] The Ellesmere manuscript shows the vernicle in the Pardoner's cap very clearly—only it looks as though the Pardoner is simply sporting the image of an attractive young man.[32]

How might we read *The Interlude* Pardoner's occluded blood? One possibility is to argue that his blood cannot be displayed because he is wounded in sodomitical affray. Blood spilt in phallic interchange between three men cannot be shown in public, even if that blood belongs to the same group as that of Becket and of Christ. In replacing Chaucer's Pardoner's vernicle with a tippet that masks his wounds, *The Interlude* erases the Pardoner's paraded relic sign and removes him from the company of those legendary figures associated with healing cruor. There is no one to wipe his face and there is no one to tend his wounds.[33] Healing cruentation is disfigured. Whatever blood remains underneath *The Interlude* Pardoner's tippet after his strenuous ablutions must be congealing. Congealed blood is dead blood. This is not the blood of the Lamb of Revelation freshly flowing in Canterbury: this is the ugly, hard blobs of dried blood that mark the sinful.[34]

Such a reading turns the blood of the queer Pardoner into pollution; a deadly deviant strain of redemptive Becketian and Christomimetic blood.[35] With this reading, the Pardoner can be claimed as a precursor of those persons victimized and excluded from normative versions of society in HIV debates over contaminated blood in the late twentieth and twenty-first centuries. He becomes an avatar of those gay persons whom a vicar publicly stated should be excluded from Holy Communion lest their AIDS-"infected" blood pollute the Eucharistic chalice.[36] An interpretation of this kind is strengthened by the narrative focalization of *The Interlude*. The narrator mediates the Pardoner's painful abjection directly, without extradiegetical commentary of any kind. The Pardoner becomes available to be read as a queer victim whose blood must be excluded from mainstream society.[37] To read the Pardoner's blood in this way makes the poem speak powerfully to gay identity politics. But while I think that this reading is entirely possible and I want to record it, I am also aware that its critical move could be seen to be queerly myopic. To cross-match Becket's Christ-like cruentation with the blood of a Chaucerian Pardoner effects more complex queer work than empathizing with (or scapegoating) a figure of ambiguous sexuality bloodied in phallic encounter. *The Interlude* asks the question not only what happens to the blood of Becket when it is seen on a Pardoner but also what happens when *The Interlude* Pardoner's blood is seen to be Becket's?

The queerness of *The Interlude* lies not so much in demonizing the blood of a deviant pardoner; more, the poem hoodwinks its readers into a queer reading of Canterbury's Becketian blood. In *The Canterbury Tales* and in *The Interlude*, the Pardoner escapes normative categorization. He questions relationships between what is literal and figurative. His association with signs and with dubious relics disturbs ontological belief.[38] To mingle the blood of this figure with the blood of Thomas Becket raises profound questions about the matter of martyred blood and about how its healing properties are represented in copious, cult-gathering display. It is not simply the case that the Pardoner's blood reverses or guys the redemptive properties of Becket's blood, or of Christ's. After all, the Pardoner does not die, and he is not a polluted object that is purged from the pilgrim assembly like one of Becket's miraculous worms or that nimble, phlegm-coated lizard. The Pardoner rides back to Southwark in the midst of the group. In *The Interlude*'s queer commentary on the Canterbury blood cult, the Pardoner's blood replicates the signs of Becket's blood to reconfigure how they appear and what they mean. So we get the head wound and knights, we get a severed body part, only a phallus is substituted for a sliced tonsure. We get a bloodied cheek, washing of blood, and laundry garments. We get Christomimesis. Only these signs are not pressed into service to tell the story of Becket exactly as the Canterbury blood propaganda machine told it in so many ways. Not only does the Pardoner's [w]rapped head still hurt, but Becket's copiously living blood is covered up so that we do not know exactly what has become of it. Is the blood under the Pardoner's tippet fresh or scabbed: dead or alive? Where has the laundered blood gone?

Pardoner Becket's blood cannot be read; its substance is impossible to make out. The pilgrims, who go to Canterbury to seek the "hooly blisful martir . . . that [h]em hath holpen whan that they were seeke" (*The General Prologue*, A.17–18), ride away from Canterbury oblivious to the fact that a version of wounded Becket, somehow bloodied—or maybe not—rides in their midst.

They cannot see the blood; they don't know that it is there. But while the characters inside the text may be oblivious to the Pardoner's bloodshed, there is a double spectatorship for this tale. Readers of *The Interlude* know about the Pardoner's head wound, and if they know about the blood industry of Canterbury Cathedral, they can see that it is Becket's. *The Canterbury Interlude* presents its readers with a circularity of signs. You can find Becket's blood on the Pardoner only if you already know about the signs of Becket's blood. If you don't know the stories of the archbishop's martyrdom, then you can't see that the Pardoner is daubed with Becket's blood. But even (or perhaps, especially) those readers in the know will realize that the poem tampers with the public evidence of Becket's healing blood. Readers who know all the stories and the signs cannot know what kind of blood might still remain on Pardoner Becket's head or what has happened to the archbishop's laundered blood. Knowing members of the audience might include clergy and officials of the ecclesiastical church and/or pilgrims to the cathedral. The Canterbury monks read the stories of Becket's martyrdom to pilgrims before the start of their tour of Trinity Chapel and interpreted for them the stained glass windows whose narratives are positioned too high to see.[39] It is those who are already most familiar with the sanctioned versions of Becket's blood who are the most disoriented. It is not simply that Becket's blood has become contaminated blood, stigmatizing a queer. It is impossible to calibrate this blood at all.

The Interlude presents readers with a scandalous series of replicated signs of replicated blood while leaving the matter of blood, what it does and how it works, opaque. Becket's blood remains as inscrutable and as enigmatic as the Pardoner's body on which it gets transfused. In its iteration from the pen of an author who surely must have known about all its work, the Canterbury Becketian blood project comes undone even as it is restated. The rehearsal of yet another narrative about Becket's blood employs ecclesiastically sanctioned protocols of its re-presentation to expose its excesses and aporiae.[40] *The Interlude* allows us to entertain the possibility that sacred blood might be manufactured into a series of carefully staged performances; that its endless mobility might allow it to settle on the brow of a sexual misfit; that the blood that ensured the canonization of a murdered archbishop might be indistinguishable from that of a sexual deviant beaten up by a red-blooded heterosexual jealous of the unwelcome attentions paid to his barmaid squeeze. Even more provocatively, insider knowledge of the signs of Canterbury blood creates a text that is an unreliable witness to Becket's blood. The eccentric positionality of the queer blood in *The Canterbury Interlude* exposes the essential queerness of Becket's vaunted cruor in the first place. For the cathedral, Becket's assassination was the occasion to create an elaborate theater of signs to authenticate miraculous blood beyond the logic of verification. With its challenge to substantiveness, *The Canterbury Interlude* exposes how Becket's martyred blood (perhaps all martyrs' blood?) is always already queer. Not so much, then, that there's now't so queer as folk: there's now't so queer as blood.

Notes

INTRODUCTION

1. Manfred Horstmanshoff, Helen King, and Claus Zittel, eds., *Blood, Sweat and Tears—The Changing Concepts of Physiology from Antiquity into Early Modern Europe* (Leiden: Brill, 2012).

2. Patricia Crawford, *Blood, Bodies and Families in Early Modern England* (Harlow: Pearson, 2004); Ariane Balizet, *Blood and Home in Early Modern Drama: Domestic Identity on the Renaissance Stage* (Oxford: Routledge, 2014).

3. Sara Read, *Menstruation and the Female Body in Early Modern England* (Basingstoke: Palgrave, 2013).

4. Cathy McClive, *Menstruation and Procreation in Early Modern France: Blood and Taboo* (Farnham: Ashgate, 2015). See also Andrew Shail and Gillian Howie, eds., *Menstruation: A Cultural History* (Basingstoke: Palgrave Macmillan, 2005).

5. Hannah R. Johnson, *Blood Libel: The Ritual Murder Accusation at the Limit of Jewish History* (Ann Arbor: University of Michigan Press, 2012)

6. Jean E. Feerick, *Strangers in Blood: Relocating Race in the Renaissance* (Toronto: University of Toronto Press, 2010).

7. Richard Sugg, *Mummies, Cannibals and Vampires: The History of Corpse Medicine from the Renaissance to the Victorians* (Abingdon, Oxon.: Routledge, 2011); Louise Noble, *Medicinal Cannibalism in Early Modern English Literature and Culture* (Basingstoke: Palgrave Macmillan, 2011).

8. Bettina Bildhauer, *Medieval Blood* (Cardiff: University of Wales Press, 2006).

9. Gail Kern Paster, *The Body Embarrassed: Drama and the Disciplines of Shame in Early Modern England* (Ithaca: Cornell University Press, 1993); Caroline Walker Bynum, *Wonderful Blood: Theology and Practice in Late Medieval Germany and Beyond* (Philadelphia: University of Pennsylvania Press, 2007).

10. Paster, *The Body Embarrassed*, 69.

11. Nancy Selleck, *The Interpersonal Idiom in Shakespeare, Donne and Early Modern Culture* (Basingstoke: Palgrave Macmillan, 2008). In *The Body Embarrassed*, Paster observes that "every subject grew up with a common understanding of his or her body

as a semipermeable, irrigated container" (8). This became a central tenet of Mary Floyd-Wilson and Garrett Sullivan Jr., eds., *Environment and Embodiment in Early Modern England* (Basingstoke: Palgrave, 2007). In this volume, Lesel Dawson observes that guilt, like lovesickness, could bind two souls across bodily boundaries (xx), and Sugg suggests that the spirits could move between bodies through the senses in *The Smoke of the Soul: Medicine, Physiology and Religion in Early Modern England* (Basingstoke: Palgrave Macmillan, 2013), 35.

12. P. D. L. Avis, "Moses and the Magistrate: A Study in the Rise of Protestant Legalism," *Journal of Ecclesiastical History* 26 (1975): 149–72. See also Thomas Fulton, "Shakespeare's *Everyman*: *Measure for Measure* and English Fundamentalism," *Journal of Medieval and Early Modern Studies* 40 (2010): 119–47. For studies of early modern legal and judicial cultures more generally, see Subha Mukherji, *Law and Representation in Early Modern Drama* (Cambridge: Cambridge University Press, 2006) and Frances Dolan, *True Relations: Reading, Literature, and Evidence in Seventeenth-Century England* (Philadelphia: University of Pennsylvania Press, 2013).

13. Giorgio Agamben, *Stanzas: Word and Phantasm in Western Culture*, trans. Giorgio Agamben (London: University of Minnesota Press, 1993), 142.

14. Agamben, *Stanzas*, 143.

CHAPTER 1

Note to epigraph: William Harvey, Dedication, *De Motu Cordis* (1628) in *The Circulation of the Blood and Other Writings*, trans. Kenneth J. Franklin and intro. Andrew Wear (London: J. M. Dent & Sons, 1990), 3. All in-text citations are to this edition.

1. This episode is recorded in William Harvey, *De Generatione Animalium* (1651), trans. and intro. Gweneth Whitteridge, *Disputations Touching the Generation of Animals* (Oxford: Blackwell Scientific Publications, 1981), 249–55. All in-text citations are to this edition. Hugh was the eldest son of the second Viscount Montgomery; Whitteridge states that this likely occurred sometime in 1641; see Whitteridge, *William Harvey and the Circulation of the Blood* (London: Macdonald, 1971), 229, and note 9, 235.

2. Cited in Whitteridge, *William Harvey*, 235, n.9.

3. Preface, *The Anatomical Exercises of Doctor William Harvey . . . Concerning the Motion of the Heart and Blood*, trans. Zachariah Wood (London, 1653), sig. A4r.

4. It could be argued that Harvey did not so much discover the circulation of the blood but demonstrated it through his experiments; others, such as Realdo Colombo at Padua, had begun to theorize the circulation of the blood prior to Harvey.

5. Christopher Hill, "William Harvey and the Idea of Monarchy," *Past and Present* 27 (1964): 56, 61–62.

6. Hill, "William Harvey," 55.

7. John Rogers, *The Matter of Revolution: Science, Poetry & Politics in the Age of Milton* (Ithaca: Cornell University Press, 1996), 20.

8. Rogers, *Matter of Revolution*, 2, 27, 20, 21.

9. Rogers, *Matter of Revolution*, 21.

10. Rogers, *Matter of Revolution*, ix; Gweneth Whitteridge, Introduction, *Disputations*, observed, similarly, that "it is difficult to maintain that Harvey's views on the relationship of heart and blood varied to any considerable extent throughout his life" (232).

11. See Wear, Introduction, *Circulation of the Blood*, 9.

12. Wear, Introduction, *Circulation of the Blood*, 9–11.

13. William Harvey, *The Anatomical Lectures of William Harvey*, ed. and trans. Gweneth Whitteridge (Edinburgh and London: E. & S. Livingstone, 1964), 295, 319, 127. All in-text citations are to this edition.

14. Cited in Thomas Wright, *Circulation: William Harvey's Revolutionary Idea* (London: Chatto & Windus, 2012), 151. No source given.

15. See Wear, Introduction, *Circulation of the Blood*, viii.

16. *The First Letter of William Harvey in the 1651–1657 Series*, in Wear, *Circulation of the Blood*, 140.

17. Hill, "William Harvey," 55, 56.

18. William Harvey, *Two Anatomical Exercitations Concerning the Circulation of the Blood, To John Riolan* (London: Francis Leach, 1653), 79.

19. Whitteridge, *William Harvey*, similarly finds no contradictions between Harvey's earlier and later theses; rather, she finds shifts in emphasis depending on whether he is discussing circulation or generation, along with many "compromises" with Aristotle, 230–33.

20. *The First Anatomical Essay to John Riolan* in Wear, *Circulation of the Blood*, 104.

21. Hill, "William Harvey," 55, 56.

22. Harvey, *A Second Essay to Jean Riolan*, in Wear, *Circulation*, 135.

23. J. Aubrey, *Brief Lives*, ed. A. Clark (Oxford, 1898), i, 300; cited in Whitteridge, *Generation of Animals*.

24. Cited in Hill, "William Harvey," 59.

25. Hill, "William Harvey," 66 and Rogers, *Matter of Revolution*, 20.

26. Rogers, *Matter of Revolution*, 20.

27. Rogers, *Matter of Revolution*, 24.

28. Harvey, *Anatomical Exercitations*, 42.

29. Sir Thomas Elyot, *The Castel of Helth* (London, 1534), f.16r.

30. Harvey, *Anatomical Lectures*, 295, 319, 127.

31. Harvey, *Anatomical Lectures*, 293; and Harvey, *Anatomical Exercitations*, 44.

32. Rogers, *Matter of Revolution*, 1–38.

33. Thomas Hobbes, *Leviathan*, ed. Richard Tuck (Cambridge: Cambridge University Press, 1996), 54.

34. Whitteridge, *Generation of Animals*, xx.

35. From Sir Charles Scarburgh's Harveian Oration, Oxford, Bodleian Library, MS Rawlinson D 815, f.6v. Cited in Whitteridge, *Generation of Animals*, xxi. On Harvey's time in Oxford see Geoffrey Keynes, *The Life of William Harvey* (Oxford: Clarendon Press, 1966), 298–317.

36. James Harrington, *The Mechanics of Nature* is published in *The Oceana of James Harrington, and his other Works*, ed. John Toland (London, 1670), xlii–xliv.

37. James Harrington, *The Commonwealth of Oceana and A System of Politics*, ed. J. G. A. Pocock (Cambridge: Cambridge University Press, 1992). All in-text citations are to this edition.

38. See Rudolf Wittkower, *Architectural Principles in the Age of Humanism* (London: Academy Editions, 1977), 28.

39. The famous phrase is John Donne's—"And new philosophy calls all in doubt"—in "The First Anniversary: An Anatomy of the World," in *The Complete Poems of John Donne*, ed. Robin Robbins (Harlow: Pearson Education, 2010), l.205. Donne's poem alludes to alchemical, astronomical, and anatomical discoveries under the mantle of "new philosophy." Donne appears mindful of current controversies about the heart and blood—"Know'st thou how blood which to the heart doth flow / Doth from one ventricle to th'other go?" (*The Second Anniversary*, ll.271–72).

40. *The First Anatomical Essay to Jean Riolan* in Wear, *Circulation of the Blood*, 104. On circular symbolism in Harvey see Walter Pagel, *William Harvey's Biological Ideas: Selected Aspects and Historical Background* (Basel and New York: S. Karger, 1967), 82–83.

41. See Wright, *Circulation*, 169.

42. See, for example, Sir Thomas Browne's eulogy to Harvey's discourse on "the little pale circle" of generation in *Pseudodoxia Epidemica*, III, 3, cited by Whitteridge, frontispiece epigraph, *Generation of Animals*, unpaginated.

43. Poem by Dr. Martin Llewellyn, cited in Whitteridge, *The Generation of Animals*, xv.

44. Gerrard Winstanley, *The Law of Freedom*, in *The Law of Freedom and Other Writings*, ed. Christopher Hill (Harmondsworth: Penguin, 1973), 347, 349.

45. Daniel Defoe, *The Complete English Tradesman* (London, 1732), 25.

46. "To the People of Maryland" by an American, June 27, 1776, in *American Archives*, ed. Peter Force, 9 vols., major compilation of documents 1774–1776, 4.6, pp. 1094–96, cited at http://www.tell-usa.org/totl/06-Rotation&otherreforms.htm#Theories, accessed September 4, 2014. See also Donald P. Kommers, John E. Finn, and Gary J. Jacobson, *American Constitutional Law: Governmental Powers and Democracy* (Lanham, MD: Rowman & Littlefield, 2004), 275.

47. Rogers, Preface, *Matter of Revolution*, ix.

CHAPTER 2

1. See Robert Klein, "Spirito peregrine," *Revue d'Études Italiennes* 11 (1965), 197–236, and Giorgio Agamben, *Stanze: La parola e il fantasma nella cultura occidentale* (Turin: Einaudi, 1977), particularly part three. On William Harvey's debunking of the notion of the sensate heart, see Margaret Healy's chapter in this volume.

2. "la paura . . . nel lago del cor" (*Inferno*, I.19–20). All quotations from *The Divine Comedy* are from *La Divina Commedia*, ed. Anna Maria Chiavacci Leonardi, 3 vols. (Milan: Mondadori, 1991–1997). Translations are from *The Divine Comedy*, trans. and ed. Robin Kirkpatrick, 3 vols. (London: Penguin, 2006–2007).

3. "e 'l sangue, ch'è per le vene disperso / fuggendo corre verso / lo cor, che 'l chiama; ond'io rimango bianco." (45–47), *Dante Alighieri: Rime*, ed. Domenico De Robertis, 3 vols. (Florence: Le Lettere, 2002). Translation mine.

4. "mi ritrovai per una selva oscura, / ché la diritta via era smarrita" (*Inferno* I.3–4).

5. I explore this more fully in my article "Dante's Stone Cold Rhymes," *Dante Studies* 121 (2003): 149–68.

6. I discuss voice as deriving from blood-based spirit in further detail in my book *The Medieval Heart* (New Haven: Yale University Press, 2010), esp. 70–82, 125–31.

7. "Ciascun si fida / del beneficio tuo sanza giurarlo, / pur che 'l voler nonpossa non ricida. / Ond'io, che solo innanzi a li altri parlo, / ti priego, se mai vedi quel paese / che siede tra Romagna e quel di Carlo, / che tu mi sie di tuoi prieghi cortese / in Fano, sì che ben per me s'adori / pur ch'i' possa purgar le gravi offese. / Quindi fu' io; ma li profondi fóri / ond'uscì 'l sangue in sul quale io sedea, / fatti mi fuoro in grembo a li Antenori, / là dov' io più sicuro esser credea / . . . / Corsi al palude, e le cannucce e 'l braco / m'impigliar sì ch'i' caddi; e lì vid' io / de le mie vene farsi in terra laco."

8. "Io fui di Montefeltro, io son Bonconte; / Giovanna o altri non ha di me cura; / per ch'io vo tra costor con bassa fronte."

9. "Oh!", rispuos' elli, "a piè del Casentino / traversa un'acqua c'ha nome l'Archiano, / che sovra l'Ermo nasce in Apennino. / Là 've 'l vocabol suo diventa vano, / arriva' io forato ne la gola, / fuggendo a piede e sanguinando il piano. / Quivi perdei la vista e la parola; / nel nome di Maria fini', e quivi / caddi, e rimase la mia carne sola." See Robin Kirkpatrick's reading of this episode, "Massacre, *Miserere* and Martyrdom," in *Vertical Readings in Dante's 'Comedy,'* vol. 1, ed. George Corbett and Heather Webb (Cambridge: Open Book Publishers, 2015), esp. 106–8.

10. "Nel mezzo della vigna [dell'anima] ha posto il vasello del cuore, pieno di sangue, per inaffiare con esso le piante, acciocchè non si secchino. . . . Di che s'inaffia? Non d'acqua ma di sangue prezioso sparso con tanto fuoco d'amore, il quale sangue sta nel vasello del cuore, come detto è." All quotations from the letters of Catherine of Siena are from *Le lettere di S. Caterina da Siena . . . con note di Niccolò Tommasèo*, ed. Piero Misciattelli, 6 vols (Florence: Giunti, 1939–1940), here letter 313, 5:16 and 21. All translations of Catherine's letters are my own.

11. For a linguistic study of the garden in Catherine's writings, see Dorotea Sliwa, "Le metafore del 'giardino' nel linguaggio mistico di Santa Caterina da Siena," in *Con l'occhio e col lume: Atti del corso seminariale di studi su S. Caterina da Siena (25 settembre–7 ottober 1995)*, ed. Luigi Trenti and Bente Klange Addabbo (Siena: Cantagalli, 1999), 131–47.

12. Auguste Hamon, "Cœur (Sacré)," in *Dictionnaire de spiritualité ascétique et mystique: Doctrine et histoire*, ed. Marcel Viller and others, 17 vols. (Paris: Beauchesne,

1932–1995), II (1953), 1023–46 (1027). On a history of devotion to the Sacred Heart, see *Cor Jesu: Commentationes in litteras encylicas Pii XII 'Haurietis aquas,'* ed. Augustinus Bea, Hugo Rahner, Henri Rondet, and Friedrich Schwendimann, 2 vols. (Rome: Herder, 1959), I.

13. Vincent of Beauvais, *Speculum naturale* (Douai, 1624; repr. Graz: Akademische Druck-und Verlagsanstalt, 1964), XXVIII.60, 2033; Thomas of Cantimpré, *Liber de natura rerum*, ed. Helmut Boese (Berlin: De Gruyter, 1973), I.47, 49.

14. Albert the Great, *De Animalibus*, ed. Hermann Stadler (Munich: Aschendorffsche Verlagsbuchhandlung, 1916).

15. Vincent of Beauvais, *Speculum naturale*, XXVIII.60, 2033; Thomas of Cantimpré, *Liber de natura rerum*, I.47, 49.

16. On Christ as mother, see Caroline Walker Bynum, *Jesus as Mother: Studies in the Spirituality of the High Middle Ages* (Berkeley: University of California Press, 1982), 110–69.

17. "Detto abbiamo che noi siamo vigna, e come ella è adornata, e come Dio vuole che sia lavorata. Ora dove ci ha posti? Nella vigna della santa Chiesa. Ine ha posto il lavoratore, cioè Cristo in terra, il quale ci ha amministrare il sangue," letter 313, 5:22–23.

18. Letter 313, 5:19.

19. Vincent of Beauvais, *Speculum naturale*, XXVIII.60, 2032.

20. "Noi membri putridi. . . . Ben vediamo che senza lui non potiamo fare. . . . Chi spregia questo dolce Vicario, spregia il sangue . . . come mi dirai tu che se tu offendi uno corpo, che tu non offenda il sangue che è nel corpo? Non sai tu, che tiene in sè il sangue di Cristo?," letter 171, 3:68. See also Catherine of Siena, *Libro della divina dottrina*, ed. Matilde Fiorilli (Bari: Laterza, 1912), 116, 233–34: "E so' ribelli a questo Sangue, perché hanno levata la reverenzia, e levatisi con grande persecuzione. Essi sono come membri putridi, tagliati dal corpo mistico della santa Chiesa."

21. *Fontes Vitae S. Catharinae Senensis Historici: Il Processo Castellano*, ed. M. H. Laurent (Milan: Bocca, 1942), 43. There is a long debate on the authenticity of letter 273, the identity of the condemned man, and the actuality of the execution. Robert Fawtier is the source of these doubts: *La double expérience de Catherine Benincasa* (Paris: Gallimard, 1948) 122–32, 220–22. Eugenio Duprè Thesedier dismisses these doubts as "original and disconcerting" in his article on Catherine in the *Dizionario biografico degli Italiani*, XXII (Rome: Istituto della Enciclopedia Italiana, 1979), 364. Anna Imelde Galletti's archival work in "Uno capo nelle mani mie: Niccolò di Toldo, Perugino," in *Atti del simposio internazionale cateriniano-bernardiniano, Siena, 17–20 aprile 1980*, ed. Domenico Maffei and Paolo Nardi (Siena: Accademia senese degli intronati, 1982), 121–28, supports the identification of the young man as Niccolò di Toldo.

22. For a succinct and thorough summary of the affair and related bibliography, see *The Letters of Catherine of Siena*, ed. Suzanne Noffke, O.P., Medieval and Renaissance Texts and Studies 202–203, 329, 355 (Tempe, AZ: Arizona Center for Medieval and Renaissance Studies, 2000–2008), I, 82–84. Niccolo's sentence may be found in *Fontes Vitae S. Catharinae Senensis Historici: Documenti*, ed. M. H. Laurent (Florence, 1936), 31.

23. "Ma la smisurata e affocata bontà di Dio lo ingannò, creandogli tanto affetto ed amore nel desiderio di Dio, che non sapeva stare senza lui, dicendo: 'Stà meco, e non mi

abandonare. E cosí non starò altro che bene; e muoio contento.' E teneva il capo suo in sul petto mio. Io allora sentiva uno giubilo e un odore del sangue suo; e non era senza l'odore del mio, il quale io desidero di spandere per lo dolce sposo Gesu," letter 273, 4:175.

24. Niccolò's gesture of laying his head upon Catherine's breast recalls Christ's comforting of John at the Last Supper: John 13.25.

25. Thomas of Cantimpre, *Liber de natura rerum* I.47, 49.

26. William of Auvergne, "De universe," in *Guillelmi Alverni Opera Omnia*, 2 vols. (Paris, 1674, reprint, Frankfurt-am-Main: Minerva, 1963), I, 1042. The translation appears with commentary in Nancy Caciola, *Discerning Spirits: Divine and Demonic Possession in the Middle Ages* (Ithaca: Cornell University Press, 2003), 189. See particularly chapter 4 and her article "Mystics, Demoniacs and the Physiology of Spirit Possession in Medieval Europe," *Comparative Studies in Society and History* 42 (2000): 268–306.

27. Notions of the spirits and the soul were frequently conflated. See Caciola, *Discerning Spirits*, 180–83. On the meaning of blood in the medieval and Renaissance periods, see Piero Camporesi, *The Juice of Life: The Symbolic and Magic Significance of Blood*, trans. Robert R. Barr (New York: Continuum, 1995).

28. "La bocca sua non diceva se non, Gesù, e Catarina. E, così dicendo, ricevetti il capo nelle mani mie, fermando l'occhio nella divina bontà, e dicendo: 'Io voglio,'" letter 273, 4:176–77.

29. "Allora si vedeva Dio-e-Uomo, come si vedesse la chiarità del sole; e stava aperto, e riceveva il sangue . . . poiché ebbe ricevuto il sangue e il desiderio suo, ed egli ricevette l'anima sua, la quale mise nella bottiga aperta del costato suo. . . . Con quanta dolcezza e amore aspettava quella anima partita dal corpo! Voltò l'occhio della misericordia verso di lei, quando venne a intrare dentro nel costato bagnato nel sangue suo, il quale valeva per lo sangue del Figliuolo di Dio. . . . Risposto che fu, l'anima mia si riposò in pace e in quiete, in tanto odore di sangue, che io non potevo sostenere di levarmi il sangue, che mi era venuto addosso, di lui," letter 273, 4:177–78.

30. On Catherine of Siena's relationships with Gregory XI and Urban VI, see Blake Beattie, "Catherine of Siena and the Papacy," in *A Companion to Catherine of Siena*, ed. C. Muessig, G. Ferzoco, and B. M. Kienzle (Leiden, Brill, 2012) 73–98.

31. "'O Dio eterno, ricevi il sacrifizio della vita mia in questo corpo mistico della santa Chiesa. Io non ho che dare altro se non quello che tu hai dato a me. Tolli il cuore dunque, e premilo sopra la faccia di questa Sposa.' Allora Dio eterno, vollendo l'occhio della clemenzia sua, divelleva il cuore, e premevalo nella santa Chiesa. E con tanta forza l'aveva tratto a sè, che, se non che subito (non volendo che 'l vasello del corpo mio fusse rotto) il ricerchiò della fortezza sua, se ne sarebbe andata la vita," letter 371, 5:277. See Karen Scott, "Mystical Death, Bodily Death: Catherine of Siena and Raymond of Capua on the Mystic's Encounter with God," in *Gendered Voices: Medieval Saints and Their Interpreters*, ed. Catherine M. Mooney (Philadelphia: University of Pennsylvania Press, 1999), 136–67. Scott compares Catherine's description of this mystical event with Raymond's, arguing that Catherine tends toward the abstract and the metaphorical, while Raymond focuses on Catherine's body, thus reversing ideas of gendered approaches to spirituality,

according to which males are understood to work in the abstract while females give attention to the bodily.

32. For analysis of Catherine's strategic use of her voice and her literary control of her texts, see Jane Tylus, *Reclaiming Catherine of Siena: Literacy, Literature, and the Signs of Others* (Chicago: University of Chicago Press, 2009).

33. "Grazia sia all'altissimo Dio eterno, che ci ha posti nel campo della battaglia, come cavalieri, a combattere per la Sposa sua," letter 371, 5:278.

34. "La dolce Sposa sua e vostra, che tanto tempo è stata tutta impallidita . . . in coloro che si pascevano e pascono al petto suo, che per li difetti loro l'hanno mostrata pallida e inferma, succhiatole il sangue d'addosso con l'amore proprio di loro," letter 346, 5:162–63.

35. See Barbara Newman, *From Virile Woman to Woman Christ: Studies in Medieval Religion and Literature* (Philadelphia: University of Pennsylvania Press, 1995) for analysis of notions of women's virility and roles as co-redeemer with Christ.

CHAPTER 3

The author would like to thank all those who responded to an earlier version of this chapter presented at the Blood Conference in Oxford (January 2014). Thanks are also due to Richard Meek, Tanya Pollard, and participants in the seminar "Shakespearean Figurations: The Theatrical Performance of Typicality" organized by Zeno Ackermann at the International Shakespeare Conference in 2014.

1. Francis Markham, *The Booke of Honour: Or Five Decads of Epistles of Honour* (London, 1625), 46.

2. See Gail Kern Paster, "Becoming the Landscape: The Ecology of the Passions in the Legend of Temperance," in *Environment and Embodiment in Early Modern England*, ed. Mary Floyd-Wilson and Garrett A. Sullivan Jr. (Harmondsworth: Palgrave, 2007), 142. See also Paster's exploration of blood, combustibility, and identity in "Nervous Tension: Networks of Blood and Spirit in the Early Modern Body," in *The Body in Parts: Fantasies of Corporeality in Early Modern Europe*, ed. David Hillman and Carla Mazzio (New York and London: Routledge, 1997), 107–25.

3. Mary Floyd-Wilson, *English Ethnicity and Race in Early Modern Drama* (Cambridge: Cambridge University Press, 2003), esp. 39–41.

4. Sara Read, *Menstruation and the Female Body in Early Modern England* (Basingstoke: Palgrave, 2013).

5. Patricia Crawford, *Blood, Bodies and Families in Early Modern England* (Harlow: Pearson Longman, 2004), 125–26.

6. Terri Clerico has, however, explored, through the semiotics of blood, the "hyperconscious rhetoric of class politics" in John Ford's plays. See "The Politics of Blood: John Ford's 'Tis Pity She's a Whore," *English Literary Renaissance* 22.3 (1992): 414. See also Paster's exploration of the fragility of blood's "power to confer distinction" in *The Body Embarrassed: Drama and the Disciplines of Shame in Early Modern England* (Ithaca: Cornell University

Press, 1993), 88; and David S. Berkeley's essay, "Severall Degrees in Bloud," in *Shakespeare's Theories of Blood, Character and Class: A Festschrift in Honor of David Shelley Berkeley*, ed. Peter C. Rollins and Alan Smith (New York: Peter Lang, 2001).

7. Berkeley, "Severall Degrees in Bloud," 7.

8. Mary Ellen Lamb, *The Popular Culture of Shakespeare, Spenser and Jonson* (London: Routledge, 2006), 2.

9. *Henry V*, 3.6.72. This and all subsequent quotations refer to Gary Taylor's edition (Oxford: Oxford University Press, 1982).

10. *Henry IV Part Two*, 2.4.226. This and all subsequent quotations refer to Rene Weis's edition (Oxford: Oxford University Press, 1997).

11. Edward Dutton Cook, *Nights at the Play: A View of the English Stage* (London, 1883), 2.230.

12. *The Politicke and Militarie Discourses of the Lord de La Noue*, trans. E[dward] A[ggas] (London, 1587), 198.

13. See, for example, Paul Jorgensen, *Shakespeare's Military World* (Berkeley: University of California Press, 1956), 73.

14. Nicolas Coeffeteau, *Table of Humane Passions with Their Causes and Effects*, trans. Edw. Grimeston (London, 1621), 552 and 609–10.

15. Coeffeteau, *Table of Humane Passions*, 555 and 550.

16. *2 Henry IV*, 2.4.191 and 5.3.93.

17. *Henry V*, 2.2.129–30.

18. Coeffeteau, *Table of Human Passions*, 323.

19. For a discussion of the "trope of vagabond veterans" in literary culture more generally, see Linda Bradley Salamon, "Vagabond Veterans: The Roguish Company of Martin Guerre and *Henry V*," in *Rogues and Early Modern English Culture*, ed. Craig Dionne and Steve Mentz (Ann Arbor: University of Michigan Press, 2004). For a summary of Elizabeth conscription, including the 1597 bill passed in order to improve recruitment, see C. G. Cruikshank, *Elizabeth's Army*, 2nd ed. (Oxford: Clarendon Press, 1966), 6–8 and 17–40.

20. Jorgensen, *Shakespeare's Military World*, 68–70.

21. Compare Hal's admonition to Falstaff in *1 Henry IV*: "thou owest God a death" (5.1.12).

22. See Jennifer Krauss, "Name-calling and the New Oxford *Henry V*," *Shakespeare Quarterly* 36.4 (1985): 523.

23. For a summary of this debate, see Krauss, "Name-calling and the New Oxford *Henry V*," 523–25.

24. See Gary Taylor, "Ancients and Moderns," *Shakespeare Quarterly* 36.4 (1985): 525.

25. Henry J. Webb, *Elizabethan Military Science: The Books and the Practice* (Madison: University of Wisconsin Press, 1965), 78.

26. Thomas Digges, *Stratioticus* (London: 1590), 93–94; see also Jorgensen, *Shakespeare's Military World*, 81.

27. The OED cites John Speed's 1611 use of the term: "An hallowed Banner of red silke, whereof the French had a wonderfull high conceit, as of that which was sent from heauen,

and called Oreflame or Auriflames." Compare the "bloody colours" that Edward of York demands in *3 Henry VI*, 2.2.172. This episode is described in Charles Edelman, *Shakespeare's Military Language: A Dictionary* (London: Athlone Press, 2000), 94.

28. See Sir John Smythe, *Instructions, Observations, and Orders Mylitarie* (London, 1594), 129–30; and Cruikshank, *Elizabeth's Army*, 54.

29. Jorgensen, *Shakespeare's Military World*, 81.

30. The word "ensign" could refer to the standard itself, as well as to the standard bearer as Taylor points out in his note to *Henry V*, 2.1.3.

31. Markham, *The Booke of Honour*, 45–890. For a survey of how the practice of exogamy was reflected in contemporary drama, see Clerico, "The Politics of Blood," 416.

32. See Taylor's note to *Henry V*, 3.1.7.

33. Compare John Stephen, "On High Birth," in *Satyrical Essayes Characters and Others* (London: 1615), 44: "High blouds likewise be the fittest receptacles for high actions; but if a sacke-cloth bee embroydred, the adiunct may deserue honor, though the ground-worke be Plebeian: and men of vp-start Parentage may, in respect of braine, take place before Nobilitie, though their persons bee odious."

34. See Jorgensen, *Shakespeare's Military World*, 74.

35. Smythe, *Instructions, Observations, and Orders Militarie*, 204–5; quoted in Jorgensen, *Shakespeare's Military World*, 74.

36. Roger Williams, *A Briefe Discourse of Warre* (London, 1590), 39.

37. *Henry V*, 4.1.188; *The Politicke and Militarie Discourses of the Lord de La Noue*, 198; quoted by Jorgensen, 73.

38. Robert Lane, "'When Blood is their Argument': Class, Character, and History-making in Shakespeare's and Branagh's *Henry V*," *English Literary History* 61.1 (1994): 27.

39. See Jonathan Dollimore and Alan Sinfield, "History and Ideology: The Instance of *Henry V*," in *Alternative Shakespeares*, ed. John Drakakis (London: Methuen, 1985), 220; and Annabel M. Patterson, *Shakespeare and the Popular Voice* (Oxford: Blackwell, 1989), 86.

CHAPTER 4

1. Hilary Mantel, *Bring Up the Bodies*, adapted by Mike Poulton (London: Nick Hern Books, 2014), 5.32, 268, 269. *Wolf Hall* and *Bring Up the Bodies* (two plays) copyright © 2013 Mike Poulton and Tertius Enterprises Ltd., published by Nick Hern Books Ltd.

2. Susan Baker, "Hamlet's Bloody Thoughts and the Illusion of Inwardness," *Comparative Drama* 21 (1987): 303–4.

3. Thomas Nashe, *Pierce Penilesse his Supplication to the Divell* (London, 1592), F3.

4. Patricia A. Cahill, *Unto the Breach: Martial Formations, Historical Trauma, and the Early Modern Stage* (Oxford: Oxford University Press, 2008), 19.

5. Maurizio Calbi, *Approximate Bodies: Gender and Power in Early Modern Drama and Anatomy* (New York: Routledge, 2005), 32, my emphasis.

6. Katharine Eisaman Maus, *Inwardness and Theater in the English Renaissance* (Chicago: University of Chicago Press, 1995), 32.

7. Maus, *Inwardness,* 90–91.

8. See, e.g., Valerie Wayne, "The Woman's Parts of *Cymbeline*," in *Staged Properties in Early Modern Drama*, ed. Natasha Korda and Jonathan Gil Harris (Cambridge: Cambridge University Press, 2002), 288–315; Andrew Sofer, *The Stage Life of Props* (Ann Arbor: University of Michigan Press, 2003), and Patricia Parker's chapter in this volume.

9. Wendy Wall, *Staging Domesticity: Household Work and English Identity in Early Modern Drama* (Cambridge: Cambridge University Press, 2002), 121.

10. Hannah Woolley, *The Compleat Servant-maid* (London, 1677), 64–70, 164–65.

11. Larger or elite households would be more likely to do their washing in-house, with designated laundry-maids and perhaps additional help.

12. See Wall, *Staging Domesticity*, 117, and also Richard Helgerson, "The Buck Basket, the Witch, and the Queen of Fairies: The Women's World of Shakespeare's Windsor," in *Renaissance Culture and the Everyday*, ed. Patricia Fumerton and Simon Hunt (Philadelphia: University of Pennsylvania Press, 1999), 162–82.

13. According to the RSC's "A Day in the Life of Running Wardrobe," "Every item of clothing that touches the skin is washed immediately after each show, which often involves up to 8 wash loads every night. . . . The recent production of *The Taming of the Shrew* . . . involved some 74 shirts for each performance," accessed September 8, 2014, http://www.rsc.org.uk/explore/running-wardrobe.aspx.

14. See the comprehensive discussion by Natasha Korda, *Labors Lost: Women's Work and the Early Modern English Stage* (Philadelphia: University of Pennsylvania Press, 2011), especially chapter 3 *passim*.

15. See Andrea Ria Stevens, *Inventions of the Skin: The Painted Body in Early English Drama, 1400–1642* (Edinburgh: Edinburgh University Press, 2013), and Lucy Munro, "'They eat each other's arms': Stage Blood and Body Parts," in *Shakespeare's Theatres and the Effects of Performance*, ed. Farah Karim-Cooper and Tiffany Stern (London: Bloomsbury, 2013), 73–93. See also Elisabeth Dutton's chapter in this volume, especially the section "Staging Croxton's Blood" (p. 185f).

16. The RSC Histories (2007–2008) used 15 liters of blood every time they staged the cycle.

17. *Wolf Hall*, 2.8, 89.

18. On the characteristically early modern state of what he terms "somatic precariousness," see David Hillman, *Shakespeare's Entrails: Belief, Scepticism and the Interior of the Body* (London: Palgrave, 2007), 1 and *passim*.

19. *Wolf Hall*, 4.24, 148.

20. Arthur Golding, *The xv books of P. Ovidius Naso, entytuled Metamorphosis* (London, 1567), L2.

21. Jonathan Sawday, "The Fate of Marsyas: Dissecting the Renaissance Body," in *Renaissance Bodies: The Human Figure in English Culture c. 1540–1660*, ed. Lucy Gent and Nigel Llewellyn (London: Reaktion, 1990), 135.

22. High-street shops, at least, do not stock men's underwear in "skin" tones.

23. John Guy, *My Heart Is My Own: The Life of Mary Queen of Scots* (London: Harper-Collins, 2004), 7. Guy's use of "tawny" is odd, as it usually refers to an orangey-brown; the word in his source is clearly red: "et ainsy fut exécutée tout en rouge" [and thus she was executed all in red], "Le vray rapport de l'exécution faicte sur la personne de la Reyne d'Escosse," in Alexandre Teulet, *Relations Politiques de la France et de l'Espagne avec L'Écosse au XVIe Siècle*, vol. 4 (Paris, 1862), 160.

24. J.B. [John Bulwer], *Anthropometamorphosis* (London, 1653), Aaaa2, quoted by Stephen Greenblatt, "Mutilation and Meaning," in *The Body in Parts: Fantasies of Corporeality in Early Modern Europe*, ed. David Hillman and Carla Mazzio (New York: Routledge, 1997), 236. "Duretto" was a hard-wearing coarse cloth.

25. See Figure 4.5.

26. Thomas Nashe, *The Unfortunate Traveller and Other Works*, edited by J. Steane (Harmondsworth: Penguin, 1978), 349.

27. Luke Wilson, "William Harvey's *Prelectiones*: The Performance of the Body in the Renaissance Theater of Anatomy," *Representations* 17 (1987): 71.

28. This is noted by Sawday, who makes no comment on the aptness of the stolen coat. As in other depictions of dissections, the textile layering within the picture is striking: Adriaenszoon's body is partially draped even as his skin is peeled away. Jonathan Sawday, *The Body Emblazoned: Dissection and the Human Body in Renaissance Culture* (London: Routledge, 1996), 150.

29. Cynthia Marshall, "Wound-man: *Coriolanus*, Gender, and the Theatrical Construction of Interiority," in *Feminist Readings of Early Modern Culture: Emerging Subjects*, ed. Valerie Traub, M. Lindsay Kaplan, and Dympna Callaghan (Cambridge: Cambridge University Press, 1996), 102.

30. Marshall, "Wound-man," 101, citing W. B. Worthen, "Deeper Meanings and Theatrical Technique: The Rhetoric of Performance Criticism," *Shakespeare Quarterly* 40 (1989): 455; my emphasis.

31. The OED gives 1609 as the first occurrence of *candidate* in the political sense, but it is found in Holland's Livy (1600).

32. Matthew 9.20–22, Mark 5.25–34, Luke 8.43–8. See Steven Connor, *The Book of Skin* (London: Reaktion, 2004), 30, 33; in her chapter in this volume, Helen Barr (p. 245) notes that on occasion this woman has been identified with St. Veronica, who later wipes away Christ's bloody sweat on the road to Calvary.

33. Munro, "'They eat each other's arms,'" in *Shakespeare's Theatres*, ed. Karim-Cooper and Stern, 84.

34. The 2014 production of *Julius Caesar* at Shakespeare's Globe in London used "Roman" costumes reminiscent of the "Peacham drawing" of *Titus Andronicus*, a toga-like drape over Elizabethan dress. The blood transferred to the other actors in the assassination scene largely stained their "togas," more robustly washable than their other garments.

35. Elaine Scarry, *The Body in Pain: The Making and Unmaking of the World* (Oxford: Oxford University Press, 1985).

CHAPTER 5

The research on which this chapter is based was funded by The Open University as part of the 2012–2013 project "Negotiating Gender in Renaissance Medicine" and by the Wellcome Trust (grant number 103177/z/13/z). Zuccolin claims 90 percent of the work, King 10 percent.

1. The translation is ours: "Seventeenth Cure, which deals with a puerperal woman who discharged menstrual blood from the nostrils and mouth. The wife of a German man who lives at the tavern was afflicted by a strong headache during the seventh month of pregnancy: to treat it we ordered the application of cupping glasses to the shoulders with scarification. That same evening she gave birth to a baby boy and a burning fever invaded her. She did not purge, was very thirsty and anxious, the outcome was uncertain. The next day, a few hours after having cut the *saphena* vein of the foot and let the blood pour out, she had a massive menstrual bleeding from the mouth and nostrils. After this haemorrhage the headache began to diminish and the whole range of symptoms began to decrease. The following day the blood began to change direction and flow back, following the right pathway, after having applied small gourds without seeds (cupping glasses), often making her drink Byzantium syrup without vinegar and having used other diverting means. When the menstrual flow appeared she proclaimed herself healed and she kept on feeling amazingly well. But her child died" (Curatio decimaseptima in qua agitur de muliere enixa, quae sanguinem menstruum per nares, et os emittebat. Uxor hominis Germani, qui ad tabernam habitat, uterum gerebat septimo mense magno capitis dolore cruciabatur, pro quo levando, cucurbitulas scapulis cum scarificatione affigi fecimus. Sed vesperi puerum peperit, et febris ardens illam invasit. Nihil purgabat, multum sitiebat, anxie agebat, res in dubio erat. Sequenti vero die, quum saphena pedis vena secta esset, et sanguis exiret, interpositis paucis horis, per os et nares sanguis menstruus illi copiosissime effluxit. Post cuius fluorem capitis dolor remitti coepit, et symptomata omnia minui. Sequenti vero die cucurbitulis seminibus admotis, et syrupo de bysantiis sine aceto saepe ebibito, ac aliis retractionibus adhibitis, sanguis diverti et retrahi coepit, ac sic rectam viam secutus fuit. Quum vero menses fluerent, se sanam dixit et basilice perseveravit: at eius puer obit), Amatus Lusitanus, *Curationum medicinalium centuriae* IV (Basileae, 1556), Centuria 2, curatio 17, 145 (first ed. Florentiae 1551).

2. Ps.-Albertus Magnus, *Women's Secrets: A Translation of Pseudo-Albertus Magnus's De Secretis Mulierum with Commentaries*, ed. Helen Rodnite Lemay (Albany, NY: State University of New York Press, 1992), 142–43. The author tells the case of a pregnant woman experiencing a heavy nosebleed just before giving birth to a stillborn child, specifying that "the blood she shed was really menstrual blood." Commentator B explains: "Since in this case the fetus was dead, it did not require nourishment, and so the menses moved upwards and were expelled through the nostrils. If a pregnant woman had a great deal of blood then a nosebleed would not harm her, but rather it would benefit her because it would relieve her. This occurs often in young women who have much blood, and especially in the beginning of the pregnancy when the fetus does not yet need a large amount of nourishment."

3. For example, these two other case histories, with opposed conclusions: (1) Michele Savonarola, *Practica Maior*, Venetiis, 1560 [1440], VI.5, De egritudinibus narium, 94rb: "And in my time I have seen a woman pregnant with a boy of the Paduan family Zabarella, who lost around 22 pounds [Ferrarese pounds, i.e., nearly one liter] of blood through the nostrils, delivered and survived together with the fetus; there exists a critical nosebleed, and this one must not be stopped unless it is overabundant, and a non-critical one" (our translation). (Et vidi diebus meis mulierem pregnantem ex masculo ex familia Zabarellorum de Padua, a qua exivit quantitas sanguinis per nares circiter lib. xxii, peperit & supervixit, & foetus ipse; & est fluxum narium quidam criticus, & talis non est compescendus, nisi superfluat: quidam vero non criticus.) (2) Thomas Bartholin, *Historiarum Anatomicarum Rariorum*, 1657, Centuria IV, Historia 36, Haemorrhagia in pregnante, 192–93: "The young wife of a merchant from Copenhagen, both of good habits and soul, suffered a quite heavy nosebleed during the seventh month of pregnancy, lasting two days continuously, so that nothing could be done to stop it, on the third day a copious vomiting of blood followed and within a span of a few hours she died" (our translation). (Juvencula uxor mercatoris Hafniensis, boni habitus et animi, septimo graviditatis mense incidit in haemorragiam narium satis copiosam, que per biduum perseveravit, continuo sanguine stillante, ut sedari nulla arte potuerit, tertio die vomitus sanguinis liberalior successit, unde paucis intejectis horis vivere desiit.)

4. Thomas Laqueur, *Making Sex: Body and Gender from the Greeks to Freud* (Cambridge, MA: Harvard University Press, 1990). Among the vast amount of secondary literature now available, see at least Joan Cadden, *Meanings of Sex Difference in the Middle Ages: Medicine, Science and Culture* (Cambridge: Cambridge University Press, 1993); Helen King, *The One-Sex Body on Trial: The Classical and Early Modern Evidence* (Aldershot: Ashgate, 2013) and her previous studies; for the medieval side, Katharine Park, "Medicine and Natural Philosophy: Naturalistic Traditions," in *The Oxford Handbook of Women and Gender in Medieval Europe*, ed. Judith M. Bennett and Ruth Mazo Karras (Oxford: Oxford University Press, 2013), 84–100.

5. To give just one example, cf. B. E. Meyers, "Chronic Epistaxis (Vicarious Menstruation?). Cauterisation of the Nose, Followed by Great General and Local Improvement," *Lancet* 158 (1901): 1666–67. Also cf. an ongoing study reported by the U.S. website eHealthMe: "Would you have Epistaxis (Nosebleed) when you have Menstruation irregular?" accessed January 6, 2017, http://www.ehealthme.com/cs/menstruation+irregular/epistaxis. The most lively nineteenth-century debate on this topic was triggered by an article by A. Wiltshire, "Clinical Lecture on Vicarious or Ectopic Menstruation, or Menses Devii," *Lancet* 126 (1885): 513–17. The letters in response to Wiltshire's article demonstrate the keen medical interest in the subject. Less than two years later the *British Gynecological Journal* devoted a whole issue to vicarious menstruation. The article written by R. Barnes ("On vicarious menstruation," *British Gynecological Journal* 2 [1886–1887]: 151–83) in defense of the theory was seriously questioned and the very existence of the phenomenon was dismissed as a simple diagnostic mistake. On this epilogue, also cf. Ornella Moscucci, *The Science of Woman, Gynaecology and Gender in England, 1800–1929* (Cambridge:

Cambridge University Press, 1990), and Gianna Pomata, "Menstruating Men: Similarity and Difference of the Sexes in Early Modern Medicine," in *Generation and Degeneration: Tropes of Reproduction in Literature and History from Antiquity to Early Modern Europe*, ed. Valeria Finucci and Kevin Brownlee (Durham, NC: Duke University Press, 2001), 109–52.

6. Cf. P. D. Mitchell, "Retrospective Diagnosis and the Use of Historical Texts for Investigating Disease in the Past," *International Journal of Paleopathology* 1.2 (2011): 81–88.

7. Vieda S. Skultans, "Research Note. Vicarious Menstruation," *Social Science and Medicine* 21.6 (1985): 713–14.

8. Martin Schurig, *Parthenologia historico-medica, hoc est Virginitatis Consideratio* (Dresden and Leipzig, 1729), 83–118; George M. Gould and Walter L. Pyle, *Anomalies and Curiosities of Medicine* (Philadelphia, 1896), especially Chapter 1.

9. On Hippocratic medical theories, see Helen King, *Hippocrates' Woman: Reading the Female Body in Ancient Greece* (London: Routledge, 1998) and below. See p. 84 in this chapter.

10. The value of combining the social history of medicine with feminist historiographies, and the move toward the recognition of gender as a spectrum rather than Laqueur's binary, informs Cathy McClive, *Menstruation and Procreation in Early Modern France: Blood and Taboo* (Aldershot: Ashgate, 2015). Sara Read's recent book on *Menstruation and the Female Body in Early Modern England* (Basingstoke: Palgrave Macmillan, 2013), despite its heuristic value, barely mentions nosebleeds and theories of anomalous bleeding and/or vicarious menstruation (131 and 146). On menstruation and male periodic bleeding throughout antiquity, the Middle Ages, and the early modern period, cf. Dale Martin, "Contradictions of Masculinity: Ascetic Inseminators and Menstruating Men in Greco-Roman Culture," in Finucci and Brownlee, *Generation and Degeneration,* 81–108; Monica H. Green, "Flowers, Poisons and Men: Menstruation in Medieval Western Europe," in *Menstruation. A Cultural History*, ed. Andrew Shail and Gillian Howe (Basingstoke: Palgrave Macmillan, 2005), 51–64 (in this same volume, see also the contributions by McClive and Stolberg, challenging any simplistic view of early modern models of menstruation, resp. 76–89 and 90–101); Willis Johnson, "The Myth of Jewish Male Menses," *Journal of Medieval History* 24 (1998): 273–95; Irven M. Resnick, "Medieval Roots of the Myth of Male Jewish Menses," *Harvard Theological Review* 93 (2000): 241–63; Peter Biller, "Views of Jews from Paris around 1300: Christian or 'Scientific?'," in *Christianity and Judaism* (Studies in Church History, 29), ed. Diana Wood (Oxford: Blackwell, 1992), 187–99; Pomata, "Menstruating Men," 109–52; Lisa Wynne Smith, "The Body Embarrassed? Rethinking the Leaky Male Body in Eighteenth-Century England and France," *Gender & History* 23.1 (2011): 26–46.

11. For the same approach, see now Wendy D. Churchill, *Female Patients in Early Modern Britain: Gender, Diagnosis, and Treatment* (Aldershot: Ashgate, 2013), esp. Chapter 3.

12. Neither the importance of menstruation in the health economy of women nor the danger of menstrual suppression and retention in historical medical sources can be overestimated. In reading these texts one cannot help but think that the womb was the sole determinant of health and disease in women. The well-known sixteenth-century physician

Laurent Joubert, author of the best-selling *The Popular Errors in Medicine*, paradigmatically devoted a chapter to fight "[a]gainst those who attribute all the diseases of children to worms and all the diseases of women to the womb" (IV.17.4). His efforts were, however, ultimately unsuccessful. In 1709 another doctor, Carolus Musitanus, poetically compared the suppression of the menses to Pandora's jar, which created endless evil diseases. The negative idea of menstruation as a divine punishment, pollution, poison, and abomination was certainly present throughout antiquity, the Middle Ages, and the Renaissance (Pliny the Elder and *Leviticus* being the main authorities). However, the majority of physicians instead took the widespread, positive view of menstruation as a healthy, necessary, and natural process. According to Stolberg, we can roughly distinguish three major explanatory models within the holistic humoral model that dominated Western medicine until the eighteenth century: the cathartic, the plethoric, and the iatrochemical. For the relation between the three see Michael Stolberg, "Menstruation and Sexual Difference in Early Modern Medicine," in Shail and Howe, *Menstruation: A Cultural History*, 90–101. For the cathartic model and its implication also see J. Barrágan Nieto, "'Secretos de las mujeres': Sangre menstrual y mujer venenosa en la Baja," in *Innovación Educativa e Historia de las Relaciones de Género*, ed. Cristina de la Rosa Cubo et al. (Vallodolid: Universidad de Valladolid, 2010), 91–102 and bibliography therein.

13. The idea that blood vessels connected the uterus with the breasts, the heart, and eventually the nose is far from being confined to antiquity. For example, the great Danish physician Thomas Bartholin (discoverer of the lymphatic system) had no doubts about this issue. After explaining the various connections between the abdominal blood vessels, he affirmed the anatomical connection between the abdomen and nostrils and highlighted it as the reason why one of the curative canons for nosebleed is the application of cupping glasses to the abdomen: "Hence the consent between the breasts and the womb is assumed, and between the abdomen and the nostrils. In nosebleed we apply indeed cupping glasses to the abdominal region" (translation ours). Cf. Thomas Bartholin, *Anatomia Reformata* (1655), lib. I, De infimo ventre, 38: "Hinc consensus mammarum cum utero putatur, abdominis cum naribus. Nam in narium haemorrhagia abdomini affigimus cucurbitulas."

14. This very same connection is evident when considering generation theory from antiquity to the Renaissance and beyond. Blood, of course, played an important role in the reproductive functions of both sexes, with breast milk and the male seed being increasingly concocted forms of it (the difference between the two is only due to a more or less refined blood digestive process). But again this is not only a matter of blood. Fertility tests of the past are prime examples of the supposed link between brain, eyes, nose, and mouth and the generative organs, both in the male and the female. Not a single doctor before the end of the Renaissance fails to mention at least some of them. See, e.g., the archetypical Hippocratic example, *Aphorisms*, V.59, and the classic example in Constantine the African, *Pantegni* (9.42). Also, medieval and renaissance physiognomy postulates a strong connection between genitals and nose/lips, especially in terms of size and texture. This is an original idea, formerly absent during antiquity (as a famous Latin proverb, quoted especially from the seventeenth century onward, puts it: "Noscitur ex labiis quantum sit virginis antrum,

Noscitur ex naso quanta sit hasta viri" / "Looking at the lips [of the mouth] the size of the vagina can be known, looking at the nose the dimension of the penis can be known" [our translation]). Medieval physiognomy also provided some tools to detect signs of virginity, alternative to the medical ones (like direct examination by midwives or urine tests), which systematically involve the shape and texture of the nose. Cf. Joseph Ziegler, "Sexuality and the Sexual Organs in Latin Physiognomy 1200–1500," in *Sexuality and Culture in Medieval and Renaissance Europe* (Studies in Medieval and Renaissance History, Third Series, Vol. II), ed. Philip M. Soergel (New York: AMS Press, 2005), 83–107.

15. However, the ideal solution would have been to avoid the initial excess—and thus the crisis—through a correct regimen of life and diet. See, e.g., Michael Stolberg, *Homo Patiens. Krankheits und Körpererfahrung in der frühen Neuzeit* (Köln/Weimar/Wien: Böhlau Verlag, 2003).

16. On the Hippocratic model, see King, *Hippocrates' Woman*. Stolberg and McClive are right to emphasise that the medical literature of the past considered all humoral bodies to be flowing, regardless of sex, but since the majority of men did not require menstruation, any plethoric leakage was pathological for them, even if it happened to be beneficial in some cases.

17. In Aristotle's *History of Animals* and *Generation of Animals*, regular menstruation is clearly singled out as the reason why women seldom experience either nosebleeds or hemorrhoids: "Of all female animals the female in man is the most richly supplied with blood, and of all animals the menstruous discharges are the most copious in woman. The blood of these discharges under disease turns into flux. Women are less subject to other [blood] diseases. Women are seldom afflicted with varicose veins, with haemorrhoids, or with bleeding at the nose, and, if any of these maladies supervene, the menses are imperfectly discharged," Aristotle, *HA*, iii, 19, 521a 29; also see *HA*, vii, 10, 587b 33, and *GA*, i, 19, 727a 12 (*The Complete Works of Aristotle*, ed. Jonathan Barnes, The Revised Oxford Translation, vol. 1 (Princeton: Princeton University Press, 1984), 827.

18. As Max Neuburger showed a hundred years ago in his seminal monograph on the subject: *The Doctrine of the Healing Power of Nature Throughout the Course of Time*, trans. Linn J. Boyd (New York: Homeopathic Medical College, 1932).

19. See Galen, *On Venesection against Erasistratus*, trans. P. Brain, *Galen on Bloodletting: A Study of the Origins, Development and Validity of his Opinions* (Cambridge: Cambridge University Press, 1986), 25–26: "Does she (nature) not evacuate all women every month, by pouring forth the superfluity of the blood? . . . Has a woman ever been known to be stricken with phrenitis, or lethargy, or spasm, or tremor, or tetany, while her menstrual periods were coming? Or did you ever hear of a woman who suffered from melancholy or madness or haemoptysis, or haematemesis, or headache, or suffocation from synanche, or from any of the major and severe diseases, if her menstrual secretions were well established?" Many other instances could be quoted.

20. As stressed by Daston and Park among many others. Cf. Lorraine Daston and Katharine Park, *Wonders and the Order of Nature, 1150–1750* (New York: Zone Books, 1998), esp. Chapters IV, V, VI (135–253).

21. Number 25, section IV.

22. The list is not exhaustive. *Aphorisms*, IV, 60: "When in fevers there is deafness, if blood runs from the nostrils, or the bowels become disordered, it carries off the disease"; IV, 74: "When there is reason to expect that an abscess will form in joints . . . it is also speedily carried off by a haemorrhage from the nose"; V, 13: "In persons who cough up frothy blood, the discharge of it comes from the lungs"; V, 32: "Haemoptysis/expectoration of blood in a woman is removed by an eruption of the menses"; VI, 12. "When a person has been cured of chronic haemorrhoids, unless one be left, there is danger of dropsy or phthisis supervening"; VII, 84: "When in quartan fevers blood flows from the nostrils it is a bad symptom."

23. In *On the Sacred Disease*, the Hippocratic writer also gives a detailed description of the major veins connecting the brain with the liver and the spleen respectively, noting in passing their connections with the nostrils: "and veins run toward it (*sc.* the brain) from all parts of the body, many of which are small, but two are thick, the one from the liver, and the other from the spleen. And it is thus with regard to the one from the liver: . . . near the ear it is concealed, and there it divides; its thickest, largest, and most hollow part ends in the brain; another small vein goes to the right ear, another to the right eye, and another to the nostril. Such are the distributions of the hepatic vein. And a vein from the spleen is distributed on the left side, upward and downward, like that from the liver, but more slender and feeble."

24. Aristotle, *Problems*, trans. W. S. Hett, Loeb Classical Library (Cambridge MA, 1936), volume 1, X.2.

25. Cf. above note 17.

26. Celsus, *On Medicine*, trans. W. G. Spencer, Loeb Classical Library (Cambridge MA, 1938), 4.27, 449; Galen, *On Diseases and Symptoms* 3, trans. Ian Johnston (Cambridge: Cambridge University Press, 2006), V.I, 283: "However, there are those [causes] stirred up from conditions of the body, when someone haemorrhages spontaneously from the nose, or when with vomiting, coughing, spitting, defecation or micturition, blood may be present. These, then, are in the whole class contrary to nature. On the other hand, in women who haemorrhage through the uterus, as has been said, the evacuation is not in the whole class contrary to nature, but only in the amount."

27. Galen, *On Diseases and Symptoms*, trans. Ian Johnston: "On the Differentiae of Symptoms," VI.III, 201.

28. Galen, *On Diseases and Symptoms*, trans. Ian Johnston: "On the Causes of Symptoms," 3, V.2. I have retained the term *diapedesis*, which remains in use. The Oxford English Dictionary has the following: "The oozing of blood through the unruptured walls of blood vessels."

29. For example, the copious annotations by the sixteenth-century physician Giovanni Costeo to the 1608 *Canon* edition.

30. Collections of recipes have instead generally proved unhelpful here, because the omnipresent recipe "ad sanguinem de naribus sistendum / to staunche blode of the nose" usually does not include any gendered difference, and only rarely do they tackle the specific issue of provoking a nosebleed. One exception is the little pamphlet that went under the

title *Dificio di ricette* (Palace of Recipes), which was published continuously in Italy from the 1520s and contains a recipe (based on yarrow) to provoke nosebleeds.

31. Richard Napier and Simon Forman, in two instances (http://www.magicand medicine.hps.cam.ac.uk/view/case/normalised/CASE11280 [2] and CASE11980, related to patients Agnes Kent and Sara Cage, aged 34 and 18 years old respectively) uses the expressions "she hath them upward at her nose" ("them" being his standard euphemism for menstrual periods) and "[tha]t w[hi]ch should goe Downew[ards] goeth out voydeth out of her nose thrice a weeke at the quantity of a pinte." Within the Casebooks, we found thirty-three cases of nosebleeds, thirteen regarding male patients and twenty regarding females (one of whom was a baby girl of three and a half months). Seventeen of them (five male and twelve female-related) provide treatment information. This evidence suggests that Napier was not trying to halt the nosebleeds with strong astringents, nor did he advise ligatures of the limbs or venesection as most academic physicians did. Instead, he contented himself with prescribing mild purges of hiera, manna, cassia, and rhubarb, and some powders to purge and cleanse the body of bad humors. Cf. Lauren Kassell et al. (eds.), *The Casebooks Project: A Digital Edition of Simon Forman's and Richard Napier's Medical Records, 1596–1634*, www.magicandmedicine.hps.cam.ac.uk [3], against which references were checked on January 11, 2017. For other instances, see also Churchill, *Female Patients*.

32. Pieter van Foreest, *Observationum et curationum medicinalium ac chirurgicarum opera omnia quatuor tomis digesta libri XXXII* (Rouen, 1653), Book 13, obs. 14, includes a very detailed reflection on the maximum loss of blood that can be sustained and provides plenty of instances taken from his own practice as well as from the previous tradition. Agreeing with the physician Leonardo Botallo, van Foreest estimates that an average healthy man can lose from six to nine pounds of blood from an open vein at one time without his life being in danger, and this evacuation can also be repeated throughout the month, but a certain weakening of the body is unavoidable. Interestingly, these authors also think that a weakening of this kind will always be milder than the loss of strength due to a continuous slow loss of blood (even a minor quantity) during many days through hemorrhoids, the womb, or the nostrils. Van Foreest also adds a kind of ethnographical note: according to him, Germans and whiter men are less likely to sustain consistent venesection in comparison with Italians and French people.

33. On Avicenna's *Canon* and nosebleeds, see Book 3, fen 5.I, Chapters 7–10, and Book 4, fen 1.II, Chapter 14, and ibid., fen 2.I, Chapters 35, 73, and 74. Helena M. Paavilainen dealt at length with the *Canon*'s section on nosebleeds in her recent *Medieval Pharmacotherapy, Continuity and Change: Case Studies from Ibn Sīnā and Some of His Late Medieval Commentators* (Leiden: Brill, 2009). Without taking into account Paavilainen's problematic assumption that the prescriptions and therapies found in the *Canon* actually reflect medical reality, we would challenge the equally problematic statement that "nosebleed provides an excellent tool for determining the rationality of medieval Arabic and Latin drug therapy" because "the ailment does require some kind of intervention, that is, it does not usually heal spontaneously." We agree that the results of treating nosebleeds are to be seen immediately, but clearly a nosebleed can also heal, and usually actually does heal, spontaneously, as

Hippocrates, Galen, Avicenna, and the whole medieval and Renaissance medical tradition recognize; hence their advice not to intervene to halt many kinds of nosebleeds, precisely because they do heal without intervention and because they were considered to be beneficial in many ways.

34. "Fluxus sanguinis a naribus aut fit per dyaboresim, id est per corosionem ex acumine humoris, aut per rixim, id est per eius subtilitatem, unde venas findit, aut per anastomasim, id est apertionem ex multitudine. Triplex igitur est causa fluxus sanguinis, secundum acumen ipsius vel subtilitas nimis liquida, vel multitudo: acumen est causa corrosionis, subtilitas est causa resudationis, multitudo est causa rupture et fractionis. . . . Et sive sit creticus sive non, aliquando fit aliquo dictorum modorum. Item sive sic sive sic, aliquando fit ab hepate, aliquando a splene, aliquando ab utroque, aliquando ab emorridis retentis vel menstruis modo debito non existentibus, et tunc bonum signum est. Unde Ippocrates: Mulieri menstruis deficientibus sanguinem a naribus fluere bonum," Gilbertus Anglicus, *Compendium medicine*, liber III, De fluxus sanguinis a naribus (Lyon, 1510), 153.

35. Michele Savonarola, *Practica Maior* (Venice, 1559), VI.5, 110r–101v. The discussion of this doubt, Savonarola informs us, is particularly useful since nobody discussed it before him in such a clear way. The answer is no: if the nosebleed is only due to the quality of the blood and not to the blood's overabundant quantity, no venesection is necessary. Old patients and children are often too weak to cope with phlebotomy. Every intelligent physician should also know that venesection is useless and dangerous in case of critical fluxes, arterial nosebleeds, and nosebleeds "qui accidit per se ipsi." In cases of arterial nosebleeds, i.e., due to the rupture of arteries in the brain, Savonarola specifies that—since they are often fatal and incurable—the physician must also avoid phlebotomy in order to avoid infamy and save his professional reputation, especially if he is young and inexperienced. A final note by Savonarola, again discussed in a deeper way with respect to Bernard de Gordon, regards the usefulness of the bath for overabundant menstruation, as opposed to its uselessness for nosebleeds. In his *De regimine pregnantium*, the author lists nosebleeds as one of the possible causes of a decrease of milk flow in breastfeeding women (ed. Belloni, 1952), 161–64.

36. See, e.g., Peter of Abano, *Conciliator* (Venice, 1565), differentia 187, 242b–243a: Utrum sanguis desuper fluens sit compescendus necne—Whether blood discharges coming from the upper part of the body are to be stopped or not.

37. Cf. this example of therapeutically induced nosebleed for lethargy: "Note, it is necessary for lethargics that people talk loudly in their presence. Tie their extremities tightly, (and) rub their palms and soles hard; and let their feet be put in salt water up to the middle of their shins, and pull the hair and nose, and squeeze the toes and fingers tightly, and cause pigs to squeal in his ears; give him a sharp clyster at the beginning of the case . . . and open the vein of the head, or nose, or forehead, and draw blood from the nose with the bristles of a boar," John of Gaddesden, *Rosa Anglica*, 8.7.

38. Van Foreest, *Observationum*. Of course there are other books accounting for isolated (male only) nosebleeds or mentioning nosebleeds given in the scholia, e.g., Book 16, *De pectoris pulmonisque morbis*, obs. 11 (a general reflection on the benefits of nosebleeds as

compared to hemoptysis), obs. 46; Book 22, *De diversis generibus profluviorum alvi*, obs. 20; Book 24, *De renum morbis*, obs. 29.

39. See, e.g., ibid., Book 9, obs. 41 or Book 13, obs. 10.

40. Johannes Arculanus, *Practica* (Venice: Bonetus Locatellus, 1497), chapter 43 (XLIII), De sanguine a naribus fluente, fol. 64rb: "sometimes they die, especially when a great quantity (of blood) is lost in a little amount of time, e.g. 25 pounds, although I have seen a woman who survived despite the uterine loss of 25 pounds of blood within three days" (our translation): "et interdum moriuntur, et precipue cum magna quantitas in parvo tempore egreditur, sicut xxv li., licet mulierem viderim evasisse posquam ob ea egresse sunt xxv li. sanguinis per matricem in tribus diebus."

CHAPTER 6

For formative discussions of a much, much earlier version of the thoughts presented in this chapter, I would like to thank Colin Burrow. Philip Hardie read it late in the day and I am enormously grateful to him for numerous suggestions and objections (this does not imply his endorsement of the final argument at every point).

1. George Eliot, *Felix Holt, the Radical*, ed. Fred C. Thomson (Oxford: Clarendon Press, 1980), 11. I am grateful to David Hillman for drawing this passage to my attention.

2. Adrian Poole, *Tragedy: A Very Short Introduction* (Oxford: Oxford University Press, 2005), 84. I will generally use "trees" and "screaming" since these features came to dominate the *topos*, but it should be noted that Eliot (following Virgil) describes bushes, and that Virgil's bush moans ("gemitus") rather than screaming, as discussed below.

3. For a discussion of some of these mythological traditions see Kenneth J. Reckford, "Some Trees in Virgil and Tolkien," in *Perspectives of Roman Poetry: A Classics Symposium*, ed. G. Karl Galinsky (Austin: University of Texas Press, 1974), 57–92.

4. See the accounts by Elizabeth Jane Bellamy, "The Broken Branch and the 'Liuing Well': Spenser's Fradubio and Romance Error in *The Faerie Queene*," *Renaissance Papers* 2 (1985): 1–12; Shirley Clay Scott, "From Polydorus to Fradubio: The History of a *Topos*," *Spenser Studies* 7 (1986): 27–57; Douglas Biow, *Mirabile Dictu: Representations of the Marvelous in Medieval and Renaissance Epic* (Ann Arbor, MI: University of Michigan Press, 1996).

5. On poetic grafting as a mixture of harsh violence and productive cooperation in the Virgilian tradition see Michael C. J. Putnam, *Virgil's Poem of the Earth: Studies in the Georgics* (Princeton: Princeton University Press, 1979), 93–94; Joseph Pucci, *The Full-Knowing Reader: Allusion and the Power of the Reader in Western Literary Tradition* (New Haven: Yale University Press, 1998), 99–108. Pucci stresses "the underlying violence of grafting with its connotations of ripping, rending, cutting or tearing" (105), drawing upon Richard F. Thomas, "Tree Violation and Ambivalence in Virgil," *Transactions of the American Philological Association* 118 (1988): 261–73, esp. 271. For a more positive, recuperative account of the practice see Dunstan Lowe, "The Symbolic Value of Grafting in Ancient Rome," *Transactions of the American Philological Association* 140 (2010): 461–88. My point is that

grafting involves a dynamic of violence *and* recuperation, which is severely troubled by the screaming, bleeding tree. The wide interest in textual grafting has partly arisen from Derrida's claim that "[t]o write is to graft. . . . Each grafted text continues to radiate back toward the site of its removal, transforming that, too, as it affects the new territory": *Dissemination*, trans. Barbara Johnson (London: Bloomsbury, 2016), 376–77. I am proposing the wounded text—the screaming, bleeding text—as an alternative and particularly unstable form of this mutual transformation.

6. Thomas M. Greene, "Rescue from the Abyss: Scève's Dizain 378," in *The Vulnerable Text: Essays on Renaissance Literature* (New York: Columbia University Press, 1986), 99–115; 100.

7. Virgil, *Aeneid*, trans. H. R. Fairclough, rev. F. P. Goold (Cambridge, MA: Harvard University Press, 1999), 3.22–30. All citations from the *Aeneid* are from this edition, though I have altered the translations in a number of places.

8. *Giraldi Cinthio on Romances, Being a Translation of the Discorse Intorno al Comporre dei Romanzi*, trans. Henry L. Snuggs (Lexington: University of Kentucky Press, 1968), 49–50. Among the many discussions of debates surrounding the marvelous and the monstrous, see Stephen Greenblatt, *Marvelous Possessions: The Wonder of the New World* (Oxford: Oxford University Press, 1991), esp. 20 on the marvelous as "thrilling, potentially dangerous, momentarily immobilizing, charged at once with desire, ignorance and fear"; and Lorraine Daston and Katherine Park, *Wonders and the Order of Nature 1150–1750* (New York: Zone, 2001).

9. Pucci, *The Full-Knowing Reader*, 101.

10. C. G. Jung, *Alchemical Studies*, trans. R. F. C. Hull (London: Routledge & Kegan Paul, 1968), 337; Maurice Bloch, "Why Trees, Too, Are Good to Think With: Towards an Anthropology of the Meaning of Life," in *The Social Life of Trees: Anthropological Perspectives on Tree Symbolism,* ed. Laura Rival (Oxford: Berg, 1998), 39–55; 52. Mary Douglas writes that humans have "a natural tendency to express situations of a certain kind in an appropriate bodily style," and it is a certain style of bodily expression that Bloch sees trees as enabling (*Natural Symbols: Explorations in Cosmology* [Harmondsworth: Penguin, 1973], 72–73).

11. Robin Nisbet, "The Oak and the Axe: Symbolism in Seneca, *Hercules Oetaeus* 1618ff.," in *Homo Viator: Classical Essays for John Bramble*, ed. Michael Whitby, Philip Hardie, and Mary Whitby (Bristol: Bristol Classical Press, 1987), 243–51; 243. For a rich account beginning with and expanding upon Nisbet, see Emily Gowers, "Talking Trees: Philemon and Baucis Revisited," *Arethusa* 38 (2005): 331–65.

12. I am grateful to Philip Hardie for these points. For the full background to the "crop of spears" as an image see Nicholas Horsfall, *Virgil, Aeneid 3: A Commentary* (Leiden: Brill, 2006), 75.

13. Lyndsay Coo, "Polydorus and the *Georgics*: Virgil *Aeneid* 3.13–68," *Materiali e discussioni per l'analisi dei testi classici* 59 (2007): 194; Marco Fucecchi, "Encountering the Fantastic: Expectations, Forms of Communication, Reactions," in *Paradox and the Marvellous in Augustan Literature and Culture*, ed. Philip Hardie (Oxford: Oxford University Press, 2009), 220.

14. Sigmund Freud, "The Uncanny," in *Art and Literature: Jensen's Gradiva, Leonardo da Vinci and Other Works*, ed. Albert Dickson (Harmondsworth: Penguin, 1985), 347.

15. René Girard, *Violence and the Sacred,* trans. Patrick Gregory (Baltimore: Johns Hopkins University Press, 1977), 33–34. See also the similar account by Mino Gabriele: "On the one hand, blood is a warm liquid that moves and nourishes the body from within, filling it with life. On the other hand, if the blood flows out of the body, this heralds death." Blood can be either "a flowing red sap" or "a liquid that quickly turns dark, thickens, and curdles" ("*Magia Sanguinis*: Blood and Magic in Classical Antiquity," in *Blood: Art, Power, Politics and Pathology*, ed. J. M. Bradburne et al. [Munich: Prestel, 2001], 33–39; 33).

16. For accounts of blood as the seat of life in a later period see Catrien Santing, "'For the Life of a Creature is in the Blood' (*Leviticus* 17:11). Some Considerations on Blood as the Source of Life in Sixteenth Century Religion and Medicine and Their Connections," in *Blood, Sweat and Tears—The Changing Concepts of Physiology from Antiquity into Early Modern Europe* (Leiden: Brill, 2012), 415–41.

17. For Virgil's account being "quite closely modeled on the beginning of Euripides's *Hecuba*" see the note to *Aeneid* 3.49 by R. D. Williams, ed., *Aeneidos Liber Tertius* (Oxford: Clarendon Press, 1962), 64. For more on the ways in which Euripides's account of Polydorus does include both tree and spear imagery, perhaps inspiring Virgil's mingling of the two, see Coo, "Polydorus and the *Georgics*," 198.

18. Abundant scholarship, especially by Hardie, has confirmed the depth and complexity of Virgil's engagement with his epic predecessor throughout his work: see his *Virgil's Aeneid: Cosmos and Imperium* (Oxford: Clarendon Press, 1986), and "Lucretian Visions in Virgil," in *Lucretian Receptions: History, the Sublime, Knowledge* (Cambridge: Cambridge University Press, 2009), 153–79. I have argued elsewhere that the fluctuating manner in which divine beings appear in the *Aeneid* is an implicit engagement with the Lucretian question of whether the gods were tangible: see *Feeling Pleasures: The Sense of Touch in Renaissance England* (Oxford: Oxford University Press, 2014), 83–92.

19. For Lucretius's enduring impact on physiological debates see Fabio Tutrone, "Between Atoms and Humours: Lucretius's Didactic Poetry as a Model of Integrated and Bifocal Physiology," in *Blood, Sweat and Tears*, 83–102.

20. The unusual grammatical construction draws particular attention to the second of these uses: Williams notes that it is the only instance of an infinitive verb with "insequi" in Classical Latin (*Aeneidos Liber Tertius*, 61). For the way in which the repetition of "et" in the sequence of Aeneas's increasingly violent wrenching complicates his motives see Horsfall, *Virgil, Aeneid 3: A Commentary*, 66.

21. See the entry in Lewis and Short, *A Latin Dictionary* (Oxford: Clarendon Press, 2002), which distinguishes two related senses: "To draw violently hither and thither something that is firm or quiet (esp. a tree, house, and the like)" and "To tear or rend to pieces, to cleave, dismember, shatter, break": the bleeding tree conflates the two senses.

22. "Otherwise with no force will you manage to win it nor rend it with hard steel."

23. Michael C. J. Putnam, "The Third Book of the *Aeneid*: From Homer to Rome," in *Virgil's Aeneid: Interpretation and Influence* (Chapel Hill: University of North Carolina

Press, 1995), 50–72; 52. For a general account of the strong sense of transgression in Aeneas's behavior see Thomas, "Tree Violation and Ambivalence in Virgil."

24. Lucretius, *De natura rerum*, trans. W. H. D. Rouse, rev. Martin Ferguson Smith (Cambridge, MA: Harvard University Press, 1975), 3.339–43. All citations and translations from this work are from this edition, with some silent alterations.

25. Hardie, "Lucretian Visions in Virgil," 170.

26. Hardie, "Lucretian Visions in Virgil," 170.

27. Thomas, it seems to me, overstates "Virgil's animism" as a straightforward belief in the *Georgics* that "vines, trees, beasts and bees, even the soil, are all sentient" ("Tree Violation and Ambivalence in Virgil," 263). I would present this instead as a form of challenging thought experiment: if *some* entities are more or less animated than we first assume them to be, must we approach them all as if they are (potentially) animate, to avoid inadvertent damage? What would it mean to inhabit the world in this fashion?

28. Citation and translation from Dante Alighieri, *Inferno*, ed. John D. Sinclair (Oxford: Oxford University Press, 1939); Canto 13, 33–34.

29. For a subtle account of the complications of speech in this episode see Leo Spitzer, "Speech and Language in *Inferno* XIII," in *Dante: A Collection of Critical Essays*, ed. John Freccero (Englewood Cliffs, NJ: Prentice Hall, 1965), 78–101. For general discussion see Charles Speroni, "The Motif of the Screaming and Bleeding Trees of Dante's Suicides," *Italian Quarterly* 9 (1965): 44–55. For a recent and subtle account of the way in which Dante's suicides are denied true corporeal personhood see Heather Webb, *Dante's Persons: An Ethics of the Transhuman* (Oxford: Oxford University Press, 2016), 4–5; cf. Webb's chapter in this volume.

30. Boccaccio makes his debt to Virgil bluntly explicit: "alla quale sangue con dolorosa voce vene appresso, non altrimenti che quando il pio Enea del non conosciuto Polidoro" ("There came forth blood and an anguished voice, not unlike the time when pious Aeneas took a branch from the unrecognized Polydorus"). Giovanni Boccaccio, *Il Filocolo*, ed. Salvatore Battaglia (Bari: G. Laterza, 1938), 456. My translation.

31. Ludovico Ariosto, *Orlando Furioso secondo la princeps del 1516: Edizione Critica*, ed. Marco Dorigatti with Gerarda Stimato (Florence: Olschki, 2006), Canto 6, Stanza 26, l.7. My translation. I would not want to overstate the comic tone of Ariosto's episode: the verb "crollar," which is repeated twice in this stanza to describe the way the hippogriff pulls the tree ("e fa crollar sì il Mirto," l.5) carries connotations of violent wrenching not dissimilar to Virgil's Lucretian "conuellere." John Harington's Elizabethan translation notably suppressed this sense of violence, noting only that the creature "pulls the tree to which the reins were tied," and that the myrtle "sore was bruised" (*Ludovico Ariosto's Orlando Furioso, translated into English Heroical Verse by Sir John Harington (1591)*, ed. Robert McNulty [Oxford: Clarendon Press, 1972], 6.25.4, 25.8).

32. *Godfrey of Bulloigne: A Critical Edition of Edward Fairfax's translation of Tasso's Gerusalemme Liberata, together with Fairfax's Original Poems*, ed. Kathleen M. Lea and T. M. Gang (Oxford: Clarendon Press, 1981), 13.41, 2, 3–4.

33. Edmund Spenser, *The Faerie Queene*, ed. A. C. Hamilton (London: Longman, 1977, rev. ed. 2006), Book I, Canto ii, stanza 30, ll.8–9, stanza 31, ll.1–3. All further references are to this edition.

34. OED, "Rift," 3c. Second edition, 1989; online version, 2011. http://www.oed.com, accessed December 2014. Quoting Richard Eden, *A treatyse of the newe India with other new founde landes and islandes, as well eastwarde as westwarde, as they are knowen and found in these oure dayes, after the description of Sebastian Munster in his boke of universall cosmographie* (London, 1553), sig. C.ii.

35. For a brief but excellent account of the wider place of blood within the humoral landscape of the poem see Michael Schoenfeldt, *Bodies and Selves in Early Modern England* (Cambridge: Cambridge University Press, 1999), 44–46.

36. Charles Grosvenor Osgood, *A Concordance to the Poems of Edmund Spenser* (Washington, DC: Carnegie Institution of Washington, 1915), 361–62.

37. The earlier poems in which the *topos* appeared were, of course, repeatedly read and interpreted in allegorical terms, but they do not announce themselves as allegories and demand to be approached as such in the same way as Spenser's. Maureen Quilligan observes that "Vergil's *Aeneid* . . . was treated like the Bible through a history of allegorical commentaries and through its presumed status as a prophetic text in its own right" (*The Language of Allegory: Defining the Genre* [Ithaca, NY: Cornell University Press, 1979], 100). *Orlando Furioso* was similarly allegorized as it made its way into English in John Harington's translation: in Ariosto's original "the allegory is fitful, and the figurative codes are constantly changing," as T. G. A. Nelson notes ("Sir John Harington and the Renaissance Debate over Allegory," *Studies in Philology* 82 [1985]: 377). Harington's treatment, however, tended to regularize this instability: his allegorizations, as Daniel Javitch observes, "reflect a more basic concern that . . . the fabulous elements in Ariosto's poem will confirm the accusation that poetry is a nurse of lies" (*Proclaiming a Classic: The Canonization of Orlando Furioso* [Princeton: Princeton University Press, 1991], 140).

38. Joe Moshenska, "The Forgotten Youth of Allegory: Figures of Old Age in *The Faerie Queene*," *Modern Philology* 110.3 (2013): 389–414; Moshenska, *Feeling Pleasures*, ch. 4, esp. 115–16, 120–22.

39. Gordon Teskey, "Death in an Allegory," in *Imagining Death in Spenser and Milton*, ed. Elizabeth Jane Bellamy, Patrick Cheney, and Michael Schoenfeldt (New York: Palgrave Macmillan, 2003), 65–77, 76.

40. Walter Benjamin, *The Origin of German Tragic Drama*, trans. John Osborne (London: Verso, 1998), 232. See also Benjamin's claim that "[a]llegory corresponds to the ancient gods in the deadness of its concrete tangibility" (230).

41. Angus Fletcher, *Allegory: The Theory of a Symbolic Mode* (Ithaca: Cornell University Press, 1964), 55; Teskey, "Death in an Allegory," 66.

42. Joseph Campana, *The Pain of Reformation: Spenser, Vulnerability, and the Ethics of Masculinity* (New York: Fordham University Press, 2012), 54, 56. This "hunger" for Christ's blood relies upon the claim, advanced by Miri Rubin among others, that the Reformation

involved, quite literally, a loss of blood: "With its criticism of the doctrine of transubstantiation, of the use of imagery in worship, and of the cult of saints and martyrs, Protestantism was to do away with many of the occasions for the contemplation of blood in vast regions of Europe" ("Blood: Sacrifice, Redemption and Iconography," in *Blood: Art, Power, Politics and Pathology*, 99).

43. As Robin Kirkpatrick writes of the bloody speech of Dante's tree, "instead of sap, blood and words issue from the gash in Piero's bark, again echoing the bloody sweat of Christ's passion" (*Dante's Inferno: Difficult and Dead Poetry* [Cambridge: Cambridge University Press, 1987], 185). A similar connection emerges in Titian's painting *Saint Jerome in Penitence* (ca. 1559) in which the figure of the crucified Christ is surrounded by trees, which themselves bleed out of sympathy. Langland in *Piers Plowman* makes the tree-as-cross typologically central: "And as Adam and alle thorugh a tree deyden / Adam and alle thorugh a tree shal turne to lyve" (William Langland, *The Vision of Piers Plowman*, ed. A. V. C. Schmidt [London: Dent, 1978], Passus 18, 359–60).

44. Campana, *The Pain of Reformation*, 60.

45. For the connections between violent mutilation and the production of meaning in this period see Stephen Greenblatt, "Mutilation and Meaning," in *The Body in Parts: Fantasies of Corporeality in Early Modern Europe*, ed. David Hillman and Carla Mazzio (London: Routledge, 1997), 221–41.

46. Poole, *Tragedy*, 84.

CHAPTER 7

My sincere thanks to Laurie Maguire, Bonnie Lander Johnson, and Eleanor Decamp, as well as the participants in this volume, for their input into this chapter.

1. For the "green lion" in Llullian and Riplean alchemy, see J. M. Rampling, "The Alchemy of George Ripley, 1470–1700" (PhD diss., History and Philosophy of Science, Cambridge University, 2009), chap. 2, esp. 49–51. For the king's blood and "the menstrual blood of our whore" (i.e., the star regulus of antimony), see William R. Newman, "'Decknamen or Pseudochemical Language'? Eirenaeus Philalethes and Carl Jung," *Revue d'Histoire des Sciences et de leurs Applications* 49 (1996): 181–82. See also Leah DeVun, *Prophecy, Alchemy, and the End of Time: John of Rupescissa in the Late Middle Ages* (New York: Columbia University Press, 2009), 73–74, 116–27.

2. On alchemical *Decknamen*, see E. O. von Lippmann, *Entstellung und Ausbrietung der Alchemie*, vol. 1 (Berlin: Springer, 1919), 11; Julius Ruska and E. Wiedemann, "Beiträge zur Geschichte der Naturwissenschaften, LXVII: Alchemistische Decknamen," *Sitzungsberichte der Physikalisch-medizinalischen Societät zu Erlangen* 56 (1924): 17–36.

3. See especially Carl Jung, "The Idea of Redemption in Alchemy," in *The Integration of the Personality*, trans. Stanley M. Dell (London: Routledge & Kegan Paul, 1940), 205–80; Newman, "'Decknamen or Pseudochemical Language'?"; and Lawrence M. Principe, *The Secrets of Alchemy* (Chicago: University of Chicago Press, 2012), 143–57.

4. For a good example of how nomenclature could change over time, see Jennifer M. Rampling, "Transmuting Sericon: Alchemy as 'Practical Exegesis' in Early Modern England," *Osiris*, vol. 29, no. 1, Chemical Knowledge in the Early Modern World (2014): 19–34.

5. This text was attributed to the theologian and natural philosopher Albertus Magnus, but was probably written by a "German follower." On this text and the tradition of the "secrets of women," see Katharine Park, *Secrets of Women: Gender, Generation, and the Origins of Human Dissection* (New York: Zone Books; Distributed by MIT Press, 2006), esp. chap. 2.

6. For a good overview of menstruation in early modern culture, see Andrew Shail and Gillian Howie, eds., *Menstruation: A Cultural History* (Basingstoke [England]; New York: Palgrave Macmillan, 2005).

7. Eirenaeus Philalethes, *Introitus*, in J. J. Manget, *Bibliotheca chemica curiosa* (Geneva, 1702) vol. II, 662; and Eirenaeus Philalethes, *An exposition upon the preface*, in *Ripley Reviv'd* (London, 1678), 28, as cited in Newman, "'Decknamen or Pseudochemical Language,'" 181–82.

8. Newman, "'Decknamen or Pseudochemical Language,'" esp. 181–83. See also Rampling, "Transmuting Sericon."

9. For the "green lion" in Llullian and Riplean alchemy, see Rampling, "The Alchemy of George Ripley, 1470–1700," chap. 2, esp. 49–51 and 56. For Philalethes, however, the green lion signified raw (impure) antimony ore ("green" because still raw), another crucial component in the philosophers' stone. Newman, "'Decknamen or Pseudochemical Language,'" 181–82.

10. Theophilus, John G. Hawthorne, and Cyril Stanley Smith, *On Divers Arts: The Foremost Medieval Treatise on Painting, Glassmaking and Metalwork* (New York: Dover; London: Constable, 1979), 189–90; Petrus Kärzenmacher, *Rechter Gebrauch der Alchemie* (1531), fol. IIIv, as cited and discussed in Pamela H. Smith, "Vermilion, Mercury, Blood, and Lizards: Matter and Meaning in Metalworking," in *Materials and Expertise in Early Modern Europe: Between Market and Laboratory*, ed. Ursula Klein and E. C. Spary (Chicago: University of Chicago Press, 2009), 43–44.

11. "den gißen in gestaltte eynß leven lyndtwurmer trachen kopffe oder waß dier gefelte ist eben gleyche." Anna Zieglerin, "Die Edele und Tewere Kunst Alchamia belagende," Niedersächsisches Landesarchiv Wolfenbüttel [hereafter NLA WO], Acta Publica des Herzogs Julius, 1 Alt 9, Nr. 306, fol. 63r–v.

12. Albert the Great, *Mineralia*, book 4, chap. 12; in *Alberti Magni opera Omnia* 5:83, as cited in Principe, *Secrets of Alchemy*, 78.

13. This discussion is heavily indebted to William R. Newman, *Promethean Ambitions: Alchemy and the Quest to Perfect Nature* (Chicago: University of Chicago Press, 2004), chap. 4.

14. "Es ist auch zu wissen, das also menschen mögen geboren werden one natürliche veter und mutter. das ist sie werden nit von weiblichem leib auf natürliche weis wie andere kinder geboren, sonder durch kunst und eines erfarnen spagirici geschiklikeit mag in mensch wachsen und geboren werden, wie hernach wird angezeigt." [Pseudo?-]Paracelsus, *De natura rerum neun Bücher*, in Sudhoff, Paracelsus, *Sämtliche Werke, 1. Abteilung:*

Medizinische, Naturwissenschaftliche Und Philosophische Schriften, ed. Karl Sudhoff, 14 vols. (Munich: R. Oldenbourg, 1922–1933), vol. 11, 313.

15. "Wie aber solches zugang und geschehen möge, ist nun sein proceß also nemlich das der sperma eines mans in verschloßnen cucurbiten per se mit der höchsten putrefaction, ventre equino, putreficirt werde auf 40 tag oder so lang bis er lebendig werde und sich beweg und rege, welchs leichtlich zu sehen ist. Nach solcher zeit wird es etlicher maßen einem menschen gleich sehen, doch durchsichtig on ein corpus. So er nun nach disem teglich mit dem arcano sanguinis humani gar weislich gespeiset und erneret wird bis auf 40 wochen und in steter gleicher werme ventris equine erhalten, wird ein recht lebendig menschlich kint daraus mit allen glitmaßen wie ein ander kint, das von einen weib geboren wird, doch vil kleiner. Dasselbig wir ein homunculum nennen und sol hernach nit anders als ein anders kint mit großem fleißen und sorg auferzogen werden, bis es zu seinen tagen und verstant kompt." [Ps.-]Paracelsus, *De natura rerum neun Bücher*, in Sudhoff, Paracelsus, Sämtliche Werke, vol. 11, 317.

16. DeVun, *Prophesy, Alchemy, and the End of Time*, 116–27 and William R. Newman, "The Philosopher's Egg: Theory and Practice in the Alchemy of Roger Bacon," *Micrologus* 3 (1995): 75–101.

17. "das ein mensch außerhalb weiblichs leibs und einer natürlichen muter möge geboren werden?" [Ps.-]Paracelsus, *De natura rerum neun Bücher*, in Sudhoff, Paracelsus, *Sämtliche Werke*, vol. 11, 316.

18. "nicht fast ungleich einer frauen die in irer monats zeit ist, die auch ein verborgen gift in augen hat." [Ps.-]Paracelsus, *De natura rerum neun Bücher*, in Sudhoff, Paracelsus, *Sämtliche Werke*, vol. 11, 318.

19. "das ist nun der aller höchsten und größesten heimlikeiten eine, die got den tötlichen und sündigen menschen hat wissen lassen. Dan es ist ein mirakel und magnale dei und ein geheimnus uber all gehimnus, sol auch bilich ein geheimnus bleiben bis zu den aler lesten zeiten, da dan nichts verborgen wird bleiben sonder ales offenbaret werden." [Ps.-]Paracelsus, *De natura rerum neun Bücher*, in Sudhoff, Paracelsus, *Sämtliche Werke*, vol. 11, 317.

20. Anna Maria Zieglerin, "die Edele und Tewere Kunst Alchamia belangende," 1. April, 1573. NLA WO 1 Alt 9, Nr. 306, fols. 64r–v (to conceive a child), 65r (for the tree), and 54v–55v (for the philosophers' stone).

21. For more detail on Anna Zieglerin and her fellow alchemists in Wolfenbüttel, see Tara Nummedal, "Anna Zieglerin's Alchemical Revelations," in *Secrets and Knowledge in Medicine and Science, 1500–1800*, ed. Elaine Yuen Tien Leong and Alisha Rankin (Aldershot, England; Brookfield, VT: Ashgate, 2011), 125–41.

22. "Ehr habe wol ein Exempel von einer rosen gebett, Wen ein menes Person des gleichen eine menstruosa ein Jed. eine rosen abbrochen, und die Irgents an ein fenster stochen od. bej einand. setzen, So verdorrete des mans rose, und des weibs wurde am dritten tage faul." "Gütliche Aussage des Philipp Sömmering," July 10, 1574, NLA WO 1 Alt 9, Nr. 308, fol. 105r.

23. "Philipps Fraw hebe gesagt, wie were eine hure." "Verhör der Anna Maria Ziegler," July 14, 1574, NLA WO 1 Alt 9, Nr. 314, fol. 11. It is unclear whether "her menses" refers to Anna's or Philipp's wife's menses.

24. "sie habe Ihr von Ihren Menstruis in warmen wein sippen gegeben, daß habe sie Ihr ins Hauß geschickt, darum daß sie Ihr gram gewesen. Wan daß einer einehme, der gehe [illegible] und Krancke." "Verhör der Anna Maria Ziegler," July 14, 1574, NLA WO 1 Alt 9, Nr. 314, fol. 22.

25. "Es were einmahl dem Theophrasto ein frawen hunbdt ins Laboratorium bracht, Da were die gleser zersprungen." "Gütliche Aussage des Philipp Sömmering," July 10, 1574, NLA WO 1 Alt 9, Nr. 308, fol. 105r.

26. "habe sie Ihme gesagt, ehr solte nicht zu seiner frawen wegen des *Menstruij* gehen." "Gütliche Aussage des Philipp Sömmering," July 10, 1574, NLA WO 1 Alt 9, Nr. 308, fol. 100r.

27. "Sie habe Philippen gesagt, der muste sich der Weiber enthalten, sonst konte ehr in d alchimisterij nicht ausrichten." "Verhör der Anna Maria Ziegler," July 14, 1574. NLA WO 1 Alt 9, Nr. 314, fol. 11r.

28. Principe, *Secrets of Alchemy*, 128–29; Nummedal, *Alchemy and Authority in the Holy Roman Empire* (Chicago: University of Chicago Press, 2007), 85–91; and Philalethes's process for purifying antimony ore, above.

29. DeVun, *Prophecy, Alchemy, and the End of Time*, 109–18.

30. To use the lion's blood to treat leprosy, Zieglerin recommended, "If you want to cleanse a leper, then every day for nine entire days give him three drops of the oil that you extracted from the tinged gold [i.e., the lion's blood]; on the ninth day, tap one of his veins, and the leprosy will run out of him, or rather out of the incision [*Aderlassloch*], like grains of sand" (Erstlych wen du eynen außßetzygen wilste reynne machen, ßo gib Ihmme neunner gantzer tage und eyn jdeß tage [marre] 3 troppen deß olleß ßo du von dem dingertten golden getzogen amme 9 tage laß Inne eyn ader schlagen, ßo loffte dehr außßatze von Imme oder auß den Aderlaßeloche mytt herrauße alß ßandte körner). Anna Maria Zieglerin, "die Edele und Tewere Kunst Alchamia belangende," April 1, 1573. NLA WO 1 Alt 9, Nr. 306, fol. 63v. For the bird: "den der ßon gottes am stamme deß heyllygen creutzes uß arme ßundern alle myt ßeynen aller heyllygeste Roßen farben blutte dyngiertte und teyl hafftig gemacht alß wirdt dieß fogeley der [yr]discher tynckktur teylhafft." Ibid., fols. 54r–55v. For a fuller discussion of this bird, see Nummedal, "Alchemical Revelations," 130–31.

31. Aussagen Heinrich Schombach gegen Anna (Newe Welt durch Fraw Annen Kund anzurichten), July 6, 1574, NLA WO 1 Alt 9, Nr. 314, fols 73–74v; Verhör der Anna Maria Ziegler, July 8, 1574, NLA WO 1 Alt 9, Nr. 314, fols. 14v–15r.

32. "Alß der graff nun erwachsen und seines vaters Theophrastij bucher bekommen, het ehr darin gefunden, dass sein vater mit höchster kunst darnach getrachtet, das ein Megdlein mucht geborn werden, die des Monatlichen flußes entfreiet, und mit der hube [?] der graff kunder zeugen wollen, die biß Immer Jungsten tage leben sollten." Philipp Sömmering's testimony Nr. 308, fol. 62.

33. "von solcher Kundern eine newe welt werden." Aussagen Heinrich Schombach gegen Anna, NLA WO 1 Alt 9, Nr. 314, fol. 74v.

34. "Philip habe es alles gesagt, und sie die fraw auch, dass sie den fluß nich habe und and[er]e viele tungende und das sie den Engeln gleich were." Heinrich Schombach

testimony, July 5, 1574, NLA WO 1 Alt 9, Nr. 313, fol. 25v. "Philip hette es alles gesagt und sie auch das sie den fluß nit hette und anderer mehr tungender und das sie den Engeln gleich sein solle, wie er auch jetz under noch nit anders vermeinet sey es andern so sey er betrogen." Heinrich Schombach testimony, July 5, 1574, NLA WO 1 Alt 9, Nr. 314, fols. 68v-69r.

35. "Was fraw Annen reinigkeit anlangt habe ehr sie wol viel gelobt, und der Mutter Gottes vergliechen, wie sie sich dan also selbst angeben. . . . Das habe ehr albereit gesagt, dass ehr Fraw Annen hoch gelobt, und sie der Junckfraw marien gleich gehalten." Philipp Sömmering's testimony, July 9, 1574, NLA WO 1 Alt 9, Nr. 308, fol. 60–61.

36. Translation from the New American Standard Bible, Genesis 3:16, accessed March 23, 2015, http://www.biblegateway.com/passage/?search=1%20Mose%203&version=NASB. The passage from the 1545 Luther Bible, 1 Mose 3:16, with which Anna Zieglerin presumably would have been familiar, reads as follows: "Und zum Weibe sprach er: Ich will dir viel Schmerzen schaffen, wenn du schwanger wirst; du sollst mit Schmerzen Kinder gebären; und dein Verlangen soll nach deinem Manne sein, und er soll dein Herr sein." Accessed March 23, 2015, http://www.biblegateway.com/passage/?search=1%20Mose%203&version=LUTH1545.

37. Beth Kreitzer, *Reforming Mary: Changing Images of the Virgin Mary in Lutheran Sermons of the Sixteenth Century*, Oxford Studies in Historical Theology (New York: Oxford University Press, 2004); Bridget Heal, *The Cult of the Virgin Mary in Early Modern Germany: Protestant and Catholic Piety, 1500–1648* (Cambridge: Cambridge University Press, 2007).

CHAPTER 8

The author would like to thank the AHRC for funding the research on which this chapter is based.

1. "Qui bene potat bene dormit / Bene dormit et nil mali cogitat / Qui nil mali cogitate salvus erit/ Erg[o] qui bene potat salvus erit": Cambridge University Library MS Add. 2830, fol. 60v. All translations, unless otherwise indicated, are my own.

2. See, for instance, Shakespeare, *Love's Labours Lost*, 1.1.4; Alexander Brome, "The Royalist's Answer," in *Poems*, ed. Roman R. Dubinski, 2 vols. (Toronto: University of Toronto Press, 1982), 1:145; John Bramhall, *A Defence of True Liberty from Antecedent and Extrinsecall Necessity*, ed. G. A. J. Rogers (London: Routledge, 1996), 196; Thomas Hobbes, *Questions Concerning Liberty, Necessity and Chance*, in *Works*, ed. William Molesworth (London: John Bohn, 1841), 5:338; H. L. Spiegel, *Twe-spraack. Ruygh-bewerp. Kort begrip. Rederijck-kunst*, ed. W. J. H. Caron (Groningen: Wolters, 1962), 159; G. A. Bredero, *Spaanschen Brabander*, ed. F. A. Stoett (Zutphen: Thieme, 1978), 92; Ludvig Holberg, *Erasmus Montanus*, in *Jeppe of the Hill*, trans. Gerald S. Argetsinger and Sven Hakon Rossel (Carbondale: Southern Illinois University Press, 1990), 162; Philippi Melancthonis, *De dialectica libri quatuor* (Leipzig: Nickel Faber, 1531), 140. See also Hans Walther, *Proverbia sententiaeque latinitatis medii aevi*, 6 vols. (Göttingen: Vandenhoeck und Ruprecht, 1963–69),

entry 23831; R. W. Dent, *Proverbial Language in English Drama Exclusive of Shakespeare* (Berkeley: University of California Press, 1984), entry H169.

3. Sanford Brown Meech, "John Drury and His English Writings," *Speculum* 9 (1934): 70–83.

4. Stanley T. Bindoff, *The House of Commons 1509–1558* (London: Secker and Warburg, 1982), 176–77; *Paston Letters and Papers of the Fifteenth Century*, ed. Norman Davis, 2 vols. (Oxford: Clarendon Press, 1971–75), 1:530.

5. "*Qui bene bibit erit beatus.* . . . Vulgo recitatur exemplum ridiculum, quod tamen referam": Augustinus Hunnaeus, *Dialecta, seu Generalia Logices Praecepta Omnia* (Antwerp: Christophorus Plantini, 1566), sig. S1.

6. "Transitus est observandus, in quo saepe dolus delitescit: *qui bene potat, bene dormit* . . . transitur ad aliud tempus: nam non in eodem tempore potatur et dormitur": Juan Luis Vives, *De disputatione*, in *Opera omnia*, ed. Gregorio Majansio, 8 vols. (London: Gregg, 1964), 3:76.

7. Eamon Duffy, *Voices of Morebath: Reformation and Rebellion in an English Village* (New Haven: Yale University Press, 2001), 8; Nicholas Orme, "Latin and English Sentences in Fifteenth-Century Schoolbooks," *Yale University Library Gazette* 60 (1985): 47–57; Joanna Bellis and Venetia Bridges, "'What shalt thou do when thou hast an english to make into latin?' A Study of the Proverb Collection of Cambridge, St John's College, MS F.26," *Studies in Philology* 112 (2015): 68–92.

8. Lincoln, Cathedral Chapter Library, MS 88 (A.3.15), fol. 129v. See George Henslow, *Medical Works of the Fourteenth Century* (London: Chapman and Hall, 1899), 79.

9. On the texts and their purpose, see Nicholas Orme, *English School Exercises, c. 1420–c. 1530*, Studies and Texts 181 (Turnhout: Brepols, 2013); Nicholas Orme, *Education and Society in Medieval and Renaissance England* (London: Hambledon, 1989), 76–98.

10. Beatrice White, *The Vulgaria of John Stanbridge and the Vulgaria of Robert Whittinton*, EETS o.s. 187 (London: Oxford University Press, 1932), 97.

11. Robert Whittinton, *Vulgaria et De institutione grammaticulorum opusculorum* (London: Wynkyn de Worde, 1520), BL C.143.a.26, fol. 30v.

12. See Ilaria Taddei, "Puerizia, Adolescenza and Giovinezza: Images and Conceptions of Youth in Florentine Society During the Renaissance," in *The Premodern Teenager: Youth in Society, 1150–1650*, ed. Konrad Eisenichler (Toronto: Centre for Reformation and Renaissance Studies, 2002), 15–26 (20–21).

13. See Luke E. Demaitre, *Doctor Bernard de Gordon: Professor and Practitioner*, Studies and Texts 51 (Toronto: Pontifical Institute of Mediaeval Studies, 1980).

14. "Unde in morbis puerorum debemus iudicare, sicut bonus medicus, si videat omnia signa bona, inde colligit non esse ipsum moriturum, sed potius evasarum": Bernhardus de Giordonio, *Tractatus de conservatione vitae humanae* (Leipzig: Johannes Rhamba and Ernestus Vogelin, 1570), 29.

15. "Seminalem in eo virtutem natura confortat . . . hinc frena laxantur luxurie et libido dominata corporibus exhaurit virtutes naturales in miseris et tam cita fatigatione debilitat, ut, cum robur corporis animique habere deberent, iam membris omnibus dissoluti. . . .

Unde consultum esset cuique prudenti connubia fluxumque libidinis differre": Thomas Cantimpratensis, *Liber de natura rerum* (Berlin: De Gruyter, 1973), 81.

16. "Videres omnes certare de munere, alias invigilare querendo victualia . . . alias futuros explorare ymbres et speculari concursus syderum. Quibus est earum adolescentia ad opera exeunt et supradicta convehunt; seniores intus operantur": ibid., 295.

17. "Adolescentia quantum ad praesens mihi occurit quod adolescentia potest accipi tripliciter. Est adolescentia naturalis, virtualis, et criminalis. . . . Criminalis idem est quod ignorantia vel levis et instabilis conditio": Petrus Berchorius, *Dictionarii seu Repertorii moralis*, 2 vols. (Venice: Hieronymus Scotus, 1574), 1:78.

18. "Carnis animalium iuuenilium sunt humidae, fluxibiles, atque molles, et ideo facilius digeruntur. Nam quando in statu veniunt, duriores fiunt, et ad digestionem et conuersionem magis ineptae . . . tunc per malas consuetudines in vitiis indurantur": ibid.

19. "Ista est sicut cera mollis faciliter recipit inpressionem siue pulchram siue turpem": ibid.

20. "Adolescentia sola est inualida viribus . . . infirma consiliis, illecebrosa delitiis, calens vitiis": Vincent of Beauvais, *De eruditione filiorum nobilium*, ed. Arpad Steiner (Menasha, WI: George Banta, 1938), 63.

21. Lynn Thorndike, "Translation of a Letter from a Physician of Valencia to His Two Sons Studying at Toulouse," *Annals of Medical History* 3 (1931): 17–20.

22. See Tara Nummedal's chapter in this volume.

23. Michael E. Goodich, *From Birth to Old Age: The Human Life Cycle in Medieval Thought, 1250–1350* (New York: University Press of America, 1989), 61.

24. See Patrick Joseph Ryan, *Master-Servant Childhood: A History of the Idea of Childhood in Medieval English Culture* (Basingstoke: Palgrave Macmillan, 2013), 82–106.

25. "Mundus constat ex quattuor elementis et quattuor temporibus et homo similiter. . . . Concordiam habet cum aere et vernali tempore, quae habent humorem et calorem, in pueritia et sanguine . . . concordat cum aqua et hieme et flegmate, quae habent frigus et humorem, in decrepita aetate—proprium est enim senibus frigidos esse": Joseph Wittig, "'Remigian' Glosses on Boethius' *Consolatio Philosophiae*," in *Source of Wisdom: Old English and Early Medieval Latin Studies in Honour of Thomas D. Hill*, ed. Charles D. Wright, Frederick M. Biggs, and Thomas N. Hall, Toronto Old English Series 16 (Toronto: University of Toronto Press, 2007), 168–200 (179).

26. Avicenna, *The Canon of Medicine of Avicenna*, trans. O. Cameron Gruner (New York: AMS, 1929), 69.

27. Martin C. Seymour, *Bartholomæus Anglicus and His Encyclopedia* (Aldershot: Variorum, 1992), 12–13.

28. "Est autem etas puerilis calide et humide, propter viarum angustiam, non invalescunt usque quo ad annum pubertatis perducantur. . . . Sunt igitur pueri carne molles corpore flexibiles, ad motum habiles atque leves, animo dociles sine cura et sollicitudine, et tutam vitam ducentes, sola iocosa appreciantes, nullum periculum magis quam ictum virge formidantes": Bartholomaeus Anglicus, *De proprietatibus rerum: texte latin et réception vernaculaire*, ed. Baudouin van den Abeele and Heinz Meyer (Turnhout: Brepols, 2005), 134.

29. On Jacopo, see Nancy G. Siraisi, *Medicine and the Italian Universities: 1250–1600* (Leiden: Brill, 2001), especially 114–39; Karine van 't Land, "Internal, Yet Extrinsic: Conceptions of Bodily Space and Their Relation to Causality in Late Medieval University Medicine," in *Medicine and Space: Surroundings and Borders in Antiquity and the Middle Ages*, ed. Patricia A. Baker, Han Nijdam, and Karine van 't Land (Leiden: Brill, 2011), 85–116.

30. "Huiusmodi operationes requirunt organa a superflua humiditate depurata, ut bene perficiantur. . . . Igitur et cetera patet consequentia et assumptum probatur, quia tales sunt operationes animales cognoscitivae quae ut patet sunt in iuuene perfectissimae": Iacobus Foroliuiensis, *Expositio et quaestiones in primum Canonem Auicennae* (Venice: Luca Antonius Iunta, 1547), fols. 211r–211v.

31. H. J. Westra, "Review of Wilson, *Glosae in Iuvenalem*," *Mittellateinisches Jahrbuch* 18 (1983): 368–69.

32. "Magistros crebis interrogationibus vexatos"; "discipulos . . . duros": Guillaume de Conches, *Glosae in Iuvenalem*, ed. Bradford Wilson, *Textes philosophiques du Moyen Age* 18 (Paris: J. Vrin, 1980), 101–2.

33. "Magistri ergo, considerantes tarditatem ingenii ex sanguine circa cor congelato procedere, pueros in sinistra manu, que magis propinque est cordi, cum instrumento de huius modi arbore facto, percutiebant. Et ita sanguis in manu commotus alium impellebat . . . et sic excitaretur ingenium": ibid., 102.

34. Kathryn L. Lynch, *The High Medieval Dream Vision* (Stanford, CA: Stanford University Press, 1988), 35–42.

35. See Arpad Steiner, "The Authorship of *De disciplina scholarium*," *Speculum* 12 (1937): 81–84.

36. Eva Matthews Sanford, "De Disciplina Scholarium: A Mediaeval Handbook on the Care and Training of Scholars," *Classical Journal* 28 (1932): 84–85.

37. "Omnia siquidem superius expedita ad scolarium informacionem sunt affixa. Nunc de eorum sagaci provisione breviter est discurrendum. Cum humana corporis condicio fleumate scilicet et sanguine et colera et melancholia constat suffulta, ab aliquo predictorum quemlibet necesse est allicere preminenciam": *De disciplina scolarium*, ed. Olga Weijers (Leiden: Brill, 1976), 108.

38. "Melancolio vero timori pigricieque . . . precavere cenas potibus mediocribusque gaudere ad nature subsidum"; "Colericus vero pallidule effigei plerumque subiectus solitudini semper supponatur, ne nimii strepitus auditu bilem in totam effundat cohortem": ibid.

39. "Sanguineus . . . omnibus sitibus potest adaptari. . . . Hunc cibariis gratissimis potibusque levioribus decet hilarari": ibid.

40. "Sanguineus vero cuius complexionis favorabilior est propago": ibid.

41. "Obliquantibus hirquis parietes solus ocillaret": ibid.

42. "Quem ludendo sepius novimus confoveri gravissima questione": ibid.

43. "Pluribus vero mentibus intimatum est gnothi se litos": ibid.

44. "Maxime vero in quibus superabundat nigra colera . . . eosque plurimum suo arbitrio committi convenient: et libertate iocisque oblectari": Petrus Paulus Vergerius, *De ingenues moribus* (Venice: Christopherus Valdefer, n.d.), fols. 8v–9.

45. Nicholas Orme, "Wheatley, William (*fl.* 1305–1317)," in *Oxford Dictionary of National Biography*, ed. Colin Matthew and Brian Harrison, 60 vols. (Oxford: Oxford University Press, 2004), 58: 422.

46. "Proprietates fleumatici patent per hos versus: Hic sompnolentus, piger ac sputamine plenus; ebes huic sensus, pinguis facie, color albus": Michael Johnson, "A Critical Edition of the Commentary by William of Wheteley on the Pseudo-Boethian Treatise De Disciplina Scolarium" (Unpub. PhD thesis, State University of New York at Buffalo, 1982), 579.

47. See Michael Johnson, "How to Achieve Discipline in the Classroom: William of Wheteley's Exposition of Pseudo-Boethius," *Acta* 8 (1981): 103–20.

48. "Item, nec gibbosus seu in aliis menbris defectuosus . . . cum natura sit fundamentum in corpora et debile fundamentum semper minetur ruinam et statum deteriorem, ex tali defectu in principio posset oriri magnus error in fine. . . . Et ideo cavendum est ne tales doctrine mancipetur": ibid., 46.

49. "Nota quod sanguis est quidam humor in corpore, hinc vocatus quia reddit hominem in quo dominatur sanus et suavis . . . cuius complexio inter omnes complexiones est favorabilior eo": ibid., 584.

50. "Item, nota quod sanguineus indifferenter se habet ad omnem locum in actu studenti. Cuius racio est quia bonum est semper sui ipsius communicativum. Communicat se bonum bonis, quia simile est illis. . . . Modo est ita quod inter omnes complexiones sanguinea complexio est melior. Et idcirco indifferenter se habet ad locum umbrosum et lucidum, strictum et amplum": ibid.

51. See Rae Thomas, Geoffrey K. Mitchell, and Laura Batstra, "Attention-Deficit/Hyperactivity Disorder: Are We Helping or Harming?" *British Medical Journal* (2013): 347.

CHAPTER 9

1. Shakespeare, William, *Romeo and Juliet*, ed. G. Blakemore Evans (Cambridge: Cambridge University Press, 2003), 3.1.180.

2. David M. Bergeron, "Sickness in *Romeo and Juliet*," *CLA Journal* 20 (1977): 356–64; Ursula Potter, "Greensickness in *Romeo and Juliet*," in *The Premodern Teenager*, ed. Konrad Eisenbichler (Toronto: CRRS Publication, 2002), 271–92; Helen King, *The Disease of Virgins: Green Sickness, Chlorosis, and the Problems of Puberty* (London: Routledge, 2004), 80; Lesel Dawson, *Lovesickness and Gender in Early Modern English Literature* (Oxford: Oxford University Press, 2008), 49–61; Hilary M. Nunn, "On Vegetating Virgins: Greensickness and the Plant Realm in Early Modern Literature," in *The Indistinct Human in Renaissance Literature*, ed. Jean E. Feerick and Vin Nardizzi (Basingstoke: Palgrave Macmillan, 2012), 159–80; Sara Read, *Menstruation and the Female Body in Early Modern England* (Basingstoke: Palgrave Macmillan, 2013), 68–69. See also Robert F. Fleissner, "Falstaff's Green Sickness unto Death," *Shakespeare Quarterly* 12 (1961): 47–55 and Laurinda S. Dixon, *Perilous Chastity: Women and Illness in Pre-Enlightenment Art and Medicine* (Ithaca, NY: Cornell University Press, 1995).

3. For the difference between lovesickness and greensickness see Helen King, *Disease of Virgins*, 36–42; Lesel Dawson, *Lovesickness and Gender*, 49–61.

4. King, *The Disease of Virgins*, 34.

5. A full list of these works would double the length of this book, but some of the titles I have in mind are: Rebecca Bushnell, *Green Desire: Imagining Early Modern English Gardens* (Ithaca, NY: Cornell University Press, 2003); Leah Knight, *Of Books and Botany in Early Modern England: Sixteenth Century Plants and Print Culture* (Surrey: Ashgate, 2009); Amy Tigner, *Literature and the Renaissance Garden from Elizabeth I to Charles II: England's Paradise* (Surrey: Ashgate, 2012); Richard Burt and John Michael Archer, eds., *Enclosure Acts: Sexuality, Property and Culture in Early Modern England* (Ithaca, NY: Cornell University Press, 1995); Margaret Pelling, *Medical Conflicts in Early Modern London: Patronage, Physicians, and Irregular Practitioners, 1550–1640* (Oxford: Oxford University Press, 2003); Vin Nardizzi, *Wooden Os: Shakespeare's Theatres and England's Trees* (Toronto: University of Toronto Press, 2013); Diane Kelsey McColley, *Poetry and Ecology in the Age of Milton and Marvell* (Surrey: Ashgate, 2007); Bruce Smith, *The Key of Green: Passion and Perception in Renaissance Culture* (Chicago: University of Chicago Press, 2008); Robert N. Watson, *Back to Nature: The Green and the Real in the Late Renaissance* (Philadelphia: University of Pennsylvania Press, 2006); Simon C. Estok, *Ecocriticism and Shakespeare: Reading Ecophobia* (New York: Palgrave, 2011); Gabriel Egan, *Green Shakespeare: From Ecopolitics to Ecocriticism* (London: Routledge, 2006).

6. "'The blood of English shall manure the ground': The almanac in *Richard II*'s vision of soil and body management," in Hilary Eklund, ed., *Ground-Work: Soil Science in Renaissance Literature* (Pittsburgh, PA: Duquesne University Press, 2017), 59–78.

7. Norman Rabkin, *Shakespeare and the Common Understanding* (New York: Free Press, 1967); Coppélia Kahn, *Man's Estate: Masculine Identity in Shakespeare* (Berkeley: University of California Press, 1981); Julia Kristeva, *Tales of Love* (New York: Columbia University Press, 1987), 98; Catherine Belsey, "The Name of the Rose in *Romeo and Juliet*," *Yearbook of English Studies* 23 (1993): 126–42.

8. Ian Maclean, *The Renaissance Notion of Women: A Study in the Fortunes of Scholasticism and Medical Science in European Intellectual Life* (Cambridge: Cambridge University Press, 1980), 46.

9. Nicholas Culpepper (quoting Fernelius) in *Directory for Midwives: The Second Part* (London: 1671), 114. See also Gail Kern Paster, *The Body Embarrassed: Drama and Disciplines of Shame in Early Modern England* (Ithaca, NY: Cornell University Press, 1993), 163–215.

10. *The problemes of Aristotle with other philosophers and phisitions. Wherein are contayned diuers questions, with their answers, touching the estate of mans bodie* (Edinburgh: 1595), 44.

11. Jacques Guillemeau, *Childbirth, or The Happy Deliverie of Women* (London, 1612).

12. Paster, *The Body Embarrassed*, 181.

13. Paster, *The Body Embarrassed*, 163–280.

14. Culpepper, *Directory for Midwives*, 159.

15. Paster, *The Body Embarrassed*, 223.

16. Culpepper, *Directory for Midwives*, 159. I infer from Culpepper's association of "unnatural" infant food with "cockering in youth" a causal relationship between the two moments of appetite formation.

17. Jacques Ferrand, *Erotomania* (London, 1640), 11.

18. Gail Kern Paster, *Humoring the Body: Emotions and the Shakespearean Stage* (Chicago: University of Chicago Press, 2004), 95.

19. Paster, *The Body Embarrassed*, 222.

20. Valerie A. Fildes, *Breasts, Bottles, and Babies: A History of Feeding* (Edinburgh: Edinburgh University Press, 1986).

21. For an analysis of child dependency on wet nurses see Fildes, *Breasts, Bottles and Babies*, 202–3.

22. Fildes, *Breasts, Bottles and Babies*, 385–97, 382.

23. Barbara Everett, *Young Hamlet: Essays on Shakespeare's Tragedies* (Oxford: Clarendon Press, 1989), 109–23.

24. Paster, *The Body Embarrassed*, 221; Fildes, *Breasts, Bottles and Babies*, 202–3.

25. Thomas Sydenham, *The Entire Works of Dr. Thomas Sydenham*, ed. John Swan (London, 1742), 607.

CHAPTER 10

1. Anon., *Arden of Faversham*, in *Three Elizabethan Domestic Tragedies: Arden of Faversham, A Yorkshire Tragedy, A Woman Killed with Kindness*, ed. Keith Sturgess (London: Penguin Classics, 2012), scene 16, 1–8.

2. Malcolm Gaskill, "Reporting Murder: Fiction in the Archives in Early Modern England," *Social History* 23.1 (1998): 9.

3. Subha Mukherji, *Law and Representation in Early Modern Drama* (Cambridge: Cambridge University Press, 2006), 109.

4. John Reynolds, *The Triumphs of Gods Revenge against the Crying and Execrable Sinne of Murther* (London, 1621), [3].

5. For an account of the various theories of cruentation and their philosophical and religious affiliations, see Francesco Paolo de Ceglia, "Saving the Phenomenon: The Reasons That Corpses Bled in the Presence of Their Murderer in Early Modern Science," in *The Corpse of Evidence: Cadavers and Proofs in Early Modern European Forensic Medicine*, ed. Francesco Paolo de Ceglia (Leiden: Brill, forthcoming). See also Mary Floyd-Wilson, *Occult Knowledge, Science and Gender on the Shakespearean Stage* (Cambridge: Cambridge University Press, 2013), 58–61.

6. Lucy Munro, "'They Eat Each Other's Arms': Stage Blood and Body Parts," in *Shakespeare's Theatres and the Effects of Performance*, ed. Farah Karim-Cooper and Tiffany Stern (London: Arden Shakespeare, 2013), 77.

7. Michael Schoenfeldt, *Bodies and Selves in Early Modern England: Physiology and Inwardness in Spenser, Shakespeare, Herbert, and Milton* (Cambridge: Cambridge University Press, 1999). See, in particular, ch. 4.

8. Early modern writers sometimes suggest that cruentation appears in texts by Homer (*Iliad*, XVII, 79–86), Plato (*Laws*, 865 d6–e10), (Pseudo) Aristotle (*Prob.* 6), and Lucretius (*De rer. nat.*, 4, 1046–1051), but in fact these texts actually describe phenomena only "vaguely comparable to cruentation" (de Ceglia, "Saving the Phenomenon"). For the origins of cruentation, see Alain Boureau, "La preuve par le cadavre qui saigne au XIIIe siècle: Entre expérience commune et savoir scolastique," *Micrologus* 7 (1999): 247–81.

9. Robert P. Brittain, "Cruentation: In Legal Medicine and in Literature," *Medical History* 9 (1965): 82.

10. Gaskill, "Reporting Murder," 9.

11. Anon., *A True Report of the Late Horrible Murther Committed by William Sherwood* (London, 1581), [6].

12. W. R., *The Most Horrible and Tragicall Murther of the Right Honorable, the Vertuous and Valerous Gentleman, John Lord Bourgh, Baron of Castell Connell* (London, 1591), sig. B.

13. Gail Kern Paster, *Humoring the Body: Emotions and the Shakespearean Stage* (Chicago: University of Chicago Press, 2004), 23.

14. Anon., *Sundrye Strange and Inhumaine Murthers, Lately Committed* (London, 1591), sig. A4v.

15. Eric Langley, "Plagued by Kindness: Contagious Sympathy in Shakespearean Drama," *Medical Humanities* 37.2 (2011): 103.

16. Gaskill, "Reporting Murder," 16.

17. Natalie Zemon Davis, *Fiction in the Archives: Pardon Tales and Their Tellers in Sixteenth-Century France* (Stanford, CA: Stanford University Press, 1987), 3–4. Quoted in Gaskill, "Reporting Murder," 3–4.

18. *The Diary of Walter Yonge, Esq.*, ed. George Roberts, Camden Society, XLI (1848), xxiii; quoted in Gaskill, "Reporting Murder," 13.

19. Ibid., 13.

20. Anon., *Five Philosophical Questions Most Eloquently and Substantially Disputed* (London, 1650), 1–2; Michael Dalton, *The Countrey Justice* (London, 1618), 266; both quoted in Gaskill, "Reporting Murder," 10.

21. Keith Thomas, *Religion and the Decline of Magic: Studies in Popular Beliefs in Sixteenth- and Seventeenth-Century England* (London: Penguin Books, repr. 1991), 261–62.

22. Lynn Alison Robson, "'No Nine Days Wonder': Embedded Protestant Narrative in Early Modern Prose Murder Pamphlets, 1573–1700" (unpublished dissertation, Warwick University, 2003), 54.

23. de Ceglia, "Saving the Phenomenon."

24. Anon., *The Bloody Husband, and Cruell Neighbour* (London, 1653), sig. A2.

25. James I, *Daemonologie* (Edinburgh, 1597), 80–81.

26. Robson, "No Nine Days Wonder," Abstract, 26.

27. Randall Martin, *Women, Murder, and Equity in Early Modern England* (New York: Routledge, 2008), 80.

28. Anon., *A Warning to Fair Women*, ed. Gemma Leggott (2011), 4.4.158–59. http://extra.shu.ac.uk/emls/iemls/resources.html.

29. William Shakespeare, *Richard III*, in *William Shakespeare: The Complete Works*, gen. eds. Stanley Wells and Gary Taylor (Oxford: Clarendon Press, 1988, 1990), 1.2.56.

30. For primitive beliefs in the revenant, see James G. Frazer, *The Fear of the Dead in Primitive Religions* (New York: Biblo and Tannen, 1933).

31. Katharine Park, "The Life of the Corpse: Division and Dissection in Late Medieval Europe," *Journal of the History of Medicine and Allied Sciences* 50 (1995): 115.

32. George Chapman, *The Revenge of Bussy D'Ambois*, in *Four Revenge Tragedies*, ed. Katharine Eisaman Maus (Oxford: Oxford University Press, 1995), 5.5.134–38.

33. de Ceglia, "Saving the Phenomenon."

34. Levinus Lemnius, *The Secret Miracles of Nature* (London, 1658), 104.

35. Francis Bacon, *Sylua syluarum: or A Naturall Historie* (London, 1627), 257. For a discussion of Bacon's views of the imagination, see Sorana Corneanu and Koen Vermeir, "Idols of the Imagination: Francis Bacon on the Imagination and the Medicine of the Mind," *Perspectives on Science* 20.2 (2012): 183–206.

36. de Ceglia, "Saving the Phenomenon."

37. Walter Charleton, *Physiologia Epicuro-Gassendo-Charltoniana, or, A Fabrick of Science Natural, upon the Hypothesis of Atoms founded by Epicurus* (London, 1654), III, ch. 15, p. 364.

38. If cruentation is the result of the victim's imagination, it could produce false results. In one story "the dead body of a young girl started to bleed when someone came close whom the girl had falsely preconceived to be her murderer," demonstrating how "it was the fixation of her still-active imagination that caused her body to bleed post-mortem." See Koen Vermeir, "Vampires as Creatures of the Imagination: Theories of Body, Soul, and Imagination in Early Modern Vampire Tracts, 1659–1755," in *Diseases of the Imagination and Imaginary Diseases in the Early Modern Period*, ed. Yasmin Haskell (Turnhout: Brepols, 2012), 365.

39. Hillary M. Nunn, *Staging Anatomies: Dissection and Spectacle in Early Stuart Drama* (Aldershot and Burlington, VT: Ashgate, 2005), 204. As John Kerrigan observes, the "drama of the Renaissance makes the 'undead' come to life" (*Revenge Tragedy: Aeschylus to Armageddon* [Oxford: Oxford University Press, 1996], 38).

40. William Shakespeare, *Titus Andronicus*, ed. Jonathan Bate, Arden Shakespeare (Walton-on-Thames: Thomas Nelson & Sons, 1997), 1.1.129.

41. Jasper Heywood, *Troas*, reprinted in *Elizabethan Seneca: Three Tragedies*, ed. James Ker and Jessica Winston, MHRA Tudor and Stuart Translations, Vol. 8 (London: Modern Humanities Research Association, 2012), "Preface to the Tragedy," l.61 (73); 4.95 (134).

42. John Marston, *Antonio's Revenge*, in *Five Revenge Tragedies: Kyd, Shakespeare, Marston, Chettle, Middleton*, ed. Emma Smith (London: Penguin Classics, 2012), 3.3.63–71.

43. Anon., *The Problemes of Aristotle* (London, 1595), [p. 45]; quoted in Floyd-Wilson, *Occult Knowledge*, 60.

44. Floyd-Wilson, *Occult Knowledge*, 60.

45. See also Ariane Balizet, who argues that "Arden's bleeding corpse is a mark of his shame, emblematizing the play's indictment of him for failing to wield and maintain his proper domestic authority" (*Blood and Home in Early Modern Drama: Domestic Identity on the Renaissance Stage* [New York: Routledge, 2014], 81).

46. Steven P. Marrone, "Magic and the Physical World in Thirteenth-Century Scholasticism," *Early Science and Medicine* 14.1 (2009): 183. See also Galeotto Marzio, *De doctrina promiscua* (Lyon, 1653) VII, 160–63.

47. For this account of lovesickness, see Lesel Dawson, *Lovesickness and Gender in Early Modern Literature* (Oxford: Oxford University Press, 2008), 26–27; 127–62.

48. John Donne, "The Ecstasy," in *John Donne*, ed. John Carey, The Oxford Authors (Oxford: Oxford University Press, 1990), ll.7–8.

49. Mukherji, *Law and Representation*, 113.

50. William Rowley, Thomas Dekker, and John Ford, *The Witch of Edmonton*, in *Three Jacobean Witchcraft Plays*, ed. Peter Corbin and Douglas Sedge (Manchester: Manchester University Press, 1986), 4.2.150; 4.2.163–64; 4.2.169.

51. William Shakespeare, *Macbeth*, in *The Complete Works*, 2.2.57.

52. Robert Miola, *Shakespeare and Classical Tragedy: The Influence of Seneca* (Oxford: Clarendon Press, 1992), 116.

53. For a discussion of early modern visual distortions see *Visions and Voice-Hearing in Historical and Literary Contexts*, ed. Hilary Powell and Corinne Saunders, forthcoming.

54. Thomas Middleton and William Rowley, *The Changeling*, ed. Michael Neill, New Mermaids (London and New York: A & C Black, 2006), 4.2.40–41; 5.2.32–33.

55. Cyril Tourneur, *The Atheist's Tragedy*, in *Four Revenge Tragedies*, ed. Maus, 5.2.202–6.

56. Thomas Fuchs observes that the experience of guilt involves incorporating the voice of the other, a process that underlies the "dialogic structure of conscience" and which results in the subject adopting "a 'meta-perspective' on one's relation towards others." "The Phenomenology of Shame, Guilt and the Body in Body Dysmorphic Disorder and Depression," *Journal of Phenomenological Psychology* 33.2 (2003): 233. For ideas about medieval and early modern voice hearing, see https://www.dur.ac.uk/hearingthevoice/ [accessed November 23, 2016].

57. Katherine Rowe, "Humoral Knowledge and Liberal Cognition in Davenant's *Macbeth*," in *Reading the Early Modern Passions: Essays in the Cultural History of Emotion*, ed. Gail Kern Paster, Katherine Rowe, and Mary Floyd-Wilson (Philadelphia: University of Pennsylvania Press, 2004), 183.

CHAPTER 11

1. See Coppélia Kahn, *Roman Shakespeare: Warriors, Wounds, and Women* (New York: Routledge, 1997), 46–76; Tina Mohler, "'Why is the body but a Swallowing Grave . . . ?': Desire Underground in *Titus Andronicus*," *Shakespeare Quarterly* 57.1 (2006): 23–44;

Danielle A. St. Hilaire, "Allusion and Sacrifice in *Titus Andronicus*," *Studies in English Literature* 49.2 (2009): 311–31; Gillian Murray Kendall, "'Lend me thy hand': Metaphor and Mayhem in *Titus Andronicus*," *Shakespeare Quarterly* 40.3 (1989): 299–316; Mary Laughlin Fawcett, "Arms/Words/Tears: Language and the Body in *Titus Andronicus*," *English Literary History* 50.2 (1983): 261–77; Louise Christine Noble, "And Make Two Pasties of Your Shameful Heads: Medicinal Cannibalism and Healing the Body Politic in Titus Andronicus," *English Literary History* 70.3 (2003): 677–708.

2. See Gail Kern Paster, *The Body Embarrassed: Drama and the Disciplines of Shame in Early Modern England* (Ithaca, NY: Cornell University Press, 1993), 83–84.

3. For example, see L. W. C., *The English Farrier, Or Country-mans Treasure* (London, 1639), which opens with advice and a diagram of veins for bloodletting horses; or chapter 4 of the 7th book of Gervase Markham's *Cavelarice, or The English Horseman* (London, 1607). Both books advise practitioners to avoid regular, seasonally driven bloodletting three to four times per year, which had been commonplace to preserve equine health, and instead to restrict bloodletting horses to urgent necessity only.

4. See James Thompson, *Helmont Disguised, OR, The Vulgar Errours of Impericall and Unskillful Practisers of Physick* (London, 1657) and George Thompson, *Aimatiasis, or, The True Way of Preserving the Bloud in its Integrity* (London, 1670), for example.

5. *An Act Concerning Barbers and Surgeons to be of One Company* (1540), Archives of the Worshipful Company of Barbers [hereafter Barbers Archive], 32 Henry VIII, A/6/1.

6. William Clowes, *A Prooved Practise for all Young Chirurgians* (London, 1588), see sig. P3r–Qiiv.

7. Simon Harward, *Harwards Phlebotomy, OR, a Treatise of Letting Bloud* (London, 1601), title page.

8. Cf. John Woodall, *Woodalls Viaticum: The Path-way to the Surgions Chest* (London, 1628), which stipulates to surgeons: "If you have *Hemoragie*, I meane bleeding or weeping of Veines or Arteries in your worke, serach for that Veine or that Artery that bleedesth. If you cannot make ligature... then apply to the end of the Veine an actually Cautery, a small one will serve but apply it very hot" (sig. B3v).

9. Richard Brome, *The Sparagus Garden* (London, 1640), sig. D3v–D4r.

10. Anon., "The Catalogue of Contented Cuckolds" (London, 1662–1692).

11. Anon., "The Northern Ladd: or, The Fair Maids Choice" ([London], 1670–1696).

12. Nicholas Gyer, *The English Phlebotomy* (London, 1592), A2r.

13. Thomas Middleton, *The Owl's Almanac*, ed. Neil Rhodes, in *The Collected Works*, ed. Gary Taylor and John Lavagnino (Oxford: Clarendon Press, 2007), 1271–1302.

14. Gyer, *English Phlebotomy*, 201.

15. Barbers' Archive, *Court Minutes*, B/1/3, 23.

16. Paster, *The Body Embarrassed*, 83.

17. Thomas Gale, *Certaine Workes of Chirurgerie* (London, 1563), 6v.

18. Sidney Young, *The Annals of the Barber-Surgeons of London* (London: Blades, 1890), 317.

19. Nashe, *Saffron-Walden*, B1v.

20. Young, *The Annals*, 23. Reflecting on the image of waste blood flowing into the sewage drain at the end of *The Changeling*, Paster comments on the doubly imbued notion of waste (Paster, *The Body Embarrassed*, 88).

21. Barbers' Archive, *Court Minutes*, B/1/2, fol. 4v.

22. Wendy Wall, *Staging Domesticity: Household Work and English Identity in Early Modern Drama* (Cambridge: Cambridge University Press, 2002), 189–95.

23. Gyer, *English Phlebotomy*, 27.

24. William Turner, *A New Boke of the Natures and Properties of all Wines* (London, 1568), Di*v*.

25. Ambroise Paré, *The Workes*, trans. Th[omas] Johnson (London, 1634), 390.

26. See p. 54 of Katharine Craik's chapter in this volume.

27. Lucy Munro, "'They eat each other's arms': Stage Blood and Body Parts," in *Shakespeare's Theatres: And the Effects of Performance*, ed. Farah Karim-Cooper and Tiffany Stern (London: Arden Shakespeare, 2013), 73–93 (esp. 80–81). Also see p. 64 of Hester Lees-Jeffries's chapter in this volume.

28. Barbers' Archive, *Charter, Act and Ordinance Book* (1604–), A/6/1.

29. Randle Holme, *Academy of Armory, or, A Storehouse of Armory and Blazon* (Chester: 1688), 438.

30. Woodall, *Woodalls Viaticum*, F2r.

31. See Harward, *Harwards Phlebotomy*, H6v-H7r.

32. Lanfranc of Milan, *A Most Excellent and Learned Woorke of Chirurgerie* (London, 1565), Ddiiiir.

33. Helkiah Crooke, *Mikrokosmographia: A Description of the Body of Man* (London, 1615), 254.

34. Harward, *Harwards Phlebotomy*, I7v.

35. Felix Plater, *Platerus Golden Practice of Physick* (London, 1664), 563; 272.

36. Woodall, *Woodalls Viaticum*, F2r.

37. Ibid., F4v.

38. John Marston, *The Dutch Courtesan*, ed. David Crane (London: A & C Black; New York: W. W. Norton, 1997); John Ford, *The Fancies, Chast and Noble* (London, 1638); Francis Beaumont, *The Knight of the Burning Pestle*, ed. Michael Hattaway, 2nd ed. (London: A & C Black; New York: W. W. Norton, 2002).

39. Holme, *Academy of Armory*, 128.

40. Thomas Middleton and Thomas Dekker, *The Meeting of Gallants at an Ordinary; or The Walks in Paul's*, ed. Paul Yachnin, in *The Collected Works*, ed. Gary Taylor and John Lavagnino, 183–94.

41. John Woodall, *The Surgions Mate* (London, 1617), E2v. Cf. Harward, *Harwards Phlebotomy*, H4v–H5r, which explains why a surgeon needs a range of launcers.

42. Gyer, *English Phlebotomy*, O5r.

43. Woodall, *Surgions Mate*, B2r.

44. Patricia Parker, "Cutting Both Ways: Bloodletting, Castration/Circumcision, and the 'Lancelet' of *The Merchant of Venice*," in *Alternative Shakespeares 3*, ed. Diana E. Henderson (London: Routledge, 2008), 95–118.

45. Quotations are taken from *Titus Andronicus*, ed. Jonathan Bate, The Arden Shakespeare: Third Series (Walton-on-Thames: Thomas Nelson, 1998).

46. Cf. Catherine Belling, "Infectious Rape, Therapeutic Revenge: Bloodletting and the Health of Rome's Body," in *Disease, Diagnosis, and Cure on the Early Modern Stage*, ed. Stephanie Moss and Kaara L. Peterson (Aldershot: Ashgate, 2004), 113–32.

47. Gyer, *English Phlebotomy*, Q7v.

48. Jean Baptiste Helmont, *Van Helmont's Works Containing his Most Excellent Philosophy, Physick, Chirurgery, Anatomy* (London, 1664), 416; 305.

49. Crooke, *Mikrokosmographia*, 129.

50. See Paster, *The Body Embarrassed*, 71–72.

51. On Shakespeare and the early modern medical world see, for example, David F. Hoeniger, *Medicine and Shakespeare in the English Renaissance* (London: Associated University Press, 1992) and Todd H. J. Pettigrew, *Shakespeare and the Practice of Physic: Medical Narratives on the Early Modern English Stage* (Newark: University of Delaware Press, 2007).

52. Stage directions stipulating "*bason*" are consistent in quarto ([1594], K1r) and Folio texts.

53. Harward, *Harwards Phlebotomy*, H7v.

54. William Davenant, *The Cruell Brother* (London, 1630), I1r.

55. Barnabe Barnes, *The Divils Charter* (London, 1607), s.d. A2v.

56. Thomas Geminus, "A Table Instructive Whan and How a Man may Conyngly Let Bloude . . ." (London 1546), para. 2, left-hand column.

57. William Bullein, *The Government of Health* (London, 1558), fol. 17–18.

58. See Paster, *The Body Embarrassed*, 98–99.

59. Patricia Parker explores the semantic nexus of "Barbary," "barbarousness," and "barber," explaining the self-consciousness of the wordplay available: "conflations of sound and interchangeable spellings were joined by the polyglot influence of languages in which different parts of the network were semantically or etymologically connected" (Patricia Parker, "Barbers and Barbary: Early Modern Cultural Semantics," *Renaissance Drama* 33 [2004]: 201–44 [201]). James Calderwood remarks that "the word 'barbarous' appears more often in *Titus* than in any other of Shakespeare's plays", but fails to register the barber association (James Calderwood, *Shakespearean Metadrama: The Argument of the Play in Titus Andronicus, Love's Labour's Lost, Romeo and Juliet, A Midsummer Night's Dream, and Richard II* [Minneapolis: University of Minnesota Press, 1971], 29.) The *Titus* references are: "barbarous Goths" (I.i.28), "Was never Scythia half so barbarous!" (I.i.134), "be not barbarous" (I.i.383), "barbarous Moor" (II.ii.78), "barbarous Tamora" (II.ii.118), "barbarous, beastly villains" (V.i.97), and again "barbarous Moor" (V.iii.4).

60. See Belling, who registers the onomastic implication but does not explore its implication: "Infectious Rape and Therapeutic Revenge," 126.

61. On barbers and sweet waters, see Phillip Stubbes, *The Second Part of the Anatomie of Abuses Conteining the Display of Corruptions* (London, 1583), G8v, and Thomas Dekker, *The Guls Horne-Booke* (London, 1609), F2v.

62. Thomas Lanfiere, *The Taunton Maids Delight* (London, 1672–1696), 4th stanza.

63. Anon., *Age Renewed by Wedlock* (London, 1693), stanza 9. ["Ladders": lathers.]

64. Galen on Chiron, trans. Thomas Gale, *Certaine Workes of Chirurgerie*, Aiiir–v.

65. See Bate's Introduction in his edition of *Titus Andronicus*, 11–12, and Katherine Rowe, *Dead Hands: Fictions of Agency Renaissance to Modern* (Stanford, CA: Stanford University Press, 1999), 73–80.

CHAPTER 12

1. See Jacobs, "Little St. Hugh," for a comparison of the abbey annals' account and that of Matthew Paris. I detail this history more fully in "The Blood Libel: Literary Representations of Ritual Child Murder in Medieval England," in *Children and Violence in the Western Tradition*, ed. Laurence Brockliss and Heather Montgomery (Oxford: Oxbow Books, 2010), 32–36.

2. Many scholars have followed Joseph Jacob in pointing out, on religious grounds, "how impossible it is for Jews to use human blood" in their rituals, and that contact with a corpse "renders a Jew impure . . . and incapable of performing any religious rite." See "Little St. Hugh of Lincoln: Researches in History, Archaeology, and Legend," in Jacob's *Jewish Ideals and Other Essays* (New York: Macmillan, 1896), 192–224. Edward I finally expelled the Jews from England in 1291 because of financial exigency: the Jews' status as financiers to the crown ensured their royal protection but also made them vulnerable to this "single and arbitrary act of spoliation." R. I. Moore, *The Formation of a Persecuting Society: Power and Deviance in Western Europe 950–1250* (Oxford: Blackwell, 1987), 44.

3. Arnold of Villanova, *Opera Omnia, cum Nicolai Taurelli Medici et philosophi in quosdam libros annotationibus* (Basil, 1585), 1241–43, cited in Willis Johnson, "The Myth of Jewish Male Menses," *Journal of Medieval History* 24.3 (1998): 275 (289). For further discussion of male menstruation see Gabriella Zuccolin and Helen King, "Rethinking Nosebleeds: Gendering Spontaneous Bleedings in Medieval and Early Modern Medicine," Chapter 5 in this collection.

4. See William Tydeman, ed., *The Medieval European Stage, 500–1500* (Cambridge: Cambridge University Press, 2001), 192.

5. Citations from the edition of the play in Greg Walker, ed., *Medieval Drama: An Anthology* (Oxford: Blackwell, 2000), 212–33, and are by line number. I have directed the play three times, most recently for the Oxford Blood Conference in January 2014. A (fixed camera) recording of this production can be seen at http://www.thebloodproject.net/performance/; it was staged in the chapel of St. John's College, Oxford, where the frisson created by the sanctified performance space compensated for the highly restricted use of stage blood dictated by the conservation requirements of a historic building.

6. See, for example, the chapters by Dawson, Decamp, Parker, Lees-Jeffries, and Lander Johnson in this collection.

7. 400, s.d.; 592, s.d., 632, s.d.

8. 435, s.d.

9. See Elisabeth Dutton, "The Croxton *Play of the Sacrament*," in *The Oxford Handbook of Tudor Drama*, ed. Thomas Betteridge and Greg Walker (Oxford: Oxford University Press, 2012), 55–71.

10. For an overview of stage directions in the early modern period, see Linda McJannet, *The Voice of Elizabethan Stage Directions: The Evolution of a Theatrical Code* (Newark, NJ: University of Delaware Press, 1999).

11. Digby, *Mary Magdalene*, Bodleian MS Digby 133, 1561 s.d. b.

12. Digby, *Conversion of St. Paul*, Bodleian MS Digby 133, 501 s.d.

13. Philip Butterworth, *Theatre of Fire: Special Effects in the Early English and Scottish Theatre* (London: Society for Theatre Research, 1998), 51.

14. Three plays of the Digby Manuscript, *Mary Magdalene*, *The Conversion of St. Paul*, and *The Slaughter of the Innocents*, are saints' plays, and the latter is of course bloody, but they contain little useful information about how bloody effects were achieved.

15. Provencal Director's Notebook, cited in Tydeman, *Medieval European Stage*, 317.

16. Peter Meredith and John Tailby, ed., *The Staging of Religious Drama in Europe in the Later Middle Ages: Texts and Documents in English Translation*, Early Drama, Art and Music Monograph Series 4 (Kalamazoo, MI: Medieval Institute Publications, 1983), 108.

17. Provencal Director's Notebook, cited in Tydeman, *Medieval European Stage*, 317.

18. Joe Moshenska, in his chapter "Screaming Bleeding Trees: Textual Wounding and the Epic Tradition," Chapter 6 in this collection.

19. The plot of *The Battle of Alcazar* requires three vials of blood and the entrails of a sheep, which has led to the suggestion that the blood would also be sheep blood; however, the ensuing reference to "dead mens heads" presumably indicates that not all of these requirements are to be taken literally.

20. Reginald Scot, *The Discoverie of Witchcraft* (London, 1584), 350.

21. Lucy Munro, "'They eat each other's arms': Stage Blood and Body Parts," in *Shakespeare's Theatres and the Effects of Performance*, ed. Farah Karim-Cooper and Tiffany Stern, The Arden Shakespeare (London: Bloomsbury, 2013), 73–93 (79–80).

22. Scot, *The Discoverie*, 350.

23. Jonathas's comment that the Christians believe on a cake (120) invokes not only the bread of the Eucharistic Host, but also the medical meaning of "cake" as an abnormal growth on the inner organs, often associated with the action of elves—an image that suggests and debases the idea of Christ's incarnation in a virgin's womb. See Dutton, "The Croxton Play," 60.

24. See Walker, *Medieval Drama*, 23, n.42.

25. The bloody cloth as a proof is a recurrent trope, ranging from bloodied wedding sheets as proof of virginity to Pyramus finding Thisbe's bloody mantle: for detailed

Notes to Pages 191–198   293

discussion see Patricia Parker, "Simular Proof, Tragicomic Turns, and *Cymbeline*'s Bloody Cloth," Chapter 13 in this collection.

26. Vigneulles *Gedenkbuch*, 244–45, describing a performance in Metz, 1513, cited in Tydeman, *Medieval European Stage*, 349. The account continues, intriguingly: "Then, enraged, he took the host and flung it in a cauldron of boiling water and it rose up in the air in a cloud and became a little child as it rose and all this was done by pulleys and *secrets*."

27. I have experimented with various means, including pouches of blood inside bread, pouches of blood hidden underneath the bread, and even an actor underneath the table on which the bread is stabbed, with blood in a syringe. None has achieved anything like the effect of "a child pissing," largely because the bread itself tends to soak up blood and prevent it from gushing.

28. "[B]lood is a substance whose physical nature and perceived significance is not intrinsic but unusually determined by its *place*. It is redolent of life and vitality so long as it remains invisible: as soon as it appears, the very fact of its appearance betokens wounding, the possible dissipation of life, and the specter of imminent death." Moshenska, "Screaming Bleeding Trees," p. 98 of Chapter 6 in this volume.

29. Andrea Stevens, "Cosmetic Transformations," in *Shakespeare's Theatres*, ed. Karim-Cooper and Stern (London: Bloomsbury, 2013), 94–117 (97).

30. Ibid., 95. Stevens cites Thomas Heywood's suggestion that the word "tragedy" derives from the Greek for "a kinde of painting."

31. For discussion of the identification of clothing with the body, see Lees-Jeffries, "Mantled in Blood," Chapter 4 in this collection.

32. Lees-Jeffries, "Mantled in Blood," writes: "It is in *Macbeth*, in contrast to *Julius Caesar*, that it is explicitly established that neither the bloody wounds nor the moment of assassination need be shown" (Chapter 4, p. 76 in this volume). However, apparently Duncan's blood *is* shown, but on Macbeth's hands.

33. Munro, "'They eat each other's arms,'" 93.

34. William Shakespeare, *Titus Andronicus*, ed. Jonathan Bate, The Arden Shakespeare (London: Routledge, 1995), 205.

35. Ibid., 3.1.282–83 n.

36. Colle, Master Brundyche's servant, invites Jonathas to seek treatment from his master: "In a pott yf yt please yow to pysse, / He can tell yf yow be curable" (568–69).

37. The significance of this is discussed in Dutton, *The Croxton Play*, 70–71.

38. This presents an argument for outdoor performance, or a reason for caution to those playing indoors: see above, note 5.

CHAPTER 13

1. The edition used for all citations of *Cymbeline* is Martin Butler, ed., *Cymbeline* (Cambridge: Cambridge University Press, 2005). Other Shakespeare plays are cited from

The Riverside Shakespeare, 2nd ed., ed. G. Blakemore Evans and J. J. M. Tobin (Boston: Houghton Mifflin, 1997).

2. Simon Palfrey, *Late Shakespeare: A New World of Words* (Oxford: Oxford University Press, 1997), 218. See also Ruth Nevo, *Shakespeare's Other Language* (London: Methuen, 1987), 87, on this moment as "a gruesome fantasy realization of Elizabethan 'dying,' to match her maidenhead with the violated head of her lover."

3. Suzanne Gossett, in her edition of Francis Beaumont and John Fletcher, *Philaster, or, Love Lies A-Bleeding* (Arden Early Modern Drama: London: A&C Black, 2009), 7, concludes, for example, that *Philaster* came before *Cymbeline*.

4. Nevo, in *Shakespeare's Other Language*, 79, noting the pun on "testimonies," observes that Posthumus "incorporates the woman's part" in the letter to Pisanio, playing the "violated virgin since he cannot be the violator that . . . he would wish to be." Janet Adelman, in *Suffocating Mothers: Fantasies of Maternal Origin in Shakespeare's Plays, Hamlet to The Tempest* (New York: Routledge, 1992), 351 n36, writes of "The incipient pun on 'testimonies'" that "The pun is reinforced by Cloten's later use of the relatively uncommon word 'testiness' in his description of his mother's hold over Cymbeline ('my mother, having power of his testiness' [4.1.20–21])."

5. Adelman, *Suffocating Mothers*, 213.

6. Adelman, *Suffocating Mothers*, 214.

7. See Ellen Spolsky, "Women's Work Is Chastity: Lucretia, *Cymbeline*, and Cognitive Impenetrability," in *The Work of Fiction: Cognition, Culture, and Complexity*, ed. Ellen Spolsky and Alan Richardson (Aldershot: Ashgate, 2004), 51–84.

8. Anne Barton, in "'Wrying but a little': Marriage, Law and Sexuality in the Plays of Shakespeare," in *Essays, Mainly Shakespearean* (Cambridge: Cambridge University Press, 1994), 3–30, writes on p. 6 that "The ambiguities of English matrimonial law" at the time make it unclear whether Innogen's hymeneal blood has been shed and that the issue in the play is not "unequivocal" (p. 20), though she also marshals evidence for her conclusion that it is likely unconsummated. Constance Jordan, in *Shakespeare's Monarchies: Ruler and Subject in the Romances* (Ithaca, NY: Cornell University Press, 1997), concluding that the union of Innogen and Posthumus is a "clandestine marriage," points out that the question of whether or not it was consummated would raise its stakes even higher, since "Clandestine marriages were not legally binding before consummation; in effect, the fact of consummation in a clandestine marriage served the same function as the act of agreeing to marriage before witnesses in a public marriage." B. J. Sokol and Mary Sokol, in *Shakespeare, Law, and Marriage* (Cambridge: Cambridge University Press, 2003), conclude that "the marriage has not been consummated" (149). David M. Bergeron, in "Sexuality in *Cymbeline*," *Essays in Literature* 10.2 (1983): 159–68, writes that "In all likelihood, though it is difficult to be sure, their marriage has not been consummated." Nevo, in *Shakespeare's Other Language*, argues that Innogen is "Wedded but not bedded." Susan Frye, in *Pens and Needles: Women's Textualities in Early Modern England* (Philadelphia: University of Pennsylvania Press, 2010), writes of the details of Innogen's bedchamber in 2.2 that "Innogen sleeps her virgin sleep enshrined within this architecture of female identity—if indeed she and Posthumus have

not yet consummated their marriage, as both the narrative and textual imagery suggest" (181). John Pitcher in his edition of *Cymbeline* (London: Penguin, 2005), 221, writes: "It seems likely that Imogen is a wedded lady (1.6.2), who has not consummated her marriage." By contrast, other prominent critics and editors have marshaled evidence in support of their conclusion that the marriage *is* consummated. Roger Warren writes in his edition of *Cymbeline* (Oxford: Clarendon Press, 1998), 32–33, with regard to Anne Barton's argument that "opposition" in Posthumus's remark that Iachimo "Found no opposition / But what he looked for should oppose, and she / Should from encounter guard" (2.4.169–71) is a specific reference to the hymen, that "none of the supporting evidence she adduces" for her arguments "unequivocally clinches it" and that it "simply means that Giacomo anticipated pleasurable physical 'opposition' to penetration, and that her behaviour was a mere prelude to intercourse ('encounter')." Valerie Wayne, in "The Woman's Parts of *Cymbeline*," in *Staged Properties in Early Modern English Drama*, ed. Jonathan Gil Harris and Natasha Korda (Cambridge: Cambridge University Press, 2002), 288–315, concurs with Warren's argument that the lines on what Innogen should "from encounter guard" do not support "Anne Barton's claim that the "opposition" Iachimo finds "refers specifically to Innogen's hymen and that she is a virgin." Martin Butler, in his 2005 New Cambridge edition of *Cymbeline* (page 26)—in contrast to Barton—concludes that "Jupiter's words are unequivocal—'in / Our temple was he married' (5.3.169–70)," and reads Posthumus's "complaint that Innogen restrained him 'of [his] lawful pleasure' (2.5.9)" as suggesting "that sexual relations between the two were fully institutionalized."

9. On the issue of whether the marriage in *Othello* is consummated or not, see, for example, T. G. A. Nelson and Charles Haines, "Othello's Unconsummated Marriage," *Essays in Criticism* 33.1 (1983) and Michael Neill, "Unproper Beds: Race, Adultery, and the Hideous in *Othello*," *Shakespeare Quarterly* 40.4 (1989): 396.

10. Karen Cunningham, *Imaginary Betrayals: Subjectivity and the Discourses of Treason in Early Modern England* (Philadelphia: University of Pennsylvania Press, 2002), 71.

11. Heather James, *Shakespeare's Troy: Drama, Politics, and the Translation of Empire* (Cambridge: Cambridge University Press, 1997).

12. Adelman, *Suffocating Mothers*, 209.

13. See Wayne, "The Woman's Parts of *Cymbeline*," 298; Frye, *Pens and Needles*, 186–87.

14. Wayne, "The Woman's Parts of *Cymbeline*," 298.

15. See Wayne, "The Woman's Parts of *Cymbeline*," 299, with 313n29, citing J. M. Nosworthy's Arden 2 edition of *Cymbeline* (London: Methuen, 1955), 197–98.

16. See Wayne, "The Woman's Parts of *Cymbeline*," 299–310, on Posthumus's "put on this" and the uses of the bloody cloth on the modern stage.

17. Wayne, "The Woman's Parts of *Cymbeline*," 301–3.

18. See Marion Lomax, *Stage Images and Traditions: Shakespeare to Ford* (Cambridge: Cambridge University Press, 1987), chapter 2. Lomax observes that "Imogen has many signs of the saint or Christ figure about her" (107), is "frequently associated with the image of a lamb (signifying innocence and sacrifice)," and is "the subject of an apparent resurrection: 'Is not this boy reviv'd from death?' (V.v.120)." And she relates the description of the

"cinque-spotted" mole (in 2.2) to the "five crimson spots" or stigmata associated with "the blood of Christ," noting that "it is ironical that this particular 'proof' should be used to condemn her for adultery" (107–8). On the latter and the stigmata, see also Peggy Muñoz Simonds, *Myth, Emblem, and Music in Shakespeare's "Cymbeline": An Iconographic Reconstruction* (Newark: University of Delaware Press, 1992), 126.

19. On Spenser's Fidelia, see James Nohrnberg, *The Analogy of "The Faerie Queene"* (Princeton, NJ: Princeton University Press, 1976), 281–82.

20. I argue that the lancing of Christ's blood is also echoed in the name of "Lancelet" in *The Merchant of Venice*, another play that transforms its biblical subtexts, in "Cutting Both Ways: Bloodletting, Circumcision/Castration, and the 'Lancelet' or Knife of *The Merchant of Venice*," in *Alternative Shakespeares 3*, ed. Diana Henderson (London: Routledge, 2008). Though it does not mention *Cymbeline*, the chapter on "Blood" (including in *The Merchant of Venice*) in Roland Greene's *Five Words: Critical Semantics in the Age of Shakespeare and Cervantes* (Chicago: University of Chicago Press, 2013), 107–42, is also very suggestive.

21. For the above, including in Spenser, see Nohrnberg, *The Analogy of "The Faerie Queene,"* 170–1, 189–90, 195. Of the resurrectional iconography of the "redcross," Nohrnberg writes on p. 170: "Since Redcrosse specifically imitates Christ, and especially the Christ who conquers sin and death, it is not insignificant that Christ himself carries a redcross pennon, attached to a long but light cross, when he enters into death and rises from the tomb. This symbol is a commonplace of the medieval iconography of the resurrection; it was a property of the miracle play on the same subject" (Nohrnberg, 170n.183: "Cf. *Howlegas*: "At Easter they should play the resurrection of our Lord; . . . and the parson plaied Christe, with a baner in his hand." Text in John Ashton, ed., *Romances of Chivalry* [London, 1887], p. 331")." See also Willy Maley, "*Cymbeline*, the Font of History, and the Matter of Britain: From Times New Roman to Italic Type," in Henderson, ed., *Alternative Shakespeares 3*, 119–37, on the crosses of St. George and St. Andrews.

22. See, for example, Donna B. Hamilton on *Cymbeline* in *Shakespeare and the Politics of Protestant England* (Lexington, KY: University Press of Kentucky, 1986).

23. Butler, ed., *Cymbeline*, 222.

24. Revelation 19:11. See also my *Shakespeare from the Margins: Language, Culture, Context* (Chicago: University of Chicago Press, 1996), 56–82, on biblical counterfeits and simulacra in *The Comedy of Errors*, *Othello*, and other texts, including "angels" as coins.

25. See Barbara Everett, "*Much Ado About Nothing*: The Unsociable Comedy," in *English Comedy*, ed. Michael Cordner, Peter Holland, and John Kerrigan (Cambridge: Cambridge University Press, 1994), 72.

26. "Stigma" (like the "stigmata" recalled by *Cymbeline*'s "bloody cloth" in 5.1) was a "note" or sign written in the skin by a needle or sharp instrument. Importantly for *Cymbeline*, the Latin of Ovid's Philomel story (the "book" Innogen has been reading in 2.2), uses "*purpureas notas*" (purple or bloody "notes") for the tongueless Philomel's writing the story of her rape. See Lynn Enterline, *The Rhetoric of the Body from Ovid to*

Shakespeare (Cambridge: Cambridge University Press, 2000), 4–5; Charlotte Scott, *Shakespeare and the Idea of the Book* (Oxford: Oxford University Press, 2007), 47–50; Elissa Marder, "Disarticulated Vices: Feminism and Philomela," *Hypatia* 7.2 (Spring 1992): 148–66.

27. *Ovid moralisé en prose (texte du quinziéme siècle),* ed. C. de Boer, Verhandelingen de Koninklijke Nederlandse Academie, 61 (Amsterdam, 1955). As Nohrnberg notes in *The Analogy of "The Faerie Queene,"* 169–70, Spenser recalls the Pyramus and Thisbe story in 1.1.46 ("apples rosie red, / As they in pure vermillion had beene dide"), where "The image is faintly Ovidian, with Redcrosse beneath the tree having the place of Pyramus beneath the mulberry." Nohrnberg also cites John Freccero, "The Sign of Satan," *Modern Language Notes* 80.1 (1965): 11–26, on the Augustinian gloss on the mulberry of Luke 17:6 in the Vulgate as "an allusion to the cross, on account of its bloody fruit" and Dante's use of the moralized Ovidian tradition in *Purgatorio* XXXII.37ff., *Purgatorio* XXVII.39, where the pilgrim responds to the name of Beatrice like Pyramus to Thisbe's, "at the time when the mulberry became red," and *Purgatorio* XXXIII.69, where the mind of the pilgrim is "a Pyramus to the mulberry." Nohrnberg also notes that the references to spouting blood in *Julius Caesar*—"an hundred spouts, / Did run pure blood" (2.2.78); "your statue spouting blood in many pipes" (2.2.85), with "dip their napkins in his sacred blood" (3.2.133)—may (given the analogy with the "sacred blood" of Christ developed by more than one critic of that play) recall this biblical-Ovidian assimilation (see also the bloodstained napkin of *3 Henry VI*, 1.4.79, 153, 157; 2.1.62).

28. On the simultaneous recall and parody of the "Ovid Moralized" tradition of Pyramus as Christ in this play, see my "Murals and Morals: *A Midsummer Night's Dream,*" in *Editing Texts: Texte edieren,* ed. Glenn W. Most (Gottingen: Vandenhoeck & Ruprecht, 1998), 190–218.

29. See Arthur Golding's translation of Ovid's *Metamorphoses,* 4.147–48, quoted in Jonathan Bate's Arden 3, ed., *Titus Andronicus* (London: Routledge, 1995), 188 (with 182 on Pyramus's "maiden blood"). See also Bate's *Shakespeare and Ovid* (Oxford: Clarendon Press, 1993), 111–13. The tragedy of Pyramus and Thisbe is also evoked in the exchange between Jessica and Lorenzo in *The Merchant of Venice* (5.1.6–9).

30. See my "What's in a Name: and More," *SEDERI* XI (2002): 101–49.

31. For these quotations see Andrew Sofer, *The Stage Life of Props* (Ann Arbor: University of Michigan Press, 2003), 65, 75, and 82, with all of Chapter 2 ("Absorbing Interests: The Bloody Handkerchief on the Elizabethan Stage"), which does not discuss *Cymbeline* but is suggestive for it.

32. See Sujata Iyengar, "Why Ganymede Faints and the Duke of York Weeps: Passion Plays in Shakespeare," *Shakespeare Survey* 67 (2014): 265–78, esp. 274, 275n54, 276–78, from which these quotations are taken. See also the discussion of bloody cloths in Ariane M. Balizet, *Blood and Home in Early Modern Drama: Domestic Identity on the Renaissance Stage* (London: Routledge, 2014), Chapter 1 ("The Bleeding Bride: Consummation and the 'Fight of Love'").

CHAPTER 14

I would like to thank Laurie Maguire for many years of friendship and collegiality; Bonnie Lander Johnson and Eleanor Decamp for extending the invitation that prompted me to write this chapter and for their engagement as it has evolved; and my fellow volume participants for provocative questions and comments, stimulating talks, and inspiring scholarship. A Fletcher Jones Foundation Distinguished Fellowship at the Huntington Library enabled me to conduct most of the research for this chapter.

1. Through the logic of resemblance that linked red wine to blood, white wine was particularly recommended to men as a remedy for "the stone" and various urinary disorders because it "provoketh urine." See William Turner, *A Book of Wines* (1568) (New York: Scholars' Facsimiles, 1941).

2. Genesis 9:4, King James version.

3. Deuteronomy 32:14; Genesis 49:11.

4. Horst Wenzel, "The Logos in the Press: Christ in the Wine-Press and the Discovery of Printing," in *Visual Culture and the German Middle Ages*, ed. Kathryn Starkey and H. Wenzel (New York: Palgrave Macmillan, 2005), 223–49, esp. 226, 227; John Variano, *Wine: A Cultural History* (London: Reaktion, 2010), 98, 100; and Russell M. Hillier, "The Wreath, the Rock and the Winepress: Passion Iconography in Milton's *Paradise Regained*," *Literature and Theology* 22.4 (2008): 387–405.

5. William Vaughan, *Directions for Health, Both Naturall and Artificiall* (London, 1617), sig. C4v; see also Tobias Whitaker, *The Tree of Humane Life, or The Blood of the Grape, proving the possibilitie of maintaining human life from infancy to extreme old age without any sicknesse by the use of wine: Republished and enlarged by the Author* (London, 1654), sig. C9v.

6. Richard Sutton, *A True Relation of the Cruelties and Barbarities of the French upon the English Prisoners of War* (London, 1690), sigs. B3v, C1v.

7. Alan C. Dessen and Leslie Thompson, *A Dictionary of Stage Directions in English Drama, 1580–1642* (Cambridge: Cambridge University Press, 1999), 251–52.

8. See, for example, Wendy Wall, *Staging Domesticity: Household Work and English Identity in Early Modern Drama* (Cambridge: Cambridge University Press, 2002), esp. 189–220, as well as the Lander Johnson, Decamp, and Zuccolin and King chapters in this volume.

9. Richard Bradley, *New Improvements of Planting and Gardening* (London, 1726): "the Sap of Plants and Trees Circulate after the Same manner as the Fluids do in Animal Bodies" (11). On blood and sap, see also Jean Feerick, "Botanical Shakespeares: The Racial Logic of Plant Life in *Titus Andronicus*," *South Central Review* 26.1&2 (2009): 82–102, esp. 98; Eve Keller, "'That Sublimest Juyce in Our Body': Bloodletting and Ideas of the Individual in Early Modern England," *Philological Quarterly* 86.1–2 (2007): 97–122; and Margaret Healy's chapter in this volume.

10. William Harvey, "The Second Anatomical Essay to Jean Riolan," in *The Circulation of the Blood: Two Anatomical Essays by William Harvey*, ed. and trans. Kenneth J. Franklin (Oxford: Blackwell Scientific Publications, 1958), 38–39.

11. Gail Kern Paster, *The Body Embarrassed: Drama and the Disciplines of Shame in Early Modern England* (Ithaca: Cornell University Press, 1993), 73 (where she discusses the Harvey passage cited above), 87.

12. [S. J.], T*he Vineyard: Being a Treatise Shewing The Nature and Method of Planting, Manuring, Cultivating, and Dressing of Vines in Foreign-Parts* (London, 1727), sig. C5v). Sir Hugh Plat advises that if you prune vines "when the sap is up," you should cover the cut with turpentine to "stay bleeding" (*Floraes Paradise* [London, 1608], sig. L3r). Worlidge extends this advice to include the idea that trees from which sap has been extracted will not yield fruit: "you must expect no Fruit from the Tree out of which you thus extract its Blood" (J. Worlidge, *Vinetum Britannicum: Or a Treatise of Cider, And other Wines and Drinks extracted from Fruits Growing in this Kingdom* [London, 1691], sig. C2r).

13. Patricia Crawford, "Attitudes toward Menstruation in Seventeenth-Century England," *Past and Present* 91.1 (1981): 47–73, esp. 59.

14. Plat, *Floraes Paradise*, sig. L3r; *The Jewel House of Art and Nature* (London, 1653), sig. V2.

15. Ralph Austen, *A Treatise of Fruit-Trees* (Oxford, 1653), sig. H4v.

16. John Evelyn, *A Philosophical Discourse of Earth* (London, 1676), sig. H7v.

17. Tobias Whitaker, *Tree of Humane Life, or the Blood of the Grape*, sigs. C1v, C2v, B3r, E6v. Whitaker may well mean beasts rather than breasts since he has been discussing the inferiority of milk (human or animal) to wine.

18. William Shakespeare, *Henry IV Part 2* (4.2.105–109) in *The Norton Shakespeare, Based on the Oxford Edition*, eds. Stephen Greenblatt et al. (New York: W. W. Norton, 1997). Subsequent Shakespeare citations refer to this edition. See also Barbara Sebek, "'More natural to the nation': Situating Shakespeare in the 'Querelle de Canary'," *Shakespeare Studies* 42 (2014): 106–21.

19. Worlidge, *Vinetum Britannicum*, sigs. D3r–v. On the medical uses of wine, see Louise Hill Curth and Tanya M. Cassidy, "'Health, Strength and Happiness': Medical Constructions of Wine and Beer in Early Modern England," in *A Pleasing Sinne: Drink and Conviviality in Seventeenth-Century England*, ed. Adam Smyth (Cambridge: D. S. Brewer, 2004), 143–59. Using wine as a solvent is an ancient tradition. See Patrick E. McGovern, *Uncorking the Past: The Quest for Wine, Beer, and Other Alcoholic Beverages* (Berkeley: University of California Press, 2009), 267.

20. [S. J.], *The Vineyard*, sig. I3v.

21. Plat, *The Jewel House of Art and Nature*, sigs. I3v–I4r. For other extensive lists, see *A True Discovery of the Projectors of the Wine Project, out of the Vintners owne orders made at their Common hall* (London, 1641), 27–28; and Walter Charleton, "The Mysterie of Vintners," in *Two Discourses* (London, 1675).

22. Gervase Markham, *The English Housewife*, ed. Michael R. Best (Kingston and Montreal: McGill-Queen's University Press, 1986), xxv.

23. Plat, *Jewel House*, sigs. I3v–I4r. Elsewhere, Plat accuses coopers of "sleights, sophistications, and parellings" and directs readers to his unpublished manuscript, *Secreta Dei pampinei* (*Floraes Paradise*, sigs. E6v–E7r).

24. John Evelyn, *Sylva, Or a Discourse of Forest-Trees . . . To which is annexed Pomona* (London, 1679), sig. Xx4r.

25. *In Vino Veritas: Or, A Conference Betwixt Chip the Cooper, and Dash the Drawer, (Being both Boozy) Discovering some Secrets in the Wine-brewing Trade* (London, 1698), 21–22.

26. Plat, *Jewel House*, sigs. I3v–I4r. On the status of blood within early modern alchemy, see Tara Nummedal's chapter in this volume.

27. *In Vino Veritas*, 16, 24.

28. *As You Like It* (Epilogue, line 3).

29. Mary Floyd-Wilson, *English Ethnicity and Race in Early Modern Drama* (Cambridge: Cambridge University Press, 2003). See also Jean E. Feerick, *Strangers in Blood: Relocating Race in the Renaissance* (Toronto: University of Toronto Press, 2010); Hillary Eklund, *Literature and Moral Economy in the Early Modern Atlantic: Elegant Sufficiencies* (Burlington, VT: Ashgate, 2015); and Gitanjali Shahani, "The Spicèd Indian Air in Early Modern England," *Shakespeare Studies* (2014): 122–37, esp. 125–26.

30. Sir Thomas Browne, *Religio Medici* (ca. 1635), in *Religio Medici, Hydriotaphia*, and *The Garden of Cyrus*, ed. R. H. A. Robbins (Oxford University Press, 1972), Second Part, section 1, 63.

31. Charles Estienne and John Liebaut, *Maison Rustique or the Country Farme*, trans. Richard Surflet (London, 1606), sig. Fff2r.

32. William Hughes, *The Compleat Vineyard: Or A most excellent Way for the Planting of Vines: Not onely according to the German and French way, but also long experimented in England* (London, 1665), sig. A3r.

33. [D. S.], *Vinetum Angliae: Or, A new and easy Way to make Wine of English Grapes and other Fruit, equal to that of France, Spain, &c with their Physical Virtues* (London, 1700), 2.

34. On the nationalism of such arguments, see Vittoria di Palma, "Drinking Cider in Paradise: Science, Improvement, and the Politics of Fruit Trees," in *A Pleasing Sinne: Drink and Conviviality in Seventeenth-Century England*, ed. Adam Smyth (Cambridge: D. S. Brewer, 2004), 161–77.

35. Worlidge, *Vinetum Britannicum*.

36. [Samuel Hartlib], *A Designe for Plentie, By an Universall Planting of Fruit-Trees* (London, n.d. [1652?]), sigs. B4r–v; see also *Vinetum Angliae*, 2.

37. William Camden, *Britain, or A Chorographicall Description of the Most flourishing Kingdomes, England, Scotland, and Ireland*, trans. Philemon Holland (London, 1637), sig. Z2r. See also Conrad Heresbach, *Foure Bookes of Husbandry*, Newly Englished, and encreased, by Barnaby Googe (London, 1601), sig. A3v.

38. Camden, *Britain*, sigs. Gg3r–v.

39. John Parkinson, *Paradisi in Sole Paradisus Terrestris. A Garden of all sorts of pleasant flowers which our English ayre will permitt to be noursed up* (London, 1629), sig. Zz6v.

40. Parkinson, *Paradisi in Sole Paradisus Terrestris*, sigs. Zz6v-Aaa1r.

41. Sir Hugh Plat, *The Second Part of the Garden of Eden* (London, 1660), sigs. E5v–E6r. Hughes repeats Plat's formulation without attribution (*The Compleat Vineyard*, sig. A2v). Also compare William Harrison, *The Description of England* [1587], ed. Georges

Edelen (Ithaca: Cornell University Press, 1968), 435, 264; Camden, *Britain*, sigs. Gg3r–v; and *Samuel Harlib His Legacie*, sig. E3r.

42. [S. J.], *The Vineyard*, sigs. A4v, A8v.

43. Thomas Pinney, *A History of Wine in America: From the Beginnings to Prohibition* (Berkeley: University of California Press, 1989), esp. 12–29; John Bonoeil, *His Majesties Gracious Letter to the Earle of South-Hampton, . . . commanding the present setting up of Silke-works, and planting of Vines in Virginia* (London, 1622).

44. Amanda Greene, "Foods That Look Like Body Parts They're Good For" (http://www.womansday.com/health-fitness/nutrition/foods-that-look-like-body-parts-theyre-good-for-109151), accessed November 5, 2016.

45. Thomas Wright, *William Harvey: A Life in Circulation* (Oxford: Oxford University Press, 2013), 164–65.

46. Robert Turner, *Botanologia: The British Physician or the Nature and Vertues of English Plants* (London, 1664), sig. A5v. The book was reprinted in 1687.

47. Daniel Botkin, *The Moon in a Nautilus Shell: From Climate Change to Species Extinction, How Life Persists in an Ever-Changing World* (Oxford: Oxford University Press, 2012), 118, 115, xviii, 129, 327.

48. Roland Greene, *Five Words: Critical Semantics in the Age of Shakespeare and Cervantes* (Chicago: University of Chicago Press, 2013).

CHAPTER 15

1. Some examples of this scene from the twelfth and thirteenth centuries include: British Library Arundel 157, fol. 18v (St. Albans, ca. 1240); British Library Lansdowne 383, fol. 8 (England, 2nd quarter 12th c.); British Library Royal 2 B II, fol. 6v (Paris, ca. 1250); British Library Royal 1 D X, fol. 14r (Oxford, before 1220); BNF Latin 12834, fol. 84 (France, ca.1266–1279); The Hague KB 76 J 18, fol. 215r (Cambray, ca. 1275–1300); St. John's College N19, fol. 5v (Flanders, 13th c.); The Walters Ms. W. 35, fol. 6v (Bruges-Ghent, ca. 1270–1280); The Walters Ms. W. 36, fol. 6v (Bruges, ca. 1250–1260). British Library Lansdowne 381, fol. 7 (Germany, ca. 1168–1189) appears to be an exception to the rule of living pigs as it shows a man standing over a pig with its mouth open lying on a table. The man is holding some kind of instrument to the pig's neck, perhaps to bleed it, yet there is no blood shown in the image.

2. For a full discussion of how to read a medieval calendar page, see "Appendix: The Calendar Page Decoded," in Bridget Ann Henisch, *The Medieval Calendar Year* (University Park: Pennsylvania State University Press, 1999).

3. The calendar cycle is common in medieval church architectural and furniture decoration as well as in manuscripts, but those other contexts will not be discussed in this chapter.

4. Colum Hourihane, ed., *Time in the Medieval World: Occupations of the Months and Signs of the Zodiac in the Index of Christian Art* (Princeton, NJ: Princeton University Press, 2007), l.

5. Representative images are collected in Hourihane, *Time in the Medieval World*.

6. The other common image for December is baking bread. It may be that the blood of the swine is related to the bread as the body and blood of Christ, but I have not explored this connection within the scope of this chapter.

7. *The Good Wife's Guide (Le Ménagier de Paris)*, trans. Gina L. Greco and Christine M. Rose (Ithaca, NY: Cornell University Press, 2009), 271–72.

8. Helmut Birkhan remarked on the great frequency of all types of blood as ingredients in the Ambras recipe collection from the fifteenth century: "Some Remarks on Medieval Cooking: The Ambras Recipe-Collection of Cod. Vind. 5486," in Melitta Weiss Adamson, ed., *Food in the Middle Ages: A Book of Essays* (Routledge, 1995), 83–98. According to Maria Dembinska, blood sausage was introduced into medieval Poland before the year 1000 from German-speaking areas: Maria Dembinska, *Food and Drink in Medieval Poland: Rediscovering a Cuisine of the Past*, rev. William Woys Weaver, trans. Magdalena Thomas (University of Pennsylvania Press, 1999), 89. The Spanish *Manual de mugeres* (1475–1525) includes instructions "to season a big blood sausage very well" using clove, cinnamon, and black pepper: Carolyn A. Nadeau, "Contributions of Medieval Food Manuals to Spain's Culinary Heritage," *Cincinnati Romance Review* 33 (2012): 74.

9. See Dolly Jørgensen, "Running Amuck? Urban Swine Management in Late Medieval England," *Agricultural History* 87 (2013): 429–51, for a discussion of swine management in the late medieval period. For general discussions of the control of butchery, see Ernest L. Sabine, "Butchering in Mediaeval London," *Speculum* 8:3 (1933): 335–53 and David R. Carr, "Controlling the Butchers in Late Medieval English Towns," *The Historian* 70 (2008): 450–61.

10. Mary Dormer Harris, ed., *The Coventry Leet Book: or Mayor's Register, Containing the Records of the City Court Leet or View of Frankpledge, AD 1420–1555, with Divers Other Matters*, 4 vols. (London: Kegan Paul, Trench, Trübner, 1907–1913), 1:42–43.

11. R. Lespinasse, ed., *Les Métiers et corporations de la ville de Paris I: XIVe–XVIIIe siècle, ordonnances générale, metiers de l'alimentation* (Paris: Imprimerie Nationale, 1886), 274, quoted in Carole Rawcliffe, "Sources for the Study of Public Health in the Medieval City," in *Understanding Medieval Primary Sources: Using Historical Sources to Discover Medieval Europe*, ed. Joel T. Rosenthal (London: Routledge, 2012), 177–95.

12. R. B. Dobson, ed., *York City Chamberlains' Account Rolls 1396–1500*, Surtees Society Publication 192 (Surtees Society: Gateshead, UK, 1980), 145–46.

13. Harris, *Coventry Leet Book*, 1:42–43.

14. Guy Geltner, "Healthscaping a Medieval City: Lucca's *Curia viarum* and the Future of Public Health History," *Urban History* 40:3 (2013): 395–415.

15. Harris, *Coventry Leet Book*, 1:32. The location is given in two land leases, BA/C/4/3/1, Dec. 1, 1448 and BA/C/4/3/2, Dec. 25, 1465, Coventry Town Archives, Coventry, UK. The second lease allowed the butchers access to draw water for the scalding house. Helena M. Chew and William Kellaway, eds., misc. roll. FF, Feb. 16, 1369–May 5, 1374 (nos. 550–99), *London Assize of Nuisance 1301–1431: A Calendar*, "British History Online," http://www.british-history.ac.uk/report.aspx?compid=35981, accessed February 14, 2013.

16. Pierpont Morgan Library, MS M.358, fol. 12r. The manuscript is a Book of Hours made in southern France ca. 1440–1450.

17. The growing interest in naturalized artistic depictions in the later medieval period has been discussed in Lynn White Jr., "Natural Science and Naturalistic Art in the Middle Ages," *American Historical Review* 52 (1947): 421–35 and Janet Backhouse, "Birds, Beasts and Initials in Lindisfarne's Gospel Books," in *St Cuthbert, His Cult and His Community to AD 1200*, ed. Gerald Bonner, David Rollason, and Clare Stancliffe (Woodbridge, Suffolk: Boydell Press, 1989), 165–74.

18. Otto Pächt, "Early Italian Nature Studies and the Early Calendar Landscape," *Journal of the Warburg and Courtauld Institutes* 13:1/2 (1950): 13–47.

19. Caroline Walker Bynum, *Wonderful Blood: Theology and Practice in Late Medieval Germany and Beyond* (Philadelphia: University of Pennsylvania Press, 2007), 210.

20. Noëlie Vialles, *Animal to Edible*, trans. J. A. Underwood (Cambridge: Cambridge University Press, 1994), 76.

21. This is not to say that pork was restricted to Christians historically in Europe. Both soldiers and common people received pork rations in the later Roman Empire, according to Sarah Bond, *Trade and Taboo: Disreputable Professions in the Roman Mediterranean* (Ann Arbor: University of Michigan Press, 2016).

22. See the image of the Judensau and discussion in Sarah Phillips, "The Pig in Medieval Iconography," in *Pigs and Humans: 10,000 Years of Interaction*, ed. Umberto Albarella, Keith Dobney, Anton Ervynck, and Peter Rowley-Conwy (Oxford: Oxford University Press, 2007), 373–87.

23. Claudine Fabre-Vassas, *The Singular Beast: Jews, Christians, and the Pig*, trans. Carol Volk (New York: Columbia University Press, 1997), 298.

24. Phillips, "The Pig in Medieval Iconography."

25. Fabre-Vassas, *The Singular Beast*, 325. There are similar paradoxes of blood being both sacred and unholy in Helen Barr's discussion of *The Canterbury Interlude* in this volume.

26. Henisch, *The Medieval Calendar Year*, 16; Hourihane, *Time in the Medieval World*, l.

27. Michael Camille, *Mirror in Parchment: The Luttrell Psalter and the Making of Medieval England* (Chicago: University of Chicago Press, 1998), 162–63.

28. Camille, *Mirror in Parchment*, 200.

29. Leah Sinanoglou, "Christ Child as Sacrifice: A Medieval Tradition and the Corpus Christi Plays," *Speculum* 48.3 (1973): 491–509.

30. Susan Boynton, "Performative Exegesis in the Fleury *Interfectio Puerorum*," *Viator* 29 (1998): 39–64.

31. See Boynton, "Performative Exegesis," and Theresa Tinkle, "Exegesis Reconsidered: The Fleury 'Slaughter of Innocents' and the Myth of Ritual Murder," *Journal of English and Germanic Philology* 102.2 (2003): 211–43.

32. Tinkle, "Exegesis Reconsidered."

33. This is exemplified in the image of a Florentine engraving from circa 1490 reproduced in Fabre-Vassas, *The Singular Beast*, figure 12A.

34. The story of "The Three Clerks" does not appear in the lives of St. Nicholas, but it became the most widely circulated story about him. For a full discussion of the legend, see Joel Fredell, "The Three Clerks and St. Nicholas in Medieval England," *Studies in Philology* 92 (1995): 181–202.

35. Karl Steele, *How to Make a Human: Animals and Violence in the Middle Ages* (Columbus: Ohio State University Press, 2011), 214.

36. Quoted in Caroline Walker Bynum, "Violent Imagery in Late Medieval Piety," *GHI Bulletin* 30 (2002): 25.

37. Steele, *How to Make a Human*, 185.

38. Bynum, "Violent Imagery in Late Medieval Piety". For a full discussion of the blood of Christ in late medieval religious belief, see Bynum, *Wonderful Blood*.

39. Bettina Bildhauer, "Medieval European Conceptions of Blood: Truth and Human Integrity," *Journal of the Royal Anthropological Institute* 19 (2013): S57–S76.

40. Bynum, *Wonderful Blood*, 5.

41. See Bynum, "Violent Imagery in Late Medieval Piety," esp. 30–31.

42. Bynum, *Wonderful Blood*, 255.

43. This is much the same as Joe Moshenska's observation in this volume about the screaming bleeding trees of Virgil and Spenser: it is through violence that we are able to hear the object speaking.

44. Fabre-Vassas, *The Singular Beast*; Michael Camille, "At the Sign of the 'Spinning Sow': the 'Other' Chartres and Images of Everyday Life of the Medieval Street," in *History and Images: Towards a New Iconology*, ed. Axel Bolvig and Phillip Lindley (Turnhout, Belgium: Brepols, 2003), 249–76; Phillips, "The Pig in Medieval Iconography."

45. As Frances Dolan demonstrates in her chapter in this volume, the agricultural practices of grape growing and winemaking also took on symbolic meaning when they were associated with blood.

CHAPTER 16

This chapter is indebted to the extensive discussions of medieval blood by Caroline Walker Bynum, *Wonderful Blood: Theology and Practice in Late Medieval Northern Germany and Beyond* (Philadelphia: University of Pennsylvania Press, 2007), and Bettina Bildhauer, *Medieval Blood* (Cardiff: University of Wales Press, 2006). References to specific points of contact will be noted in situ.

1. This work is also known as *The Prologue to the Tale of Beryn* and was edited for the Early English Text Society under the title *The Tale of Beryn with a Prologue of the merry Adventure of the pardoner with a Tapster at Canterbury* by F. J. Furnivall and W. G. Stone (EETS OS 1901). For ease of reference I quote from the more recent edition by John Bowers, ed., *The Canterbury Tales: Fifteenth-Century Continuations and Additions* (Kalamazoo, MI: Medieval Institute Publications, 1992), in which Bowers calls the Prologue *The*

Canterbury Interlude. Although not included in early printed versions of Chaucer's works, *The Interlude* and *Beryn* were printed in John Urry's posthumous *The Works of Geoffrey Chaucer, Compared with the Former Editions, and Many Valuable MSS. Out of which, Three Tales are Added which were Never Before Printed* (London, 1721). Thomas Wright included a version of Urry's text in his *The Canterbury Tales of Geoffrey Chaucer: A New Text with Illustrative Notes in Early English Poetry, Ballads and Popular Literature of the Middle Ages* (London: Percy Society, 1847 and 1857, vols. 24, 26). But W. W. Skeat excluded *Beryn* from his Chaucer canon, *The Chaucer Canon, with a Discussion of the Works Associated with the Name of Geoffrey Chaucer* (Oxford: Clarendon Press, 1900), 143.

2. A pardoner was a person licensed by the church to sell pardons to contrite sinners as a part of making satisfaction, making amends for sin. The pardon was intended as an act of penance and offered no guarantees about the eventual state of one's soul.

3. Discussion of Chaucer's Pardoner is extensive. Most relevant to the concerns of this chapter are Carolyn Dinshaw, *Chaucer's Sexual Poetics* (Madison: University of Wisconsin Press, 1989), 157–84, and Robert S. Sturges, *Chaucer's Pardoner and Gender Theory: Bodies of Discourse* (London: Macmillan, 2000), 36–70.

4. Cambridge University Library MS Gg.4. 27, fol.290r. The illustration is reproduced in *Poetical Works: A Facsimile of Cambridge University Library MS Gg. 4.27*, ed. M. B. Parkes and Richard Beadle (Cambridge: D. S. Brewer, 1980).

5. Cain's murder of Abel is told in Genesis 4:10. Bettina Bildhauer discusses how the spilling of Cain's blood was seen as original sin from which all evil started; blood flowing to the ground seen as a deflowering of the earth and the violation of a prohibition against murder, *Medieval Blood*, 66.

6. Walker Bynum, *Wonderful Blood*, 244–58.

7. David M. Halperin argues that "queer" does not designate a class of already objectified pathologies or perversions; rather it describes a horizon of possibility whose precise extent and heterogeneous scope cannot in principle be delimited in advance. *Saint Foucault: Towards a Gay Hagiography* (New York; Oxford: Oxford University Press, 1995), 62.

8. For the blood and flying mitre, see the miniature in an English psalter ca. 1250, Walters Art Gallery, Baltimore: http://www.answers.com/topic/thomas-becket#ixzz390N8apgY, accessed August 8, 2014. For dubbing ceremonies, the illustration in British Library MS Harley 5312 fol. 28v shows a knight raising his sword behind Becket's shoulders as he kneels at the altar. See also British Library MS Harley 5102 fol. 32 showing a knight pointing his sword high upon Becket's brow.

9. J. C. Robertson and J. B. Shepherd, eds., *Materials for the History of Thomas Becket, Archbishop of Canterbury* (London: Rolls Series, 1875–1885), 3, 151–52.

10. *Materials for the History of Thomas Becket*, 2.438.

11. *Materials for the History of Thomas Becket*, 2.15.

12. Michael Swanton, ed., *The Lives of Thomas Becket* (Manchester: Manchester University Press, 2001), 203.

13. E. A. Abbott, *St Thomas of Canterbury: His Death and Miracles* (London: Adam and Charles Black, 1898), 158. William of Canterbury also dwells on the Christological significance of the blood and water, *Materials for the History of Thomas Becket*, 1.1–2.

14. The wounding of Christ with the spear in his side is told in John 19:34: "one of the soldiers with a spear opened his side, and immediately there came out blood and water." Walker Bynum discusses the medieval commentary on the purifying and redemptive blood from Longinus's wound to Christ's sides at several points in *Wonderful Blood*, 4, 13, 65, 78–79, and 165. This is a moment encapsulated in a brilliant pun in *Piers Plowman*, B.18.86: "The blood sprong doun by þe spere and vnspered þe kny3tes ei3en." Text quoted from William Langland, *Piers Plowman: A Parallel-Text Edition of the A, B, C and Z Versions*, ed. A. V. C. Schmidt (London: Longman, 1995).

15. *Materials for the History of Thomas Becket*, 2.43.

16. Paul Binski, *Becket's Crown: Art and Imagination in Gothic England 1170–1300* (New Haven: Yale University Press, 2004), 8.

17. Binski, *Becket's Crown*, 7–11. Walker Bynum notes the belief that church walls erupted in blood when sanctuary was violated, *Wonderful Blood*, 181.

18. Abbott, *St Thomas of Canterbury*, 234.

19. A selection of these miracles can be found in Abbott, *St Thomas of Canterbury*, 244–328, and in Swanton, *The Lives of Thomas Becket*, 204–10.

20. Abbott, *St Thomas of Canterbury*, 244.

21. Richard Gameson, "The Early Imagery of Thomas Becket," in *Pilgrimage: The English Experience from Becket to Bunyan*, ed. Colin Morris and Peter Roberts (Cambridge: Cambridge University Press, 2002), 49.

22. For the fruit trees see the account of Muriel of Canterbury in Abbott, *St Thomas of Canterbury*, 262; for the four-footed lizard vomited by Agnes of Canterbury, see Abbott, *St Thomas of Canterbury*, 265 (the story records that when the lizard was plunged in phlegm and placed on an upper windowsill, it disappeared); and for the worm spewed by Henry, son of a knight in Essex, see Abbott, *St Thomas of Canterbury*, 274.

23. Anne J. Duggan notes: "the pilgrim demand for tangible tokens of their pilgrimage created a veritable industry for the manufacture of ampullae, badges and small figurines," in *Thomas Becket,* Reputations (London: Arnold, 2004), 234. Sarah Blick discusses how badges that reproduced the ampullae were thought to ensure the wearer's safe return home, "Reconstructing the Shrine of Thomas Becket in Canterbury Cathedral," in *The Art and Architecture of the Late Medieval Pilgrimage in Northern Europe and the British Isles*, ed. Sarah Blick and Rita Tekippe (Leiden: Brill, 2005), 405–41, 453.

24. For discussion and illustration see Madeleine Harrison Caviness, *The Windows of Christ Church Cathedral Canterbury* (London: Oxford University Press, 1981): Kellet, 201–2; Plate XV, figs. 325–30; Valognes, 187–88; figs. 272–2a; Sunieve, 194–95, 197; figs. 295–300a; Etheldreda, 184–85; figs. 267–70; Jervaux, 191–92; figs. 286–87. Color photographs are available in M. A. Michael and Sebastian Strobl, *Stained Glass of Canterbury Cathedral* (London: Scala, 2004), 118–19, 130–31, 144–47, 116–17, 138–39.

25. For the staff as a detachable phallus invested with sodomitical association see Robert S. Sturges, "The Pardoner in Canterbury: Class, Gender and Urban Space in *The Prologue to the Tale of Beryn*," *College Literature* 33 (2006): 52–76 (68–69).

26. In *Piers Plowman*, Christ rides into Jerusalem barefoot, without spurs or a spear, as a "knyȝt þat comeþ to be dubbed." The wounds that Christ will acquire from the nail driven into his feet are likened to gilt spurs on slashed overshoes, B.18.11–14.

27. The edge of the pan cuts Jak's vein and sinews in two. While Becket's blood heals the leg wounds of William of Kellet and Roger of Valognes, eight days later, Jak's injury gets worse; the bone has become so badly infected that the Hosteller has more pain than when the wound was fresh (lines 587–90).

28. The thigh could also be understood as a figurative reference to the genitals; see MED "thigh" (n)., 1d.

29. For examples, see Douglas Gray, ed., *A Selection of Religious Lyrics* (Oxford: Clarendon Press, 1975), 45/8, 23/29, 30/15–18, and 28/17–18.

30. *The Riverside Chaucer*, ed. Larry D. Benson et al. (Oxford: Oxford University Press, 2008), 3rd rev. ed.

31. James F. Rhodes, "The Pardoner's Vernicle and His Vera Icon," *Modern Language Studies* 13 (1983): 34–40.

32. Ellesmere, Huntingdon MS EL 26 C 9, fol. 138r. A digitized copy of Ellesmere is available at http://hdl.huntington.org/cdm/ref/collection/p15150coll7/id/2838

Sturges discusses the Pardoner's vernicle as a simulacrum that threatens the difference between the true and the false, the real and the imaginary, in *Bodies of Discourse*, 70. He argues that it is all the more disturbing that the Pardoner's vernicle sports the face of Christ as a young man in a woman's garment because Jesus in drag suggests that the Logos itself, like the phallus, is only a masquerade (80).

33. The isolation of the Pardoner contrasts strongly with the populated scenes of the healing miracles in written narratives and in the stained glass windows.

34. Walker Bynum discusses the contrast between Christ's present, living blood from a fresh wound and the coagulated blood of unrepentant sinners that is dead, *Wonderful Blood*, 166–69.

35. Bildhauer discusses how blood produces not only the domain of intelligible bodies but also a domain of unthinkable, abject, unliveable bodies, *Medieval Blood*, 8–10.

36. In the 1980s *The Sun* newspaper quoted the Rev. Robert Stimpson as saying "I would ban all practising homosexuals who are most in danger of catching AIDS from taking normal communion," cited in Simon Whatney, *Policing Desire: Pornography, AIDS and the Media* (London: Cassell, 1997), 3rd ed., 94.

37. Walker Bynum analyzes how blood created filiation and community, *Wonderful Blood*, 72, 157 and establishes boundaries by accusing dissidents and outsiders, 249.

38. I argue this more fully in my *Transporting Chaucer* (Manchester: Manchester University Press, 2014), 34–44.

39. *Materials for the History of Becket,* 3.151. In light of this practice, it is intriguing that a central episode of *The Interlude* describes "lewd sottes" (including the Pardoner) trying, and failing, to read the significance of a stained glass window. There is no monk to help them (ll.147–58), though a monk does teach them about the names and significance of holy relics, line 167.

40. In her reading of mystical responses to the wounds in Christ's body, Karma Lochrie argues that queer reading seeks out those dissonances, gaps, and excesses of meaning that signal heteronormative protocols of representation and that enable a disruption of those same protocols, "Mystical Acts, Queer Tendencies," in *Constructing Medieval Sexuality*, ed. Karma Lochrie, Peggy McCracken, and James A. Schultz (Minneapolis: University of Minnesota Press, 1997), 180–200, 180.

Bibliography

PRIMARY: MANUSCRIPTS

Archives of the Worshipful Company of Barbers. *An Act Concerning Barbers and Surgeons to be of One Company* (1540). 32 HENRY VIII, A/6/1.
Archives of the Worshipful Company of Barbers. *Court Minutes*. B/1/2, B/1/3.
British Library. MS Harley 5312 fol. 28v.
British Library. MS Harley 5102 fol. 32.
Cambridge University Library. "The Canterbury Tales." MS Gg.4. 27.
Cambridge University Library. MS Add. 2830.
Digby. *Conversion of St. Paul*. Bodleian MS Digby 133.
Digby. *Mary Magdalene*. Bodleian MS Digby 133.
Huntingdon. "The Ellesmere Manuscript." MS EL 26 C 9.
Lincoln. Cathedral Chapter Library. MS 88: A.3.15.
Pierpont Morgan Library. 15th Century Book of Hours. MS M.358.
Zieglerin, Anna Maria. "die Edele und Tewere Kunst Alchamia belagende." Niedersächsisches Landesarchiv Wolfenbüttel. Acta Publica des Herzogs Julius. 1 Alt 9, Nr. 306.
Zieglerin, Anna Maria. "Gütliche Aussage des Philipp Sömmering." Niedersächsisches Landesarchiv Wolfenbüttel. 1 Alt 9, Nr. 308.
Zieglerin, Anna Maria. "Verhör der Anna Maria Ziegler." Niedersächsisches Landesarchiv Wolfenbüttel. 1 Alt 9, Nr. 314.

PRIMARY: PRINTED TEXTS

A[gga], E[dward], trans. *The Politicke and Militarie Discourses of the Lord de La Noue*. London, 1587.
Albert the Great. *De Animalibus*. Edited by Hermann Stadler. Munich: Aschendorffsche Verlagsbuchhandlung, 1916.
Alighieri, Dante. *La Divina Commedia*. Edited by Anna Maria Chiavacci Leonardi. 3 vols. Milan: Mondadori, 1991–1997.

Alighieri, Dante. *Inferno*. Edited by John D. Sinclair. Oxford: Oxford University Press, 1939.
Anglicus, Bartholomaeus. *De proprietatibus rerum: texte latin et réception vernaculaire*. Edited by Baudouin van den Abeele and Heinz Meyer. Turnhout: Brepols, 2005.
Anglicus, Gilbertus. *Compendium medicine*, liber III, De fluxus sanguinis a naribus. Lyon, 1510.
Anon. *Age Renewed by Wedlock*. London, 1693.
Anon. *The Bloody Husband, and Cruell Neighbour*. London, 1653.
Anon. "The Catalogue of Contented Cuckolds." London, 1662–1692.
Anon. *De disciplina scolarium*. Edited by Olga Weijers. Leiden: Brill, 1976.
Anon. *Five Philosophical Questions Most Eloquently and Substantially Disputed*. London, 1650.
Anon. *In Vino Veritas: Or, A Conference Betwixt Chip the Cooper, and Dash the Drawer, (Being both Boozy) Discovering some Secrets in the Wine-brewing Trade*. London, 1698.
Anon. "The Northern Ladd: or, The Fair Maids Choice." [London], 1670–1696.
Anon. *Opera Nuova Intitolata Difficio di Ricette*. Venice: 1574.
Anon. *The Problemes of Aristotle with other Philosophers and Phisitions*. London, 1595.
Anon. *Sundrye Strange and Inhumaine Murthers, Lately Committed*. London, 1591.
Anon. *A True Report of the Late Horrible Murther Committed by William Sherwood*. London, 1581.
Anon. *A Warning to Fair Women*. 1599.
Arculanus, Johannes. *Practica*. Venice: Bonetus Locatellus, 1497.
Ariosto, Ludovico. *Orlando Furioso secondo la princeps del 1516: Edizione Critica*. Edited by Marco Dorigatti with Gerarda Stimato. Florence: Olschki, 2006.
Arnold of Villanova. *Opera Omnia, cum Nicolai Taurelli Medici et philosophi in quosdam libros annotationibus*. Basil, 1585.
Aubrey, John. *Brief Lives*. Edited by A. Clark. Oxford, 1898.
Austen, Ralph. *A Treatise of Fruit-Trees*. Oxford, 1653.
Avicenna. *The Canon of Medicine of Avicenna*. Translated by O. Cameron Gruner. New York: AMS, 1929.
Bacon, Francis. *Sylua Syluarum: or A Naturall Historie*. London, 1627.
Barnes, Barnabe. *The Divils Charter*. London, 1607.
Barnes, Jonathan. *The Complete Works of Aristotle*. The Revised Oxford Translation. Vol. 1. Princeton: Princeton University Press, 1984.
Bartholin, Thomas. *Anatomia Reformata*. 1655.
Bartholin, Thomas. *Historiarum Anatomicarum Rariorum*. 1657.
Beaumont, Francis. *The Knight of the Burning Pestle*. Edited by Michael Hattaway. 2nd ed. London: A&C Black; New York: W. W. Norton, 2002.
Beaumont, Francis, and John Fletcher. *Philaster, or, Love Lies A-Bleeding*. Edited by Suzanne Gossett. Arden Early Modern Drama: London: A&C Black, 2009.
Benson, Larry D. et al., eds. *The Riverside Chaucer*. 3rd rev. ed. Oxford: Oxford University Press, 2008.

Berchorius, Petrus. *Dictionarii seu Repertorii moralis*. 2 vols. Venice: Hieronymus Scotus, 1574.
Boccaccio, Giovanni. *Il Filocolo*. Edited by Salvatore Battaglia. Bari: G. Laterza, 1938.
Bonoeil, John. *His Majesties Gracious Letter to the Earle of South-Hampton, . . . commanding the present setting up of Silke-works, and planting of Vines in Virginia*. London, 1622.
Bowers, John, ed. *The Canterbury Tales: Fifteenth-Century Continuations and Additions*. Kalamazoo, MI: Medieval Institute Publications, 1992.
Bradley, Richard. *New Improvements of Planting and Gardening*. London, 1726.
Brain, P., trans. *Galen on Bloodletting: A Study of the Origins, Development and Validity of His Opinions*. Cambridge: Cambridge University Press, 1986.
Bramhall, John. *A Defence of True Liberty from Antecedent and Extrinsecall Necessity*. Edited by G. A. J. Rogers. London: Routledge, 1996.
Bredero, G. A. *Spaanschen Brabander*. Edited by F. A. Stoett. Zutphen: Thieme, 1978.
Brome, Alexander. *Poems*. Edited by Roman R. Dubinski. 2 vols. Toronto: University of Toronto Press, 1982.
Brome, Richard. *The Sparagus Garden*. London, 1640.
Browne, (Sir) Thomas. *Religio Medici* (ca. 1635). In *Religio Medici, Hydriotaphia*, and *The Garden of Cyrus*. Edited by R. H. A. Robbins. Oxford University Press, 1972.
B[ulwer], J[ohn]. *Anthropometamorphosis*. London, 1653.
C., L. W. *The English Farrier, Or Country-mans Treasure*. London, 1639.
Camden, William. *Britain, or A Chorographicall Description of the Most flourishing Kingdomes, England, Scotland, and Ireland*. Translated by Philemon Holland. London, 1637.
Cantimpratensis, Thomas. *Liber de natura rerum*. Berlin: De Gruyter, 1973.
Celsus, Aulus Cornelius. *On Medicine*. Translated by W. G. Spencer. Loeb Classical Library. Cambridge, MA, 1938.
Charleton, Walter. *Physiologia Epicuro-Gassendo-Charltoniana, or, A Fabrick of Science Natural, upon the Hypothesis of Atoms founded by Epicurus*. London, 1654.
Charleton, Walter. *Two Discourses*. London, 1675.
Clowes, William. *A Prooved Practise for all Young Chirurgians*. 1588.
Coeffeteau, Nicolas. *Table of Humane Passions with Their Causes and Effects*. Translated by Edw. Grimeston. London, 1621.
Cook, Edward Dutton. *Nights at the Play: A View of the English Stage*. London, 1883.
Corbin, Peter, and Douglass Sedge, eds. *Three Jacobean Witchcraft Plays*. Manchester: Manchester University Press, 1986.
Crooke, Helkiah. *Mikrokosmographia: A Description of the Body of Man*. London: 1615.
Culpepper, Nicholas. *Directory for Midwives: The Second Part*. London, 1671.
Dalton, Michael. *The Countrey Justice*. London, 1618.
Davenant, William. *The Cruell Brother*. London, 1630.
Davis, Norman, ed. *Paston Letters and Papers of the Fifteenth Century*. 2 vols. Oxford: Clarendon Press, 1971–1975.
De Robertis, Domenico, ed. *Dante Alighieri: Rime*. 3 vols. Florence: Le Lettere, 2002.
Defoe, Daniel. *The Complete English Tradesman*. London, 1732.

Dekker, Thomas. *The Guls Horne-Booke*. London, 1609.
Derrida, Jacques. *Dissemination*. Translated by Barbara Johnson. London: Bloomsbury, 2016.
Digges, Thomas. *Stratioticus*. London, 1590.
Donne, John. *The Complete Poems of John Donne*. Edited by Robin Robbins. Harlow: Pearson Education, 2010.
Donne, John. *John Donne*. Edited by John Carey. The Oxford Authors. Oxford: Oxford University Press, 1990.
Eden, Richard. *A treatyse of the newe India with other new founde landes and islandes, as well eastwarde as westwarde, as they are knowen and found in these oure dayes, after the description of Sebastian Munster in his boke of universall cosmographie*. London, 1553.
Eliot, George. *Felix Holt, the Radical*. Edited by Fred C. Thomson. Oxford: Clarendon Press, 1980.
Elyot, Sir Thomas. *The Castel of Helth*. London, 1534.
Estienne Charles, and John Liebaut. *Maison Rustique or the Country Farme*. Translated by Richard Surflet. London, 1606.
Evelyn, John. *A Philosophical Discourse of Earth*. London, 1676.
Evelyn, John. *Sylva, Or a Discourse of Forest-Trees . . . To which is annexed Pomona*. London, 1679.
Ferrand, Jacques. *Erotomania*. London, 1640.
Ford, John. *The Fancies, Chast and Noble*. London, 1638.
Foroliuiensis, Iacobi. *Expositio et quaestiones in primum Canonem Auicennae*. Venice: Luca Antonius Iunta, 1547.
Franklin, Kenneth J., trans. and intro. by Andrew Wear. *The Circulation of the Blood and Other Writings*. London: J. M. Dent & Sons, 1990.
Gale, Thomas. Certaine Workes of Chirurgerie. London, 1563.
Galen of Pergamon. *On Diseases and Symptoms*. Edited and translated by Ian Johnston. Cambridge: Cambridge University Press, 2006.
Galen of Pergamon. *On Venesection against Erasistratus*. Translated by P. Brain in *Galen on Bloodletting: A Study of the Origins, Development and Validity of His Opinions*. Cambridge: Cambridge University Press, 1986.
Geminus, Thomas. "A Table Instructive Whan and How a Man may Conyngly Let Bloude of the Necessary Veynes of Mans Body Very Profitable for all Chirurgeons and Barbers." London, 1546.
de Giordonio, Bernhardus. *Tractatus de conservatione vitae humanae*. Leipzig: Johannes Rhamba and Ernestus Vogelin, 1570.
Golding, Arthur. *The xv books of P. Ovidius Naso, Entytuled Metamorphosis*. London, 1567.
Gould, George M., and Walter L. Pyle. *Anomalies and Curiosities of Medicine*. Philadelphia, 1896.
Greene, Robert. *The Defence of Conny Catching*. London, 1592.
Guillaume de Conches. *Glosae in Iuvenalem*. Edited by Bradford Wilson. Textes philosophiques du Moyen Age 18. Paris: J. Vrin, 1980.

Guillemeau, Jacques. *Childbirth, or The Happy Deliverie of Women*. London, 1612.
Gyer, Nicholas. *The English Phlebotomy*. London, 1592.
Harrington, James. *The Commonwealth of Oceana and A System of Politics*. Edited by J. G. A. Pocock. Cambridge: Cambridge University Press, 1992.
Harrington, James. *The Oceana of James Harrington, and his other Works*. Edited by John Toland. London, 1670.
Harrison, William. *The Description of England* [1587]. Edited by Georges Edelen. Ithaca, NY: Cornell University Press, 1968.
[Hartlib, Samuel]. *A Designe for Plentie, By an Universall Planting of Fruit-Trees*. London, n.d. [1652?].
Harvey, William. *De Generatione Animalium* (1651). Translated by Gweneth Whitteridge. In *Disputations Touching the Generation of* Animals. Oxford: Blackwell Scientific Publications, 1981.
Harvey, William. *The Anatomical Exercises of Doctor William Harvey . . . Concerning the Motion of the Heart and Blood*. Translated by Zachariah Wood. London, 1653.
Harvey, William. "The Second Anatomical Essay to Jean Riolan." In *The Circulation of the Blood: Two Anatomical Essays by William Harvey*, edited and translated by Kenneth J. Franklin. Oxford: Blackwell Scientific Publications, 1958.
Harvey, William. *Two Anatomical Exercitations Concerning the Circulation of the Blood, To John Riolan*. London: Francis Leach, 1653.
Harward, Simon. *Harwards Phlebotomy, OR, a Treatise of Letting Bloud*. London, 1601.
Helmont, Jean Baptiste. *Van Helmont's Works Containing his Most Excellent Philosophy, Physick, Chirurgery, Anatomy*. London, 1664.
Henslow, George. *Medical Works of the Fourteenth Century*. London: Chapman and Hall, 1899.
Heresbach, Conrad. *Foure Bookes of Husbandry*. Newly Englished, and encreased, by Barnaby Googe. London, 1601.
Hill, Christopher, ed. *The Law of Freedom and Other Writings*. Harmondsworth: Penguin, 1973.
Hobbes, Thomas. *Questions Concerning Liberty, Necessity and Chance*. In *Works*, edited by William Molesworth. London: John Bohn, 1841.
Holberg, Ludvig. *Jeppe of the Hill*. Translated by Gerald S. Argetsinger and Sven Hakon Rossel. Carbondale: Southern Illinois University Press, 1990.
Hughes, William. *The Compleat Vineyard: Or A most excellent Way for the Planting of Vines: Not onely according to the German and French way, but also long experimented in England*. London, 1665.
Hunnaeus, Augustinus. *Dialecta, seu Generalia Logices Praecepta Omnia*. Antwerp: Christophorus Plantini, 1566.
[J., S.]. *The Vineyard: Being a Treatise Shewing The Nature and Method of Planting, Manuring, Cultivating, and Dressing of Vines in Foreign-Parts*. London, 1727.
James I. *Daemonologie*. Edinburgh, 1597.
Joubert, Laurent. *Popular Errors*. Translated by Gregory de Rocher. Tuscaloosa: University of Alabama Press, 1989.

Kärzenmacher, Petrus. *Rechter Gebrauch der Alchemie.* 1531.
Ker, James, and Jessica Winston, eds. *Elizabethan Seneca: Three Tragedies.* MHRA Tudor & Stuart Translations. Vol. 8. London: Modern Humanities Research Association, 2012.
Kirkpatrick, Robin, trans. *The Divine Comedy.* 3 vols. London: Penguin, 2006–2007.
Lanfiere, Thomas. *The Taunton Maids Delight.* London, 1672–1696.
Lanfranco. *A Most Excellent and Learned Woorke of Chirurgerie.* London, 1565.
Langland, William. *Piers Plowman: A Parallel-Text Edition of the A, B, C and Z Versions.* Edited by A. V. C. Schmidt. London: Longman, 1995.
Langland, William. *The Vision of Piers Plowman.* Edited by A. V. C. Schmidt. London: Dent, 1978.
Laurent, M. H., ed. *Fontes Vitae S. Catharinae Senensis Historici: Il Processo Castellano.* Milan: Bocca, 1942.
Lea, Kathleen M., and M. Gang, eds. *Godfrey of Bulloigne: A Critical Edition of Edward Fairfax's Translation of Tasso's Gerusalemme Liberata, together with Fairfax's Original Poems.* Oxford: Clarendon Press, 1981.
Lemnius, Levinus. *The Secret Miracles of Nature.* London, 1658.
Lucretius. *De Rerum Natura.* Translated by W. H. D. Rouse and revised by Martin Ferguson Smith. Cambridge, MA: Harvard University Press, 1975.
Lusitanus, Amatus. *Curationum medicinalium centuriae* IV. Basileae, 1556.
Manget, J. J. *Bibliotheca chemica curiosa.* Geneva, 1702.
Mantel, Hilary. *Bring up the Bodies.* Adapted by Mike Poulton. London: Nick Hern Books, 2014.
Markham, Francis. *The Booke of Honour: Or Five Decads of Epistles of Honour.* London, 1625.
Markham, Gervase. *Cavelarice, or The English Horseman.* London, 1607.
Markham, Gervase. *The English Housewife.* Edited by Michael R. Best. Kingston and Montreal: McGill–Queen's University Press, 1986.
Marston, John. *The Dutch Courtesan.* Edited by David Crane. London: A&C Black; New York: W. W. Norton, 1997.
Marzio, Galeotto. *De doctrina promiscua.* Lyon, 1653.
Maus, Katharine Eisaman, ed., *Four Revenge Tragedies.* Oxford: Oxford University Press, 1995.
McNulty, Robert, ed. *Ludovico Ariosto's Orlando Furioso, translated into English Heroical Verse by Sir John Harington (1591).* Oxford: Clarendon Press, 1972.
Melancthonis, Philippi. *De dialectica libri quatuor.* Leipzig: Nickel Faber, 1531.
Middleton, Thomas. *The Collected Works.* Edited by Gary Taylor and John Lavagnino. Oxford: Clarendon Press, 2007.
Middleton, Thomas, and William Rowley. *The Changeling.* Edited by Michael Neill, New Mermaids. London and New York, 2006.
Misciattelli, Piero, ed. *Le lettere di S. Caterina da Siena . . . con note di Niccolò Tommasèo.* 6 vols. Florence: Giunti, 1939–1940.

Nashe, Thomas. *Pierce Penilesse his Supplication to the Divell*. London, 1592.
Nashe, Thomas. *The Unfortunate Traveller and Other Works*. Edited by J. Steane. Harmondsworth: Penguin, 1978.
Noffke O. P., Suzanne, trans. and ed. *The Letters of Catherine of Siena*. Vol. 1. Tempe: Arizona Center for Medieval and Renaissance Studies, 2000–2008.
Paracelsus. *Sämtliche Werke, 1. Abteilung: Medizinische, Naturwissenschaftliche Und Philosophische Schriften*. Edited by Karl Sudhoff. 14 vols. Munich: R. Oldenbourg, 1922–1933.
Paré, Ambroise. *The Workes*. Translated by Th[omas] Johnson. London, 1634.
Parkes, M. B., and Richard Beadle, eds. *Poetical Works: A Facsimile of Cambridge University Library MS Gg. 4.27*. Cambridge: D. S. Brewer, 1980.
Parkinson, John. *Paradisi in Sole Paradisus Terrestris. A Garden of all sorts of pleasant flowers which our English ayre will permitt to be noursed up*. London, 1629.
Peter of Abano. *Conciliator*. Venice, 1565.
Philalethes, Eirenaeus. *Ripley Reviv'd*. London, 1678.
Plat, (Sir) Hugh. *Floraes Paradise*. London, 1608.
Plat, (Sir) Hugh. *The Jewel House of Art and Nature*. London, 1653.
Plat, (Sir) Hugh. *The Second Part of the Garden of Eden*. London, 1660.
Plater, Felix. *Platerus Golden Practice of Physick*. London, 1664.
R., W. *The Most Horrible and Tragicall Murther of the Right Honorable, the Vertuous and Valerous Gentleman, John Lord Bourgh, Baron of Castell Connell*. London, 1591.
Reynolds, John. *The Triumphs of Gods Revenge against the Crying and Execrable Sinne of Murther*. London, 1621.
Rhodes, James F. "The Pardoner's Vernicle and His Vera Icon." *Modern Language Studies* 13 (1983): 34–40.
Roberts, George. *The Diary of Walter Yonge, Esq*. Camden Society, XLI: 1848.
[S., D.]. *Vinetum Angliae: Or, A new and easy Way to make Wine of English Grapes and other Fruit, equal to that of France, Spain, &c with their Physical Virtues*. London, 1700.
Savonarola, Michele. *Practica Maior*. Venice, 1559.
Schurig, Martin. *Parthenologia historico-medica, hoc est Virginitatis Consideratio*. Dresden and Leipzig, 1729.
Scot, Reginald. *The Discoverie of Witchcraft*. London, 1584.
Shakespeare, William. *The Complete Works*. Edited by Gary Taylor and Stanley Wells. Oxford: Oxford University Press, 1998.
Shakespeare, William. *Cymbeline*. Edited by Martin Butler. Cambridge: Cambridge University Press, 2005.
Shakespeare, William. *Cymbeline*. Edited by John Pitcher. London: Penguin, 2005.
Shakespeare, William. *The Norton Shakespeare, Based on the Oxford Edition*. Edited by Stephen Greenblatt et al. New York: W. W. Norton, 1997.
Shakespeare, William. *Riverside Shakespeare*. Edited by G. Blakemore Evans and J. J. M. Tobin. 2nd ed. Boston: Houghton Mifflin, 1997.
Shakespeare, William. *Romeo and Juliet*. Edited by G. Blakemore Evans. Cambridge: Cambridge University, 2003.

Shakespeare, William. *Titus Andronicus*. Edited by Jonathan Bate, the Arden Shakespeare. Walton-on-Thames Surry: Thomas Nelson & Sons, 1997.

Spenser, Edmund. *The Faerie Queene*. Edited by A. C. Hamilton. London: Longman, 1977, rev. ed. 2006.

Spiegel, H. L. *Twe-spraack. Ruygh-bewerp. Kort begrip. Rederijck-kunst*. Edited by W. J. H. Caron. Groningen: Wolters, 1962.

Smith, Emma, ed. *Five Revenge Tragedies: Kyd, Shakespeare, Marston, Chettle, Middleton*. London: Penguin Classics, 2012.

Smythe, John (Sir). *Instructions, Observations, and Orders Mylitarie*. London, 1594.

Snuggs, Henry L., trans. *Giraldi Cinthio on Romances, Being a Translation of the Discorse Intorno al Comporre dei Romanzi*. Lexington: University of Kentucky Press, 1968.

Stubbes, Phillip. *The Second Part of the Anatomie of Abuses Conteining the Display of Corruptions*. London, 1583.

Sturgess, Keith, ed. *Three Elizabethan Domestic Tragedies: Arden of Faversham, A Yorkshire Tragedy, A Woman Killed with Kindness*. London: Penguin Classics, 2012.

Sutton, Richard. *A True Relation of the Cruelties and Barbarities of the French upon the English Prisoners of War*. London, 1690.

Sydenham, Thomas. *The Entire Works of Dr. Thomas Sydenham*. Edited by John Swan. London, 1742.

Teulet, Alexandre. *Relations Politiques de la France et de l'Espagne avec L'Écosse au XVIe Siècle*. Vol. 4. Paris, 1862.

Thomas of Cantimpré, *Liber de natura rerum*. I. Edited by Helmut Boese. Berlin: De Gruyter, 1973.

Thompson, George. *Aimatiasis, or, The True way of Preserving the Bloud in its Integrity*. London, 1670.

Thompson, James. *Helmont Disguised, OR, The Vulgar Errours of Impericall and Unskillful Practisers of Physick*. London, 1657.

Tuck, Richard, ed. *Leviathan*. Cambridge: Cambridge University Press, 1996.

Turner, Robert. *Botanologia: The British Physician or the Nature and Vertues of English Plants*. London, 1664.

Turner, William. *A Book of Wines*. London, 1568. Reprinted in New York, New York: Scholars' Facsimiles, 1941.

Turner, William. *A New Boke of the Natures and Properties of all Wines*. London, 1568.

Urry, John, ed. *The Works of Geoffrey Chaucer, Compared with the Former Editions, and Many Valuable MSS. Out of which, Three Tales are Added which were Never Before Printed*. London, 1721.

van Foreest, Pieter. *Observationum et curationum medicinalium ac chirurgicarum opera omnia quatuor tomis digesta libri XXXII*. Rouen, 1653.

Vaughan, William. *Directions for Health, Both Naturall and Artificiall*. London, 1617.

Vincent of Beauvais. *De eruditione filiorum nobelium*. Edited by Arpad Steiner. Menasha, WI: George Banta, 1938.

Bibliography

Vincent of Beauvais. *Speculum natural*. Douai, 1624; repr. Graz: Akademische Druck-und Verlagsanstalt, 1964.

Virgil. *Aeneid*. Translated by H. R. Fairclough and revised by F. P. Goold. Cambridge, MA: Harvard University Press, 1999.

Vives, Ludovicus. *De disputatione*, in *Opera Omnia*. Edited by Gregorio Majansio. 8 vols. London: Gregg, 1964.

Walker, Greg, ed. *Medieval Drama: An Anthology*. Oxford: Blackwell, 2000.

Whitaker, Tobias. *The Tree of Humane Life, or the The Blood of the Grape, proving the possibilitie of maintaining human life from infancy to extreme old age without any sicknesse by the use of wine: Republished and enlarged by the Author*. London, 1654.

White, Beatrice, ed. *The Vulgaria of John Stanbridge and the Vulgaria of Robert Whittinton*. EETS O.S. 187. London: Oxford University Press, 1932.

Whitteridge Gweneth, trans and ed. *The Anatomical Lectures of William Harvey*. Edinburgh and London: E. & S. Livingstone, 1964.

Whittinton, Robert. *Vulgaria et De institutione grammaticulorum opusculorum*. London: Wynkyn de Worde, 1520.

William of Auvergne. "De universe." In *Guillelmi Alverni Opera Omnia*. 2 vols. I. Paris, 1674; reprint, Frankfurt-am-Main: Minerva, 1963.

Williams, Roger. *A Briefe Discourse of Warre*. London, 1590.

Williams, R. D., ed. *Aeneidos Liber Tertius*. Oxford: Clarendon Press, 1962.

Woodall, John. *The Surgions Mate*. London, 1617.

Woodall, John. *Woodalls Viaticum: The Path-way to the Surgions Chest*. London, 1628.

Woolley, Hannah. *The Compleat Servant-maid*. London, 1677.

Worlidge, J. *Vinetum Britannicum: Or a Treatise of Cider, And other Wines and Drinks extracted from Fruits Growing in this Kingdom*. London, 1691.

Wright, Thomas. *The Canterbury Tales of Geoffrey Chaucer: A New Text with Illustrative Notes in Early English Poetry, Ballads and Popular Literature of the Middle Ages*. London: Percy Society, 1847 and 1857, Vols. 24 and 26.

SECONDARY

Abbot, E. A. *St Thomas of Canterbury: His Death and Miracles*. London: Adam and Charles Black, 1898.

Adelman, Janet. *Suffocating Mothers: Fantasies of Maternal Origin in Shakespeare's Plays, Hamlet to The Tempest*. New York: Routledge, 1992.

Agamben, Giorgio. *Stanzas: Word and Phantasm in Western Culture*. Translated by Giorgio Agamben. London: University of Minnesota Press, 1993.

Agamben, Giorgio. *Stanze: La parola e il fantasma nella cultura occidentale*. Turin: Einaudi, 1977.

Anidjar, Gil. *Blood: A Critique of Christianity*. New York: Columbia University Press, 2014.

Ashton, John, ed. *Romances of Chivalry*. London, 1887.
Avis, P. D. L. "Moses and the Magistrate: A Study in the Rise of Protestant Legalism." *Journal of Ecclesiastical History* 26 (1975): 149–72.
Backhouse, Janet. "Birds, Beasts and Initials in Lindisfarne's Gospel Books." In *St Cuthbert, His Cult and His Community to AD 1200*, edited by Gerald Bonner, David Rollason, and Clare Stancliffe, 165–74. Woodbridge, Suffolk: Boydell Press, 1989.
Baker, Susan. "Hamlet's Bloody Thoughts and the Illusion of Inwardness." *Comparative Drama* 21 (1987): 303–17.
Balizet, Ariane. *Blood and Home in Early Modern Drama: Domestic Identity on the Renaissance Stage*. New York: Routledge, 2014.
Barnes, R. "On Vicarious Menstruation." *British Gynecological Journal* 2 (1886–1887): 151–83.
Barr, Helen. *Transporting Chaucer*. Manchester: Manchester University Press, 2014.
Barton, Anne. *Essays, Mainly Shakespearean*. Cambridge: Cambridge University Pres, 1994.
Bate, Jonathan. *Shakespeare and Ovid*. Oxford: Clarendon Press, 1993.
Bellamy, Elizabeth Jane. "The Broken Branch and the 'Liuing Well': Spenser's Fradubio and Romance Error in *The Faerie Queene*." *Renaissance Papers* 2 (1985): 1–12.
Belling, Catherine. "Infectious Rape, Therapeutic Revenge: Bloodletting and the Health of Rome's Body." In *Disease, Diagnosis, and Cure on the Early Modern Stage*, edited by Stephanie Moss and Kaara L. Peterson, 113–32. Aldershot: Ashgate, 2004.
Bellis, Joanna, and Venetia Bridges. "'What shalt thou do when thou hast an english to make into latin?' A Study of the Proverb Collection of Cambridge, St. John's College, MS F.26." *Studies in Philology* 112 (2015): 68–92.
Belsey, Catherine. "The Name of the Rose in *Romeo and Juliet*." *Yearbook of English Studies* 23 (1993): 126–42.
Benjamin, Walter. *The Origin of German Tragic Drama*. Translated by John Osborne. London: Verso, 1998.
Bennett, Judith M., and Ruth Mazo Karras, eds. *The Oxford Handbook of Women and Gender in Medieval Europe*. Oxford: Oxford University Press, 2013.
Bergeron, David M. "Sexuality in *Cymbeline*." *Essays in Literature* 10.2 (1983): 159–68.
Bergeron, David M. "Sickness in *Romeo and Juliet*." *CLA Journal* 20 (1977): 356–64.
Berkeley, David S. "Severall Degrees in Bloud." In *Shakespeare's Theories of Blood, Character and Class: A Festschrift in Honor of David Shelley Berkeley*, edited by Peter C. Rollins and Alan Smith, 7–18. New York and Oxford: Peter Lang, 2001.
Biale, David. *Blood and Belief: The Circulation of a Symbol Between Jews and Christians*. Berkeley: University of California Press, 2007.
Bicks, Caroline. *Midwiving Subjects in Shakespeare's England*. Aldershot: Ashgate, 2003.
Bildhauer, Bettina. *Medieval Blood*. Cardiff: University of Wales Press, 2006.
Bildhauer, Bettina. "Medieval European Conceptions of Blood: Truth and Human Integrity." *Journal of the Royal Anthropological Institute* 19 (2013): S57–S76.
Biller, Peter. "Views of Jews from Paris around 1300: Christian or 'Scientific?'." In *Christianity and Judaism* (Studies in Church History, 29), edited by Diana Wood, 187–99. Oxford: Blackwell, 1992.

Bindoff, Stanley T. *The House of Commons 1509–1558*. London: Secker and Warburg, 1982.
Binski, Paul. *Becket's Crown: Art and Imagination in Gothic England 1170–1300*. New Haven: Yale University Press, 2004.
Binski, Paul. *Medieval Death: Ritual and Representation*. Ithaca, NY: Cornell University Press, 1996.
Biow, Douglas. *Mirabile Dictu: Representations of the Marvelous in Medieval and Renaissance Epic*. Ann Arbor: University of Michigan Press, 1996.
Blick, Sarah. "Reconstructing the Shrine of Thomas Becket in Canterbury Cathedral." In *The Art and Architecture of the Late Medieval Pilgrimage in Northern Europe and the British Isles*, edited by Sarah Blick and Rita Tekippe, 405–41. Leiden: Brill, 2005.
Bloch, Maurice. *Natural Symbols: Explorations in Cosmology*. Harmondsworth: Penguin, 1973.
Bloch, Maurice. "Why Trees, Too, Are Good to Think With: Towards an Anthropology of the Meaning of Life." In *The Social Life of Trees: Anthropological Perspectives on Tree Symbolism*, edited by Laura Rival, 39–55. Oxford: Berg, 1998.
Bolvig, Axel, and Phillip Lindley, eds. *History and Images: Towards a New Iconology*. Turnhout, Belgium: Brepols, 2003.
Bond, Sarah. *Trade and Taboo: Disreputable Professions in the Roman Mediterranean*. Ann Arbor: University of Michigan Press, 2016.
Botkin, Daniel. *The Moon in a Nautilus Shell: From Climate Change to Species Extinction, How Life Persists in an Ever-Changing World*. Oxford: Oxford University Press, 2012.
Boureau, Alain. "La preuve par le cadavre qui saigne au XIIIe siècle: Entre expérience commune et savoir scolastique." *Micrologus* 7 (1999): 247–81.
Boynton, Susan. "Performative Exegesis in the Fleury *Interfectio Puerorum*." *Viator* 29 (1998): 39–64.
Bradburne, James M., James Clifton, MAK Frankfurt, and Schirn Kunstall, eds. *Blood: Art, Power, Politics and Pathology*. New York: Prestel, 2001.
Brittain, Robert P. "Cruentation: In Legal Medicine and in Literature." *Medical History* 9 (1965): 82–88.
Brockliss, Laurence, and Heather Montgomery, eds. *Children and Violence in the Western Tradition*. Oxford: Oxbow Books, 2010.
Buckley, Thomas, and Alma Gottlieb, eds. *Blood Magic: The Anthropology of Menstruation*. Berkeley: University of California Press, 1988.
Burt, Richard, and John Michael Archer, eds. *Enclosure Acts: Sexuality, Property and Culture in Early Modern England*. Ithaca, NY: Cornell University Press, 1995.
Bushnell, Rebecca. *Green Desire: Imagining Early Modern English Gardens*. Ithaca, NY: Cornell University Press, 2003.
Butterworth, Philip. *Theatre of Fire: Special Effects in the Early English and Scottish Theatre*. London: Society for Theatre Research, 1998.
Caciola, Nancy. *Discerning Spirits: Divine and Demonic Possession in the Middle Ages*. Ithaca, NY: Cornell University Press, 2003.
Caciola, Nancy. "Mystics, Demoniacs and the Physiology of Spirit Possession in Medieval Europe." *Comparative Studies in Society and History* 42 (2000): 268–306.

Cadden, Joan. *Meanings of Sex Difference in the Middle Ages: Medicine, Science and Culture.* Cambridge: Cambridge University Press, 1993.
Cahill, Patricia A. *Unto the Breach: Martial Formations, Historical Trauma, and the Early Modern Stage.* Oxford: Oxford University Press, 2008.
Calbi, Maurizio. *Approximate Bodies: Gender and Power in Early Modern Drama and Anatomy.* New York: Routledge, 2005.
Calderwood, James. *Shakespearean Metadrama: The Argument of the Play in Titus Andronicus, Love's Labour's Lost, Romeo and Juliet, A Midsummer Night's Dream, and Richard II.* Minneapolis: University of Minnesota Press, 1971.
Camille, Michael. "At the Sign of the 'Spinning Sow': The 'Other' Chartres and Images of Everyday Life of the Medieval Street." In *History and Images: Towards a New Iconology,* edited by Axel Bolvig and Phillip Lindley, 249–76. Turnhout, Belgium: Brepols, 2003.
Camille, Michael. *Mirror in Parchment: The Luttrell Psalter and the Making of Medieval England.* Chicago, IL: University of Chicago Press, 1998.
Campana, Joseph. *The Pain of Reformation: Spenser, Vulnerability, and the Ethics of Masculinity.* New York: Fordham University Press, 2012.
Camporesi, Piero. *The Juice of Life: The Symbolic and Magic Significance of Blood.* Translated by Robert R. Barr. New York: Continuum, 1995.
Carlino, Andrea. *Books of the Body: Anatomical Ritual and Renaissance Learning.* Translated by John Tedeschi and Anne C. Tedeschi. London: University of Chicago Press, 1999.
Carr, David R. "Controlling the Butchers in Late Medieval English Towns." *The Historian* 70 (2008): 450–61.
Carsten, Janet. *Blood Will Out: Essays on Liquid Transfers and Flows.* Oxford: Wiley Blackwell, 2013.
Caviness, Madeleine Harrison. *The Windows of Christ Church Cathedral Canterbury.* London: Oxford University Press, 1981.
de Ceglia, Francesco Paola, ed. *The Corpse of Evidence: Cadavers and Proofs in Early Modern European Forensic Medicine.* Leiden: Brill, forthcoming.
Churchill, Wendy D. *Female Patients in Early Modern Britain: Gender, Diagnosis, and Treatment.* Aldershot: Ashgate, 2013.
Clerico, Terri. "The Politics of Blood: John Ford's '*Tis Pity She's a Whore.*" *English Literary Renaissance* 22.3 (1992): 405–24.
Connor, Steven. *The Book of Skin.* London: Reaktion, 2004.
Coo, Lyndsay. "Polydorus and the *Georgics*: Virgil *Aeneid* 3.13–68." *Materiali e discussioni per l'analisi dei testi classici* 59 (2007): 193–99.
Cordner, Michael, Peter Holland, and John Kerrigan, eds. *English Comedy.* Cambridge: Cambridge University Press, 1994.
Corneanu, Sorana, and Koen Vermeir. "Idols of the Imagination: Francis Bacon on the Imagination and the Medicine of the Mind." *Perspectives on Science* 20.2 (2012): 183–206.
Covington, Sarah. *Wounds, Flesh and Metaphor in Seventeenth-Century England.* Basingstoke: Palgrave Macmillan, 2009.

Crawford, Patricia. "Attitudes toward Menstruation in Seventeenth-Century England." *Past and Present* 91.1 (1981): 47–73.
Crawford, Patricia. *Blood, Bodies and Families in Early Modern England*. Harlow: Pearson Longman, 2004.
Cruikshank, C. G. *Elizabeth's Army*. 2nd ed. Oxford: Clarendon Press, 1966.
Cunningham, Karen. *Imaginary Betrayals: Subjectivity and the Discourses of Treason in Early Modern England*. Philadelphia: University of Pennsylvania Press, 2002.
Curth, Louise Hill, and Tanya M. Cassidy. "'Health, Strength and Happiness': Medical Constructions of Wine and Beer in Early Modern England." In *A Pleasing Sinne: Drink and Conviviality in Seventeenth-Century England*, edited by Adam Smyth, 142–59. Cambridge: D. S. Brewer, 2004.
Daston, Lorraine, and Katherine Park. *Wonders and the Order of Nature 1150–1750*. New York: Zone, 2001.
Davis, Natalie Zemon. *Fiction in the Archives: Pardon Tales and Their Tellers in Sixteenth-Century France*. Stanford, CA: Stanford University Press, 1987.
Dawson, Lesel. *Lovesickness and Gender in Early Modern Literature*. Oxford: Oxford University Press, 2008.
de Boer, C., ed. *Ovid moralisé en prose (texte du quinziéme siècle)*. Verhandelingen de Koninklijke Nederlandse Academie, 61. Amsterdam, 1955.
Decamp, Eleanor. *Civic and Medical Worlds in Early Modern England: Performing Barbery and Surgery*. Basingstoke: Palgrave Macmillan, 2016.
Demaitre, Luke E. *Doctor Bernard de Gordon: Professor and Practitioner*. Studies and Texts 51. Toronto: Pontifical Institute of Mediaeval Studies, 1980.
Dembinska, Maria. *Food and Drink in Medieval Poland: Rediscovering a Cuisine of the Past*. Revised by William Woys Weaver and translated by Magdalena Thomas. University of Pennsylvania Press, 1999.
Dent, R. W. *Proverbial Language in English Drama Exclusive of Shakespeare*. Berkeley: University of California Press, 1984.
Dessen Alan C., and Leslie Thompson. *A Dictionary of Stage Directions in English Drama, 1580–1642*. Cambridge: Cambridge University Press, 1999.
DeVun, Leah. *Prophecy, Alchemy, and the End of Time: John of Rupescissa in the Late Middle Ages*. New York: Columbia University Press, 2009.
Dinshaw, Carolyn. *Chaucer's Sexual Poetics*. Madison: University of Wisconsin Press, 1989.
Dixon, Laurinda S. *Perilous Chastity: Women and Illness in Pre-Enlightenment Art and Medicine*. Ithaca, NY: Cornell University Press, 1995.
Dobson, R. B., ed. *York City Chamberlains' Account Rolls 1396–1500*. Surtees Society Publication 192. Gateshead, UK: Surtees Society, 1980.
Dolan, Frances. *True Relations: Reading, Literature, and Evidence in Seventeenth-Century England*. Philadelphia: University of Pennsylvania Press, 2013.
Dollimore, Johnathan, and Alan Sinfield. "History and Ideology: The Instance of *Henry V*." In *Alternative Shakespeares*, edited by John Drakakis, 206–27. London: Methuen, 1985.

Duffy, Eamon. *Voices of Morebath: Reformation and Rebellion in an English Village.* New Haven, CT: Yale University Press, 2001.
Duggan, Anne J. *Thomas Becket.* Reputations. London: Arnold, 2004.
Dutton, Elisabeth. "The Croxton *Play of the Sacrament.*" In *The Oxford Handbook of Tudor Drama,* edited by Thomas Betteridge and Greg Walker, 55–71. Oxford: Oxford University Press, 2012.
Edelman, Charles. *Shakespeare's Military Language: A Dictionary.* London: Athlone Press, 2000.
Egan, Gabriel. *Green Shakespeare: From Ecopolitics to Ecocriticism.* London: Routledge, 2006.
Eklund, Hillary. *Literature and Moral Economy in the Early Modern Atlantic: Elegant Sufficiencies.* Burlington, VT: Ashgate, 2015.
Enterline, Lynn. *The Rhetoric of the Body from Ovid to Shakespeare.* Cambridge: Cambridge University Press, 2000.
Estok, Simon C. *Ecocriticism and Shakespeare: Reading Ecophobia.* New York: Palgrave, 2011.
Everett, Barbara. *Young Hamlet: Essays on Shakespeare's Tragedies.* Oxford: Clarendon Press, 1989.
Fabre-Vassas, Claudine. *The Singular Beast: Jews, Christians, and the Pig.* Translated by Carol Volk. New York: Columbia University Press, 1997.
Fawcett, Mary Laughlin. "Arms/Words/Tears: Language and the Body in *Titus Andronicus.*" *English Literary History* 50.2 (1983): 261–77.
Fawtier, Robert. *La double expérience de Catherine Benincasa.* Paris: Gallimard, 1948.
Feerick, Jean E. "Botanical Shakespeares: The Racial Logic of Plant Life in *Titus Andronicus.*" *South Central Review* 26.1&2 (2009): 82–102.
Feerick, Jean E. *Strangers in Blood: Relocating Race in the Renaissance.* Toronto: University of Toronto Press, 2010.
Feerick, Jean E., and Vin Nardizzi, eds. *The Indistinct Human in Renaissance Literature.* Basingstoke: Palgrave Macmillan, 2012.
Fildes, Valerie A. *Breasts, Bottles, and Babies: A History of Feeding.* Edinburgh: Edinburgh University Press, 1986.
Finucci, Valeria, and Kevin Brownlee, eds. *Generation and Degeneration: Tropes of Reproduction in Literature and History from Antiquity to Early Modern Europe.* Durham, NC: Duke University Press, 2001.
Fleissner, Robert F. "Falstaff's Green Sickness Unto Death." *Shakespeare Quarterly* 12 (1961): 47–55.
Fletcher, Angus. *Allegory: The Theory of a Symbolic Mode.* Ithaca, NY: Cornell University Press, 1964.
Floyd-Wilson, Mary. *English Ethnicity and Race in Early Modern Drama.* Cambridge: Cambridge University Press, 2003.
Floyd-Wilson, Mary. *Occult Knowledge, Science and Gender on the Shakespearean Stage.* Cambridge: Cambridge University Press, 2013.
Floyd-Wilson, Mary, and Garrett A. Sullivan Jr., eds. *Environment and Embodiment in Early Modern England.* Harmondsworth: Palgrave Macmillan, 2007.

Freccero, John. "The Sign of Satan." *Modern Language Notes* 80.1 (1965): 11–26.
Fredell, Joel. "The Three Clerks and St. Nicholas in Medieval England." *Studies in Philology* 92 (1995): 181–202.
Freud, Sigmund. "The Uncanny." In *Art and Literature: Jensen's Gradiva, Leonardo da Vinci and Other Works*, edited by Albert Dickson, 339–76. Harmondsworth: Penguin, 1985.
Frye, Susan. *Pens and Needles: Women's Textualities in Early Modern England*. Philadelphia: University of Pennsylvania Press, 2010.
Fucecchi, Marco. "Encountering the Fantastic: Expectations, Forms of Communication, Reactions." In *Paradox and the Marvellous in Augustan Literature and Culture*, edited by Philip Hardie, 213–30. Oxford: Oxford University Press, 2009.
Fuchs, Thomas. "The Phenomenology of Shame, Guilt and the Body in Body Dysmorphic Disorder and Depression." *Journal of Phenomenological Psychology* 33:2 (2003): 223–43.
Fumerton, Patricia, and Simon Hunt, eds. *Renaissance Culture and the Everyday*. Philadelphia: University of Pennsylvania Press, 1999.
Gager, Kristin Elizabeth. *Blood Ties and Fictive Ties: Adoption and Family Life in Early Modern France*. Princeton: Princeton University Press, 1996.
Galletti, Anna Imelde. "Uno capo nelle mani mie: Niccolò di Toldo, Perugino." In *Atti del simposio internazionale caterniano-bernardiniano, Siena, 17–20 aprile 1980*, edited by Domenico Maffei and Paolo Nardi. Siena: Accademia senese degli intronati, 1982.
Gaskill, Malcolm. "Reporting Murder: Fiction in the Archives in Early Modern England." *Social History* 23.1 (1998): 1–30.
Geltner, Guy. "Healthscaping a Medieval City: Lucca's *Curia viarum* and the Future of Public Health History." *Urban History* 40.3 (2013): 395–415.
Gent, Lucy, and Nigel Llewellyn, eds. *Renaissance Bodies: the Human Figure in English Culture c. 1540–1660*. London: Reaktion, 1990.
Girard, René. *Violence and the Sacred*. Translated by Patrick Gregory. Baltimore: Johns Hopkins University Press, 1977.
Goodich, Michael E. *From Birth to Old Age: The Human Life Cycle in Medieval Thought, 1250–1350*. New York: University Press of America, 1989.
Gowers, Emily. "Talking Trees: Philemon and Baucis Revisited." *Arethusa* 38 (2005): 331–65.
Gowland, Angus. *The Worlds of Renaissance Melancholy: Robert Burdon in Context*. Cambridge: Cambridge University Press, 2006.
Gray, Douglas, ed. *A Selection of Religious Lyrics*. Oxford: Clarendon Press, 1975.
Grazer, James G. *The Fear of the Dead in Primitive Religions*. New York: Biblo and Tannen, 1966.
Green, Monica H. "Flowers, Poisons and Men: Menstruation in Medieval Western Europe." In *Menstruation: A Cultural History*, edited by Andrew Shail and Gillian Howe, 51–64. Basingstoke: Palgrave Macmillan, 2005.
Greenblatt, Stephen. *Marvelous Possessions: The Wonder of the New World*. Oxford: Oxford University Press, 1991.

Greenblatt, Stephen. "Mutilation and Meaning." In *The Body in Parts: Fantasies of Corporeality in Early Modern Europe*, edited by David Hillman and Carla Mazzio, 221–42. New York and London: Routledge, 1997.

Greene, Roland. *Five Words: Critical Semantics in the Age of Shakespeare and Cervantes*. Chicago: University of Chicago Press, 2013.

Guy, John, *My Heart Is My Own: The Life of Mary Queen of Scots*. London: HarperCollins, 2004.

Halperin, David M. *Saint Foucault: Towards a Gay Hagiography*. New York; Oxford: Oxford University Press, 1995.

Hamilton, Donna B. *Cymbeline* in *Shakespeare and the Politics of Protestant England*. University Press of Kentucky, 1986.

Hamon. Auguste. "Cœur (Sacré)." In Vol. 2 of *Dictionnaire de spiritualité ascétique et mystique: Doctrine et histoire*, edited by Marcel Viller and others, 17 vols. Paris: Beauchesne, 1932–1995 (1953).

Hardie, Philip. *Lucretian Receptions: History, the Sublime, Knowledge*. Cambridge: Cambridge University Press, 2009.

Hardie, Philip. *Virgil's Aeneid: Cosmos and Imperium*. Oxford: Clarendon Press, 1986.

Harkness, Deborah E. "A View from the Streets: Women and Medical Work in Elizabethan London." *Bulletin of the History of Medicine* 81.1 (2008): 52–85.

Harris, Mary Dormer, ed. *The Coventry Leet Book: or Mayor's Register, Containing the Records of the City Court Leet or View of Frankpledge, AD 1420–1555, with Divers Other Matters*. 4 vols. London: Kegan Paul, Trench, Trübner, 1907–1913.

Haskell, Yasmin, ed. *Diseases of the Imagination and Imaginary Diseases in the Early Modern Period*. Turnhout: Brepols, 2012.

Heal, Bridget. *The Cult of the Virgin Mary in Early Modern Germany: Protestant and Catholic Piety, 1500–1648*. Cambridge: Cambridge University Press, 2007.

Henisch, Bridget Ann. *The Medieval Calendar Year*. University Park: Pennsylvania State University Press, 1999.

Hill, Christopher. "William Harvey and the Idea of Monarchy." *Past and Present* 27 (1964): 54–72.

Hillier, Russell M. "The Wreath, the Rock and the Winepress: Passion Iconography in Milton's *Paradise Regained*." *Literature and Theology* 22.4 (2008): 387–405.

Hillman, David. *Shakespeare's Entrails: Belief, Scepticism and the Interior of the Body*. London: Palgrave, 2007.

Hillman, David, and Carla Mazzio, eds. *The Body in Parts: Fantasies of Corporeality in Early Modern Europe*. New York and London: Routledge, 1997.

Hoeniger, David F. *Medicine and Shakespeare in the English Renaissance*. London and Toronto: Associated University Press, 1992.

Horsfall, Nicholas. *Virgil, Aeneid 3: A Commentary*. Leiden: Brill, 2006.

Horstmanshoff, Manfred, Helen King, and Claus Zittel, eds. *Blood, Sweat and Tears— The Changing Concepts of Physiology from Antiquity into Early Modern Europe*. Leiden: Brill, 2012.

Hourihane, Colum, ed. *Time in the Medieval World: Occupations of the Months and Signs of the Zodiac in the Index of Christian Art*. Index of Christian Art Resources 3. Princeton, NJ: Index of Christian Art in Association with Pennsylvania University Press, 2007.

Hunt, Tony. *The Medieval Surgery*. Woodbridge: Boydell, 1992.

Iyengar, Sujata. "Why Ganymede Faints and the Duke of York Weeps: Passion Plays in Shakespeare." *Shakespeare Survey* 67 (2014): 265–78.

Jacob, Joseph, ed. *Jewish Ideals and Other Essays*. New York: Macmillan, 1896.

James, Heather. *Shakespeare's Troy: Drama, Politics, and the Translation of Empire*. Cambridge: Cambridge University Press, 1997.

Javitch, Daniel. *Proclaiming a Classic: The Canonization of Orlando Furioso*. Princeton: Princeton University Press, 1991.

Johnson, Christopher, Bernhard Jussen, David Warren Sabbean, and Simon Teuscher, eds. *Blood and Kinship: Matter for Metaphor from Ancient Rome to the Present*. New York and Oxford: Berghahn, 2013.

Johnson, Hannah R. *Blood Libel: The Ritual Murder Accusation at the Limit of Jewish History*. Michigan: University of Michigan Press, 2012.

Johnson, Michael. "A Critical Edition of the Commentary by William of Wheteley on the Pseudo-Boethian Treatise De Disciplina Scolarium." Unpublished PhD thesis, State University of New York at Buffalo, 1982.

Johnson, Michael. "How to Achieve Discipline in the Classroom: William of Wheteley's Exposition of Pseudo-Boethius." *Acta* 8 (1981): 103–20.

Johnson, Willis. "The Myth of Jewish Male Menses." *Journal of Medieval History* 24 (1998): 273–95.

Jordan, Constance. *Shakespeare's Monarchies: Ruler and Subject in the Romances*. Ithaca, NY: Cornell University Press, 1997.

Jørgensen, Dolly. "Running Amuck? Urban Swine Management in Late Medieval England." *Agricultural History* 87 (2013): 429–51.

Jorgensen, Paul. *Shakespeare's Military World*. Berkeley: University of California Press, 1956.

Jung, C. G. *Alchemical Studies*. Translated by R. F. C. Hull. London: Routledge & Kegan Paul, 1968.

Jung, C. G. *The Integration of the Personality*. Translated by Stanley M. Dell. London: Routledge & Kegan Paul, 1940.

Kahn, Coppélia. *Man's Estate: Masculine Identity in Shakespeare*. Berkeley: University of California Press, 1981.

Kahn, Coppélia. *Roman Shakespeare: Warriors, Wounds, and Women*. New York and London: Routledge, 1997.

Karim-Cooper, Farah, and Tiffany Stern, eds. *Shakespeare's Theatres and the Effects of Performance*. London: Bloomsbury, 2013.

Keller, Eve. *Generating Bodies and Gendered Selves: The Rhetoric of Reproduction in Early Modern England*. Seattle: University of Washington Press, 2007.

Keller, Eve. "'That Sublimest Juyce in Our Body': Bloodletting and Ideas of the Individual in Early Modern England." *Philological Quarterly* 86.1–2 (2007): 97–122.

Kendall, Gillian Murray. "'Lend me thy hand': Metaphor and Mayhem in *Titus Andronicus*." *Shakespeare Quarterly* 40.3 (1989): 299–316.
Kern Paster, Gail. "Becoming the Landscape: The Ecology of the Passions in the Legend of Temperance." In *Environment and Embodiment in Early Modern England*, edited by Mary Floyd-Wilson and Garrett A. Sullivan Jr., 137–52. Harmondsworth: Palgrave, 2007.
Kern Paster, Gail. *The Body Embarrassed: Drama and the Disciplines of Shame in Early Modern England*. Ithaca, NY: Cornell University Press, 1993.
Kern Paster, Gail. *Humoring the Body: Emotions and the Shakespearean Stage*. Chicago: University of Chicago Press, 2004.
Kern Paster, Gail, Katherine Rowe, and Mary Floyd-Wilson, eds. *Reading the Early Modern Passions: Essays in the Cultural History of Emotion*. Philadelphia: University of Pennsylvania Press, 2004.
Kerrigan John. *Revenge Tragedy: Aeschylus to Armageddon*. Oxford: Oxford University Press, 1996.
Kerwin, William. *Beyond the Body: The Boundaries of Medicine and English Renaissance Drama*. Amherst and Boston: University of Massachusetts Press, 2005.
Keynes, Geoffrey. *The Life of William Harvey*. Oxford: Clarendon Press, 1966.
King, Helen. *The Disease of Virgins: Green Sickness, Chlorosis, and the Problems of Puberty*. London: Routledge, 2004.
King, Helen. *Hippocrates' Woman: Reading the Female Body in Ancient Greece*. London: Routledge, 1998.
King, Helen. *The One-Sex Body on Trial: The Classical and Early Modern Evidence*. Aldershot: Ashgate, 2013.
Kirkpatrick, Robin. *Dante's Inferno: Difficult and Dead Poetry*. Cambridge: Cambridge University Press, 1987.
Kirkpatrick, Robin. "Massacre, *Miserere* and Martyrdom." In Vol. 1 of *Vertical Readings in Dante's "Comedy,"* edited by George Corbett and Heather Webb. Cambridge: Open Book Publishers, 2015.
Kirschbaum, Leo. "Shakespeare's Stage Blood and Its Critical Significance." *PMLA* 64.3 (1949): 517–29.
Klein, Robert. "Spirito peregrine." *Revue d'Études Italiennes* 11 (1965): 197–236.
Knight, C. *Blood Relations: Menstruation and the Origins of Culture*. New Haven, CT: Yale University Press, 1991.
Knight, Leah. *Of Books and Botany in Early Modern England: Sixteenth Century Plants and Print Culture*. Surrey: Ashgate, 2009.
Kommers, Donald P., John E. Finn, and Gary J. Jacobson. *American Constitutional Law: Governmental Powers and Democracy*. Lanham, MD: Rowman & Littlefield, 2004.
Korda, Natasha. *Labors Lost: Women's Work and the Early Modern English Stage*. Philadelphia: University of Pennsylvania Press, 2011.
Korda, Natasha, and Jonathan Gil Harris, eds. *Staged Properties in Early Modern Drama*. Cambridge: Cambridge University Press, 2002.

Krauss, Jennifer. "Name-calling and the New Oxford *Henry V*." *Shakespeare Quarterly* 36.4 (1985): 523–25.

Kreitzer, Beth. *Reforming Mary: Changing Images of the Virgin Mary in Lutheran Sermons of the Sixteenth Century*. Oxford Studies in Historical Theology. New York: Oxford University Press, 2004.

Kristeva, Julia. *Tales of Love*. Columbia: Columbia University Press, 1987.

Lamb, Mary Ellen. *The Popular Culture of Shakespeare, Spenser and Jonson*. London: Routledge, 2006.

Land, Karine van 't. "Internal, Yet Extrinsic: Conceptions of Bodily Space and Their Relation to Causality in Late Medieval University Medicine." In *Medicine and Space: Surroundings and Borders in Antiquity and the Middle Ages*, edited by Patricia A. Baker, Han Nijdam, and Karine van 't Land, 85–116. Leiden: Brill, 2011.

Lane, Robert. "'When Blood is their Argument': Class, Character, and Historymaking in Shakespeare's and Branagh's *Henry V*." *English Literary History* 61.1 (1994): 27–52.

Langley, Eric. "Plagued by Kindness: Contagious Sympathy in Shakespearean Drama." *Medical Humanities* 37.2 (2011): 103–9.

Laoutaris, Chris. *Shakespearean Maternities: Crises of Conception in Early Modern England*. Edinburgh: Edinburgh University Press, 2008.

Laqueur, Thomas. *Making Sex: Body and Gender from the Greeks to Freud*. Cambridge MA: Harvard University Press, 1990.

Lederer, Susan E. *Flesh and Blood: Organ Transplantation and Blood Transfusion in 20th Century America*. Oxford: Oxford University Press, 2008.

Lespinasse, R., ed. *Les Métiers et corporations de la ville de Paris I: XIVe–XVIIIe siècle, ordonnances générale, metiers de l'alimentation*. Paris: Imprimerie Nationale, 1886.

Lindemann, Mary. *Medicine and Society in Early Modern Europe*. 2nd ed. Cambridge: University of Cambridge Press, 2010.

von Lippmann, E. O. *Entstellung und Ausbrietung der Alchemie*, vol. 1. Berlin: Springer, 1919.

Lochrie, Karma, Peggy McCracken, and James A. Schultz, eds. *Constructing Medieval Sexuality*. Minneapolis: University of Minnesota Press, 1997.

Lomax, Marion. *Stage Images and Traditions: Shakespeare to Ford*. Cambridge: Cambridge University Press, 1987.

Lowe, Dunstan. "The Symbolic Value of Grafting in Ancient Rome." *Transactions of the American Philological Association* 140 (2010): 461–88.

Lynch, Kathryn L. *The High Medieval Dream Vision*. Stanford, CA: Stanford University Press, 1988.

MacDonald, Helen. *Human Remains: Dissection and Its Histories*. New Haven, CT: Yale University Press, 2005.

Maclean, Ian. *The Renaissance Notion of Women: A Study in the Fortunes of Scholasticism and Medical Science in European Intellectual Life*. Cambridge: Cambridge University Press, 1980.

Maley, Willy. "*Cymbeline*, the Font of History, and the Matter of Britain: From Times New Roman to Italic Type." In *Alternative Shakespeares 3*, edited by Diana E. Henderson, 119–37. London; New York: Routledge, 2008.
Marder, Elissa. "Disarticulated Vices: Feminism and Philomela." *Hypatia* 7.2 (Spring 1992): 148–66.
Marshall, Cynthia. "Wound-man: *Coriolanus*, Gender, and the Theatrical Construction of Interiority." In *Feminist Readings of Early Modern Culture: Emerging Subjects*, edited by Valerie Traub, M. Lindsay Kaplan, and Dympna Callaghan, 93–118. Cambridge: Cambridge University Press, 1996.
Martin, Dale. "Contradictions of Masculinity: Ascetic Inseminators and Menstruating Men in Greco-Roman Culture." In *Generation and Degeneration: Tropes of Reproduction in Literature and History from Antiquity to Early Modern Europe,* edited by Finucci and Brownlee, 81–108. Durham, NC: Duke University Press, 2001.
Martin, Randall. *Women, Murder, and Equity in Early Modern England.* New York: Routledge, 2008.
Matthew, Colin, and Brian Harrison, eds. *Oxford Dictionary of National Biography.* 60 vols. Oxford: Oxford University Press, 2004.
Maus, Katharine Eisaman. *Inwardness and Theater in the English Renaissance.* Chicago: University of Chicago Press, 1995.
McClive, Cathy. *Menstruation and Procreation in Early Modern France: Blood and Taboo.* Aldershot: Ashgate, 2015.
McColley, Diane Kelsey. *Poetry and Ecology in the Age of Milton and Marvell.* Surrey: Ashgate, 2007.
McCracken, Peggy. *The Curse of Eve, the Wound of the Hero: Blood, Gender, and Medieval Literature.* Philadelphia: University of Pennsylvania Press, 2003.
McGovern, Patrick E. *Uncorking the Past: The Quest for Wine, Beer, and Other Alcoholic Beverages.* Berkeley: University of California Press, 2009.
McJannet, Linda. *The Voice of Elizabethan Stage Directions: The Evolution of a Theatrical Code.* Newark, NJ: University of Delaware Press, 1999.
Meech, Sanford Brown. "John Drury and His English Writings." *Speculum* 9 (1934): 70–83.
Meredith, Peter, and John Tailby, eds. *The Staging of Religious Drama in Europe in the Later Middle Ages: Texts and Documents in English Translation.* Early Drama, Art and Music Monograph Series 4. Kalamazoo, MI: Medieval Institute Publications, 1983.
Meyers, B. E. "Chronic Epistaxis (Vicarious Menstruation?). Cauterisation of the Nose, Followed by Great General and Local Improvement." *Lancet* 158 (1901): 1666–67.
Michael, M. A., and Sebastian Strobl. *Stained Glass of Canterbury Cathedral.* London: Scala, 2004.
Miller, Kathleen. *The Literary Culture of Plague in Early Modern England.* Basingstoke: Palgrave Macmillan, 2016.
Miola, Robert. *Shakespeare and Classical Tragedy: The Influence of Seneca.* Oxford: Clarendon Press, 1992.

Mitchell, P. D. "Retrospective Diagnosis and the Use of Historical Texts for Investigating Disease in the Past." *International Journal of Paleopathology* 1.2 (2011): 81–88.

Mohler, Tina. "'Why is the body but a Swallowing Grave. . .?': Desire Underground in *Titus Andronicus*." *Shakespeare Quarterly* 57.1 (2006): 23–44.

Mooney, Catherine M., ed. *Gendered Voices: Medieval Saints and Their Interpreters*. Philadelphia: University of Pennsylvania Press, 1999.

Moore, R. I. *The Formation of a Persecuting Society: Power and Deviance in Western Europe 950–1250*. Oxford: Blackwell, 1987.

Morris, Colin, and Peter Roberts, eds. *Pilgrimage: The English Experience from Becket to Bunyan*. Cambridge: Cambridge University Press, 2002.

Moscucci, Ornella. *The Science of Woman, Gynaecology and Gender in England, 1800–1929*. Cambridge: Cambridge University Press, 1990.

Moshenska, Joe. *Feeling Pleasures: The Sense of Touch in Renaissance England*. Oxford: Oxford University Press, 2014.

Moshenska, Joe. "The Forgotten Youth of Allegory: Figures of Old Age in *The Faerie Queene*." *Modern Philology* 110.3 (2013): 389–414.

Moss, Stephanie, and Kaara L. Peterson. *Disease, Diagnosis, and Cure on the Early Modern Stage*. Aldershot: Ashgate, 2004.

Muessig, C., G. Ferzoco, and B. M. Kienzle, eds. *A Companion to Catherine of Siena*. Leiden, Brill, 2012.

Mukherji, Subha. *Law and Representation in Early Modern Drama*. Cambridge: Cambridge University Press, 2006.

Muñoz Simonds, Peggy. *Myth, Emblem, and Music in Shakespeare's "Cymbeline": An Iconographic Reconstruction*. Newark, NJ: University of Delaware Press, 1992.

Munro, Lucy. "'They eat each other's arms': Stage Blood and Body Parts." In *Shakespeare's Theatres and the Effects of Performance*, edited by Farah Karim-Cooper and Tiffany Stern, 73–93. London: Bloomsbury, 2013.

Nadeau, Carolyn A. "Contributions of Medieval Food Manuals to Spain's Culinary Heritage." *Cincinnati Romance Review* 33 (2012): 59–77.

Nardizzi, Vin. *Wooden Os: Shakespeare's Theatres and England's Trees*. Toronto: University of Toronto Press, 2013.

Neill, Michael. "Unproper Beds: Race, Adultery, and the Hideous in *Othello*." *Shakespeare Quarterly* 40.4 (1989): 383–412.

Nelson, T. G. A. "Sir John Harington and the Renaissance Debate over Allegory." *Studies in Philology* 82 (1985): 359–79.

Nelson, T. G. A. and Charles Haines. "Othello's Unconsummated Marriage." *Essays in Criticism* 33.1 (1983).

Neuburger, Max. *The Doctrine of the Healing Power of Nature Throughout the Course of Time*. Translated by Linn J. Boyd. New York: Homeopathic Medical College, 1932.

Nevo, Ruth. *Shakespeare's Other Language*. London: Methuen, 1987.

Newman, Barbara. *From Virile Woman to Woman Christ: Studies in Medieval Religion and Literature*. Philadelphia: University of Pennsylvania Press, 1995.

Newman, William R. "Decknamen or Pseudochemical Language? Eirenaeus Philalethes and Carl Jung." *Revue d'Histoire des Sciences et de leurs Applications* 49 (1996): 181–82.

Newman, William R. "The Philosopher's Egg: Theory and Practice in the Alchemy of Roger Bacon." *Micrologus* 3 (1995): 75–101.

Newman, William R. *Promethean Ambitions: Alchemy and the Quest to Perfect Nature*. Chicago: University of Chicago Press, 2004.

Nieto, J. Barrágan. "'Secretos de las mujeres': Sangre menstrual y mujer venenosa en la Baja." In *Innovación Educativa e Historia de las Relaciones de Género*, edited by Cristina de la Rosa Cubo et al., 91–102. Vallodolid: Universidad de Valladolid, 2010.

Nisbet, Robin. "The Oak and the Axe: Symbolism in Seneca, *Hercules Oetaeus* 1618ff." In *Homo Viator: Classical Essays for John Bramble*, edited by Michael Whitby, Philip Hardie, and Mary Whitby, 243–51. Bristol: Bristol Classical Press, 1987.

Noble, Louise. "'And Make Two Pasties of Your Shameful Heads': Medicinal Cannibalism and Healing the Body Politic in Titus Andronicus." *English Literary History* 70.3 (2003): 677–708.

Noble, Louise. *Medicinal Cannibalism in Early Modern English Literature and Culture*. Basingstoke: Palgrave Macmillan, 2011.

Nohrnberg, James. *The Analogy of "The Faerie Queene."* Princeton: Princeton University Press, 1976.

Nummedal, Tara. *Alchemy and Authority in the Holy Roman Empire*. Chicago: University of Chicago Press, 2007.

Nummedal, Tara. "Anna Zieglerin's Alchemical Revelations." In *Secrets and Knowledge in Medicine and Science, 1500–1800*, edited by Elaine Yuen Tien Leong and Alisha Rankin, 125–41. Aldershot: Ashgate, 2011.

Nunn, Hilary M. "On Vegetating Virgins: Greensickness and the Plant Realm in Early Modern Literature." In *The Indistinct Human in Renaissance Literature*, edited by Jean E. Feerick and Vin Nardizzi, 159–80. Basingstoke: Palgrave Macmillan, 2012.

Nunn, Hilary. *Staging Anatomies: Dissection and Spectacle in Early Stuart Drama*. Aldershot: Ashgate, 2005.

Orme, Nicholas. *Education and Society in Medieval and Renaissance England*. London: Hambledom, 1989.

Orme, Nicholas. *English School Exercises, c. 1420–c. 1530*. Studies and Texts 181. Turnhout: Brepols, 2013.

Orme, Nicholas. "Latin and English Sentences in Fifteenth-Century Schoolbooks." *Yale University Library Gazette* 60 (1985): 47–57.

Osgood, Charles Grosvenor. *A Concordance to the Poems of Edmund Spenser*. Washington, DC: Carnegie Institution of Washington, 1915.

Paavilainen, Helena M. *Medieval Pharmacotherapy, Continuity and Change: Case Studies from Ibn Sīnā and Some of His Late Medieval Commentators*. Leiden: Brill, 2009.

Pächt, Otto. "Early Italian Nature Studies and the Early Calendar Landscape." *Journal of the Warburg and Courtauld Institutes* 13.1/2 (1950): 13–47.

Pagel, Walter. *William Harvey's Biological Ideas: Selected Aspects and Historical Background.* Basel and New York: S. Karger, 1967.
Palfrey, Simon. *Late Shakespeare: A New World of Words.* Oxford: Oxford University Press, 1997.
Park, Katherine. "The Life of the Corpse: Division and Dissection in Late Medieval Europe." *Journal of the History of Medicine and Allied Sciences* 50 (1995): 111–32.
Park, Katharine. "Medicine and Natural Philosophy: Naturalistic Traditions." In *The Oxford Handbook of Women and Gender in Medieval Europe*, edited by Judith M. Bennett and Ruth Mazo Karras, 84–100. Oxford: Oxford University Press, 2013.
Park, Katharine. *Secrets of Women: Gender, Generation, and the Origins of Human Dissection.* New York and Cambridge, MA: Zone Books; Distributed by the MIT Press, 2006.
Parker, Patricia. "Barbers and Barbary: Early Modern Cultural Semantics." *Renaissance Drama* 33 (2004): 201–44.
Parker, Patricia. "Cutting Both Ways: Bloodletting, Castration/Circumcision, and the 'Lancelet' of *The Merchant of Venice*." In *Alternative Shakespeares 3*, edited by Diana E. Henderson, 95–118. London; New York: Routledge, 2008.
Parker, Patricia. "Murals and Morals: *A Midsummer Night's Dream*." In *Editing Texts: Texte edieren*, edited by Glenn W. Most, 190–218. Gottingen: Vandenhoeck & Ruprecht, 1998.
Parker, Patricia. *Shakespeare from the Margins: Language, Culture, Context.* Chicago, IL: University of Chicago Press, 1996.
Parker, Patricia. "What's in a Name: and More." *SEDERI* XI (2002): 101–49.
Patterson, Annabel M. *Shakespeare and the Popular Voice.* Oxford: Blackwell, 1989.
Pelling, Margaret. *Medical Conflicts in Early Modern London: Patronage, Physicians, and Irregular Practitioners, 1550–1640.* Oxford: Oxford University Press, 2003.
Pettigrew, Todd H. J. *Shakespeare and the Practice of Physic: Medical Narratives on the Early Modern English Stage.* Newark, NJ: University of Delaware Press, 2007.
Phillips, Sarah. "The Pig in Medieval Iconography." In *Pigs and Humans: 10,000 Years of Interaction*, edited by Umberto Albarella, Keith Dobney, Anton Ervynck, and Peter Rowley-Conwy, 373–87. Oxford: Oxford University Press, 2007.
Pinney, Thomas. *A History of Wine in America: From the Beginnings to Prohibition.* Berkeley: University of California Press, 1989.
Poole, Adrian. *Tragedy: A Very Short Introduction.* Oxford: Oxford University Press, 2005.
Porter, Roy. *Blood and Guts: A Short History of Medicine.* London: Penguin, 2003.
Potter, Ursula. "Greensickness in *Romeo and Juliet*." In *The Premodern Teenager*, edited by Konrad Eisenbichler, 271–92. Toronto: CRRS Publications, 2002.
Powell, Hilary, and Corinne Saunders, eds. *Visions and Voice-Hearing in Historical and Literary Contexts.* Forthcoming.
Principe, Lawrence M. *The Secrets of Alchemy.* Chicago, IL: University of Chicago Press, 2012.
Pucci, Joseph. *The Full-Knowing Reader: Allusion and the Power of the Reader in Western Literary Tradition.* New Haven: Yale University Press, 1998.

Purkiss, Diane. *The Witch in History: Early Modern and Twentieth Century Representations.* Abingdon, Oxon: Routledge, 1996.
Putnam, Michael C. J. *Virgil's Aeneid: Interpretation and Influence.* Chapel Hill: University of North Carolina Press, 1995.
Putnam, Michael C. J. *Virgil's Poem of the Earth: Studies in the Georgics.* Princeton, NJ: Princeton University Press, 1979.
Quilligan, Maureen. *The Language of Allegory: Defining the Genre.* Ithaca, NY: Cornell University Press, 1979.
Rampling, Jennifer M. "Transmuting Sericon: Alchemy as 'Practical Exegesis' in Early Modern England." *Osiris*, vol. 29, no. 1, Chemical Knowledge in the Early Modern World (2014): 19–34.
Rawcliffe, Carole. "Sources for the Study of Public Health in the Medieval City." In *Understanding Medieval Primary Sources: Using Historical Sources to Discover Medieval Europe*, edited by Joel T. Rosenthal, 177–95. London: Routledge, 2012.
Rawcliffe, Carole. *Urban Bodies: Communal Health in Late Medieval Towns and Cities.* Woodbridge: Boydell Press, 2013.
Read, Sara. *Menstruation and the Female Body in Early Modern England.* Basingstoke: Palgrave, 2013.
Reckford, Kenneth J. "Some Trees in Virgil and Tolkien." In *Perspectives of Roman Poetry: A Classics Symposium*, edited by G. Karl Galinsky, 57–92. Austin: University of Texas Press, 1974.
Resnick, Irven M. "Medieval Roots of the Myth of Male Jewish Menses." *Harvard Theological Review* 93 (2000): 241–63.
Robertson, J. C., and J. B. Shepherd, eds. *Materials for the History of Thomas Becket, Archbishop of Canterbury.* London: Rolls Series, 1875–1885.
Robsin, Lynn Alison. "'No Nine Days Wonder': Embedded Protestant Narrative in Early Modern Prose Murder Pamphlets, 1573–1700." Unpublished dissertation, Warwick University, 2003.
Rogers, John. *The Matter of Revolution: Science, Poetry & Politics in the Age of Milton.* Ithaca, NY: Cornell University Press, 1996.
Rose, E. M. *The Murder of William of Norwich: The Origins of the Blood Libel in Medieval Europe.* Oxford: Oxford University Press, 2015.
Rosenthal, Joel T., ed. *Understanding Medieval Primary Sources: Using Historical Sources to Discover Medieval Europe.* London: Routledge, 2012.
Rowe, Katherine. *Dead Hands: Fictions of Agency Renaissance to Modern.* Stanford, CA: Stanford University Press, 1999.
Ruska, Julius, and E. Wiedemann. "Beiträge zur Geschichte der Naturwissenschaften, LXVII: Alchemistische Decknamen." *Sitzungsberichte der Physikalisch-medizinalischen Societät zu Erlangen* 56 (1924): 17–36.
Ryan, Patrick Joseph. *Master-Servant Childhood: A History of the Idea of Childhood in Medieval English Culture.* Basingstoke: Palgrave Macmillan, 2013.
Sabine, Ernest L. "Butchering in Mediaeval London." *Speculum* 8.3 (1933): 335–53.

Salamon, Linda Bradley. "Vagabond Veterans: The Roguish Company of Martin Guerre and *Henry V*." In *Rogues and Early Modern English Culture*, edited by Craig Dionne and Steve Mentz, 261–93. Ann Arbor: University of Michigan Press, 2004.

Sanford, Eva Matthews. "De Disciplina Scholarium: A Mediaeval Handbook on the Care and Training of Scholars." *Classical Journal* 28 (1932): 82–95.

Santing, Catrien. "'For the Life of a Creature is in the Blood' (*Leviticus* 17:11). Some Considerations on Blood as the Source of Life in Sixteenth Century Religion and Medicine and Their Connections." In *Blood, Sweat and Tears—The Changing Concepts of Physiology from Antiquity into Early Modern Europe*, edited by Manfred Horstmanshoff, Helen King, and Claus Zittel, 415–41. Leiden: Brill, 2012.

Saunders, Corinne. "Bodily Narratives: Illness, Medicine and Healing in Medieval Romance." In *The Boundaries in Medieval Romance*, edited by Neil Cartlidge, 175–90. Cambridge: D. S. Brewer, 2008.

Sawday, Jonathan, *The Body Emblazoned*: *Dissection and the Human Body in Renaissance Culture*. London: Routledge, 1996.

Sawday, Jonathan. "The Fate of Marsyas: Dissecting the Renaissance Body." In *Renaissance Bodies: The Human Figure in English Culture c. 1540–1660*, edited by Lucy Gent and Nigel Llewellyn, 111–35. London: Reaktion, 1990.

Scarry, Elaine. *The Body in Pain: The Making and Unmaking of the World*. Oxford: Oxford University Press, 1985.

Schoenfeldt, Michael. *Bodies and Selves in Early Modern England*: *Physiology and Inwardness in Spenser, Shakespeare, Herbert, and Milton*. Cambridge: Cambridge University Press, 1999.

Scott, Charlotte. *Shakespeare and the Idea of the Book*. Oxford: Oxford University Press, 2007.

Scott, Shirley Clay. "From Polydorus to Fradubio: The History of a *Topos*." *Spenser Studies* 7 (1986): 27–57.

Sebek, Barbara. "'More natural to the nation': Situating Shakespeare in the 'Querelle de Canary'." *Shakespeare Studies* 42 (2014): 106–21.

Selleck, Nancy. *The Interpersonal Idiom in Shakespeare, Donne and Early Modern Culture*. Basingstoke: Palgrave Macmillan, 2008.

Seymour, Martin C. *Bartholomæus Anglicus and His Encyclopedia*. Aldershot: Variorum, 1992.

Shahani, Gitanjali. "The Spicèd Indian Air in Early Modern England." *Shakespeare Studies* (2014): 122–37.

Shail, Andrew, and Gillian Howie, eds. *Menstruation: A Cultural History*. Basingstoke: Palgrave Macmillan, 2005.

Silverman, Lisa. *Tortured Subjects: Pain, Truth, and the Body in Early Modern France*. Chicago, IL: University of Chicago Press, 2001.

Sinanoglou, Leah. "Christ Child as Sacrifice: A Medieval Tradition and the Corpus Christi Plays." *Speculum* 48:3 (1973): 491-509.

Siraisi, Nancy G. *Medicine and the Italian Universities: 1250–1600*. Leiden: Brill, 2001.

Skultans, Vieda S. "Research Note. Vicarious Menstruation." *Social Science and Medicine* 21.6 (1985): 713–14.

Sliwa, Dorotea. "Le metafore del 'giardino' nel linguaggio mistico di Santa Caterina da Siena." In *Con l'occhio e col lume: Atti del corso seminariale di studi su S. Caterina da Siena (25 settembre–7 ottobre 1995)*, edited by Luigi Trenti and Bente Klange Addabbo, 131–47. Siena: Cantagalli, 1999.

Smith, Bruce. *The Key of Green: Passion and Perception in Renaissance Culture*. Chicago, IL: University of Chicago Press, 2008.

Smith, Pamela H. "Vermilion, Mercury, Blood, and Lizards: Matter and Meaning in Metalworking." In *Materials and Expertise in Early Modern Europe: Between Market and Laboratory*, edited by Ursula Klein and E. C. Spary, 43–44. Chicago, IL: University of Chicago Press, 2009.

Smyth, Adam. *A Pleasing Sinne: Drink and Conviviality in Seventeenth-Century England*. Cambridge: D. S. Brewer, 2004.

Soergel, Philip M., ed. *Sexuality and Culture in Medieval and Renaissance Europe*. Studies in Medieval and Renaissance History, Third Series, Vol. II. New York: AMS Press, 2005.

Sofer, Andrew. *The Stage Life of Props*. Ann Arbor: University of Michigan Press, 2003.

Sokol, B. J., and Mary Sokol. *Shakespeare, Law, and Marriage*. Cambridge: Cambridge University Press, 2003.

Speroni, Charles. "The Motif of the Screaming and Bleeding Trees of Dante's Suicides." *The Italian Quarterly* 9 (1965): 44–55.

Spitzer, Leo. "Speech and Language in *Inferno* XIII." In *Dante: A Collection of Critical Essays*, edited by John Freccero, 78–101. Englewood Cliffs, NJ: Prentice Hall, 1965.

Spolsky, Ellen and Alan Richardson, eds. *The Work of Fiction: Cognition, Culture, and Complexity*. Aldershot: Ashgate, 2004.

St. Hilaire, Danielle A. "Allusion and Sacrifice in *Titus Andronicus*." *Studies in English Literature* 49.2 (2009): 311–31.

Steele, Karl. *How to Make a Human: Animals and Violence in the Middle Ages*. Columbus: Ohio State University Press, 2011.

Steiner, Arpad. "The Authorship of *De discisplina scholarium*." *Speculum* 12 (1937): 81–84.

Stephen, John. *Satyrical Essayes Characters and Others*. London, 1615.

Stevens, Andrea Ria. *Inventions of the Skin: The Painted Body in Early English Drama, 1400–1642*. Edinburgh: Edinburgh University Press, 2013.

Stolberg, Michael. *Homo Patiens. Krankheits und Körpererfahrung in der frühen Neuzeit*. Köln/Weimar/Wien: Böhlau Verlag, 2003.

Stolberg, Michael. "Menstruation and Sexual Difference in Early Modern Medicine." In *Menstruation: A Cultural History*, edited by Andrew Shail and Gillian Howie, 90–101. Basingstoke: Palgrave Macmillan, 2005.

Sturges, Robert S. *Chaucer's Pardoner and Gender Theory: Bodies of Discourse*. London: Macmillan, 2000.

Sturges, Robert S. "The Pardoner in Canterbury: Class, Gender and Urban Space in *The Prologue to the Tale of Beryn*." *College Literature* 33 (2006): 52–76.

Sugg, Richard. "'Good Physic but Bad Food': Early Modern Attitudes to Medicinal Cannibalism and Its Suppliers." *Social History of Medicine* 19.2 (2006): 225–40.

Sugg, Richard. *Mummies, Cannibals and Vampires: The History of Corpse Medicine from the Renaissance to the Victorians*. Abingdon, Oxon: Routledge, 2011.

Sugg, Richard. *Murder After Death: Literature and Anatomy in Early Modern England*. Ithaca, NY: Cornell University Press; Bristol: University Presses Marketing, 2007.

Sugg, Richard. *The Smoke of the Soul: Medicine, Physiology and Religion in Early Modern England*. Basingstoke: Palgrave Macmillan, 2013.

Swanton, Michael, ed. *The Lives of Thomas Becket*. Manchester: Manchester University Press, 2001.

Sylla, Edith Dudley, and William R. Newton. *Evidence and Interpretation in Studies on Early Science and Medicine*. Leiden: Brill, 2009.

Taddei, Ilaria. "Puerizia, Adolescenza and Giovinezza: Images and Conceptions of Youth in Florentine Society During the Renaissance." In *The Premodern Teenager: Youth in Society, 1150–1650*, edited by Konrad Eisenichler, 15–26. Toronto: Centre for Reformation and Renaissance Studies, 2002.

Taylor, Gary. "Ancients and Moderns." *Shakespeare Quarterly* 36.4 (1985): 525–27.

Thesedier, Eugenio Duprè. *Dizionario biografico degli Italiani*, XXII. Rome: Istituto della Enciclopedia Italiana, 1979.

Teskey, Gordon. "Death in an Allegory." In *Imagining Death in Spenser and Milton*, edited by Elizabeth Jane Bellamy, Patrick Cheney, and Michael Schoenfeldt, 65–77. New York: Palgrave Macmillan, 2003.

Theophilus, John G. Hawthorne, and Cyril Stanley Smith. *On Divers Arts: The Foremost Medieval Treatise on Painting, Glassmaking and Metalwork*. New York; Dover Publications; London: Constable, 1979.

Thomas, Keith. *Religion and the Decline of Magic: Studies in Popular Beliefs in Sixteenth and Seventeenth-Century England*. London: Penguin Books, repr. 1991.

Thomas, Rae, Geoffrey K. Mitchell, and Laura Batstra. "Attention-Deficit/Hyperactivity Disorder: Are We Helping or Harming?" *British Medical Journal* (2013): 347 (18–20).

Thomas, Richard F. "Tree Violation and Ambivalence in Virgil." *Transactions of the American Philological Association* 118 (1988): 261–73.

Thorndike, Lynn. "Translation of a Letter from a Physician of Valencia to His Two Sons Studying at Toulouse." *Annals of Medical History* 3 (1931): 17–20.

Tigner, Amy. *Literature and the Renaissance Garden from Elizabeth I to Charles II: England's Paradise*. Surrey: Ashgate, 2012.

Tinkle, Theresa. "Exegesis Reconsidered: The Fleury 'Slaughter of Innocents' and the Myth of Ritual Murder." *Journal of English and Germanic Philology* 102.2 (2003): 211–43.

Tracy, Larissa. *Torture and Brutality in Medieval Literature: Negotiations of National Identity*. Cambridge: D. S. Brewer, 2012.

Tydeman, William ed. *The Medieval European Stage, 500–1500*. Cambridge: Cambridge University Press, 2001.

Tylus, Jane. *Reclaiming Catherine of Siena: Literacy, Literature, and the Signs of Others.* Chicago, IL: University of Chicago Press, 2009.
Vaught, Jennifer C. *Rhetorics of Bodily Disease and Health in Medieval and Early Modern England.* London and New York: Routledge, 2016.
Vergerii, Petrii Pauli. *De ingenues moribus.* Venice: Christopherus Valdefer, n.d.
Vialles, Noëlie. *Animal to Edible.* Translated by J. A. Underwood. Cambridge: Cambridge University Press, 1994.
Wailoo, Keith, *Drawing Blood: Technology and Disease Identity in Twentieth-Century America.* London: Johns Hopkins University Press, 1997.
Walker Bynum, Caroline. *Jesus as Mother: Studies in the Spirituality of the High Middle Ages.* Berkeley: University of California Press, 1982.
Walker Bynum, Caroline. *The Resurrection of the Body in Western Christianity, 200–1336.* New York, 1995.
Walker Bynum, Caroline. "Violent Imagery in Late Medieval Piety." *GHI Bulletin* 30 (2002): 3–36.
Walker Bynum, Caroline. *Wonderful Blood: Theology and Practice in Late Medieval Germany and Beyond.* Philadelphia: University of Pennsylvania Press, 2007.
Wall, Wendy. *Staging Domesticity: Household Work and English Identity in Early Modern Drama.* Cambridge: Cambridge University Press, 2002.
Walther, Hans. *Proverbia sententiaeque latinitatis medii aevi.* 6 vols. Göttingen: Vandenhoeck und Ruprecht, 1963–1969.
Watson, Robert N. *Back to Nature: The Green and the Real in the Late Renaissance.* Philadelphia: University of Pennsylvania Press, 2006.
Wear, Andrew ed. *Medicine in Society.* Cambridge: Cambridge University Press, 1991.
Webb, Heather. *Dante's Persons: An Ethics of the Transhuman.* Oxford: Oxford University Press, 2016.
Webb, Heather. "Dante's Stone Cold Rhymes." *Dante Studies* 121 (2003): 149–68.
Webb, Heather. *The Medieval Heart.* New Haven, CT: Yale University Press, 2010.
Webb, Henry J. *Elizabethan Military Science: The Books and the Practice.* Madison: University of Wisconsin Press, 1965.
Wenzel, Horst. "The Logos in the Press: Christ in the Wine-Press and the Discovery of Printing." In *Visual Culture and the German Middle Ages*, edited by Kathryn Starkey and H. Wenzel, 223–49. New York: Palgrave Macmillan, 2005.
Westra, H. J. "Review of Wilson, *Glosae in Iuvenalem*." *Mittellateinisches Jahrbuch* 18 (1983): 368–69.
Whatney, Simon. *Policing Desire: Pornography, AIDS and the Media.* 3rd ed. London: Cassell, 1997.
White, Lynn, Jr. "Natural Science and Naturalistic Art in the Middle Ages." *American Historical Review* 52 (1947): 421–35.
Whitteridge, Gweneth. *William Harvey and the Circulation of the Blood.* London: Macdonald, 1971.

Wittkower, Rudolf. *Architectural Principles in the Age of Humanism.* London: Academy Editions, 1977.
Wittig, Joseph. "'Remigian' Glosses on Boethius' *Consolatio Philosophiae.*" In *Source of Wisdom: Old English and Early Medieval Latin Studies in Honour of Thomas D. Hill,* edited by Charles D. Wright, Frederick M. Biggs, and Thomas N. Hall. Toronto Old English Series 16, 168–200. Toronto: University of Toronto Press, 2007.
Wilce, James M. "Medical Discourse." *Annual Review of Anthropology* 38 (2009): 199–215.
Wilson, Luke. "William Harvey's *Prelectiones*: The Performance of the Body in the Renaissance Theater of Anatomy." *Representations* 17 (1987): 62–95.
Wiltshire, A. "Clinical Lecture on Vicarious or Ectopic Menstruation, or Menses Devii." *Lancet* 126 (1885): 513–17.
Worthen, W. B. "Deeper Meanings and Theatrical Technique: The Rhetoric of Performance Criticism." *Shakespeare Quarterly* 40 (1989): 440–55.
Wright, Thomas. *Circulation: William Harvey's Revolutionary Idea.* London: Chatto & Windus, 2012.
Wynne Smith, Lisa. "The Body Embarrassed? Rethinking the Leaky Male Body in Eighteenth-Century England and France." *Gender & History* 23.1 (2011): 26–46.
Young, Sidney *The Annals of the Barber-Surgeons of London.* London: Blades, 1890.
Ziegler, Joseph. "Sexuality and the Sexual Organs in Latin Physiognomy 1200–1500." In *Sexuality and Culture in Medieval and Renaissance Europe* (Studies in Medieval and Renaissance History, Third Series, Vol. II), edited by Philip M. Soergel, 83–107. New York: AMS Press, 2005.
Zorach, Rebecca. *Blood, Milk, Ink, Gold: Abundance and Excess in the French Renaissance.* Chicago, IL: University of Chicago Press, 2005.

ELECTRONIC TEXTS AND ONLINE RESOURCES

Amanda Greene. "Foods That Look Like Body Parts They're Good For." http://www.womansday.com/health-fitness/nutrition/foods-that-look-like-body-parts-theyre-good-for-109151.
"British History Online." http://www.british-history.ac.uk/report.aspx?compid=35981.
The Casebooks of Richard Napier and Simon Forman. http://www.magicandmedicine.hps.cam.ac.uk/the-casebooks/search/cases.
Lander Johnson, Bonnie, Decamp, Eleanor, and Laurie Maguire. "The Blood Project." http://www.thebloodproject.net.
"Wellcome Library." http://wellcomelibrary.org.

Contributors

Helen Barr is Professor of English Literature at the University of Oxford. She is the author of *Transporting Chaucer* (Manchester University Press, 2014), *The Digby Poems: A New Edition of the Lyrics* (University of Exeter Press, 2009), *Socioliterary Practice in Late Medieval England* (Oxford University Press, 2001), *Signes and Sothe: Language in the Piers Plowman Tradition* (Boydell and Brewer, 1994), and *The Piers Plowman Tradition* (London: Dent, 1993).

Katharine A. Craik is Reader in Early Modern Literature at Oxford Brookes University. Her book *Reading Sensations in Early Modern England* was published by Palgrave in 2007 and she is co-editor, with Tanya Pollard, of *Shakespearean Sensations: Experiencing Literature in Early Modern England* (Cambridge University Press, 2013). Craik is Principal Investigator on *Watching*, a critical-creative arts project funded by the Wellcome Trust to explore the Renaissance history of sleep. She is currently working on ideas of vividness and vitality in Shakespeare's plays and is editing a collection of essays entitled *Shakespeare and Emotion* for Cambridge University Press.

Lesel Dawson is a Senior Lecturer in English at the University of Bristol. She is the author of *Lovesickness and Gender in Early Modern Literature* (Oxford University Press, 2008) and as co-editor is currently preparing a collection, *Revenge and Gender in Classical, Medieval, and Renaissance Literature* (Edinburgh University Press, 2018).

Eleanor Decamp is author of *Civic and Medical Worlds: Performing Barbery and Surgery* (Palgrave Macmillan, 2016), a contributor to *The Senses in Early Modern England, 1558–1660* (Manchester University Press, 2015), and co-convenor of the Blood Project with Bonnie Lander Johnson.

Frances E. Dolan is Distinguished Professor of English Literature at the University of California, Davis. She has published five books, including *True Relations: Reading, Literature, and Evidence in Seventeenth-Century England* (University of Pennsylvania Press, 2013), *Marriage and Violence* (University of Pennsylvania Press, 2008), and *Whores of Babylon: Catholicism, Gender, and Seventeenth-Century Print Culture* (Cornell University Press, 1999). Her current project is tentatively entitled *Digging the Early Modern: How Alternative Agriculture Remembers the Seventeenth Century*.

Elisabeth Dutton is Professor of Medieval English at the University of Fribourg. Her publications include *Julian of Norwich: The Influence of Late-Medieval Devotional Compilations* (Boydell and Brewer, 2008) and an edition of Julian of Norwich (Yale University Press, 2008); she is co-editor of *John Gower: Trilingual Poet* (Boydell and Brewer, 2010) and of *Drama and Pedagogy in Medieval and Early Modern English* (Narr, 2015); and she has published numerous articles on early drama. She is an experienced theater director who has established the Early Drama at Oxford project, examining plays written and performed in Oxford colleges in the early modern period, and she leads the Medieval Convent Drama project: these research projects explore the drama of very different institutions through archival work and performance research.

Margaret Healy is Professor of Literature and Culture at the University of Sussex. She has published widely on the cultural history of the body and the interfaces between literature, medicine, and science. Healy is the author of *Shakespeare, Alchemy and the Creative Imagination: The Sonnets and A Lover's Complaint* (Cambridge University Press, 2011); *Fictions of Disease in Early Modern England: Bodies, Plague and Politics* (Palgrave, 2001); and *Richard II* (Northcote House, 1998). She is co-editor of *Renaissance Transformations: The Making of English Writing 1500–1650* (Edinburgh University Press, 2009); *The Intellectual Culture of the British Country House 1500–1700* (Manchester, 2015); and a special issue of the journal *Textual Practice:* "Prosthesis in Medieval and Early Modern Culture" (2016).

Dolly Jørgensen is Professor of History at University of Stavanger in Norway. She has co-edited the volumes *Northscapes: History, Technology and the Making of Northern Environments* (University of British Columbia Press, 2013), *New Natures: Joining Environmental History with Science and Technology*

Studies (University of Pittsburgh Press, 2013), and *Visions of North in Premodern Europe* (Brepols, 2017).

Helen King is Professor Emerita of Classical Studies at the Open University. She has published widely and collaboratively. Her monographs include *The One-Sex Body on Trial: Using the Classical and Early Modern Evidence* (Ashgate, 2013*)*, *Midwifery, Obstetrics and the Rise of Gynaecology: The Uses of a Sixteenth-Century Compendium* (Ashgate, 2007), and *Hippocrates' Woman: Reading the Female Body in Ancient Greece* (Routledge, 1998).

Bonnie Lander Johnson is Fellow, Lecturer, and Director of Studies at Selwyn College, Cambridge University. She is the author of *Chastity in Early-Stuart Literature and Culture* (Cambridge University Press, 2015) and numerous articles on early modern drama and its theological, medical, and environmental contexts. She is currently writing a book on Shakespeare and botany.

Hester Lees-Jeffries is University Lecturer in English Literature at the University of Cambridge and a Fellow of St. Catharine's College. She is the author of *Shakespeare and Memory* (Oxford University Press, 2013) and *England's Helicon: Fountains in Early Modern Literature and Culture* (Oxford University Press, 2007). She is currently working on a book entitled *Textile Shakespeare*.

Joe Moshenska is Associate Professor of English Literature at the University of Oxford and a Fellow of University College. He is the author of *Feeling Pleasures: The Sense of Touch in Renaissance England* (Oxford University Press, 2014) and *A Stain in the Blood: The Remarkable Voyage of Sir Kenelm Digby* (William Heinemann, 2016). He is currently completing a monograph, *Iconoclasm as Child's Play*.

Tara Nummedal is Associate Professor of History and Italian Studies at Brown University. She is the author of *Alchemy and Authority in the Holy Roman Empire* (University of Chicago Press, 2007). Her second book on Anna Zieglerin is forthcoming.

Patricia Parker is the Margery Bailey Professor in English and Professor of Comparative Literature at Stanford University. She is the author of four books: *Inescapable Romance* (Princeton University Press, 1979), *Literary Fat*

Ladies: Rhetoric, Gender, Property (Methuen, 1987), *Shakespeare from the Margins* (University of Chicago Press, 1996), and *Shakespearean Intersections: Language, Contexts, Critical Keywords* (University of Pennsylvania Press, 2018); and co-editor of five collections of essays on criticism, theory, and cultural studies, including *Shakespeare and the Question of Theory* and *Women, Race and Writing in the Early Modern Period*. She is currently General Editor of the open-access *Stanford Global Shakespeare Encyclopedia* online.

Ben Parsons is Lecturer in Medieval and Early Modern Literature at the University of Leicester. He is co-author of the critical anthology *Comic Drama in the Low Countries* (Boydell and Brewer, 2012), and author of the monograph *Punishment in Medieval Education* (Boydell and Brewer, 2018).

Heather Webb is Reader in Medieval Italian Literature and Culture at the University of Cambridge. She is the author of *The Medieval Heart* (Yale University Press, 2010) and *Dante's Persons: An Ethics of the Transhuman* (Oxford University Press, 2016). With Dr George Corbett, she is editor of *Vertical Readings in Dante's Comedy*, 3 vols. (Open Book Publishers 2015–2017).

Gabriella Zuccolin was Wellcome Trust Research Fellow at the Department of History and Philosophy of Science at the University of Cambridge and is now Fellow at Villa I Tatti, The Harvard University Center for Italian Renaissance Studies, in Florence. She has published several essays on the interconnected realms of medicine and philosophy as fostered by medieval Italian universities and courtier milieus. She is currently working on a book entitled *Women's Medicine between Script and Print, 1450–1600*.

Index

1 Henry VI, 62
2 Henry IV, 43–58
3 Henry VI, 207

adolescence and adolescents, 7, 123–133, 146, 139
agricultural images, 231, 233 (*fig. 15.4*), 236
agricultural manuals, 135, 211–212, 214 (*see also* vineyard; wine)
alchemy and alchemical texts, 6–8, 24, 25–26, 111–122, 133, 216–218, 223 (*see also* homunculus, the; philosopher's stone, the)
allegory, 104–105, 129
All's Well That Ends Well, 74
amenorrhea, 81, 87 (*see also* menstruation)
amputation, 66, 179, 185–186, 195
anatomy, 18, 67, 70, 127–130, 213 (*see also* body, the)
animal(s), 6, 15, 18, 20, 22, 26–27, 64, 85, 91, 94, 104, 111, 113–114, 117, 129, 136, 157, 173, 188–189, 211, 224–225, 228–234, 265 (*n*17), 298 (*n*9) (*see also* dog; horse; lamb; lion; pig)
animate and inanimate, the, 44, 92, 97–99, 102, 103, 107, 117
anti-Semitism, 184, 185
Antonio's Revenge, 159–160
apparition(s), 152, 156, 185, 189, 194 (*see also* ghost[s])

appetite(s), 7–8, 44, 133, 135, 136–148, 159
Arden of Faversham, 151–152, 157, 160–162
Aristo, Ludovico, 93
aristocrat(s), 43, 45, 48, 53, 55, 57, 142, 227
Aristotle, 16, 18, 19–20, 22–23, 26–27, 36, 39, 80, 84, 85–86, 112, 138, 160, 265 (*n*17), 283 (*n*10)
As You Like It, 206–207, 218
Atheist's Tragedy, The, 164
atomist physiology, 99–101
Aubrey, John, 22
Avicenna, 36, 86–87, 89, 128, 267–268 (*n*33)

Bacon, Francis, 158, 170
Bacon, Roger, 115
ballads, 170–171, 180, 181
baptism, 203, 228, 240
barber(s) and barbery, 10, 169–182
barber-surgeon and barber-surgery, 169–171, 177, 182
Bartholomew of England, 66–67, 128–129
basin, the, 167–182, 214, 224, 228
barber's basin, the, 176–177
Beaumont, Francis, 199
Becket, Thomas, 10–11, 238–248
beer, 212 (*see also* cider; vineyard; water; wine)
Benedict of Canterbury, 239–240

Index

biblical narratives, 35, 203–205, 207, 213 (*see also* sin)
   Deuteronomy, 212
   Genesis, 136, 156, 212
   Isaiah, 190, 203
   Matthew, 184, 232, 244, 245
   Revelation, 203, 240
bleeding, 5, 8, 12, 36, 48, 50, 62, 66, 76, 79–91, 92–110, 135, 139, 152–155, 158, 160, 163–164, 167–182, 184–189, 193, 196, 199–200, 224, 230–234, 244 (*see also* cruentation; menses; menstruation)
blood
   advertising blood, 168, 170, 172–174, 179
   blood and belief, 183–197
   blood and fluidity, 98, 128–129, 133, 192
   blood and intellect, 127, 129–130
   blood and liquidity, 131–133
   congealed blood, 28, 157, 174, 245
   blood and temperature, 18, 19, 21–23, 26, 32, 37, 41, 48, 81, 88, 96, 100, 108, 114, 128–130, 133, 144, 152, 158–160, 178, 185–187, 214–215, 220 (*see also* bleeding; blood and temperature, blood-degree; blood shed; bloodletting; bloodline[s]; bloodstain[s]; bodily affliction[s], hemorrhage; gore; stigmata; transformation)
   blood as fertilizer, 117, 214–215
   blood as filth, 96, 104, 229
   blood as food, 7, 31, 117, 136, 143–144, 213, 218, 222, 224, 228, 234, 236
   blood and metaphor, 3, 12, 25, 43, 63, 66, 133, 135, 137, 222–223, 232
   blood and metonymy, 207, 234
   blood brother, 54
   blood of the green lion, 111, 113, 274 (*n*1), 275 (*n*9)
   blood miracle, 242
   blood outside the body, 8, 69, 174, 191, 214

blood spouting, 180, 206, 297 (*n*27)
blood type, 46, 48, 50, 58
blood's fecundity, 114
blood-degree, 43–58
hymeneal blood, 199–201, 205–206, 294 (*n*8)
life-giving blood, 18–19, 37, 38, 41, 236
menstrual blood, 6–7, 80–82, 85, 87–88, 90–91, 111–112, 137, 138, 200, 261 (*n*1), 263 (*n*12), 265 (*n*19)
queer blood, 11, 238–248, 305 (*n*7), 308 (*n*40)
royal blood, 16, 66, 111, 198
sacred blood, 207, 238, 247, 297 (*n*27), 303 (*n*25)
smell of blood, the, 39, 77, 164, 174, 192, 213
stage blood, 62, 65, 77, 152, 185–196, 291 (*n*5)
bloodless, 230
bloodletting, 64, 79, 84–86, 89, 167–182, 199, 213, 225, 288 (*n*3)
bloodletting instruments (*see* cupping [glasses]; evacuation; leeching; scarification)
bloodline(s), 43–45, 48
bloodshed, 8, 9, 54, 55, 57, 64, 65, 75, 77, 94, 103–104, 193, 199, 214, 240, 243, 247, 261 (*n*2), 294 (*n*8)
bloodstain(s), 61–78, 163, 184, 190, 193, 195, 202, 297 (*n*27)
blood type, 46, 48, 50, 58
Boccaccio, Giovanni, 93, 102, 272 (*n*30)
bodily affliction(s) (*see also* body, the)
   amenorrhea, 81, 87
   choler/choleric, 45–48, 53, 57–58, 87, 131, 158
   crisis, 83–85, 265 (*n*15)
   disease, 7, 28, 83, 85, 86–87, 89–91, 119, 126, 135, 137, 138, 142, 182, 219, 264 (*n*12), 265 (*n*17), 266 (*n*22)
   endometriosis, 82

Index

fever, 84, 88, 90, 261 (*n*1), 266 (*n*22)
greensickness, 126, 135–140, 144–147, 283 (*n*3)
headache, 88, 89, 244, 261 (*n*1), 265 (*n*19)
hemorrhage, 82, 84, 86, 88, 261 (*n*1), 266 (*n*22)
hemorrhoid(s), 84, 85–86, 88–89, 91, 184, 265 (*n*17), 266 (*n*22)
inflammation, 46, 83, 175
leprosy, 112, 119, 240–241, 277 (*n*30)
ligature, 89, 267 (*n*31), 288 (*n*8)
malaria, 241
melancholy/melancholic, 87, 131, 139, 142, 145, 265 (*n*19)
nosebleed(s), 79–91, 128, 241, 261 (*n*2), 262 (*n*3), 263 (*n*10), 264 (*n*13), 265 (*n*17), 266 (*n*30), 267 (*n*31), 268 (*n*33, 35, 37, 38)
phlegmatic, 87, 131–132
plethora, 2, 83–84, 88, 91, 168, 176, 264 (*n*12), 265 (*n*16)
pleurisy, 28
sanguine, 16, 44, 68, 78, 87, 131–132
virgins' disease, the, 135, 139–140
body, the (*see also* bodily affliction[s]; Christ, the)
    anatomy, 18, 67, 70, 127–130, 213
    blood vessels, 20, 35, 86, 128, 264 (*n*13)
    body parts, 62, 196, 222, 234
    brain, the, 17, 18, 21, 32, 36, 83, 86, 87, 88, 89, 90–91, 127, 129, 222, 239–240, 258 (*n*33), 264 (*n*14), 266 (*n*23), 268 (*n*35)
    breast and breastfeeding, 7–8, 38, 41, 69, 82, 89, 139–145, 148, 213, 215, 240, 255 (*n*24), 268 (*n*35), 283 (*n*13, 14), 299 (*n*17)
    cardiovascular system, the, 18
    crown, 239, 241, 242
    dismemberment, 178, 180, 232, 271 (*n*21)
    dissection, 69–70, 260 (*n*28)
    dug, 143–144, 146
    eyes, 31, 39, 82, 83, 87, 116, 126, 131, 140, 146, 152, 160–166, 217, 240, 264 (*n*14), 266 (*n*23)
    flesh, 9, 11, 28, 34, 63, 66, 68–70, 75, 83, 95, 102, 105, 116, 126, 128–129, 136, 140, 147, 154, 212, 215, 230, 231–233
    genitals, 83, 89, 91, 200, 222, 243, 264 (*n*14), 307 (*n*28)
    hand(s), 16, 39, 62, 75–77, 89, 96, 101, 102, 103, 129, 130, 159–160, 163–164, 168, 174, 180–182, 184–188, 192–197, 198, 202, 213, 244
    head, 11, 38–39, 61, 66, 127, 167, 180, 187, 199, 225, 236, 239, 242–244, 246–247, 268 (*n*37), 294 (*n*2)
    heart, the, 3, 15–30, 31–42, 46, 74, 129–130, 141, 158, 160, 163, 215, 251 (*n*10), 252 (*n*39, 1), 264 (*n*13)
    intestine, 227–228
    leg(s), 55, 170, 224, 229, 241, 307 (*n*27)
    liver, the, 17–18, 36, 87–91, 179
    maternal body, the, 139
    menses, 7, 81–82, 85, 112, 116–118, 137–138, 140, 146, 184, 261 (*n*2), 264 (*n*12), 265 (*n*17), 266 (*n*22), 276 (*n*23)
    mole, 202, 205, 296 (*n*18)
    mouth, 31, 79–80, 102, 153, 156, 195–196, 206, 229, 261 (*n*1), 264 (*n*14), 265 (*n*14)
    neck, 72
    nose, 79–91, 128, 229, 241, 261 (*n*2), 262 (*n*3, 5), 263 (*n*10), 264 (*n*13), 265 (*n*14, 17), 266 (*n*22, 30), 267 (*n*31), 268 (*n*33, 35, 37, 38)
    one-sex model, the, 80–83
    phallus, 242, 246, 307 (*n*25)
    pregnant body, the, 80, 112, 117, 138–139, 261 (*n*1, 2), 262 (*n*3)
    prostheses, 188
    semen/sperm, 84, 114–116, 215
    severed body, 66, 195–196, 239, 241, 246

body, the (*continued*)
  skin, 5, 9, 65–69, 74, 76–78, 82, 84, 103–104, 137, 168, 259 (*n*13), 260 (*n*22, 28), 296 (*n*26)
  skull, 105, 163, 239, 241, 244
  spirit(s), the (*see* spirit[s] and *spiritus*)
  spleen, 87–89, 91, 178–179, 266 (*n*23)
  sweat, 28, 48, 69, 75, 84, 187–188, 245, 260 (*n*32), 274 (*n*43)
  throat, 34, 176, 178, 198
  tongue, 74, 141, 163, 165, 168, 180, 202, 296 (*n*26)
  urine, 64, 84, 86, 88, 174, 211, 265 (*n*14), 298 (*n*1)
  womb, 7, 8, 82, 87, 88, 90, 118–120, 137–144, 147–148, 168, 263 (*n*12), 267 (*n*32), 292 (*n*23)
  (*see also* Eucharistic host, the; homunculus, the; tree[s])
Botkin, Daniel, 222
brain, the, 17, 18, 21, 32, 36, 83, 86, 87, 88, 89, 90–91, 127, 129, 222, 239–240, 258 (*n*33), 264 (*n*14), 266 (*n*23), 268 (*n*35)
bread, 11, 183, 184, 188, 191, 196, 232, 292 (*n*23), 293 (*n*27), 302 (*n*6)
breast and breastfeeding, 7–8, 38, 41, 69, 82, 89, 139–145, 148, 213, 215, 240, 255 (*n*24), 268 (*n*35), 283 (*n*13, 14), 299 (*n*17)
Bring Up The Bodies, 61–62
Bulwer, John, 69, 72 (*fig. 4.4*)
butchery and the butcher, 10, 173–174, 178, 180, 202, 213, 224–237, 302 (*n*9)

Calvinist theology, 157
cannibalism, 32, 213, 223
Canterbury Cathedral, 238, 240, 247
Canterbury Interlude, The, 11, 238, 238–248
Canterbury Tales, The, 11, 238, 245, 246
cardiovascular system, the, 18
Catherine of Siena, 3, 35–42
cauterization, 89, 170, 288 (*n*8)

Celsus, 86
Charles I, 15, 16, 214
Charleton, Walter, 158, 160
Chaucer, Geoffrey, 11, 183, 238, 242, 245, 246, 305 (*n*1)
  Canterbury Tales, The, 11, 238, 245, 246
Chiron, 181–182
choler/choleric, 45–48, 53, 57–58, 87, 131, 158
Christ, the, 6, 35–41, 62, 75, 107, 119–120, 183–185, 187–191, 194, 196–197, 203–205, 212, 231–234, 236, 237, 239, 240, 242, 243–246, 254 (*n*16), 256 (*n*35), 274 (*n*43), 295 (*n*18), 296 (*n*21), 297 (*n*27, 28), 302 (*n*6), 304 (*n*38), 306 (*n*14), 307 (*n*26, 32)
church, (the), 4, 35–37, 40–42, 68, 74, 160, 184, 189, 194, 197, 227–228, 231–232, 234, 239, 241, 247, 301 (*n*3), 305 (*n*2), 306 (*n*17)
cider, 215, 216–217, 219 (*see also* beer; water; wine)
clothes, 61, 63–64, 68, 69, 185, 190, 192, 194, 197, 202
  cuff, 63–64
  doublet, 6, 69
  ruff, 50, 63–64
  shirt, 62–68, 74, 76, 78, 259 (*n*13)
  toga, 74, 260 (*n*34)
Clowes, William, 170
color, 51, 52, 63, 66, 68, 74, 77–78, 88, 92, 94, 96, 98, 102, 104, 119, 137, 159–160, 185, 186, 187, 189–190, 192, 199, 203, 205, 207, 211, 217, 222, 239–241, 257 (*n*27), 260 (*n*23), 271 (*n*15), 297 (*n*27) (*see also* humor[s], the, and the humoral system; paint)
comedy, 195, 201, 204, 207
communion, 54, 212, 242, 245, 307 (*n*36) (*see also* Eucharist, the)
Coriolanus, 65–66, 70, 72, 74–77, 192, 295 (*n*8), 296 (*n*20)
crisis, 83–85, 265 (*n*15)

Index

Croxton *Play of the Sacrament*, 183–197, 203, 345
Crucifixion, (the), 107, 183, 191, 207, 231, 239
cruentation, 8, 10, 151–166, 245–246, 284 (*n*5), 285 (*n*8), 286 (*n*38)
Culpepper, Nicholas, 139, 142, 284 (*n*16)
cupping (glasses), 79, 84, 89, 168, 261 (*n*1), 264 (*n*13)
Cymbeline, 198–207, 294 (*n*4), 297 (*n*31)

Dante Alighieri, 3, 4, 31–42, 93, 102, 107, 253 (*n*5), 272 (*n*29), 274 (*n*43), 297 (*n*27)
death, 6, 7, 34, 38–40, 42, 48, 49, 55, 64–65, 72, 75, 94, 97–108, 119, 137–138, 140, 146–148, 154–159, 163, 164, 170, 175, 183, 191, 198–207, 214, 228, 230–237, 239, 271 (*n*17), 293 (*n*28), 295 (*n*18), 296 (*n*21)
diet, 125, 127, 144, 167, 215, 218, 221, 265 (*n*15)
dissection, 69–70, 260 (*n*28)
Doctor Faustus, 62
dog, 118, 138, 214, 242–243
Donne, John, 162, 252 (*n*39)
Drury, John, 124

earl of Essex, 68
earth, the, 26, 28, 33, 35, 37, 40, 48, 96, 107, 136–138, 140–141, 143–144, 147–148, 190, 223, 238, 305 (*n*5)
ecocriticism, 135, 222
Eliot, George, 92–94, 108, 269 (*n*2)
Elizabethan, 49, 51, 52, 102, 257 (*n*19), 260 (*n*34)
Elyot, Sir Thomas, 23
endometriosis, 82
Erasistratus, 85
Etheledreda of Canterbury, 241
Eucharist, the, 2, 10, 36, 211, 240, 242 (*see also* communion; Eucharistic host, the)

Eucharistic host, the, 184–185, 189–197, 292 (*n*23)
Euripides, 99, 271 (*n*17)
Evelyn, John, 214, 216, 217
evacuation, 79, 83–85, 89, 168, 266 (*n*26), 267 (*n*32)
execution, 17, 38, 39, 41, 69, 164, 193–194, 213, 254 (*n*21)

Faerie Queene, The, 93, 95, 99, 103–105, 203–204, 297 (*n*27) (*see also* Spenser, Edmund)
Fagarola, Pedro, 127
fertility, 94, 117, 120, 121, 137–138, 264 (*n*14)
Fletcher, John, 199
flux, 120, 129 (*see also* menses; menstrual blood; menstruation)
folklore, 82, 97
foreignness, 217–221
Forman, Simon, 87, 267 (*n*67) (*see also* Napier, Richard)
Freud, Sigmund, 98, 145
Fulmerston, Edmund, 123–125, 127

Gale, Thomas, 172
Galen (of Pergamon), 1, 2, 4, 18–20, 23, 36, 80, 83–86, 88, 91, 112, 136–138, 168, 182, 265 (*n*19), 266 (*n*26), 268 (*n*33)
garden(s), 24, 35, 37, 41–42, 135, 141, 142, 218, 220, 221, 253 (*n*11)
gender, 1, 2, 5, 44, 79–91, 112, 116
genre, 62, 86, 136, 199
geohumoralism, 218, 220
ghost(s), 155, 157, 159–160, 164–165, 194–195 (*see also* apparition[s])
Gilbert the Englishman, 87
gore, 48, 104–108, 159–160, 193–194, 213–214, 222
greensickness, 126, 135–140, 144–147, 283 (*n*3)
Guillemeau, Jacques, 134, 138
Gyer, Nicholas, 171–172, 174, 175, 177–178

Hamlet, 64
Harrington, James, 17, 24–25, 27–29
Harvey, William, 2, 3, 15–30, 168, 213–214, 251 (*n*10, 19)
Harward, Simon, 170, 175
health, 1, 3, 7, 9, 12, 25, 29, 30, 32, 41, 83, 86, 88, 91, 112, 123, 125, 132, 137–138, 215, 217–219, 222, 229, 241–242, 263 (*n*12), 288 (*n*3)
heart, the, 3, 15–30, 31–42, 46, 74, 129–130, 141, 158, 160, 163, 215, 251 (*n*10), 252 (*n*39, 1), 264 (*n*13)
Henry V, 43–58
Hill, Christopher, 17, 21, 22, 23
Hippocrates of Kos, 83, 88, 139, 265 (*n*16), 268 (*n*33)
Hobbes, Thomas, 17, 24, 28–29
homunculus, the, 114–118, 120
horse, 49, 68, 89, 114, 115, 168, 233
Hugh of Jervaux, 241
humor(s), the, and the humoral system, 1, 2, 44–46, 50, 83–85, 88, 91, 115, 128–132, 135, 137, 138, 140, 142, 144, 154, 168, 174, 214–215, 264 (*n*12), 265 (*n*16), 267 (*n*31), 273 (*n*35)
   bile, 130–131
   black bile, 130, 132
   blood (*see* blood)
   phlegm, 128, 130, 246
   (*see also* choler/choleric; melancholy/melancholic; phlegm and phlegmatic; sanguine)
hymeneal blood, 199–201, 205–206, 294 (*n*8)

identity, 2, 4, 5, 8, 9, 12, 33–34, 43–45, 50–54, 65, 82, 75, 223, 246 (*see also* personhood; selfhood; subjectivity)
impurity, 98, 113, 119, 216–217, 275 (*n*9), 291 (*n*2)

In Vino Veritas, 217
infidelity, 199–201
insignia, 51, 125

Jews, 114, 170, 183–197, 230, 232, 234, 239, 291 (*n*2)
Julius Caesar, 75–76, 192, 260 (*n*34), 297 (*n*27)
Jung, Carl, 97, 111
Juvenal, 129

Kempe, Margery, 233
Kern Paster, Gail, 1, 4, 44, 140, 142, 145, 154, 172, 214, 249 (*n*11), 256 (*n*2), 289 (*n*20)
kingship, 20
Kyd, Thomas, 206
Lamb and lamb, 114, 202–204, 232, 240, 245

lancet, 177, 180
Laqueur, Thomas, 80–81, 263 (*n*10)
laundress, the, 63–64, 259 (*n*11)
laundry, 63–65, 75, 244, 246
leeching, 84, 168
leprosy, 112, 119, 240–241, 277 (*n*30)
lion and "green lion," 48, 111, 113–114, 117–120, 206
liver, the, 17–18, 36, 87–91, 179
love, 35, 38, 39, 41, 55, 75, 134–141, 144, 146–148, 152, 162, 205, 206, 250 (*n*11), 283 (*n*3), 287 (*n*47)
Lucretius, 95, 99–101, 103, 108, 271 (*n*19)
Lusitanus, Amatus, 79–80, 85

Macbeth, 76, 163–165, 174, 183–197, 293 (*n*32)
malaria, 241
Markham, Francis, 43, 44, 46, 52–53, 57
Markham, Gervase, 288 (*n*3)
Marston, John, 159

Index

martyr(s), 68, 183, 202, 231–234, 238–248, 274 (n42)
Mary, Queen of Scots, 68
medicine, 12, 18, 80, 83, 86, 88, 90–91, 112, 119, 125, 136, 137, 138, 140–141, 143, 145–148, 175, 182, 185, 213–214, 215, 221, 263 (n10), 264 (n12)
medieval calendar, the, 10, 224–237, 301 (n2, 3)
melancholy/melancholic, 87, 131, 139, 142, 145, 265 (n19)
menses, 7, 81–82, 85, 112, 116–118, 137–138, 140, 146, 184, 261 (n2), 264 (n12), 265 (n17), 266 (n22), 276 (n23)
menstrua (*see* menstrual blood)
menstrual blood, 6–7, 80–82, 85, 87–88, 90–91, 111–112, 137, 138, 200, 261 (n1), 263 (n12), 265 (n19) (*see also* menstruation)
menstruation, 80–91, 112, 118, 120, 184, 202, 262 (n5), 263 (n10), 264 (n12), 265 (n17), 268 (n35), 275 (n6), 291 (n3) (*see also* amenorrhea; menstrual blood)
Merchant of Venice, The, 170, 296 (n20), 297 (n29)
Merry Wives of Windsor, The, 64
Metamorphoses, 205–206
Middle Ages, the, 81, 83, 86, 114, 128, 130, 168, 228, 230, 231, 263 (n10), 264 (n12)
Middleton, Thomas, 62, 159, 164, 171, 177
Midsummer Night's Dream, A, 205–207
milk, 7, 113, 134, 136, 139, 141–148, 213, 230, 240, 264 (n14), 268 (n35), 299 (n17)
Milton, John, 212
Much Ado About Nothing, 204, 207
murderer, the, 8, 10, 151–166, 191, 193, 238, 239, 286 (n38)

nakedness, 62, 65, 77, 153
Napier, Richard, 87, 267 (n31) (*see also* Forman, Simon)

Nashe, Thomas, 62, 69–70, 172
natura rerum, De, 95, 100–101, 114–118
nature, 6, 24, 53, 82–87, 91, 114, 116, 120, 132, 138, 140, 158, 206, 221–223, 230, 231, 265 (n19), 266 (n26)
nosebleed(s), 79–91, 128, 241, 261 (n2), 262 (n3), 263 (n10), 264 (n13), 265 (n17), 266 (n30), 267 (n31), 268 (n33, 35, 37, 38)

Othello, 77, 191, 200–202, 206–207, 295 (n9)
Ovid, 93, 168, 205–206

pain, 77, 88, 108, 121, 143 (*see also* bodily affliction[s]; suffering)
paint, 64, 68, 188–189, 192–193, 195–196 (*see also* color)
Paracelsus, 114, 118–120
pedagogy and pedagogical discourse, 3, 7, 8, 124–128, 132–133
performance, 10, 46, 63, 76, 155, 174, 181, 186, 202, 204, 247, 259 (n13), 293 (n26)
personhood, 4, 6, 33, 35, 42, 45–46, 49–50, 52, 58, 75, 95, 272 (n29) (*see also* identity; selfhood; subjectivity)
Philaster, 199
philosopher's stone, the, 113–115, 119, 121, 275 (n9)
phlebotomy (*see* bloodletting; cupping [glasses]; leeching; scarification)
phlegm and phlegmatic, 87, 128, 130–132, 246
pig, 224–237
pilgrim(s) and pilgrimage, 11, 240–242, 244–247, 297 (n27), 306 (n23)
plants, 34, 35, 92, 93, 97–98, 100, 101, 114, 117, 121, 138, 140–141, 143–144, 146, 211, 213, 218, 221–222 (*see also* agricultural images; agricultural manuals; tree[s]; vineyard)

plants (*continued*)
  grapevines, 214
  plant anatomy, 213
  pruning, 214, 228, 299 (*n*12)
Plat, Sir Hugh, 214, 216–217, 220, 299 (*n*12), 301 (*n*41)
Play of the Sacrament, the (*see* Croxton *Play of the Sacrament*)
plethora, 2, 83–84, 88, 91, 168, 176, 264 (*n*12), 265 (*n*16)
pleurisy, 28
poison(ous), 65, 112, 116–117, 119, 137–140, 141, 143–148, 159, 173, 198, 264 (*n*12)
pregnant body, the, 80, 112, 117, 138–139, 261 (*n*1, 2), 262 (*n*3)
purging, 2, 7, 79–80, 84, 112, 137, 179, 184, 215, 241, 246, 261 (*n*1), 267 (*n*31)

rape, 180–182, 206, 296 (*n*26)
receptacles for blood 168, 173–177, 179, 181
  ampulla, 240–242, 306 (*n*23)
  basin (*see* basin, the)
  pan, 227–229, 234, 307 (*n*27)
  phial, 240–242, 244
  porringer, 174–175
  saucer, 175–176, 179
recipe(s), 113–121, 175, 228, 266 (*n*30), 302 (*n*8) (*see also* diet)
redemption, 11, 112, 114–16, 118, 119, 120, 153, 157, 165, 204
Reformation, the, 2, 4, 11, 107, 212, 223
relic(s), 202, 238, 245–246, 308 (*n*39)
Renaissance, 12, 43, 74, 81, 82, 86, 87, 88, 91, 97, 99, 103–104, 134, 264 (*n*12), 268 (*n*33, 39)
reproduction, 1, 6, 7, 82, 112, 114, 116, 118, 120, 264 (*n*14)
revenge, 8, 152, 156, 157–160, 164, 168, 178, 180, 182, 196, 199–200, 201, 204, 207
Revenge of Bussy D'Ambois, The, 157
Richard III, 157, 164–165
Richard of Sunieve, 241

ritual, 74, 193, 217, 291 (*n*1)
Roger of Valognes, 241, 307 (*n*27)
Romeo and Juliet, 7, 134–148, 205
royal blood, 16, 66, 111, 198

sacrament, the, 36, 107, 189, 194, 203, 213 (*see also* Croxton *Play of the Sacrament*)
sacred blood, 207, 238, 247, 297 (*n*27), 303 (*n*25)
sacrifice, 40–41, 159, 201–204, 212, 230–232, 234, 236–237, 285 (*n*18)
salvation, 33, 35, 36, 38–41, 156, 234, 237
sanguine, 16, 44, 68, 78, 87, 131–132
sanitation, 225, 229
scarification, 69, 79, 168, 261 (*n*1)
Schurig, Martin, 82
selfhood, 4, 5, 9, 33, 46 (*see also* identity; personhood; subjectivity)
senses, the, 31, 39, 40, 101, 108, 127, 132, 141, 250 (*n*11), 271 (*n*21)
sexual intercourse, 200, 202 (*see also* rape; sexuality; sodomy)
sexuality, 2, 6–7, 137–138, 201–202, 246
Shakespeare, William, 4, 7, 9, 12, 44–46, 51–53, 56–58, 64, 65, 67, 68, 72, 74–78, 134–139, 157, 159, 168, 170, 178–179, 185, 192, 195–196, 198, 200–201, 204, 205, 207
1 Henry VI, 62
2 Henry IV, 43–58
3 Henry VI, 207
All's Well That Ends Well, 74
As You Like It, 206–207, 218
Coriolanus, 65–66, 70, 72, 74–77, 192, 295 (*n*8), 296 (*n*20)
Cymbeline, 198–207, 294 (*n*4), 297 (*n*31)
Hamlet, 64
Henry V, 43–58
Julius Caesar, 75–76, 192, 260 (*n*34), 297 (*n*27)

Index

Macbeth, 76, 163–165, 174, 183–197, 293 (*n*32)
Merchant of Venice, The, 170, 296 (*n*20), 297 (*n*29)
Merry Wives of Windsor, The, 64
Midsummer Night's Dream, A, 205–207
Much Ado About Nothing, 204, 207
Othello, 77, 191, 200–202, 206–207, 295 (*n*9)
Richard III, 157, 164–165
Romeo and Juliet, 7, 134–148, 205
Taming of the Shrew, The, 181
Titus Andronicus, 65, 74, 159, 168, 178–182, 195, 205, 260 (*n*34)
sin, 6, 8, 9, 32, 112, 118, 121, 152–153, 156, 163, 166, 202, 234, 296 (*n*21), 305 (*n*2, 5)
slaughterhouse, 230
smell of blood, the, 39, 77, 164, 174, 192, 213
sodomy, 243, 245, 307 (*n*25)
soul, the, 4, 8, 16–19, 22–24, 27, 32, 34–36, 39–42, 77, 100–101, 118–119, 126, 140, 154, 157–158, 214, 231, 255 (*n*27), 262 (*n*3), 305 (*n*2)
sovereignty, 17
Spenser, Edmund, 44, 93, 103–108, 203–204, 273 (*n*37), 291 (*n*21), 297 (*n*27), 304 (*n*43) (see also *Faerie Queene, The*)
spirit(s) and *spiritus*, 8, 17–18, 20–28, 31–32, 39–41, 46, 48, 101, 157–162, 164, 166, 172, 212–216, 250 (*n*11), 253 (*n*6), 255 (*n*27)
spiritual, 4, 31, 33–35, 38, 41–42, 45, 152, 157, 162, 224, 228, 236
St. Veronica, 245, 260 (*n*32)
stage blood, 62, 65, 77, 152, 185–196, 291 (*n*5)
stage directions, 62, 65, 66, 75, 77, 141, 179, 185–196, 212, 290 (*n*52), 292 (*n*10)
stigmata, 203–205, 296 (*n*18)
subjectivity, 74, 153, 162 (see also identity; personhood; selfhood)

suffering, 87, 89, 92, 94, 97, 102–103, 107–108, 137, 159, 168, 175, 178, 233–234 (see also bodily affliction[s]; pain)
supernatural, 102, 156
surgeon (or chirurgian), 10, 55, 169–182
surgery, 18, 69, 169, 171, 175, 180, 182

Taming of the Shrew, The, 181
Tasso, Torquato, 93, 102–103
teaching (see pedagogy and pedagogical discourse)
textiles, 61–78, 260 (*n*28)
Thomas of Monmouth, 183–184
"Three Clerks, The," 232, 304 (*n*34)
Titus Andronicus, 65, 74, 159, 168, 178–182, 195, 205, 260 (*n*34)
transformation(s), 2, 54, 72 (*fig. 4.4*), 75, 77, 82, 93, 95–100, 102, 104, 105, 107, 119, 133, 139, 153, 181, 184, 201, 203, 207, 217, 223, 224, 232, 270 (*n*5), 296 (*n*20)
transfusion, 215, 247
transubstantiation, 11, 189, 215–217, 223, 274 (*n*43)
treatment and cure, 2, 85, 87, 117, 120, 176, 182, 241, 261 (*n*1), 277 (*n*30)
tree(s), 5, 92–108, 117, 129, 135, 188, 206, 213–214, 234, 241, 271 (*n*17), 272 (*n*27), 274 (*n*43), 297 (*n*27), 299 (*n*12), 306 (*n*22) (see also plants)

van Foreest, Pieter, 89–90, 267 (*n*32)
venesection, 88, 90, 267 (*n*31), 268 (*n*35) (see also bloodletting)
Vesalius, Andreas, 18, 69, 71 (*fig. 4.3*), 73 (*fig. 4.5*)
Vincent of Beauvais, 35, 37, 127
vineyard, 35–37, 217, 219–221 (see also wine)
violence, 75, 94, 98, 100–102, 107, 108, 126, 134, 152, 161, 179, 193, 195, 197, 234, 269 (*n*5), 272 (*n*31)

Virgil, 32, 93–108, 271 (*n*17, 18), 272 (*n*30)
   Aeneid, The, 93–100, 271 (*n*18)
virgin, 113, 137, 146, 201, 239, 265 (*n*14), 292 (*n*23), 295 (*n*8)
Virgin Mary, the, 120, 121
virgins' disease, the, 135, 139–140
voice, 31, 93–94, 98, 107–108, 154, 156, 164–165, 253 (*n*6), 256 (*n*32), 272 (*n*30)

Walker Bynum, Caroline, 306 (*n*14, 17), 307 (*n*34, 37)
Wall, Wendy, 63, 173, 298 (*n*8)
war, 44, 51, 53–54, 57, 62, 66, 177, 193, 198, 203, 212
Warning to Fair Women, A, 157, 162
waste, 2, 9–10, 138, 214, 222–223, 229, 289 (*n*20)
water, 6, 35, 64, 76, 89, 100–101, 106, 112, 117, 128, 154, 176, 181, 184, 193, 224, 229, 236, 239–244, 268 (*n*37) (*see also* beer; cider; vineyard; wine)
weaning, 8, 136, 141–148

weapon(s), 56, 58, 65, 77, 97, 163, 177, 178
   axe, 164, 225, 227, 236, 241
   knife, 163, 178–180, 190, 202, 224–237
   spear(s), 96–99, 239, 243, 270 (*n*12), 271 (*n*17), 306 (*n*14), 307 (*n*26)
   staff, 242–244
   sword(s), 76, 177, 198, 201, 239, 242–243, 305 (*n*8)
Whitaker, Tobias, 214–215, 299 (*n*17)
William of Kellet, 241, 307 (*n*27)
wine, 3, 10, 11, 23, 64, 118, 164, 190, 203, 211–223, 240, 304 (*n*45) (*see also* beer; vineyard)
Winstanley, Gerrard, 18, 24, 28
Witch of Edmonton, The, 163
Woodall, John, 175–177, 288 (*n*8)
wormwood, 142–145, 148

youth, 7, 8 123–133, 135, 137, 141, 284 (*n*16) (*see also* adolescence and adolescents)

Zieglerin, Anna, 114, 117–121, 277 (*n*30), 278 (*n*36)

Acknowledgments

We had been warned by numerous colleagues that editing a collection of essays would be one of the greatest administrative and "personnel" challenges of our careers. But it has not been so. In compiling this book we have been privileged to work with generous and patient scholars whose writing and thinking we have long admired. We owe a huge debt of thanks to all of the book's contributors—for trusting us with their work, for generating some of the most stimulating conversation we have known, and for being such good company.

Blood Matters is only one of the fruits of the Blood Project, which we began in Oxford in 2012. Others include Elisabeth Dutton's production of the Croxton *Play of the Sacrament*, Zachary Beer's beautiful series of paintings on blood and print typologies, and the Blood Conference at Oxford University where many of the ideas contained here were first advanced.

To everyone who has joined us in our work from all corners of the globe and offered their thoughts and labor, we are most grateful: Tamara Atkin, Barbara Baert, Ariane Balizet, Helen Barr, Matthew Beresford, Elma Brenner, Madelaine Caudron, Francesco Paolo de Ceglia, Angelo Lo Conte, Paul Craddock, Katharine Craik, Stephen Curtis, Lesel Dawson, Frances Dolan, Elisabeth Dutton, David Fuller, Indira Ghose, Angus Gowland, Erin Griffey, Dolly Jørgensen, William Kerwin, Margaret Healy, Hester Lees-Jeffries, Chris Laoutaris, Anne Leone, Rebecca Maryan, Francesca Matteoni, Arabella Milbank, Kathleen Miller, Joe Moshenska, Lucy Munro, Mike Murphy, Harry Newman, Tara Nummedal, Patricia Parker, Ben Parson, Kaara Peterson, Diane Purkiss, Sara Read, Madeline Ruegg, Jennifer Rust, Corinne Saunders, Sarah Star, Andrea Stevens, Chris Stone, Jessica Sun, Larissa Tracy, and Penelope Wood. We would also like to thank those who helped to organize the Oxford event and chair panels: Alex da Costa, Micah Coston, Sian Decamp, Peter Friend, and Emma Smith. Thanks too to St. Anne's College, Oxford, for accommodating us, and St. John's College, Oxford, and chaplain for the use of the chapel.

We are very grateful to the funders of the Blood Project: the Wellcome Trust, the Society for Renaissance Studies, the John Fell Fund, the Faculty of English at Oxford, and Green Templeton College, Oxford.

The fact that this collection is in print is down to the support of Jerry Singerman and his staff at Penn Press—we owe much thanks to them all.

However, neither this book nor the wider Blood Project would have been possible without the guidance, vision, and friendship of Laurie Maguire, to whom this collection is dedicated and without whom we might both have lost our intellectual way some time ago.